HOMO, 99 and 44/100% NONSAPIENS

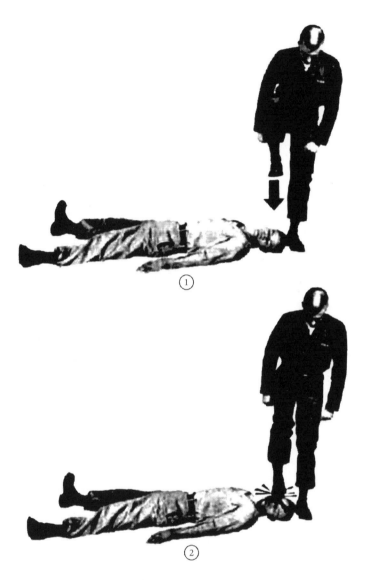

Figure 41. Heel Stomp

HOMO,
99 and 44/100%
NON
SAPIENS

REVISED WITH NEW INTRODUCTION

GERALD B. LORENTZ

APOP / UNDERWORLD AMUSEMENTS

ISBN: 978-0-9885536-3-7

Designed by Kevin I. Slaughter

With deep gratitute to the team of proofreaders:
MRDA, B.E., R.A., D.N.

This edition published in co-operation with Apop of St. Louis, who arranged for the reprinting and new foreword.

APOP
www.ApopRecords.com

UNDERWORLD AMUSEMENTS
www.UnderworldAmusements.com

CONTENTS

FOREWORD

I am indebted to Dustin Newman for resurrecting *HOMO, 99 and 44/100% NONSAPIENS*, without whom the book may have gone into Limbo. Ecclesiastes contains these words: "To every thing there is a season, and a time to every purpose under the heaven..." They are beautiful words, and they are true. Incidentally, I read the Bible not as a sourcebook for knowledge, but for its poetic beauty and lofty allegorical flights of imagination. Neither the season nor the time was right when my book was first published two decades ago. Scientific ideas like biological evolution are as old as Ancient Greece, but their time had not come until after the Age of Enlightenment and the coming of Darwin; even then, they met with bitter opposition from religious fanatics. Hopefully, NOW, in this age of computers and high technology, the moment for publishing is auspicious.

The word "science" is derived from the Latin word *scientia*, which means "having knowledge", or "to know". The essence of science is the passion for knowledge which is precisely what *HOMO, 99 and 44/100% NONSAPIENS* is all about. The essence of this book is an aversion to ignorance and a craving for unlimited knowledge. For many tens of thousands of years, human beings believed that our Earth was both flat and the center about which the sun revolved. It's a natural belief because that's exactly the way our senses perceive it. However, as we now know, it is NOT true. Our senses deceive us. Our senses also tell us that a hard rock of granite is solid. Here, again, our senses deceive us because we know from science that it is almost entirely empty space. The sensation of solidity is caused by the strong electromagnetic forces of repulsion at the atomic and molecular level.

Science had its birth in Ancient Greece, but it was short lived. It became a victim of Political Correctness when Rome conquered Greece and when Christianity gave it the *coup de grace* with theological precepts enforced by *Index Librorum Prohibitorum*, Torquemada, the Popes, and the Inquisition. After Constantine I converted to

Christianity, the Western World held the belief that the Bible was the only source of true knowledge. It culminated during the Holy Roman Empire era. The presumptuous concept that mere MAN has curative powers was blasphemous because it was an irreverent incursion into the exclusive domain of God's Will. Only the Almighty, man's Creator, could cure disease, and access to God's Will was through PRAYER. Unfortunately, despite many centuries of prodigious praying, worshipping, and devotion to GOD, the faithful continued to die from plagues and diseases unremittingly. This dismal failure of prayer presented no problem to the faithful because that, too, was God's Will. It was always a no-lose proposition for God. With a scenario like that, fiasco was transformed into success and became self-perpetuating.

The fact that medical problems were stubbornly unresponsive to all prayer for thousands of years should nudge a rational person into considering one of two possibilities: namely, either God doesn't give a hoot about human illness, or maybe, just maybe, He doesn't exist. In 1798 AD, there was a departure from the norm. Medical science was resurrected after a very long hibernation since the glory days of Hippocrates (460 BC - 377 BC), but it faced ecclesiastical discountenance. Edward Jenner, while pursuing the scientific method, a discovery of the Age of Reason, found that smallpox could be prevented by means of inoculations with lesions from cowpox. EUREKA! Simple inoculations performed the very medical miracles that prayer had sought for thousands of years. Enlightened man could do what gods could never do. The power of Nature's immune system eclipsed the powers of all the gods. Medical science was so effective that, today, smallpox inoculations have eradicated that devastating disease from the face of the globe, and it only required a relatively few short years of concerted effort. How much sapience does it require to understand that quick success like that is far superior to millenniums of failure? Perhaps more than many people possess.

Just as Jenner opened the eyes of the world to bona fide "miracles" of medical science, *HOMO, 99 and 44/100% NONSAPIENS* attempts to open the eyes of the reader to commonly held misconceptions and ignorance in general. For example, that white light is a simple color like red and blue is a common misconception. The prism (and rainbows) prove that white light is a composite of ALL visible colors. That Genesis tells us the true story of the origin of life and the world was a misconception for millennia. The Bible is mythology, not a textbook. Only science has the ability to tell us the true story of our origins. The fact, as we know it today, is that Nature created man, and man created gods—thousands of them. India has been called the land of a million gods. All ancient societies created gods, whether they were in Polynesia, Africa, Europe, Asia, or the Americas. The Aztec gods were very cruel. Even the Hebrew God of the Old Testament was cruel. Jesus put a kindly face on God, but his cult was rejected by his own people, and he was crucified. Gentiles accepted Jesus and transformed the Jewish cult into one of the major religions of the world. When Constantine I converted to Christianity, Jesus replaced the Roman Emperors as God, who had usurped that title from the Roman gods Jupiter, Juno, Mars, and Venus.

Religion inspired the judicial practice of trial by combat to determine guilt or innocence of the accused. It was called *judicium Dei* (judgment of God). It was firmly believed that God, in His infinite power and wisdom, would perform miracles to guarantee victory to the innocent contestant. When science inspired trial (justice) by forensic evidence, it was a giant leap from darkness into light, but it could only happen after the diminution of strong religious influences. Our Founding Fathers were sapient indeed when they insisted on separation of church and state. What are the credentials of Science? It gave the world computers, TVs, automobiles, walks on the moon, atomic energy, medical miracles, etc., etc. Religion gave us dogmatism, intellectual stagnation, antagonism to science, religious wars, Crusades and Islamic terrorists; but, in fairness, it also gave us saints like Francis of Assisi and Mother Theresa. It gave hope for an afterlife and helped to alleviate the terrible pains of bereavement. The psychological benefits, while good, did not compensate for the institutionalization of ignorance; and saints, while admirable, did not give the world modern technology, prodigious wealth, or medical science, like antibiotics or pharmacology, that save millions of human lives.

—Gerald B. Lorentz, 11/18/06

Everyone likes, "Somewhere over the rainbow—"

Chapter 1

BORN TO KILL

About one and a half or two million years ago, an event unique to the solar system, and possibly to the universe itself, occurred on the planet Earth. It was the ushering-in of a biological upheaval that disturbed the balance of nature and introduced unprecedented strife, disruption, suffering, and mindless slaughter in the world of nature. Thousands of animal species were exterminated as a result. It caused the extinction of one hundred species of birds and forty species of mammals since A.D. 1600 alone. It was responsible for the extinction of one species per year since A.D. 1900, and the rate is rapidly accelerating. It may even be responsible for the eventual extinction of the human race.

The horse, the camel, and the rhinoceros were native to North America, but they were exterminated from the New World because of this fateful incident. Fortunately, some of the animals managed to escape annihilation by fleeing across a land-bridge along the site of the present Bering Strait. Horses were not seen in the Americas again until they were reintroduced by the Spaniards. Camels and rhinoceroses were also reintroduced, but as curiosities for visitors at zoos. When the event of which we speak irrupted upon the Hawaiian Islands, it had, as it had everywhere, catastrophic consequences on the ecosystem. It caused the extinction of forty-five species of animals, including the flightless rail and the flightless ibis.

This event, which we call the Biological Revolution of Lower Pleistocene times, had the same dire consequences on human life as it had on all animal life. It accounts for the deaths of at least 70 million human beings during the first three-quarters of the twentieth century; but this is a mere statistic, and it has no impact on our comprehension unless we translate it into a graphic mental image. If we were to accord each dead human victim the simple dignity of a number, and count each dead victim at the rate of one per second, forty hours per week, IT WOULD REQUIRE NINE AND ONE THIRD YEARS TO COMPLETE THE COUNT. If we were to enunciate each victim's name, IT WOULD REQUIRE TWENTY YEARS TO COMPLETE THE MACABRE ROLL CALL. IF WE WERE TO PLACE THE BODIES OF THESE DEAD VICTIMS END TO END, THEY WOULD ENCIRCLE THE EARTH MORE THAN THREE TIMES.

What was this cataclysmic Revolution of the Lower Pleistocene epoch? It was the incursion into the animal kingdom of a sinister, homicidal, vicious organism—A BORN KILLER. Incredibly, this killer is seldom recognized as the mad, stupid killer which it is, in spite of the obvious facts of its compulsion for mindless slaughter.

The passenger pigeon was once the most common bird in the world. In 1810, the noted ornithologist Alexander Wilson described an impressive flight of a flock of these pigeons which covered an area of several miles and took hours to pass over the sky, shadowing the Earth as it did so. This one flock numbered over two billion birds. By A.D. 1900, the born killer had nearly exterminated the entire species. The last passenger pigeon in the world died in the Cincinnati Zoo September 1, 1914.

The born killer also exterminated the great auk, the dodo bird, the moa, the huia bird (the male and female were inspirations of working partnerships), the giant elephant bird of Madagascar (its eggs were three feet in circumference and contained at least two gallons of fluid), Steller's sea cow, the quagga (a kind of horse), et cetera, et cetera. This congenital killer has countless other species teetering on the brink of extinction, among which are the great apes, the whales, lions, elephants, otters, tigers, pheasants, cranes, et cetera, et cetera.

The vicious killer of which we speak is on exhibition at the Honolulu Zoo. He can be seen in the first cage as one enters the main entrance and turns to the right. The nameplate on his cage identifies him as "THE MOST DANGEROUS ANIMAL IN THE WORLD." When a visitor walks up to the cage, and looks into it, he sees bars, and then he notices that there is a mirror on the back wall of the cage. HE SEES HIMSELF. *Homo sapiens* (Latin for "wise man") is, indeed, the most dangerous animal in the world, and often the most stupid. He almost hunted the rhinoceros to extinction for the second time in history, not for food, but for the nonexistent aphrodisiac properties which he foolishly supposed existed in their ground-up horns. He would have exterminated himself long ago, had he not been programmed to reproduce his kind at a faster rate than he was programmed to destroy it.

Anthropologists identify the hominoid irruption of Lower Pleistocene times as *Homo erectus* (erect man). He was a meat-eating hunter, a predator, but he was also an opportunist, which means he became omnivorous when there were no opportunities for killing his fellow animals. He had a common ancestry with the great apes, but he became uniquely human when he broke company with them by becoming the only killer ape. Anthropologist Richard Leakey believes that *Homo habilis* (skillful man) was the first true man. He dates his appearance at 2 million years ago.

Homo (man) proved to be as much a thorn as a flower of creation. He evolved as just another vicissitude of some 3 billion years of erratic biological evolution. He was a fortuitous event in that his emergence depended upon random events like genetic mutations, genetic shuffling in sexual reproduction, and genetic drift (Sewall Wright effect), rather than purposeful design. Desmond Morris calls this creature, who boasts the dubious honor of being the primate with the biggest penis and the biggest brain, the "Naked Ape."

Homo's kinship to the apes is irrefutable. Fetal and juvenile apes look astonishingly human. The shape and features of a juvenile chimpanzee's head resemble a human being more than they resemble an adult chimpanzee. The evolution of man was near completion once nature created our primitive ape-man ancestor. Modern man is essentially a precocious fetal ape. Nature merely employed the principle of neoteny by genetically arresting the normal skeletal development of the juvenile ape into an adult ape, eliminated its body hair (Naked Ape), induced a tumorous growth of his cerebrum, and Voila! Nature presented the world with a human being. The difference between man and ape is one of degree, not of kind. ✓

It does not require much imagination to recognize man's close kinship to the apes. It requires a tremendous amount of prejudice and ignorance NOT to recognize it. Morphologically, a human being is an overgrown, stunted ape. When a strand of man's DNA is unwrapped and matched to a chimpanzee's DNA, it is found to differ by less than two percent. Man's close genetic kinship to a chimp is unquestioned by knowledgeable people. Man and chimpanzees are subject to the same diseases. There is no difference between man and chimp's blood serum albumin.

Contrary to common belief, man is not the only animal that can communicate by means of language. Apes can communicate in sign language. Dr. Francine Patterson's gorilla, Koko, had a vocabulary of eight hundred words, and an IQ of ninety at the age of eight-and-a-half, which made it superior to some human beings. According to W.C. Watt of the University of California, "The history of our planet will be obliged to record that the first species to learn the language of another species was not man but chimpanzee."

Man is NOT the only tool-making animal. Jane Goodall describes how chimps design tools such as termite probes from twigs, and sponges from leaves. Many other animals are tool-users. The Egyptian vulture makes a tool of a rock by picking it up and slamming it on ostrich eggs so it can break them and eat the contents. The sea otter uses rocks as anvils to crack open shellfish to get to the meal inside. Apes use sticks to reach bananas. Archer fish shoot down insects from foliage by spitting droplets of water at them. Crows pull up the lines of ice fishermen to eat the bait.

Evolution was once referred to as a theory, but it was also once a theory that the Earth revolves around the Sun. Today, evolution is as much recognized as a fact as the revolution of the Earth around the sun—except by people of colossal ignorance, that is. Even most anti-evolution religious zealots possess the knowledge that they originated from a single-cell sperm from their fathers and a single-cell ovum from their mothers, and they evolved through nine months of uterine evolution as zygotes, embryos, and fetuses in their mother's wombs, during which time they were fish with gills and flippers, then animals with tails, then finally fetuses barely distinguishable from an ape's fetus.

Anti-evolution religious zealots can virtually see nine-month ontogenetic evolution take place before their very eyes, but they cannot extrapolate this knowledge into the recognition that ontogeny recapitulates phylogeny. Every human infant has the morphology of an ape, namely, long arms, short legs, a very large head, and scarcely any lower jaw. If the fact of the nine-month uterine evolution from a single cell to a human being is evident to all but the benighted, why should it be so difficult to accept the fact of the same evolution taking place on Earth over a period of 3 billion years? Just how sapient is Homo Sapiens if, as evidence indicates, he has a natural affinity for mythology, legends, and puerile fables, but a natural aversion to scientific facts?

About two hundred and fifty thousand years ago (possibly five hundred thousand) the cerebral tumefaction in the neotenic naked ape qualified him for the questionable, self-conferred title of Homo Sapiens. Essentially, he then had the same brain as modern man. It was the brain that made him unique among all animals, because it enabled him to kill at a distance and become the paragon of predators-the ultimate killer. His killing prowess progressed from the spear, the bow and arrow, the gun, the bomb dropped from an airplane, to a hydrogen bomb in the head of an intercontinental missile. In making man, Nature, like a mad inventress, created a creature out of electrons and protons, and then programmed it to fulfill its destiny by self-destructing into its constituent electrons and protons in a nuclear Armageddon. *wow — why would Nature leave that option open?*

Killing is as natural as sex for the human being. He evolved red in tooth and claw in Nature's arena of struggle for existence. He kills for food, for territory, for God, for country, for honor, for sport, for revenge, or for whatever reason he can invent to satisfy his killer instinct. If a human freak, a non-killer, were to demonstrate in front of a butcher shop to protest human savagery as manifested by the slaughter of his fellow creatures, to protest the gory display and barbarous eating of his fellow creatures' flesh, he would probably be carted off to an insane asylum. It is unthinkable for man to question the morality involved in slaughtering his fellow animals for food because he is a natural predator and a natural killer. If man had evolved as a strict herbivore, it would be unthinkable to kill other animals and place parts of their bodies for sale in meat markets. Can you imagine a pack of sheep attacking and eating a wolf, or a herd of wolves grazing peacefully on the grasslands? Man, like all predatory animals, was born to kill.

It is unthinkable for man to question the establishment of an army and navy or the morality of war. Man's predatory instincts drive him to wage war, just as the salmon's spawning instincts drive them to struggle upstream. War is so fundamental that even we "peace-loving" Americans must create a War Department, which is now euphemistically called the Department of Defense. We have no Department of Peace. We are a "peace-loving" nation, but we have an uncanny propensity to get involved whenever and wherever a war is fought. If there isn't a good idealistic reason for our involvement in a war, we are compelled to invent one.

There is an unparalleled intensity of excitement and exotic thrill experienced by soldiers psyched for combat. Soldiers report that the hunt and the kill of man by man eclipses all highs of human experience. War grants the moral and legal license for the hunt and kill. It is always glorified and rationalized as a fight for country, for freedom, for socialism, for glory, or for God. War is glorious when it is won, but ignominious when it is lost. Napoleon, Hitler, and Mussolini were national heroes while they were winning wars. They were not discredited by their countrymen until they lost.

When President Ronald Reagan spoke of the tragedy of the Vietnam War, he was not addressing himself to the fifty-eight thousand slain Americans, or the million slaughtered Vietnamese. He was addressing himself to the TRAGEDY OF DEFEAT. Inflation and unemployment made Prime Minister Margaret Thatcher's popularity plummet. Victory in the Falkland War made it soar. President Reagan's victory over the tiny nation of Grenada gave his popularity a huge boost. There is no thrill greater than victory in war.

Myth-mongers take issue with categorizing man as a carnivore and a predator, but the billions of slaughtered and devoured cows, pigs, sheep, and fowl must surely concur, as would the countless millions of human victims of human wars, if they had tongue. All of us who have teeth wear the predator's badge. Our four upper front teeth are called incisors. The two on either side of them are called canines. These teeth are the bloody tools of a carnivore. They don't look as lethal as the fangs on a viper, or the teeth of a saber-toothed tiger, but there is no need. Man's cerebrum enabled him to supplant them with far more deadly weapons. Knives, swords, cleavers, and machetes are far more deadly. Most predators can easily outrun the fastest man, but even the cheetah is slower than a tortoise when it is pursued by a human bullet.

Predators and carnivores are facts of animal life. There are predatory birds, predatory fish, predatory insects, predatory quadrupeds, and predatory bipeds, but man is the king of all predators. It seems that half of all living creatures (predators) must survive by preying on the other half of all living creatures (herbivores). Being eaten alive is obviously a terrifying experience. Ask anyone who has been attacked by a hungry shark, tiger or bear. It is rather curious that religious zealots who believe in an omnipotent and all-loving God avoid the question "Why did the God of Love create a world in which half of all living creatures can survive only by eating the other half?" One other germane question pricks the intellect: "Why did the God of Love create man with incisors and canines, the weapons of a killer, and then command him to be a creature of love?" It's like creating a worm and then commanding it to fly.

The human being is a strange, contradictory, illogical killer. For example, the United States suffered no pangs of conscience when it dropped two atomic bombs on Japan and cruelly incinerated some two hundred thousand fellow human beings, most of whom were decent, innocent civilians; but she goes into hand-wringing, soul-searching paroxysms of conscience when required to protect her society from the most vicious of its public enemies by surgically excising them like malignant cancers. The slaughter of the Japanese was applauded not only for bringing the enemy to its knees, but also for "saving lives." Slaughtering hundreds of thousands of Japanese was humane, but executing a single heinous murderer is inhumane. Predators display one kind of behavior toward the in-group, and another kind of behavior toward the out-group. Killing one's fellow man is unacceptable in the in-group, but in the out-group, it is not only acceptable, it is a solemn duty and obligation—when it is sanctioned by war. That is the law of the predator.

There is no greater honor than to kill for one's country or for one's God. Sgt. Alvin York became a popular hero, and he received the highest decorations of the American and French governments for killing twenty-five German soldiers in the Argonne Forest during World War I. He believed that he fought for God and country, but the Kaiser believed that the same God was the leader of the German army. The Crusaders were bestowed with the Church's highest honors for killing infidel Mohammedans. Violence is part and parcel of human nature. Some North American Indians regarded the use of the bow and arrow, the spear, and the war-club as man's noblest employments. Benito Mussolini wrote, "War alone brings up to its highest tension all human energy and puts the stamp of nobility upon the peoples who have the courage to face it." The great heroes of history are the mass murderers of history: Alexander the Great, Charlemagne, Genghis Khan, Napoleon, and so forth.

During the first three-quarters of this century alone, more than 70 million people were killed as a result of wars, revolutions, insurrections, rebellions, massacres, assassinations, executions, exterminations, genocides, and so forth. To name some of those wars we have the Boer War, Balkan Wars, Russo-Japanese War, World War I, World War II, Italo-Ethiopian War, Israeli-Arab Wars, Korean War, Vietnam War, Chinese Civil Wars, Spanish Civil War, Sino-Japanese Wars, Turkish-Italian War, Mexican Civil War, Lebanon Civil War, Honduras Civil War, et cetera. This is not to mention the hundreds of revolutions, rebellions, and insurrections in South America and Asia—and this century is far from over.

As we mentioned, it would require twenty years just to recite the roll call of the dead "heroes" of this century, and if their bodies were laid end to end, they would encircle the Earth more than three times. Each dead person was a hero to someone or some country. George Washington was a hero to the patriots, but a traitor to the Loyalists and English, who would have hanged him, if they could have captured him, in which case, and provided the Revolution had failed, we Americans would all despise him as a traitor today. The moral to this statement is that, in the world of predators, there is no substitute for victory.

According to Lane, Goldman, and Hunt's *World's History*, World War I "killed about 13 million soldiers and sailors and approximately the same number of civilians. A grim reminder of wartime hate and fear, the blockade of Germany continued for seven months after the Armistice. The Germans claim that keeping the blockade killed eight hundred people a day." World War I, "the war to end wars," begot a far more cataclysmic war—World War II. According to World History by Smith, Mussey, and Lloyd, the cost of World War II "has been appalling. Altogether, 85 million men had been under arms, and of this number, 14 million had been killed. There were 56 million other casualties." Millions of civilians were slaughtered by blockbuster bombs, anti-personnel bombs, fire bombs, artillery fire, two atomic bombs, and many other infernal instruments of death and destruction.

Hitler exterminated 6 million Jews in his genocidal Holocaust of World War II. More than a million Kampucheans were massacred by the Khmer Rouge between 1975 and 1979. Probably uncounted millions slaughtered each other in India following a rising tide of religious hatred among Moslems, Sikhs, and Hindus, which forced the nation to disjoint into Pakistan, Bangladesh, and India. Idi Amin massacred and tortured some three hundred thousand of his fellow Ugandans during the Seventies. Thousands are tortured and murdered almost daily in Central and South America. Catholics and Protestants are murdering each other in Northern Ireland. Arabs and Jews are killing each other in the Middle East.

Lenin and Stalin killed many millions of their fellow Russians, some by ruthless murder, some as the result of forcing communism upon unwilling peasants, which resulted in food shortages. Coerced communism aggravated the severity of the famine of 1921, causing 5 million Russians to perish from starvation. However, in spite of the millions upon millions of global killings, murders and slaughters of man by man, and natural disasters like earthquakes, floods, typhoons, and droughts, which account for many millions more deaths, there are over 4.5 billion human beings alive in the world today. The birth rate always meets the compensatory demand after a war or a natural disaster. Man is automated with a sex instinct to insure the replenishment of losses sustained because of his murderous predatory instincts and natural disasters.

The ancient Greek philosopher Heraclitus said, "War is the father of all and the king of all; and some he has made gods, some men, some bond and some free." How true! Indian wars were the father of the American colonies. The American Revolutionary War was the father of the United States as an independent nation. The Mexican War and the Spanish-American War were the father of today's sprawling, transcontinental United States. World War I and World War II were the father of the United States as a superpower. The history of the world is a history of wars. It is the history of people preying on people, and people resisting predation. It is the struggle of competing societies to survive in a world of natural biological and sociopolitical strife. That is why it is difficult to turn a single page of history without reading of war, combat, strife, revolution, uprising, invasion, insurrection, strike or some form of violence.

The father of scientific history, the ancient Greek of the fifth century B.C., Thucydides, believed that history repeats itself. History does, in fact, prove that all people on all continents replicated common themes. Nation-building by means of predation, followed by empire-building by means of predation, constitute the basic motif of the history of "civilized" man, from the time of the Ancient Egyptian Empire to modern times of the two World Wars. World War I was a clash between the great imperial powers. World War II was an attempt by Hitler and Mussolini to build a vast empire in Europe and Africa, and Japan to build a great empire in the Far East.

Life evolved to higher orders from the simple protozoa, and culminated in man by means of struggle for existence, natural selection, and survival of the fittest. Similarly, human societies evolved to higher orders from simple tribes, kingdoms, nations, empires, and superpowers by means of struggle for existence (war) and survival of the fittest (society). The process by which sociopolitical evolution has taken place; that is, war, has been bloody, brutal, and savage. The human carnage has been astronomical. The human suffering has been incalculable.

Circa 4000 B.C., many little kingdoms formed along the Nile river in North-East Africa following many minor wars of unification. After a series of major wars of conquest, and by means of them, they combined into two larger kingdoms. These two kingdoms fought each other bitterly until they became united into the nation of Egypt about 3400 B.C. The pharaohs, using slave labor, began the Egyptian Pyramid Era at this time. Then, between 2500 B.C. and 1500 B.C., the rich nobles engaged in a power struggle which severely weakened the pharaohs. About 1500 B.C., Thutmose III formed a powerful army of chariots and archers. He re-established the rule of the pharaohs and conquered many surrounding nations. HE CREATED THE FIRST KNOWN MILITARY EMPIRE. Rebellions broke up the empire by 1150 B.C.

Before 3000 B.C., the Suzerains came from the plateau of central Asia, conquered the area along the mouths of the Tigris and Euphrates rivers, and developed a civilization of city-kingdoms. The expanding wealth and progress of the Sumerians invited invasion from nomadic Semitic tribes such as the Hebrews, Phoenicians, Arameans, and Chaldeans, as well as the nomadic Aryan tribes from Asia. Wealth (loot) attracts predators by a kind of tropism, as light attracts moths. The Sumerian city-kingdoms constantly fought among themselves. (Tribes and city-kingdoms fighting among themselves is a common theme in history) Consequently, they became weakened and easy prey for Sargon of Akkad. Akkad was a country north of Sumer. Sargon defeated the Sumerians and set up the first Semitic kingdom. After considerable fighting, the nation of Sumer-and-Akkad was created, circa 2500 B.C. This nation then conquered much of Western Asia, but it was defeated by other Semitic invaders before 2000 B.C.

Circa 2500 B.C., a tribe of Amorites conquered the town of Babylon. A century later, Hammurabi, an Amorite king, conquered all of Shiner and the entire region became known as Babylonia. A tribe called Kassites conquered Babylon about 1750 B.C., and civilization was halted in that area for a thousand years

To the north of Babylon, and about 2900 B.C., a small settlement called Assur began to form into the kingdom of Assyria which was being constantly invaded from both the north and the south for over a thousand years. In defending themselves, the Assyrians became hardened to war, and this induced them to build a powerful military machine. This military machine afforded them power, and power in the hands of a natural predator means predation and conquest. By 750 B.C., the Assyrians had established a large empire which included Israel. Sennacherib, their king of biblical fame (705 B.C. to 681 B.C.), built a magnificent capital at Nineveh, but he also beat a path of destruction in the Ancient World. The Assyrians plundered mercilessly and punished rebels with extreme cruelty.

Assyrian soldiers were rewarded for every enemy head they brought in from the battlefield. Prisoners were forced to kneel, and their heads were either bashed in or cut off while scribes counted the slaughtered victims. The king presided while booty was distributed in proportion to each soldier's score of battered corpses and bashed heads. Defeated nobles received special treatment. Their feet were tied. Then their hands, feet, noses, and ears were sliced off. Their bleeding bodies were thrown from high towers. Their children were skinned alive, or slowly roasted over a scorching fire.

When Ashurbanipal conquered revolting Babylon, he had the tongues of the captives torn out of their mouths, and then their heads were clubbed to a pulp. Women and children were massacred in bloody orgies. The victims of the human predators were left for hungry vultures to gorge themselves. Curiously, some modern anthropologists condone those brutal slaughters as exigencies of overpopulation, but they do not advocate a nuclear holocaust as a modern remedy, probably because it would involve them and their kin.

The Assyrians were weakened by constant war and rebellions, which made it possible for the Chaldeans and their allies, the Medes, to conquer them. Nineveh fell in 612 B.C. The glory of the Chaldean conquerors (Neo-Babylonia) lasted less than one hundred years, but during that time, their ruler, Nebuchadnezzar, built a gorgeous palace which was roofed with the famous Hanging Gardens of Babylon. He conquered and destroyed Jerusalem and took thousands of select Hebrews into their famed "Babylonian captivity."

The Medes gobbled up an empire which included Persia, east of the Tigris, by 700 B.C. Cyrus united the Persian tribes by conquests and then conquered the Medes in 552 B.C. Surrounding countries, including Lydia, Chaldea, and Egypt, became so fearful of their own freedom because of the rapid success of Cyrus that they formed an alliance against him, but to no avail. Cyrus conquered Lydia and all Asia Minor to the Mediterranean, including Chaldea and Babylon. Shortly after the death of Cyrus, his son, Cambyses, conquered Egypt (525 B.C.). The Great Persian Empire was now at its peak.

It is important to remember that empires are predatory dominions of one nation over other nations, and nations, themselves, are predatory dominions of one kingdom or tribe over other kingdoms and tribes, and all such dominions are achieved by predatory wars of conquest.

The Scythians were hardy horsemen occupying the area of the Ukraine who, by 514 B.C., became sufficiently audacious to challenge the Persian Empire. The ritual of the Scythian warrior called upon him to drink blood from his first fallen foe. Scythian worship of the god of war included the bleeding to death of their victims whose right hands and arms were hacked from their bodies and hurled triumphantly into the air in honor of their god. They made leather-bound drinking cups from the skulls of their enemies.

The Ancient Greek historian Herodotus relates that the Scythians scalped their slain foe, and "scraped the scalp clean of flesh and, softening it by rubbing between the hands, uses it thenceforth as a napkin. The Scyth is proud of these scalps and hangs them from his bridle rein; the greater the number of such napkins that a man can show, the more highly is he esteemed among them." They make cloaks by sewing together the scalps of their slain enemy. Bear in mind that the Scythians were human beings exactly like us. They merely lived in an age and a society of different prejudices, beliefs, and customs.

When the Persian Empire expanded into the regions of the Greek city-states, war with the Greeks became inevitable. The Greeks were Indo-Europeans, or Aryans, who had invaded the home of Cretan Civilization from out of the northern grasslands. The island of Crete was the center of a well-developed civilization which began about 3000 B.C. By 2000 B.C., it had conquered most of the Aegean islands. It expanded into what is modern Greece about 1500 B.C. This civilization and era became known as the Mycenaean Age and flourished from 1500 to 1200 B.C.

Indo-European tribesmen from the north invaded the region of modern Greece around 1500 B.C. By 1000 B.C., these Indo-Europeans completely conquered the Aegean world, including the coast of Asia Minor. This brought them (the Ancient Greeks) into conflict with the expanding Persian Empire. The conquering Indo-Europeans from the north (the Ancient Greeks) developed a fantastic civilization such as the world had never known. It was superior to the civilization of Europe in the Middle Ages, and superior to anything black Africa developed even in modern times. It was the civilization of Aristotle, Plato, Socrates, Homer, Euclid, Pythagoras, Herodotus, Aristophanes, Hippocrates, and countless other contributors to philosophy, science, medicine, art, history, law, and literature which form the basis of all modern Western civilization.

The Persians conquered western Asia Minor (Ionia), but the Ionian cities quickly rebelled. Athens sent twenty ships to help them, but they were repulsed. The Persians sacked Miletus along with many other cities, killed the men, and carried the women and children back to Persia as slaves. This was a normal practice in those days. In 490 B.C., the Persians sent a fleet with invasion troops to Attica, a region near Athens and Marathon, where a bloody battle ensued. The Athenians won this famous Battle of Marathon. Pheidippides made the first Marathon run when he ran twenty-five miles to Athens with the glad tidings of victory.

Ten years later, the Persians invaded Greece again. The Greeks lost at Thermopylae, but won the brilliant naval victory at Salamis in 480 B.C. A year later, the Greek city-states were definitively saved from Persian conquest after victories at the Battle of Plataea and the naval engagement at Mycale. Flushed with victory, the Athenians promptly converted the Delian (DEFENSE) League of Greek city-states into their own empire. The power of Athens now aroused the fear and suspicion of another powerful city-state; namely, Sparta, whereupon Sparta and Athens lunged into a prolonged and bloody conflict called the Peloponnesian Wars.

Endless conflicts between the Greek city-states so weakened them that they became easy prey for Philip II of Macedonia. His conquest of the Greek city-states (with the exception of Sparta) was completed upon his victory at Chaeronea in 338 B.C. Throughout history, we read of people being torn apart by internal jealousies, fears, hatreds, and wars, then becoming weak and easy prey for conquest by an outside power. Human beings are natural predators, and the law of the predator mandates predation, with the mechanical certainty of a tropism, upon any signals of weakness.

Two years after Philip's great victory, he was murdered, and his twenty year-old son, Alexander, set out to conquer the world, disseminate Greek culture, and establish the Empire of Alexander the Great. He defeated the Persians at Granicus in 334 B.C. He then conquered Egypt, and turned to Asia to complete the conquest of the Persian Empire. He was in the midst of preparations for the conquest of India when he caught a fever and died at the age of thirty-three in 323 B.C.

We should never lose sight of the fact that the building of military empires always entailed a horrible toll on human life, incredible human suffering, and wholesale mayhem. As one small example, when the Thebans refused to become Alexander the Great's mercenaries, he massacred ten thousand of their men, women, and children. Any town that did not yield to him and join forces with him for further conquests was completely destroyed, and its inhabitants were either murdered or sold into slavery. To eliminate any threat to his personal power, he assassinated his stepmother and stepbrother. He was not above murdering some of his closest generals and advisers.

We are reminded of Joseph Stalin's murder of Kirov in 1934, and the murder of thousands of his old Bolshevik cronies during the infamous purges from 1937 to 1939. It is conjectured that his Soviet secret police imprisoned or murdered at least a million people. Power-hungry tyrants are as viable today as at any time in ancient history. There has been no diminution in the killing of man by man with the progress of civilization—quite the contrary! Human intelligence has been unable to restrain human predatory instincts. It has only truckled to them and rendered man an ever more vicious and dangerous killer.

For forty years after Alexander the Great's death, his generals fought bloody wars in a power struggle for acquisition of the Empire. It was ultimately divided into three parts. The European portion (Macedonia and Greece) went to Antigonus. The Asian portion consisting of the former Persian Empire went to Seleucus. The African portion (Egypt) went to Ptolemy (Cleopatra, storied queen of Egypt and lover of Marc Antony, was the last of the Ptolemaic line). In the meanwhile, the Romans were in the process of building one of the greatest empires in the history of the world. It was accomplished, naturally, by the usual human slaughter, and the accompanying human maiming, blood-letting, suffering, and agony.

In the seventh century B.C., Italy consisted of three peoples: the Italic tribes (early settlers of diverse origins), the Etruscans (immigrants by sea from Lydia in Asia Minor), and Greek colonizers. They waged vicious wars against each other for control of Italy. Rome was a little village of Italic tribes (Latins) in 1000 B.C. The Romans learned civilization from the Etruscans and the Greeks. The idiosyncratic attributes of the Romans were ability as builders of such structures as roads, bridges, and viaducts, and their amazing tenacity in war. They suffered many defeats, but they persevered with such doggedness that they drove out invaders from Gaul, and defeated and united all Italian tribes including the tough Samnites.

Etruscan kings ruled Rome from 750 B.C., but the Latins revolted and expelled the Etruscans in 500 B.C. A long internal struggle ensued between the common people (plebs) and the nobles (patricians). The plebs won a snatch of power and became more willing to fight for conquests because they could now share in the conquered farm lands, and they could now claim war prisoners as slaves for themselves. In other words, they could share in the loot and booty of conquest. The lure of booty gave them an incentive for even greater conquests. As a result, Rome became master of all Italy after the defeat of a last ditch alliance of Gauls, Etruscans, and Samnites in 295 B.C. at the battle of Sentinum, and the surrender of the Greeks in 270 B.C.

Even a cursory discussion of Ancient Rome is incomplete if it fails to include Carthage. Phoenician seafarers (Semites akin to the ancient Jews) founded a colony on the North African coast, near

Sicily, in the ninth century B.C. It was called Carthage. Carthage seized colonies in Spain, Sardinia, Corsica, and Sicily, just as European nations seized colonies in the New World after the fifteenth century A.D. The seafaring Carthaginians controlled the sea. This sea power was an impediment to Roman trade in the Mediterranean. The two expanding predatory powers, Rome and Carthage, became hell-bent on a collision course, and three Punic (from Poen)—Greek and Roman name for Phoenicia) Wars resulted.

The First Punic War (264-241 B.C.) was caused by Roman jealousy over Carthaginian expansion in Sicily, and Rome's own desire to expand into Sicily in a kind of manifest destiny. Rome realized the necessity of becoming a sea power during her struggles to wrest Sicily from Carthage. She built four fleets, but they were destroyed by the Carthaginians. She then invented the grappling hook, with which she could lash her ships to enemy ships and convert a sea battle into a land battle of hand-to-hand combat, at which the Romans excelled. The Carthaginians were forced to sue for peace, and Sicily became a Roman province.

Victory made the Romans more arrogant and greedy than ever. They seized Corsica and Sardinia. Rome interpreted the Carthaginian attempt to rebuild an empire in Spain as a threat to her interests and unleashed the Second Punic War (218-201 B.C.). Hannibal was the Carthaginians' ablest general. He crossed the Alps, starting from the Carthaginian colony in Spain, passed through Gaul (modern France), and entered Italy from the rugged Alps. It was a fantastic feat to move an army of sixty thousand, including thirty-seven elephants, and eight thousand mounted fighters, through such forbidding terrain. He suffered great losses, but they were largely due to inclement weather. Nevertheless, the lure and promise of loot and booty for his soldiers was irresistible. It enabled him to annihilate the Roman army at Cannae in 216 B.C. He killed fifty thousand Romans and captured twenty thousand others. The dying Romans, having had their tendons slashed from behind, begged to be killed.

Hannibal won continuing victories on the Roman home ground of Italy for fifteen years, but Roman tenacity finally won the day. The Romans appeased the wrath of their gods by entombing vestal virgins alive, and fought on with renewed vigor. The Carthaginians appeased their god, Baal-Haman, by daily sacrifices of up to hundreds of living children to devouring flames, as their cries were drowned out in the noise of trumpets and cymbals. The Roman general, Scipio, who replaced Fabius the Cunctator, defeated the Carthaginians in Africa. Hannibal had been called home to defend the homeland, where he was soundly defeated in the Battle of Zama in 202 B.C. The war was costly for Rome. The Second Punic War ravaged about half of the Italian farms, destroyed four hundred towns, and killed three hundred thousand men.

By 149 B.C., Roman vindictiveness and avarice reached their zenith. The rapid recovery of Carthaginian prosperity excited Roman envy and fear. Now nothing could placate the senatorial magnates except the utter destruction of Carthage and the complete expropriation of her territory. Cato personified this sentiment when he orated, "*Delenda Est Carthago!*" (Carthage must be destroyed!) In a series of treacherous acts, Rome managed to disarm Carthage, but she still mustered the strength to resist the siege of her city for three years in this, the Third Punic War (149-146 B.C.). Upon the horrible and frightful butchery of her five hundred thousand population, which reduced it to fifty-five thousand, Carthage was forced to surrender. The survivors were sold into slavery and the magnificent city was razed, plowed under, and sown with salt. In 146 B.C., Carthage was wiped from the face of the Earth. Rome reigned supreme. It was brutal, but it was effective—as effective as the annihilation of the American Indians was in eliminating them from world history and elevating the United States to supremacy.

Slaves were abundant and cheap in the Roman Empire. One hundred and fifty thousand prisoners of war were sold into slavery after one military victory alone. Slaves were worked to exhaustion from morning until night, often flogged, and always poorly fed. At night, they were chained in basement dungeons. If they revolted, they were crucified. During the year 30 B.C., there were four hundred thousand slaves in the city of Rome alone. It was said that some Romans owned twenty thousand slaves. Almost all work was performed by slaves. Their plight was one of inhuman cruelty. Seneca told of the instruments of torture used on slaves, the savage punishments, the tearing apart of human limbs, and the branding of the slaves' foreheads. A rational creature may well suspect that membership in the human race is more a disgrace than an honor.

The vast majority of Romans were not interested in art, science, or literature. They derived their pleasure from drooling over gladiatorial combats, in which slaves and criminals were made either to fight each other to the death in the blood-soaked Flavian amphitheater, or to fight feral beasts in an arena of splattered gore and shredded flesh. Even though they caused their fellow human beings to be killed for sport and merriment, the Romans considered themselves to be kindly people because they gave the victorious gladiator a slight chance to live. Throughout the ancient world it was always considered moral and just to slaughter war captives, criminals, and disobedient slaves. Hence, giving one of them even a one-in-a-thousand chance to live was an act of love and charity.

Romans are cited for their contributions to jurisprudence, but Roman law was Draconian. It permitted a father to torture, imprison, sell, or kill any of his children. The law decreed death for libel, perjury, and fraud. Rebellious slaves were severely punished; for example, six thousand followers of Spartacus were crucified along the Appian way, and their rotting bodies were left to hang on the crosses for months as a warning to other slaves.

Julius Caesar expanded the Roman Empire by conquering Gaul (modern France). He made himself the first emperor, thus ending the republic. Octavian defeated Marc Antony in 31 B.C., in the naval battle of Actium, and added Egypt to the Empire in 30 B.C. Octavian arrogated the titles of Augustus and Imperator. Claudius defeated and added Britain to the Empire during his reign (A.D. 41-51). There were isolated revolts, civil wars, and bloody skirmishes, but the Romans were so firmly in the saddle for two hundred years after Octavian's victory in 31 B.C., that the era was called Pax Romana (Roman Peace). It was peace or death. When the Jews revolted in A.D. 70, about one million of them were killed. Jerusalem and the temple were destroyed. Fleeing Jews had their bellies slit open in searches for swallowed coins. Survivors either sought refuge by killing themselves, died as unwilling gladiators, or were sold as slaves.

Death came, as it must to all things, to the Roman Empire. Barbarians invaded the Empire, leaving devastation everywhere. The Huns, defeated in the East by the Han emperors of China, moved westward, spreading death and destruction wherever they went. They forced the Sarmatians to leave their homeland and move into the Balkans, which, in turn, forced the native Goths to flee and invade the Roman frontiers. Alaric the Visigoth sacked Rome in A.D. 400. In A.D. 429, Gaiseric the Vandal conquered Spain and North Africa. His pirate fleet controlled the Mediterranean, and he raided Sicily in A.D. 440. He sacked Rome in A.D. 455. Attila the Hun was hard on the heels of the fleeing German tribes. The Huns were horsemen and deadly accurate mounted archers, who struck terror in the hearts of their prey. Attila built an empire of conquered German tribes. When he died in A.D. 453, his many sons scrambled for loot (the Empire). They fought bitterly among themselves. The predatory struggle for existence was keen, and the selection of the fittest was relentless.

Rome decayed and was ripe for a fall. Corruption was rampant. Agriculture came to a standstill. Sex ran riot. The dole replaced hard work. Inflation went wild. It was difficult to feed children, and so parents engaged in the massive killing of their infants by exposure. In A.D. 166, the Asiatic Plague killed half of the people in the Empire. The Plague of A.D. 260 to A.D. 265 killed five thousand people a day for many weeks. The holocausts of war, plague, abortion, and infanticide sapped the vitality of the Empire. The Roman Empire in the West officially came to an end in A.D. 476 when Odoacer, a German general, became emperor.

The Roman Empire of sorts in the East, under the name of the Byzantine Empire, with its capitol at Constantinople (Istanbul), survived another one thousand years. The name of this Empire was derived from Byzantium, the city Constantine I rebuilt and renamed as Constantinople (City of Constantine) in A.D. 330. The Turks changed its name to Istanbul in 1930.

History is the process of sociopolitical evolution (AND REPETITION), the general pattern of which is the same for all peoples all over the world, and for the same reason seeds of the same species of plant have the same patterns of development, no matter when or where they are planted; that is, because they contain the same entelechy. In the Far East, Chinese farmers created civilizations along the river valleys, much as the Egyptians had along the Nile, the Sumerians had along the Tigris and Euphrates, and the Latins had along the Tiber. The civilized farmers and city people along these rivers created conspicuous wealth, which lured nomads into attacking them and looting it. Military leaders arose to defend the people against marauding nomads, but when they became powerful, they promptly conquered their neighboring tribesmen and made themselves kings of centralized kingdoms.

Greed is concomitant with power in the human predator; and so, these leaders were driven by their instincts to conquer surrounding kingdoms like common brigands and to unify them into huge personal possessions which we read in history as EMPIRES. Successful conquest is a tremendous ego-inflater; and so, these conquerors conferred impressive titles upon themselves, such as EMPEROR, IMPERATOR, AUGUSTUS, GREAT (Alexander, Peter, Frederick, et cetera), MAGNIFICENT (Sulayman), even GOD. When Christians refused to worship the Roman emperors they incurred persecution. The Japanese emperor was worshipped as a descendant of the sun goddess until World War II.

Ch'in Shih Huang Ti unified China in 221 B.C. by conquering or terrorizing other Chinese kingdoms. He proclaimed himself the "First Sovereign Emperor of Ch'in." The word China is derived from Chin. He boasted that his dynasty would last "10,000 generations." (Sounds like Hitler's boast that the Third Reich would last one thousand years.) It was said that one of Ch'in Shih Huang Ti's generals slaughtered four hundred thousand soldiers of a rival kingdom after it surrendered. He built the Great Wall of China, which was said to be the "longest Cemetery on Earth" because tens of thousands of its slave builders were reputed to have been buried in its foundations, and many were bricked up alive for not working at breakneck speed. When he died, several hundred maidens were buried alive with his body to keep him company in the hereafter. The workmen who built his elaborate mausoleum were also buried alive with his body "lest they should live to reveal the secret passage to the grave." The Ch'in

Dynasty barely survived his death by five years. Rival princes quickly established rival kingdoms.

The civilized Chinese kingdoms were attacked by Tartar, Mongol, and Hun nomads, just as the civilized Egyptians, Sumerians, Cretans, and Latins were attacked by Semitic, Indo-European, and German nomads. These attacks prompted the Chinese to build the Great Wall of China as a defense against invading nomads, but it was also a monument to an egomaniacal emperor's vanity. The wall was three thousand seven hundred miles long through rugged mountains, forty feet high, and contained twenty-five thousand towers.

Protective walls as defenses against human predation are common in history. Notable walls of antiquity were those of Thebes, Troy, Jericho, Babylon, and the Hadrian Wall. The wall at Caracassonne, France, is an example of a medieval wall. Defensive walls were even built in modern times; for example, the French Maginot Line, and the German Siegfried Line.

We who study history objectively are driven to two inescapable conclusions: 1) The fact that man has ALWAYS preyed upon his fellow man, either as man upon man, tribe upon tribe, kingdom upon kingdom, nation upon nation, or empire upon empire, proves that he is a territorial predator who is driven to predation by the relentless compulsion of instinct. Human intelligence in this Age of Science did not countermand predation and violence. It intensified it by transforming tooth and claw into ever deadlier blockbuster bombs and nuclear weapons. 2) The stupidity of the human animal exceeds the stupidity of all other animals. No other animal will kill or die at the beck and call of fanatical tyrants as, for example, the Germans killed and died for Hitler. No other animal will murder its species for sacrifices to its gods, for holy wars, willingly die for silly promises of eternal life, or follow goofball religious nuts into senseless bloodbaths.

After the fall of the Roman Empire (Western), the Franks (a German tribe), under the leadership of Clovis, conquered the territory known today as Western Germany and France. In keeping with the old familiar refrain in history, civil wars followed his death in A.D. 511. In A.D. 687, Pepin conquered the areas in the North.

His son, Charles, conquered and united the entire Frankish realm. This was at the time the Mohammedans were trying to conquer the world in the name of their God, Allah. Allah spurred them on with insensate fury and an unquenchable thirst for blood, as only religious fanaticism can. Hordes of Mohammedans poured into Spain, and then into France, from the coast of Africa. Charles defeated them in the Battle of Tours. After this victory, he became known as Charles Martel (Charles the Hammer) because of his ferociousness in battle. His grandson, Karl, became known as Charlemagne (Charles the Great).

The most vicious killers of history are honored by having "GREAT" suffixed to their names, a few of which were Alexander the Great, Peter the Great, and Catherine the Great.

"Charlemagne," in the words of Dagobert D. Runes, "was one of the most vicious and bloodthirsty conquerors of the Dark Ages, forever engaged in conquestorial enterprises and multiple feats of almost childish self-aggrandizement." He conquered the Saxons and encouraged their conversion to Christianity by such intimidating acts as decapitating four thousand, five hundred of them on the Aller River. He enslaved so many Slavs that the modern word "slave" is coined from the word "Slav." He emulated Mohammed by spreading the Christian religion with the sword. Many good people in Europe and America worship Christ today only because of Charlemagne's brutality. The Pope was grateful for his service of increasing the power and wealth of the Church by proselytizing the populations, and he proved it by crowning him "Emperor of the Romans" in A.D. 800. The Roman Catholic Church canonized him as a saint on December 28, 1164.

Charlemagne didn't relish his crowning by the Pope because it placed him in a subservient position. He wanted suzerainty over both the state and the Church. After Charlemagne's death, his sons and grandsons fought the usual bitter battles for inheritance of the Empire. In A.D. 843, it was divided into three realms by the Treaty at Verdun. The realm in the east became Germany, and the realm in the west became France. These two realms have waged war over boundary disputes ever since. It was a bone of contention in the two

World Wars. In the interval, and before A.D. 900, Charlemagne's former Empire split up into warring tribes, and the primitive tribal wars of the German people began all over again.

A new wave of barbarian invasions by Saracens, Slavs, Magyars, and Norsemen now began. They murdered and plundered with gusto. Violent disorder gave rise to the need for skilled warriors to defend against the marauders. A warrior class evolved from former officers of the kings and from bandits. The kings had lost their power. The warriors became the fighting nobles in the Age of Knights from A.D. 1000 to 1300. A three-class society developed: 1) The workers, or serfs (practically slaves); 2) The fighters or military nobility; and 3) The prayers or clergy.

The class divisions were rigid. If a serf killed an enemy nobleman, even in war, he was not decorated. He was executed by his own commander for the crime of a commoner killing a person of high rank. High office in the Church was held only by noblemen. Most of the people were impoverished. Serfs were sold with the land. They were chattel. The children of the serfs were the property of the lord. The lord enjoyed many special privileges among which was the legal right to spend the first night of his vassal's wedding with the vassal's bride. This legal right was called "DROIT DU SEIGNEUR" and "JUS PRIMAE NOCTIS."

Force was the law of the feudal world, and warfare was the principal occupation of the age. Any sign of weakness immediately invited attack by a neighbor. Constant fighting turned most of Europe into a wasteland. Wars and banditry made trade and travel hazardous. The principal occupation of the knights was plundering their rivals' serfs. The Church became land wealthy from do nations and from inheritances. The faithful believed that by willing their property to the Church, they would assure salvation for themselves, plus top status in Heaven. Men of high descent were expected to respond to insults, real or imagined, by fighting duels of honor, a practice which persisted as late as 1804 when Alexander Hamilton was killed in a duel with Aaron Burr for the alleged insult of having called Burr "a dangerous man." Alexander's son Philip had similarly died in a duel in A.D. 1801. It was obviously not an unbiased observer who flattered man with the designation *Homo Sapiens* (wise man).

In A.D. 1095, Pope Urban II persuaded Christians to kill fewer of each other and more of the infidel Mohammedans. The incentive for dying and for killing was the promised guarantee of eternal salvation. The goal was the liberation of the Holy Land from the infidel Moslems. And so began the Crusades, in which the Christians slaughtered the infidel Mohammedans in the name of Christ, and the Mohammedans slaughtered the infidel Christians in the name of Allah. The motivation for the Moslems was the same as for Christians—the promise of instant Heaven. Mohammed called Heaven the "GARDEN OF DELIGHTS", in which the believer would be clothed in robes of shimmering silk, as he reclined on couches of exquisite designs, while being attended by beautiful girls. It was an alluring paradise for a man. Women never counted for much in the Islamic world. The war cry of the Christians was, "God wills it!" The war cry of the Mohammedan generals was, "Victory or paradise is before you. The devil and hell-fire are behind you. Charge!" You couldn't induce the most stupid animal, either alive or extinct, to kill or die for such childish nonsense.

Mankind has always proudly killed and died for the mythological gods created by his fertile imagination. One pious knight jubilantly wrote to the Pope, "The Crusaders rode in the blood of Moslems up to the knees of their horses." How better to honor the Prince of Peace and the God of Love—human style? Under the guidance of Peter the Hermit, a motley horde of plunderers marched to liberate the Holy Land. Many were slaughtered en route by the Hungarians. Many died for various reasons. The survivors were massacred by the Turks. In A.D. 1099, the Crusaders took Jerusalem, then murdered the inhabitants with shocking barbarity. In A.D. 1183, Moslems substituted Christian prisoners for goats in the sacrificial slaughter of the annual pilgrimage rites in Mecca. Saladin recaptured Jerusalem in A.D. 1187.

Other Crusades followed, the most bizarre of which was the Children's Crusade. It was reasoned that the Crusades had failed because of the sinfulness of the Crusaders, and that God would look with more favor on children because of their pristine innocence. With that logic in mind, and with the help of Pope Innocent III, a twelve-year-old named Stephen, after hearing "the voice of God" talk to him, organized fifty thousand children to do "God's work" of liberating the Holy Land. They were emotionally devastated when they reached the Mediterranean, and God failed to part the waters as biblical legend related He had done for the children of Israel.

Some merchant seamen offered to take the young crusaders to Palestine free of charge. Five thousand accepted the offer. It came to pass that God didn't look with favor on the children either. Two ships were wrecked. Five did reach Moslem ports, but the merchant mariners sold the children into slavery. In A.D. 1291, Sultan Khalil drove the Crusaders completely out of Palestine and massacred or enslaved sixty thousand prisoners. The Moslems held the Holy Land until after World War I when Britain took it as a Protectorate. Allah had held suzerainty over Christ in the Holy Land for over six hundred years.

England and France were natural enemies since the Norman invasion of A.D. 1066. William the Conqueror unified Normandy (by war, of course). Then he crossed the English Channel and defeated the English at the Battle of Hastings. He became King of England, then conquered the rest of the country with his motley regiment which burned crops and houses, savagely murdered menfolk, and killed cattle. Thus it was that the King of England controlled both England and French Normandy, and a long enmity arose between England and France. By the time of Henry II of England, less than one hundred years later, the English kings held ten times as much of France as the French kings.

The French kings wanted to expel the English from France. The English coveted even more of France; hence, the hostility. This hostility was the basis for the Hundred Years' War, which exacted a terrible toll in human lives. The English had conquered almost all of France after their victories at Crecy in A.D. 1346, and Agincourt in A.D. 1415. Joan of Arc now entered the scene, and circumstances began to ameliorate for France. She heard "divine voices" which inspired her to lead the French to victory at Orleans in A.D. 1429. The French were now convinced that God was on their side; so they fought with super-charged ferocity. Joan led the French to many victories, but she was taken prisoner; and, through English treachery and conspiracy, condemned on the charge of heresy; and burned at the stake. Nevertheless, Joan of Arc had done her work of inspiring the French and uniting them. The French and English began to hate each other as never before, and their mutual slaughters were to continue unabatedly for several hundred years, or until they found even better qualified enemies.

It should be noted that the French were Franks who were German tribesmen. The Normans, or Norsemen, were also German tribesmen. After the fall of the Roman Empire, Britain was invaded by Angles, Saxons, and Jutes—all German tribesmen. The very name England means "Angle-land" or "Land of the Angles" (Germans). Much of the carnage in Europe until the present time was the slaughter of Germans by Germans. King George I of England could speak no English, only German. Old English and German were nearly identical languages. Even today, many words are similar; for example, "*bruder*" and "brother", "*mutter*" and "mother", "*vater*" and "father", "*papier*" and "paper", "*mann*" and "man", "*land*" and "land", "*und*" and "and", "*maus*" and "mouse", "*natur*" and "nature", *et cetera*. The French retained more of the Latin influence in their language: a relic of the Roman Empire, in which Latin was the official language. The Italians, Spanish, Portuguese, and Romanians all preserved their linguistic links to the ancient Roman Empire.

The rivalry between England and France was very keen during the Age of Imperialism when conquest was ostensibly undertaken in the name of national honor, but actually for loot and plunder. It became a contest among the nations of Europe to see which could gobble up the most colonies. The imperialistic powers waged war on each other, like hyenas and lions fighting over the carcass of the prey.

In A.D. 1756, England's William Pitt set out to defeat the French in America, in India, and on the high seas. He succeeded in Canada at the Battle on the Plains of Abraham in Quebec (1759), which claimed the lives of both Montcalm and Wolfe. He achieved success in India with Robert Clive's defeat of Dupleix and Lally in 1763. Complete success was enjoyed when the French were driven from the seas. The defeated French were bitter and sought revenge. That was the principal reason France quickly recognized American Independence and sent Lafayette to help us defeat the English.

Napoleon Bonaparte revived subdued French militancy. France and England again lunged for each other's jugular in a series of vicious wars. Napoleon instilled loyalty and bellicose frenzy in his troops by the traditional method of appealing to their predatory instincts and promising them loot. Said he to his troops, "Fruitful provinces will soon lie at your mercy. There you will find honor, profit, and wealth." The promise of booty has been almost as effective as the promise of eternal paradise to arouse man's killer instinct. Predatory instincts manifest themselves at every opportunity, such as after natural disasters. Even the New York blackouts of a few years ago attracted looters by the droves, not because of economic deprivation, but because of the compulsion of predatory instincts.

Napoleon built an empire in continental Europe through the usual employment of cunning, intrigue, ruthlessness, assassinations, murders, and massacres. He planned to invade England, but Admiral Nelson thwarted his plans at Trafalgar in 1805. Nevertheless, Napoleon won control of most of continental Europe, and world domination was within his grasp. His plan was to destroy England economically; and so, he instituted his Continental System, which forbade all countries from trading with England.

England was inaugurating the Industrial Revolution, and trade was vital to her; but industrial products were also vital to the world, including Napoleon who, himself, broke the Continental System when it served his purposes. Russia wanted the fruits of the Industrial Revolution; and so, she defied Napoleon by renewing trade with England. Napoleon retaliated in 1812 by invading Russia with six hundred thousand men. Russian winter, and Russian tactics of retreating, leaving nothing but scorched earth, coalesced to deal disaster to Napoleon. His tattered, starving, freezing troops retreated from Moscow, but most of them died. Only twenty thousand half-dead men managed to return to France. This fiasco was repeated by Hitler in 1943 with the rout of Gen. Friedrich von Paulus at Stalingrad and three hundred thousand German casualties.

Napoleon rebuilt an army of five hundred thousand soldiers, lost the crucial and gory Battle of the Nations at Leipzig in 1813, and again retreated into France but with only ninety thousand survivors. This time the jig was up. Napoleon was exiled to the island of Elba, off Italy. Trouble brewed in France. It gave Napoleon renewed inspiration. He escaped in 1815, gathered an army of one hundred twenty-five thousand men, and met Wellington at the Battle of Waterloo where he was defeated, but not without the help of the German (Prussian) General Blucher and his army of one hundred twenty thousand men. The English did not call the Germans "Huns" at that time. The Germans were their very good friends and allies.

This is the eternally recurrent irony of history. Today's allies, who must be loved by government decree, are tomorrow's enemies, who must be slaughtered by government decree, and vice versa. Only a few years ago, Japanese and Americans were killing each other, as were Germans and Americans. Today, they embrace each other. The English did not hate the Germans until Germany became a powerful industrial and military nation which posed a threat to her control of one-quarter of the Earth. The English boasted that the sun never set on the British Empire, and they meant to keep it that way.

After Waterloo, Napoleon was exiled on Saint Helena, where he died or was murdered five years later (1821). Forgotten are the 100 million people in Europe who suffered frightfully from his pillagings, burnings, and killings. The human misery, despair, tears, torment, and pain he caused are interred with his bones, but the glory of his conquests live on for time immemorial. This is as it must be. A predatory animal must glorify the greatest of its predators. It is only a question of time when Hitler's atrocities will also be forgotten, and his memory as another conquering Napoleon or Alexander the Great will live in glory as an inspiration to the predatory race of human beings.

Human tribes, kingdoms, or cities do not normally unite into a nation as a result of rational considerations. The ruler of each tribe, kingdom, or city wants desperately to maintain his power, and he will violently resist anyone or anything that will diminish it. Only a greater military or police power strong enough to wrest away the local power can unite population groups into nations. This power must be wielded by war and violence, rather than by reason, because man is an irrational animal. England was united because of many bloody wars of aggression against Scotland, Wales, and Ireland. The Republic of Ireland eventually escaped union into the United Kingdom, but only by struggling through centuries of cruel wars. Freebooting lords from England first seized lush, green Ireland in the Age of Knights (A.D. 1000-1300). The Emerald Isle was attractive loot.

Otto Von Bismarck once said, "The great questions of the day will not be settled by speeches or by majority decisions...but by iron and blood." So saying, he unified the Prussian segment of the German people into the German nation by blood and iron. The other segment, the Austrian, built an empire all its own in the way all empires were built—by blood and iron. (Hitler united Austria and Germany in 1938. This Anschluss was nullified in 1943.) Bismarck picked a fight with the Empire of Austria-Hungary in 1866, and annexed several German states as a consequence of victory. He tricked France into declaring war on Germany in 1870. After several bloody battles, and with the French losing one hundred twenty thousand men in two days, the French surrendered at Sedan. Germany gained Alsace-Lorraine and also the undying hatred of France which helped precipitate World War I after which France retook Alsace-Lorraine only to lose it to Hitler in 1940, but Germany lost it to France again in 1944.

Only self-serving, prejudicial, irrational blindness can prevent an intelligent being from realizing that man is a cruel, stupid, territorial predator—a born killer. The human brain proves itself to be an organ of stupidity far more often than it proves itself an organ of intelligence. Man's brain evolved on nature's proving ground of competing predators. The brain of the superior predator had survival value, and it was selected for reproduction and encoded in the DNA strands of the double helix. Man's brain did not evolve in an ivory tower of philosophic intellects contemplating the solution to the riddle of the Universe.

Italy was unified after a long series of wars and revolutions. Camillo Cavour started the process by masterminding the Austro-Sardinian War of 1859. Giuseppe Garibaldi organized his "Red Shirts," fought against Austria which held Italian states, and conquered Sicily, whereupon he became its dictator. (We are reminded of Mussolini, who organized his "Black Shirts" to re-establish the Roman Empire and national glory. Hitler organized his "Brown Shirts" to establish the Third Reich as successor to the German Empire of 1871-1918 which was the Second Reich.) Italy was partially unified in 1866 when she joined Prussia in one of her wars against another German power and arch rival, Austria. With the defeat of Austria, Italian territory held by Austria was given to Italy by Prussia. Further unification took place when the Papal States were annexed after the defeat of the Pope in Rome in 1871. The Pope retaliated by excommunicating the King of Italy and making himself "the prisoner of the Vatican." Final unification took place after World War I with the breakup of the Austro-Hungarian Empire.

The United States was unified as British Colonies as a consequence of many wars such as the Pequot War (1637), King Philip's War (1675-1676), King William's War (1689-1697), Queen Anne's War (1702-1713), War of Jenkin's Ear (1739-1741), King George's War (1744-1748), French and Indian War (1756-1763), *et cetera*. The United States was unified as an independent nation by the American Revolution and the War of 1812. Unification was preserved by the American Civil War. The Hawaiian Islands were unified by Kamehameha the Great in 1810 when he conquered all the reigning chiefs and drove rival troops to their deaths over Oahu's Pali cliffs. He created a dynasty that ended with the death of Kamehameha V in 1872.

The brutal killings, mayhem, and intense suffering that accompanied the predatory wars of national unification are forgotten. Only the glory of victory lives forever for posterity to celebrate—the Fourth of July, for example. Such are the ways of predatory animals. They are not the ways of rational creatures.

We have time and space to barely scratch the surface regarding man slaughtering man in satisfying his predatory appetite for power, empire, and national unification. The planet Earth has been a human slaughterhouse since the dawn of history; and, when we speak of human slaughterhouses, we cannot overlook the Mongol Empire, which reached its zenith in A.D. 1300. Temujin (A.D. 1167-1227) exterminated the Tartars, destroyed the Kereit people, and assumed the title of Genghis Khan (Indomitable Emperor). He went on to forge one of the world's greatest empires. It encompassed the vast territory from all of China, Russia, most of Asia, and eastern Europe, to Hungary. In twelve years of warfare, Genghis Khan accounted for the slaughter of more than 18 million people in China alone. Any survivor of a Mongol invasion was a potential rebel. The solution to the problem of possible rebellion was simple—mass slaughter of all survivors. It is said that human blood never dried on the Khan's hands. His wars left a trail of human carnage that makes Hitler's Holocaust look like a Sunday school picnic.

Batu Khan, a grandson of Genghis Khan, was one of the most sadistic murderers in history. According to Sir Robert K. Douglas, Batu Khan broke the resistance of the defenders of Ryazan in December of 1237, whereupon the Boyars and all inhabitants, regardless of age and sex, were slaughtered with the savage cruelty of Mongol revenge. Some were impaled, shot at with arrows for sport, flayed, or had splinters of wood driven under their fingernails. Priests were roasted alive. Nuns and maidens were ravished in churches. Not a single eye remained open to shed tears for the blood bath.

Tamerlane (Khan Timur the Lame) claimed to be a descendant of Genghis Khan. He made Hitler look like Saint Francis of Assisi. He drew his inspiration from the Koran, which he quoted as, "O Prophet, make war upon infidels and unbelievers, and treat them with severity." This cruel, Turkic, Islamic conqueror and master of intrigue and treachery subdued every state from Mongolia to the Mediterranean. He crossed the Indus and massacred or enslaved all who could not flee from him. When he captured Delhi, he slaughtered one hundred thousand people in cold blood and then plundered the city. He built pyramids of their skulls. In 1386, he ordered the massacre of all the inhabitants of Isfahan. He ordered the decapitation of the slain knights of Saint John in Smyrna, and used the heads as missiles which were catapulted on the enemy. His sons and grandsons fought over succession to his Empire. His descendant, Bahur, founded the Moslem line of Indian emperors known as the Great Moguls.

Will Durant wrote in his *Story of Civilization*, "The Mohammedan conquest of India is probably the bloodiest story in history." Sultan Balkan punished rebels by skinning them alive, stuffing their skins with straw, and hanging them from Delhi's gates. Sultan Ahmad Shar feasted lavishly whenever the slaughter of Hindus exceeded twenty thousand a day. Firoz Shah put a bounty on infidels and paid off on one hundred and eighty thousand Hindu heads. Circa A.D. 1600, Mogul Emperor Jahangir impaled rebels' heads on a forest of spears, exhibited them to his rebellious son, and then blinded him. The fanatic Qutb-ud-din Aibak slaughtered hundreds of thousands of "infidels." This inhuman cruelty forced many Hindus to convert to Mohammedanism, which set the stage for the continuation of religious hatred and slaughter to this very day. It caused the breakup of India into the states of Pakistan and Bangladesh.

Rurik the Norseman was the founder of Russia in the ninth century A.D. He came from Sweden and conquered the Slavic tribes in central Europe. In 1237, the Mongol Batu Khan, conquered and destroyed all the chief Russian cities except Novgorod and Pskov. The Mongols established the Empire of the Golden Horde in south and east Russia, which lasted until A.D. 1480. By A.D. 1300, the Ottoman Turks had conquered much of the Mongol Empire; and, by A.D. 1454, they conquered the Byzantine Empire, which brought an end to the Eastern Roman Empire. By A.D. 1500, the Russian Prince of Moscow, Ivan the Terrible, became powerful enough to defeat the Mongol overlords and assume the title of Czar (Caesar). His Cossack leader Yermak conquered Siberia. The czars continued a series of cruel wars of conquest and extermination until the Russian Empire extended from the Pacific Ocean to Germany.

Peter the Great and Catherine the Great were among the honored butcherers of history who helped make Russia sprawl over one-sixth of the Earth's surface. England contained Russia's further expansion out of fear of the threat to her own empire. England never permitted Russia to gain her most cherished goal, Constantinople and control of the Dardanelles and Bosporus. She wanted to bottle up Russia's naval power in the Black Sea. That was the reason England and France drove Russia out of the Ottoman Empire in 1854 and waged the Crimean War.

A vicious Russo-Turkish war was fought from 1877 to 1878 because Russia came to the aid of her Slavic cousins, who were subjects of the Ottoman Empire. The Slavs were Christians like the Russians, and they were being brutalized by their Turkish overlords who were Mohammedans.

Ottoman Sultan Abd Al-Hamid II attempted to exterminate the Christian Armenians. One million Armenians were massacred between 1895 and 1915. In 1915, Turkish Interior Minister Talaat Pasha decreed Armenian genocide with the order, "Destroy completely all Armenians living in Turkey . . . No regard must be paid to age, or sex, or to scruples of conscience." Armenian babies were thrown into pits and buried alive. The women were raped, their breasts were hacked off, and they were murdered by Turkish gendarmes.

Struggles of the Balkan countries for freedom and independence from the tyranny of the Ottoman Empire, in addition to imperial rivalries, led to the Balkan Wars; which, in turn, led to World War I. World War I sowed the seeds of World War II. It is said that unpreparedness invites war, as it did in World War II, but preparedness invited World War I prior to which Europe was a bristling armed camp. Only one thing really causes war—the predatory nature of man, the territorial carnivore. The history of the human race is a history of predation, strife, and war.

The history of mankind has passed through five phases: 1) Human beings formed tribes, just as apes form troops because of their gregarious instincts. Like all animals, man tends to breed faster than the food supply permits. The need for Lebensraum, plus his territorial and predatory instincts, have thrust him into endless wars of conquest. 2) Macho leaders motivated by acquisitive instincts forced their tribesmen to unite into kingdoms by means of bloody conquests. 3) The same predatory instincts caused kingdoms to unify into nations—also by means of bloody conquests. 4) Nations with superior predatory competence, and led by charismatic super predators, gobbled up colonies and territories to create EMPIRES, at the cost of great human carnage and suffering. 5) National charismatic "heroes" emerged who "liberated" imperialistically united peoples by means of sanguinary revolutions.

As an example of the five phases, and putting British history in a nutshell: 1) Germans, Picts, and Celts formed tribes, invaded the British Isles, and waged constant war on each other. 2) Local conquerors united the tribes into Northumbria, Cambria, Wessex, *et cetera*. Invaders such as Romans, Danes, Norsemen, *et cetera*, conquered the British Isles. 3) King Alfred the Great's conquests began the history of England as a nation, and William the Conqueror's conquests accelerated the process. 4) England, under the monarchies, having conquered Wales, Scotland, and Ireland, created the British Empire, with the help of macho "heroes" like Sir Francis Drake, James Wolfe, Robert Clive, Cecil Rhodes, and Benjamin Disraeli. 5) National heroes emerged, and national wars of liberation broke up the British Empire. For example, George Washington and the American Revolution; rebellions in Ontario and Quebec which led to Lord Durham's Report and Canadian self-government; Arthur Griffith and Irish rebellions, which led to the formation of the Free State of Eire; Jomo Kenyatta and the Mau-Mau uprisings, and so forth. THROUGHOUT ALL FIVE PHASES THE ONE CONSTANT IS BLOODSHED AND HUMAN CARNAGE.

Nearly every revolution is followed by a period of vengeance and terror in the name of justice. Mass slaughters followed the French, Russian, and Mao Tse-tung Revolutions. Iran's recent Islamic Revolution was true to form. The Shah and his SAVAK's atrocities were replaced by the Ayatollah Khomeini's atrocities. Liberation from colonial rule in Africa was followed by bloody power struggles. Bloodbaths followed the liberation of Indo-China.

Nothing really changed in modern times. It is said that headhunters still ply their grisly trade in the jungles of Transkei, South Africa. The Ache Indians are still hunted down and enslaved in Paraguay. In 1976, the dictator, General Alfredo Stroessner, tortured and killed Ache Indians in a Nazi-style "final solution." In 1972, Libya's Qaddafi staged a heroes' welcome for the Palestinian terrorists who massacred eleven Israeli athletes at the Munich Olympics, and he paid the terrorist organization a 10 million dollar bonus. Until recently, the Cinta Largas tribe in Brazil was bombed and strafed from the air, and the survivors were gunned down by hunting parties so that loggers could clear the tribe's lands.

The Sandinistas conducted a bloodbath of Miskito Indians in 1982, in order to clear a zone on the Nicaragua-Honduras border. Over a thousand Bengalis were slaughtered and butchered by native tribesmen in Tripura in 1980. In 1983, India's state of Assam exploded in paroxysms of communal and religious hatred, resulting in the death of thousands. The Iraqi-Iranian war accounted for four hundred thousand human lives between 1980 and 1984, and the slaughter is accelerating. Daily slaughters occur in struggles for Basque, Corsican, Kurd, and Karen independence. Americans, Russians and Cubans are supplying Central Americans with deadly weapons, with which they are slaughtering each other. Murders and massacres in Lebanon between Moslem sects and Christians are daily occurrences.

No, nothing has changed in modern times. The nauseating atrocities of history are sickeningly repetitive. Those who extol the virtues of the Noble Savage and think that the American Indians were placid, at peace, and in harmony with nature before "they were brutalized by Europeans" are simply ignorant of history. The Aztec Indians in the twelfth century were nomadic tribes of invaders from the north. By the fifteenth century, they had established a Great Empire in Mexico and Central America by means of ruthless conquest of the Huastic, Mixtec, Zapotec, and Tlaxcala Indian nations. The Aztecs slaughtered at least seventy-five thousand prisoners of war and ate them during one year alone, but they may have butchered as many as two hundred fifty thousand members of neighboring tribes whom they cooked in huge vats, and then gorged themselves on the human flesh. After the Aztecs had exterminated the local wildlife they became cannibals and fed on human flesh, but the Spaniard Hernando Cortex was not to be outdone by their savagery. He murdered Emperor Montezuma, tortured and hanged Emperor Cuauhtemoc (Montezuma's brother and successor), and conquered the Aztec Empire for Spain in A.D. 1525 by committing atrocities which were horrible, even by Aztec standards.

The Inca Indians had established a great empire in South America, which was centered at Cuzco, Peru, at the time of Christopher Columbus. They had conquered the Cuismancu Empire in the fifteenth century, which, in turn, had conquered the Mochica civilization which had flourished from 100 B.C. to A.D. 800. The greatest Incan conquests were made by Pachacuti and his son, Topa, between A.D. 1471 and 1493. The Empire encompassed the entire Andean area from Quito, Ecuador, to the Rio Maule in Chile. This empire, like most empires, was merciless to its enemies, but Conquistador Francisco Pizarro outdid the Incas in cruelty and treachery. He murdered Inca Emperor Atahualpa, conquered the Empire for Spain in A.D. 1537, and wrote another bloody chapter in the history of predation by man on man.

The Iroquois Indians from New York drove the Cherokee as far south as Georgia, and raided the Far West to the Black Hills. When the Sioux of Minnesota and Wisconsin acquired horses in 1600, they became a raiding nation and conquered more territory than Charlemagne ever held. When the Indians acquired horses and guns from the Spaniards, they used them in their predatory wars against neighboring tribes. The Comanche and Apache fought each other, as the English and French fought each other in Europe, and the Mongols and the Chinese fought each other in Asia. Everywhere on Earth, the human animal displayed the same aggressive patterns of behavior as robots programmed for predation. The only reason American Indians and African blacks did not have global empires is that they lacked predatory competency.

The barbaric slaughter and mutilation of man by man has remained undiminished throughout human history. The only variable is man's technological capacity for massive slaughter. His brain has eliminated his anatomical need for tooth and claw, and supplanted them with the ultimate tooth and claw—nuclear weapons. Because modern man does not have direct contact with his war victims, as when he drops bombs and napalm from aircraft, or lobs warheads on his enemies from missiles; and does not experience the horrible mutilation, torture, and enormities he inflicts upon his fellow man as a person-to-person contact affair, he feels a kind of moral immunity and loses the sense of his barbarity. But, sense of barbarity or not, man always feels justified when he slaughters his fellow man. It is for God, country, freedom, democracy, socialism, honor, or glory. That is the hallmark of a true predator and born killer.

Good and evil are phantasmata. Hitler did not think of himself as evil. He, like all human beings, thought of his enemies as evil. When the Church burned heretics at the stake, it thought itself the epitome of goodness, and the heretics the abysm of depravity. Vladimir Lenin and Joseph Stalin thought of capitalism as evil, and American presidents think of Communism as evil. All think themselves supremely good. All want to propagate their political, economic, and religious faiths. The Hebrews thought they were divinely ordained to conquer Canaan and slaughter its inhabitants—it's in the Bible. Is there really any hope for creatures who compulsively slaughter each other because of predatory greed and irrational will-o'-the-wisps?

Such is the tragedy of the human race. The human brain is wired for predation and for the rationalization of predation. In the words of Havelock Ellis, "The sun and the moon and the stars would have disappeared long ago . . . had they happened to be within the reach of predatory human hands." Genetically determined diversity, especially religious, mandates ideational divisions into conflicting camps, with one's own camp representing good, virtue, justice, right, and God, and one's opponents representing evil, vice, injustice, wrong, and the Devil.

The United States felt obliged to fight World War I to make the world safe for democracy; but the USSR feels obliged to make the world safe for socialism. The United States felt it was incumbent upon her to fight Holy Wars in Korea and Vietnam to save the world from monolithic Communism; but the USSR feels it is incumbent upon her to save the world from imperialistic capitalism. Predatory instincts drive human beings to territorial, bloody struggles, rationalized as exigencies of national interests.

We Americans believe that we are nonpareils—that we are a God-fearing nation upon which God has shed His grace, and that our nation is dedicated to liberty, equality, and justice for all. We believe that our nation was founded on the most noble of principles and the most sublime of ideals. We believe that we are a peace-loving people who only go to war in defense of freedom, justice, and honor. Is this a reality or a fantasy? Let us check the facts!

Chapter 2

THE LAND OF THE FREE AND THE HOME OF THE BRAVE

Is the Land of the Free and the Home of the Brave ONE NATION UNDER GOD? If it is, it took a long time for our nation to make the discovery. The words, "under God" were not added to the Pledge of the Allegiance to the Flag by an act of Congress until 1954. "In God We Trust" was not adopted as the national slogan until 1956.

Christian zealots would have us believe that their religion played a major role in the founding of our republic, but some of our Founding Fathers would have been surprised to learn this. Ben Franklin wrote, "Revealed religion had no weight with me. . . Serving God is doing good to man, but praying is thought an easier serving, and therefore most generally chosen." He once published a defense of atheism. Thomas Jefferson noted, "Millions of innocent men and women, since the introduction of Christianity, have been burnt, tortured, fined and imprisoned . . . [its effect is] to make one half of the world fools and the other half hypocrites." He also predicted, "The day will come when the mystical generation of Jesus by the Supreme Being as his father, in the womb of a virgin, will be classified with the fable of the generation of Minerva in the brain of Jupiter." He admitted to being a materialist.

James Madison, the father of the Constitution, never became a church member. He defended the dissenters from the Anglican church and helped to disestablish it in Virginia. George Washington attended church infrequently and was said to be a lifelong nonbeliever. John Adams was actually hostile to religion. Thomas Paine voiced strong opposition to organized religion and belief in the Bible in his work, *Age of Reason.* Said he, "I do not believe in the creed professed by the Jewish Church, by the Roman Church, by the Greek Church, by the Turkish Church, by the Protestant Church, nor by any church that I know of. My own mind is my own church." Abe Lincoln belonged to no church. In a letter to Judge J. A. Wakefield, he wrote, "My earlier views of the unsoundness of the Christian scheme of salvation and the human origin of the scriptures, have become clearer and stronger with advancing years . . ."

Chauvinistic Americans delight in blustering about the "high ideals and noble principles" upon which our country has been founded. If they were high ideals, and if we are more concerned with fact than fiction, the logical inference is that slavery must be a high ideal, and the extermination of Indian culture along with Indian populations must be a noble undertaking based upon the "noble principle" of Machiavellian *Machtpolitik*: that is, might makes right. Chauvinists must also admit to the implied high ideal that women should be excluded from legal and economic rights. Those who oppose slavery, oppose the subjugation of the female, oppose the robber barons, and oppose the principle that might makes right, should deplore the loathsome tacit principles and ideals upon which our country had been founded, and which required two hundred years of intense struggle and suffering to partially reverse.

If chauvinists are indifferent to the facts of history, but impressed by the empty words in the Declaration of Independence, they should also be impressed by the empty words in the USSR's Constitution of 1936, which "guarantees" every Soviet citizen freedom of religion, freedom to form trade unions, freedom from discrimination, *et cetera*. If the USSR is judged by deeds rather than rhetoric, why not the USA? It would have been rather difficult to convince the millions of enslaved Negroes or the tens of millions of dispossessed, brutalized, and slaughtered American Indians of the high ideals and noble principles upon which our country had been founded.

The United States is a European creation, with cultural roots in Ancient Greece, Ancient Rome, and especially in English law, politics, and economics. Her legal and political roots are in the Magna Carta, Model Parliament, and English and French political philosophy. Her economic roots are in the Industrial Revolution and rugged individualism. Every nation must have territory as a precondition to its existence. Just as it was incumbent upon Joshua to conquer the Canaanites to win the Hebrew Promised Land (territory), it was necessary for our forefathers to conquer the American Indians to win the New World Promised Land (territory).

The Indians fought hard against our plundering forefathers. They had occupied the Americas for over thirty thousand years. Naturally they felt a sense of ownership for the land. Consequently, they refused to roll over and die so that our ancestors could create THE AMERICAN DREAM for themselves. It may have been an American Dream for Europeans who profited from the rapine; but for the American Indians who were victims of predation, it was THE AMERICAN NIGHTMARE.

When Christopher Columbus first visited San Salvador (Watlings Island) in 1492, the Tainos Indians showered him with gifts. Columbus wrote to Ferdinand and Isabella, "So tractable, so peaceable, are these people that I swear to your majesties there is not in the world a better nation. They love their neighbors as themselves, and their discourse is ever sweet and gentle, and accompanied with a smile; and though it is true that they are naked, yet their manners are decorous and praiseworthy." THEY WERE OBVIOUSLY EASY PREY. Columbus kidnapped several of them, and hauled them off to Spain. The Spanish returned to loot and burn villages, and to capture hundreds of men, women, and children for the European slave market. Within a decade whole tribes and hundreds of thousands of Indians were exterminated.

The implementation of the American Dream for Europeans by expropriating Indian homelands and exterminating native Indians was about as noble as the Holy Wars of the eleventh through the thirteenth century in which pious Crusaders slaughtered infidel Moslems for Christ, and God-intoxicated Moslems slaughtered infidel Christians for Allah.

The slaughter of Indians by Europeans began almost immediately upon the "discovery" of America. As one example of the horrible extermination of Indians, Cortes's siege of Tenochtitlan caused the beleaguered defenders to die like flies from hunger, thirst, and disease. There were so many dead human bodies strewn about the streets and houses that, according to Bernal Diaz, "I do not know how to describe it . . . We could not walk without treading on the bodies and heads of dead Indians. The stench was so bad that no one could endure it." Tenochtitlan was razed, and upon its ruins stands modern Mexico City. In like manner, the United States of America stands upon the ruins of Indian culture and the remains of hunted-down Indians, a monument to the triumph of human greed assisted by guns and cannons. The United States exists today as a proud nation, but should not the robbery, slaughter, and genocide inflicted upon the Indian people somehow impugn her pride?

As children, we were taught that the Indians were the bad guys, and we were the good guys. Our history books told us that the savage Indians scalped our forefathers, but neglected to mention that our predatory ancestors placed a bounty on Indians' heads, and payment was upon presentation of Indian scalps. General Sheridan's statement, "The only good Indian is a dead Indian!" became an American aphorism. Role-reversal, and the restructuring of facts into self-serving myths, constitute normal human behavior. Patriotism demands it. It's not rational behavior, but man isn't a rational creature.

Reay Tannahill's book, *Flesh and Blood*, gives us an idea of the incomprehensible magnitude of the slaughter of Indian human beings by European human beings in reporting that, before the coming of the Conquistador Cortex in A.D. 1519, there were an estimated 25 million Indians in central Mexico alone; but, by A.D. 1605, only a little over one million survived. The horror of it should make a compassionate person want to disown his membership in the human race.

If anyone has any doubts about the genocide committed on the Indians, just look around you. How many Indians do you see in this the land of the American Indians where they flourished for over thirty thousand years? In the words of Tecumseh, an Indian chief of the Shawnee tribe who died in battle in A.D. 1813, "Where today are the Pequot? Where are the Narragansett, the Mohican, the Pokanoket, and many other once powerful tribes of our people? They have vanished before the avarice and the oppression of the White Man, as snow before a summer sun. Will we let ourselves be destroyed in our turn . . . Our homes, our country bequeathed to us by the Great Spirit . . . and everything that is dear and sacred to us?" America was the Great Spirit's Promised Land for the Indians just as Canaan was Jehovah's Promised Land for the Hebrews.

To add insult to atrocity, in spite of their long residence in America, the surviving Indians were not even granted full citizenship in the United States until 1924. The original, true Americans were not legal Americans for over thirty thousand years. They have been legal Americans for less than sixty years. Only a madman or a complete ignoramus can boast of the high ideals, noble principles, and justice upon which the United States was founded, but madness and ignorance are not alien to the human race.

Indian chief Black Hawk was captured in 1832, and taken East to be displayed like an animal in a zoo for the edification of the curious. When he died in 1838, his skeletal remains were kept as a souvenir on display in the office of the governor of the Iowa Territory. In like manner, the severed head of Chief Metacom of the Wampanoags was on public exhibition at Plymouth for twenty years. Former President Andrew Jackson made an illustrious career of killing thousands of Cherokees, Chickasaws, Choctaws, Creeks, and Seminoles before he became president. High ideals and noble principles? If Jack the Ripper quoted Jesus while he committed murder, would that confer nobility upon him?

To touch a bit more on THE AMERICAN NIGHTMARE for the Indian people, we quote historians Nevins and Commager: "The frontiersmen . . . constantly encroached on Indian lands, in defiance of treaty; they destroyed the game on which the Indians depended for food and clothing; and many were ready to slay any redskin on sight. When the Indians tried to defend themselves, war ensued." The white man massacred the Indians in terrible orgies of savagery. Very few massacres were exposed to the scrutiny of history as were the Massacres at Sand Creek in 1864, in which Col. John Chivington indiscriminately slaughtered and mutilated hundreds of Cheyenne men, women and children; and Wounded Knee in 1890, in which United States troops opened fire on men, women and children of the Sioux tribe, killing two hundred of them.

Seemingly endless bloodcurdling wars of extermination were waged on the hapless Indians by our freebooting forefathers, among which were: Pequot Indian War (1637), King Philip's War (1675-6), Yamasee India War (1763), Creek Indian War (1814), several Seminole Indian Wars, Black Hawk War (1832), Sioux, Apache and Comanche Wars, *et cetera, et cetera*. It required many wars to dispossess and exterminate the Indians. Young Abe Lincoln was a captain in the Black Hawk War, one of the most brutal affairs in the history of the world. The starving Black Hawk Indians entered Wisconsin to raise corn and live in peace. Two thousand militiamen cut them to ribbons while they pleaded for peace. One rifleman wrote, "It was a horrid sight to witness little children, wounded and suffering the most excruciating pain, although they were of the savage enemy."

The white man's predatory avarice not only led to terrible atrocities against the red man, it also induced bloody conflicts within his own race. The New York/New Jersey area was a battleground for New Sweden and New Amsterdam. England seized the entire region, including former Swedish colonies, after the Second Dutch War (1664-67). Pennsylvania was also disputed territory for the English, Dutch, and Swedes. British forces seized the Delaware area in 1664. Spain claimed the entire eastern half of the present United States. The British fought and defeated the Spaniards in such battles as Bloody Marsh in Georgia. The French and English colonists fought each other in the King William's War, the Queen Anne's War, and the King George's War. The military might of England finally established the thirteen original colonies from which the United States was born.

Our illustrious ancestors attempted to enslave the surviving Indians, but they were not successful. The Indians could be robbed of their lands, and even of their bodies, but not of their souls. They were driven into concentration camps called reservations like animals herded into corrals. How innocuous a vicious crime appears when it is couched in deceptive euphemisms! African blacks were more amenable to slavery than Indians. Therefore, they were destined for involuntary servitude. According to Dagobert Runes, 50 million blacks lost their lives being hunted like animals by slave traders, and yet they fared better than the Indians. A comparison in the number of blacks to the number of Indians in any of our major cities gives evidence to that fact.

Blacks now comprise about 13 percent of our total population, and the figure is growing. When the white man conquered Africa, he did not exterminate the natives. The black man outnumbers the white man by a huge majority in black Africa. This fact permits sanctimonious Americans to sermonize on the principle of one man, one vote for South Africa as they had for former Rhodesia. Would the sanctimonious hypocrites make the same demand for justice in America if our ancestors had not exterminated the Indians, and the Indians now outnumbered the white man by an equal majority? The Indian problem was eliminated by eliminating the Indians. Hitler stole a page from American history.

Two hundred years of serfdom for the Aleuts (natives of the Aleutian Islands) did not end until 1983. The Aleuts were enslaved by Russian fur traders in the eighteenth century, and became federal wards of the United States government after Alaska was acquired in 1867. According to historian Claus Naske at the University of Alaska, "There are many black chapters in (American) history, but this one (serfdom of the Aleuts) is among the blackest." Until 1964, the Aleuts needed a pass from the government to leave the islands. They couldn't own their homes. They survived by clubbing to death thousands of seals each summer for the federal government.

According to AIM (American Indian Movement), the federal government made more than three hundred treaties with the surviving Indians, but they were made to be broken by "the great forked-tongue liars." The treaties made "in perpetuity" were honored until gold or oil was discovered on Indian property, or until the white man wanted a railroad to go through Indian property, or until the white man simply wanted to feed his greed by invasions and aggressions beyond the frontier.

The Indian Intercourse Act of 1834 provided for a free Indian Territory in Oklahoma, Kansas, and Nebraska. The creation of the Kansas and Nebraska Territories in 1854 decimated the Indian Territory, and the 1907 admission of Oklahoma into the union as a state completed the extinction of the Indian Territory in the same manner that the Mexican Cession of 1848, and the Texas Annexation of 1845, completed the confiscation of Mexican territory.

Taiwan got a taste of the sanctity of American treaties rather recently. Every nation abrogates treaties when deemed in the national interest. But the patriotic delusion persists. Our side can be trusted, but not the other side. We can encircle Russia with our military arsenal of destruction on her borders, but she had better stay clear of the New World. When the Monroe Doctrine is quoted one part is never quoted: -the part that pledges that the United States will never interfere in the political affairs of Europe We do not permit the USSR to proclaim its own Monroe Doctrine. To be a patriotic American, we must love America, no matter what evil she perpetrates, and hate Russia, no matter what good she fosters. American arrogance is readily identified even by friendly foreigners, who know us as the "Ugly American" or the "Gringo."

Actually, who can trust whom? After World War I, the Allies (France, Britain, and the United States) blockaded Russia and sent Allied troops into Russia to defeat the Red Army. American expeditionary forces marched into Siberia in 1919. Trotsky crushed the enemy, and the Allies withdrew. There is evidence that Hitler was partially financed by British and American capital for the purpose of containing Communism, the arch enemy of capitalism. Our Indian treaties, like the Hitler-Stalin Nonaggression Pact, are respected only so long as they serve national interests. It should never be forgotten that all human beings—Americans, Russians, Japanese, or whatever—are motivated (or automated) by the same predatory instincts. Predators are natural opportunists.

We never tire of calling Hitler a madman, a vicious fiend, and a power-hungry monster for doing what human beings have always done. He wanted to build a German Empire, but empire-building has been characteristic of "civilized" man from the dawn of history to Modern America. Have we forgotten about our own America Empire? Hitler's war cry of aggression was "LEBENSRAUM FOR THE GERMAN PEOPLE." The American war cry of aggression was, "MANIFEST DESTINY." Sanctimony disguised the aggression by calling it "THE WHITE MAN'S

BURDEN." The purpose in all cases was identical—TERRITO-RIAL EXPANSION!

The United States wanted California and the New Mexico Territory for its empire, and offered to buy them from Mexico, but Mexico refused to sell. Almost as Hitler wanted parts of Czechoslovakia and Poland, but they refused to yield, and so he ordered his troops into those countries. President Polk did the same. He coveted territory, and so he ordered Captain John C. Fremont and Colonel Stephen W. Kearny to march their troops into California and New Mexico. Kearny advanced over the Santa Fe trail to Santa Fe, and then joined forces with Commodore Robert F. Stockton in Southern California. General Winfield Scott, with the cooperation of the United States Navy, marched his troops into Mexico, then captured Vera Cruz and Mexico City. The rapine of Mexico was as speedy and efficient as Hitler's conquests. The American Empire expanded, and Mexico shrank. But, we, the good guys, had a conscience, and, to assuage it, we paid Mexico 15 million dollars. We were magnanimous, as predators go.

Is it an exaggeration to compare the expansion of the American Empire with Hitler's expansion of Germany? Only if we forget the genocide committed on the Indian people, and only if our penchant for self-aggrandizement deludes us into thinking we can do no wrong. President Teddy Roosevelt unashamedly admitted that he stole the Panama Canal Zone. In a speech in 1912 he said, "I took Panama. It was the only way the canal could be constructed." The end justified the means. Panama had joined the Colombian Union in 1821, after Simon Bolivar, the Liberator of South America from Spain, cleared New Granada of loyalist forces. Roosevelt fomented a revolution of the Panamanians in Colombia, following Colombia's refusal to ratify the Hay-Herran Treaty which would have provided the United States with the proposed Canal Zone.

Roosevelt sent cruisers steaming to the coast of Colombia and landed American marines in Colón to prevent Colombia from squashing the revolt. It was oblique, but it was naked aggression nevertheless. Once the Revolution was a *fait accompli*, the Panamanians were putty in his hands. They signed an accommodating treaty in 1903 which gave the United States the Canal Zone for a nominal fee. The treaty granted exclusive use, occupation, and control of the Canal Zone by the United States in perpetuity. However, violent confrontation and the threat of war led to the new Panama Canal Treaties in 1977-78 which will return sovereignty to Panama by the end of this century.

The imperialistic attitude of the United States was exemplified by President Grant in 1881 when he spoke of "an American canal, on American soil, to the American people." It has a ring of familiarity. Hitler made similar speeches to the German people, promising them territorial gifts "to the German people and for the German people."

Adolf Hitler wrote in *Mein Kampf*, "The right to soil and territory can become a duty if decline seems to be in store for a great nation unless it extends its territory." Hitler went on to say, "What we have to fight for is . . . the freedom and independence of the fatherland, in order to enable our people to mature for the fulfillment of the mission which the Creator of the Universe has allotted them." Doesn't this sound like the justification for empire given by our forefathers: that is, MANIFEST DESTINY? John L. O'Sullivan coined the phrase in 1845 when he wrote of "the fulfillment of our manifest destiny to overspread the continent allotted by Providence for the free development of our yearly multiplying millions." Adolf Hitler could not have said it better.

Teddy Roosevelt added a number of satellite countries, or virtual protectorates, in the Caribbean to the American Empire. United States troops occupied Santo Domingo in 1905. Haiti and Nicaragua were occupied by the United States for many years, pursuant to our infamous "dollar diplomacy."

Did the Philippines, Guam, and Puerto Rico ask to become parts of the American Empire? About as much as Latvia, Estonia, and Lithuania asked to become parts of the Russian Empire! The Philippines, Guam, and Puerto Rico were confiscated from Spain following the Spanish-American War of 1898. The acquisition was pulled off by President McKinley after much rationalizing designed to euphemize theft with the word "liberation." For cosmetic reasons, 20 million dollars were paid to Spain for the Philippines, BUT THE FILIPINOS WERE PAID NOTHING. Money can obviously purchase virtue. Acquisition, the Big Stick, Gunboat Diplomacy, and Dollar Diplomacy were official United States policies. They were the policies of an imperialistic aggressor nation.

To further examine the "noble principles" upon which the United States was founded, let us analyze the American Revolution. It seems reasonable to say that if the American Revolution were such a praiseworthy undertaking, most of the colonists would have favored it, but such is not the case. Only about 33 percent favored it. In sharp contrast, a huge majority of Vietnamese favored Ho Chi Minh's Revolution. About 33 percent of the American colonists remained loyal to the Crown, but even this percentage does not represent the actual number of loyalists (Tories) because they were severely harassed, cruelly persecuted, tarred and feathered, and their property was confiscated by the patriots; that is, intimidated. At least one hundred thousand loyalists fled the noble American Revolution. Many of the persecuted loyalists fled to Canada. Some fled to the West Indies, Florida, and England. The remaining 33 percent of the colonists were indifferent to the Revolution.

In the late spring of 1776, six of the thirteen colonial delegates to the Continental Congress were instructed to vote AGAINST separation from Britain. Tens of thousands of American Tories were hostile to the American patriots. The Anglican clergy was almost solidly behind the British king. The loyalists outnumbered the patriots in several of the large cities. Fifty thousand loyalists took up arms and joined British regiments. When George Washington had only nine thousand troops in 1780, eight thousand Americans were fighting side by side with the redcoats. According to Tom Burnam's, *The Dictionary of Misinformation*, "At times there were more Americans fighting for the King than against him."

Loyalists were so convinced that the American Revolution was wrong that they did everything they could to sabotage it. They circulated counterfeit Continental currency to destroy rebel economy. They distributed propaganda leaflets to dissuade the Revolutionists. Loyalists supplied the Redcoats with food at the very time George Washington's soldiers were starving. American Tories shouted their opposition: "Damn the rebel!" Others screamed, "I wish they were all scalped—damn Congress to Hell!" Pennsylvania Tory Samuel Shoemaker visited Windsor Castle and came away saying, "I wish some of my violent countrymen could have such an opportunity. They would be convinced that George III has not one grain of tyranny in his composition. A man of his fine feelings, so good a husband, so kind a father, cannot be a tyrant."

It is a matter of historical record that the American Revolution was an unilateral, illegal revolt of a minority, largely in the upper class, who stood to profit personally. Even the French of Quebec, who hated the English bitterly after their defeat by England (James Wolfe) in 1759, refused to support the American colonists in their revolt. The American expedition into Canada was a disaster. Two attempts to invade Florida also failed. The Floridians remained loyal to Great Britain. At least 66 percent of the colonists did NOT think that the American Revolution was justified. High principles and noble causes meant opposite things to the patriots and the loyalists. George Washington, the rebel who would have been hanged, hated, and forgotten, had he lost or been captured, lived to become a national hero.

The American Revolutionists did not want their wealth diminished by George III's and Parliament's taxes to fund intercolonial wars and maintain British garrisons in America. They wanted to enrich themselves. Hence, the slogan, "No taxation without representation!"

God-fearing Christians who fled Europe for religious freedom wanted freedom to persecute other religious sects. When the Puritans came to power in England after the Puritan Revolution (1642-46), and Oliver Cromwell ruled England, they were ruthless persecutors of all other religious sects. When they were driven from power in 1660 after the death of Cromwell, and they, themselves, were persecuted, they fled to America, where they enjoyed the freedom to continue their own persecutions. They conducted witch-hunts, enacted Blue Laws, and suppressed religious freedom. The Massachusetts Bay Colony's "Body of Liberties" made blasphemy a crime punishable by death. Joseph Smith, the founder of the Mormon Church, was persecuted, forced to flee for his life several times, and was finally murdered at Carthage, Illinois on June 27, 1844.

After the Revolution, George Washington returned to the comforts of wealth. He returned to his Mount Vernon Estates and to the luxuries afforded by slaves. Haym Salomon, a merchant banker and passionate supporter of the Revolution, had helped finance it. He distributed his own money to relieve distress among Philadelphia's poor, lent money to delegates to the Continental Congress, including James Madison, Thomas Jefferson and James Monroe, but he died penniless with the United States government owing him at least six hundred thousand dollars. The Revolution was also good to Thomas Jefferson. He owned several thousand acres of land and one hundred fifty slaves. He was the aristocrat of Monticello, and he had a comfortable retreat in his second home at Poplar Forest in Bedford County. The American Revolution was NOT a poor man's revolution like the French and Russian Revolutions.

There was a sharp contrast between the George Washington/Thomas Jefferson Revolution and the Ho Chi Minh Vietnamese Revolution. Washington had the support of 33 percent of his people. Ho Chi Minh had the support of from 85 to 90 percent of his people. Some 25,000 Americans died in their Revolution. More than one million Vietnamese died in theirs. Some 8,445 Americans were wounded in their fight for independence. Many millions of Vietnamese were maimed in their struggle. Americans fought an eight-year revolution for independence. The Vietnamese fought a twenty-eight-year revolution. Uncounted Vietnamese villages were razed and plowed by Americans, reminiscent of Rome's destruction of ancient Carthage in the Third Punic War.

SEVEN MILLION TONS OF BLOCKBUSTING DEATH AND DESTRUCTION WERE RAINED UPON THE VIETNAMESE BY AMERICAN BOMBERS, NOT COUNTING FRENCH BOMBINGS. Relative losses to American patriots were negligible. George Washington fought six years for the British before he became a turncoat. Ho Chi Minh's entire life of seventy-nine years in near poverty was devoted to the struggle for freedom and independence of his country from colonial rule. Washington and Jefferson owned many slaves. Ho Chi Minh owned no slaves. BUT

GEORGE WASHINGTON WAS A NOBLE MAN, AND HO CHI MINH WAS A VILLAIN.

The French and British Canadians had another opportunity to win freedom from England and join the noble undertaking of the American Dream during the War of 1812, when the armies of the United States again invaded Canada. What did the French and British Canadians, who not only hated each other with a passion but also were under the thumb of the British Crown, do? They closed ranks and fought side by side against the American invaders. They fought fiercely and bravely, expelled the American aggressors from Canada, and remained loyal to the British Crown. Today, the Canadians celebrate their cherished victories over the American aggressors with as much patriotic fervor as we celebrate the Fourth of July and our victories over the British. The lofty principles and noble cause of the United States were neither lofty nor noble to the Canadians. They wanted no part of them.

To the Russians, their cause in overthrowing the czars and establishing a socialist state was noble. To monarchs, their cause in suppressing democracy was noble because it was God's will, a conclusion derived from belief in the divine right of kings. To Hitler, his cause was noble because of his belief in "the natural right of the master race to dominate." To some religious fanatics, killing infidels is a noble cause because it glorifies God. The reality is that the human being, the most absurd of all animals, distills endless delusions in the cerebral tumor he calls a brain, and he has a compulsion to kill in service to his delusions. That which is the greatest good to one human being is the greatest evil to another, and so they must annihilate each other because the organ of human stupidity, the human brain, orchestrates the burlesque.

How did the "lofty principles" on which America was founded, and which were hammered out in Philadelphia's City Tavern rather than Philadelphia's Independence Hall, benefit the ordinary man: the teeming millions of American workers? Let us examine the facts, subversive as they are to the American Myth.

Forgetting black slavery for the moment, let us look at the plight of the white worker. Early American WHITE capitalists exploited

WHITE workers with incredible cruelty. The white worker received no more kindness at the hands of the white capitalists than the black slave did at the hands of the white plantation owner. If anything, many black slaves on the plantation had it BETTER than the inhumanely exploited factory and mine workers. Man has always exploited his fellow man, and he never cared particularly what race he belonged to. When most people lived on small farms, they raised large families to obtain cheap labor. Parents exploit their own children, and children exploit their own parents. It all depends upon the power structure, and it varies with the times. There is little discrimination when it comes to exploitation. Frenchmen exploit Frenchmen, Germans exploit Germans, and blacks exploit blacks. It was blacks who rounded up black slaves in Africa, for the profit in selling them to white slave traders. There was nothing personal in it. It was simply business, and it is the business of predators to exploit.

During the early days of capitalism, young children of only five years of age were forced to work fourteen or more hours a day, seven days a week, in cold factories and dank mines. They were forced to slave away for a mere pittance, and they were brutally whipped when they fell asleep from exhaustion. Women and children toiled long hours in filthy coal mines, and they went down on all fours, like beasts of burden, in order to pull heavy carloads of coal through low and narrow tunnels. Between 1890 and 1900, child workers tripled in the South. All laws which attempted to regulate child labor were set aside by the United States Supreme Court, right on through the first quarter of the twentieth century (*Hammer vs. Dagenhart*, 1918, and *Baily vs. Drezel Furniture Co.*, 1922).

Dire poverty, or near-poverty and exhaustion, was the lot of the drab worker in the Land of the Free, while he provided ease and comfort for his opulent employer. As in today's Communist countries, workers were denied the right to form labor unions. They were slaves in every sense of the word. They owed their souls to their affluent employers. White workers, including women and small children, were mere means to greater wealth for white men of power. Workers were never thought of as ends in themselves. The American worker won the right to organize by the same process that the Russian peasants, the French serfs, and all oppressed people won freedom; that is, by acts of violence. Predators do not let go of spoils without a fight. America's motto has always been, "To the victor (successful predator) belongs the spoils."

In Haymarket Square in Chicago in 1886, when three hundred forty thousand workers struck for an eight-hour day, violence erupted and a bomb was exploded. At the Carnegie Steel Company in Homestead, Pennsylvania, in 1892, a strike for union recognition became a clash between company-employed strikebreakers, including armed guards, and strikers. It resulted in considerable loss of life on both sides. The American Railway Union strike and the Pullman Company boycott of 1894, ignited by a 25 percent wage cut, led to violence and mass destruction of property, and the calling out of two thousand federal troops. Strikes, the hiring of strikebreakers, and accompanying violence were commonplace. Between 1913 and 1914, United Mine Workers were machine-gunned in West Virginia. Similar gunplay also occurred in Colorado. The National Guard machine-gunned miners' tent colonies. The miners fought back. There was a sickening loss of life and property. Strikebreaking was the order of the day. The National Guard was called out in 1934, when West Coast maritime workers, under the leadership of Harry Bridges, went on strike, and rioting took place following the employers' hiring of strikebreakers.

The American courts consistently ruled that labor unions were illegal until 1842. Organizing a union was considered criminal conspiracy, much as it is in Poland and in other Communist countries today. After the Civil War, unionism was attacked by the courts as a tort, that is, a civil wrong, the remedy against which was injunctions and restraining orders. The Sherman Act of 1890 and the Clayton Act of 1914 made all combinations in restraint of trade or commerce illegal, and unions were considered combinations that restrained trade and commerce because of the use of their weapons, the strike. The United States Supreme Court held that the Sherman Act applied to organized labor in its 1908 decision. In spite of a 1914 Congressional Act favorable to labor, the Supreme Court upheld the spirit of its 1908 decision in its 1921 decision. America was the working man's hell during those years of ruthless capitalistic exploitation. IT WAS THE AMERICAN NIGHTMARE, NOT THE AMERICAN DREAM.

The law of the predator decrees the exploitation of the weak by the strong. When the wolf and the lamb both have total freedom, it is the lamb that discovers its flesh and bones being crunched between powerful jaws. Freedom is a noble ideal for the wolf. Restraint of the wolf's freedom is a noble ideal for the lamb. When the *laissez-faire* capitalist was free to wield his natural economic power over his workers, he was the wolf that devoured the lamb, that is, the worker. When protective labor legislation, such as the Wagner Act of 1935, transferred predatory power to organized labor by legalizing its weapon (the strike), organized labor became a potential wolf. Employers struggled to survive the crippling effects of prolonged strikes. Union wages became confiscatory, but the ultimate quarries were not capitalists; they were consumers because confiscatory wages were passed onto them by means of higher prices.

When human beings think of freedom, they think of freedom for themselves, not for other persons. The American patriot of 1776 wanted freedom for himself, not for blacks, women, or workers. When Frenchmen fought Hitler, and they spouted slogans of LIBERTY, FRATERNITY, AND EQUALITY, it was for themselves, not for the millions of Vietnamese whom they held in virtual colonial slavery. When smokers demand freedom, it is for themselves. Smokers' Rights are predator rights. They couldn't care less about nonsmokers, whose breathing space they assault with pollutants and contaminants. This is perfectly natural because it expresses the compulsive, instinctive nature of predators and predator morality. The ideal of total freedom can be realized only in the jungle, and the lion is king of the jungle. Civilized societies must restrict the freedom of a man to swing his fists to the point where another man's nose begins. If the greatest good to the greatest number is democracy's ideal, freedom can be its nemesis.

We conveniently suffer amnesia of our history when we rhapsodize about the noble principles upon which our country has been founded. We forget our predatory subjugations of Indians, blacks, workers, and women. BLACK SLAVERY was a respected and honored American institution which was sanctioned by the Constitution and the Supreme Court of the United States. Blacks were not guaranteed the right to vote until passage of the New Voting Rights Act of 1965. If it required two hundred years for the United States to see the error in its ways in denying civil and human rights to all its citizens, either the United States is a nation of very stupid people or a nation of very immoral people.

Most Americans are familiar with the Declaration of Independence, at least the histrionic words which read, "We hold these Truths to be self-evident, that all Men are created equal, that they are endowed by their Creator with certain unalienable Rights . . . That to secure these Rights, Governments are instituted among Men, deriving their just Powers from the Consent of the Governed." Thomas Jefferson who wrote those inspiring words was, himself, a slaveholder. If he really believed that all men are created equal, he certainly didn't indicate it in his *Notes on the State of Virginia*, where he wrote that the Negro "is in reason much inferior, as I think one could scarcely be found capable of tracing and comprehending the investigations of Euclid." George Washington was also a slaveholder along with our other Founding Fathers, nearly all of whom were dyed-in-the wool racists. When our aristocratic Founding Fathers thought of freedom and equality, it was for themselves alone, not for the poor, not for women, not for blacks, and certainly not for the native Indians. Like the Magna Carta which protected the knights and barons, not the serfs, the American Constitution protected the upper class, not the poor.

Abe Lincoln's "government of the people, by the people, and for the people" did not include blacks, Indians, or women. He definitely was not an abolitionist. He wished merely to contain slavery. His very words (Aug 22, 1862) were: "My paramount object in this struggle [Civil War] is to save the Union, and is not either to save or destroy slavery. If I could save the union without freeing any slave, I would do it . . ." He was against integrating blacks into the nation's social and political fabric. His emancipation plan called for sending the freed slaves back to Africa, but the border slave states were unwilling to inaugurate it.

Abe Lincoln, the Great Emancipator, was an advocate of Apartheid. He made this abundantly clear in his opening speech at the Fourth Joint Debate at Charleston, Illinois, Sept. 18th, 1858, when he said, "I will say then, that I am not, nor ever have been in favor of bringing about in any way the social and political equality of the white and black races; that I am not, nor ever have been, in favor of making voters or jurors of Negroes, nor of qualifying them to hold office, nor to intermarry with white people; and I will say in addition to this that there is a physical difference between the white and black races which I believe will forever forbid the two races living together on terms of social and political equality. And inasmuch as they cannot so live, while they do remain together, there must be the position of superior and inferior, and I, as much as any other man, am in favor of having the superior position assigned to the white race ... I give him [Judge Douglas] the most solemn pledge that I will to the very last stand by the law of this state, which forbids the marrying of white people with Negroes" (*Complete Works of Abraham Lincoln*, edited by John G. Nicolay & John Hay, Volume IV, published by Francis D. Tandy Company, New York, 1905, pp. 89-91).

The right to vote was contingent upon one's wealth after the American Revolution. In 1789, none of the thirteen states gave the poor man the right to vote. Women were not allowed to vote until 1920. Blacks were not guaranteed the right to vote until passage of The New Voting Rights Act in 1965. Intelligent blacks objected to being drafted into the armed forces and sent to die for the supposed freedom of other people because they, themselves, were denied that very freedom. Some rebelled against Christianity, a white man's religion, because it preached acceptance of the status quo. The white man's God of Love was devoid of the love to permit the black man to worship in the white man's church.

The Constitution of the United States, itself, fully legitimatized slavery and implied the legal denial of the blacks' right to vote in Article IV, Section 2: "No person held in Service to Labour in one State, under the Laws thereof, escaping into another, shall, in Consequence of any Law or Regulation therein, be discharged from such Service or Labour, but shall be delivered up on Claim of the Party to who such

Service or Labour may be due." The United States Supreme Court upheld the constitutionality of the institution of slavery and non-citizen status of blacks as late as 1856-7 with its Dred Scott Decision, which declared that Congress had no power to exclude slavery from the territories. In view of the fact that the Declaration of Independence held that ALL men are created equal, that government derives its just powers from the consent of the governed, and the slaves were certainly governed, how could intelligent people argue for the existence or preservation of slavery, or the denial of the right to vote for the black? Human reason was equal to the task.

Human reason can justify or prove absolutely anything when there is a commitment to belief. To those who profited from slavery, the arguments for slavery were sound. There were legal precedents for slavery dating back to Roman law which held that a slave is mere chattel and has no rights whatsoever. Before the advent of the Industrial Revolution, the cheap labor of slaves was extremely profitable for the southern plantation owners. Profit provided an incentive for the rational defense of slavery. The apparent contradiction of all men being created equal and the existence of slavery was resolved by denying that blacks are human beings; but if human beings, then substandard human beings. Religious hypocrites had their own smug rationale. Blacks, they said, were being punished according to Biblical prophecy and God's principles of absolute justice.

The Biblical justification for slavery is as follows: Blacks are descendants of Ham, on whom God placed a curse through Noah because he had pruriently ogled his father's (Noah's) naked body while Noah was sleeping off a wine drunk. Ham's brothers behaved with proper filial decorum by covering his nakedness with a cloak. When Noah sobered up and learned what had happened, he was angry and placed a curse on Ham saying, "Cursed be Cannan (Ham), a servant of servants shall he be unto his brethren." According to Talmudic and Midrashic sources, Noah told Ham, "Your seed will be ugly and dark-skinned." From henceforth, Ham was accused of being "the notorious world-darkener. " The biblical explanation for the dark skin of blacks and the justification for their condition of slavery should sound ridiculous to a rational person; but it isn't any more ridiculous than the story of the creation of Eve from Adam's rib; or the damnation of mankind because of Adam and Eve's eating of the forbidden fruit. Ridiculous fables are not exclusively for children.

In 1562, John Hawkins became the first Englishman to run slave ships between Africa and America. He enlarged his fleet of slave ships in 1564. It was so profitable to England that Queen Elizabeth knighted him. He took for his crest a manacled black. His flagship of the slave ship fleet was named JESUS. Sometimes, the ships ran short of water, and many thousands of the slaves were dumped overboard. Under the terms of the Peace of Utrecht (A.D 1713), subtitled the Asiento contract, Spain was obligated to grant Britain the sole right of supplying at least four thousand eight hundred Negro slaves per year to the Spanish colonies. In the century ending in the year 1776, the English had supplied no fewer than 3 million black slaves to the various colonies. At least 12 percent died from the horrors of each sea passage. The human suffering was incredible, but the treaty was so profitable to the British slave trade that Handel was commissioned to compose a special *Te Deum* to be sung in the churches in its honor.

The conscience of Britain was awakened in 1833 by the Industrial Revolution. Labor-saving machines could now produce goods cheaper and more efficiently than slaves. Slavery suddenly became obsolete. Therefore, it was abolished. The Industrial Revolution advanced more slowly in America; and so, it required another thirty years, and a gory Civil War, before it was legally abolished in the Land of the Free and the Home of the Brave. *De facto* slavery lingered on for another hundred years.

The industrialization of the North made slavery as anachronistic as the horse and buggy in today's society. The people of the North could well afford to feel smugly self-righteous, liberal, and magnanimous in their advocacy of Emancipation; but they were not so magnanimous in their treatment of "free" working men, working women, and working children. The North demanded the abolition of slavery in the name of God, justice, and the Constitution; while, at the same time, the South demanded the preservation of the institution of slavery in the name of God, justice, and the Constitution. Moral indignation was felt only by those who couldn't profit from slavery, much as moral indignation is felt by Americans against Apartheid in South Africa. Morality is a creature of expediency. That is why murder is the highest virtue in times of war, but the worst crime in times of peace. Concepts of virtue vary widely. A frigid woman is inclined to see virginity as a virtue, whereas a nymphomaniac would see it as a vice. Eating pork has been taboo for Jews and Arabs because it was the only pre-scientific way to deal with trichinosis.

Pre-Civil War North and South had different economic interests. The South was a source of food and raw material, and a market for the manufactures of the North. The South was to the North what colonies were to colonial empires. The Civil War was to the South what the Revolutionary War was to the Thirteen Colonies. When the South lost hope of ever controlling Congress and was hurt by tariff, as the Thirteen Colonies were hurt by taxation, it wanted to secede from the Union. Thus began the War for Southern Independence, otherwise known as the War of the Rebellion, the War of Secession, or the Civil War.

Ideals played no real part in the Civil War. They were mere fig leaves. Materialistic needs are normally disguised as moral aspirations. Lincoln's Emancipation Proclamation was not an awakening of the moral conscience of the nation. It was an awakening of military necessity to weaken the South. The North wanted to unite the South as desperately as North Vietnam wanted to unite South Vietnam. The Confederacy was denied its freedom to exist as an independent nation in a bloodletting contest of brother killing brother, father killing son, and son killing father.

General Sherman wrote, "I began to regard the death and mangling of a couple thousand men as a small affair, a kind of morning dash." The gruesome carnage of the Civil War accounted for seventy-five thousand battle deaths and sixty thousand related deaths, not to mention the accompanying mayhem, agony, broken bodies, and twisted minds. The North's conquest of the Confederate States of America was completed at Appomattox on April 9, 1865. The independent nation under the presidency of Jefferson Davis survived four years. The United States (North) no longer had to fear a powerful nation on her southern border which would soon have expanded southward towards the Caribbean and become a threat to her existence.

The modern Western world now holds that slavery is an unspeakable evil, a crime against human rights, and a crime against humanity. If slavery is all that evil, and *Homo sapiens* (wise man) is an intelligent creature, why did it require nearly 2 million years for the genus *Homo* to reach this conclusion? Slavery is an institution as old as history. It was considered entirely moral by most societies until very recently, that is, until the Industrial Revolution. There is nothing either in the Old Testament or in the New Testament to indicate that slavery is evil—QUITE THE CONTRARY!

The Church Fathers accepted and even justified slavery as the consequence of original sin. Thomas Aquinas, the eminent Church theologian, sanctified slavery on the grounds that justice demands that inferior men be subject to superior men. According to him, weak minds are intended by nature to be bondsmen. Aristotle reasoned that slavery is the proper consequence of the natural inequality of men. Will Durant wrote that slavery is "an institution that has lasted throughout known history appeared inevitable and eternal, even to honest moralists." The Popes, themselves, had slaves. Will Durant wrote in *The Age of Faith*, "Thousands of captured Slavs and Saracens were distributed among monasteries as slaves; and slavery on church lands and papal estates continued till the eleventh century. Canon law sometimes estimated the wealth of church lands in slaves rather than in money; like secular law, it considered the slave as a chattel." The United States recognized slavery as a legal institution well past the second half of the nineteenth century.

Slavery didn't go out of style because of moral progress. It was economic progress that gave the death knell to slavery. The Industrial Revolution made slavery evil; not *The Bible*; not Moses; nor Christ; nor the Church; nor any moral leader. Slavery is obviously obsolete when a machine can do better, faster, and cheaper work than a slave; and the economic system provides surrogate slaves through the magic of the price-wage-profit system. It was simply stupid to feed and clothe a black slave and his family when a "free" white factory or mine worker could be hired at a starvation wage. If America were deprived of the labor-saving devices of the Industrial Revolution today, Negroes would be back in slavery tomorrow.

Should we condemn the slavery of times past when it was proclaimed moral and just by all the most honored moralists in the history of ethics? Should the score of the 1902 Rose Bowl football game be changed on the basis of the 1984 rules? Some philosophasters argue that blacks should be compensated for the injustice inflicted upon them, but it was not injustice when slavery existed. It is only injustice by TODAY'S rules. Slavery is normal and just for a natural predator who lacks the alternative of mechanical slaves. Justice is a human invention which serves specific human interests. Nothing is so evil that it had not been thought good at some time, and nothing is so good that it had not been thought evil at some time.

Parents once had the moral and legal right to kill their own children. Now it's a crime. Human sacrifices to the gods was once thought a sacred duty. Abortion was illegal in America a few years ago. Today, it is legal. A few years ago, it was illegal for blacks and whites to intermarry. Today, it is legal. A few years ago, fornication was a crime. Today, it is perfectly legal. Ancient tribes of India ate their parents as a sign of respect and honor. Human headhunting was popular in Africa, India, the Middle East, and South America. South American Indians shrank the human heads of their hunted-down victims for use as trophies, and it was considered moral and proper. It was thought honorable for Alexander Hamilton and Aaron Burr to try to kill each other in a duel.

Slavery has been upheld by the churches, by moral leaders, by philosophers, by theologians, by the Bible, by the United States Supreme Court, and by the United States Constitution. The Old Testament clearly upheld slavery in Leviticus 25:44 16: "Both thy bondsmen and thy bondsmaids, which thou shalt have, shall be of the heathen that are round about you; of them ye shall buy bondsmen and bondsmaids . . . And ye shall take them as an inheritance for your children after you, to inherit them for a possession; they shall be your bondsmen forever." The New Testament implies the legitimacy of slavery in Titus 2:9: "Exhort servants to be obedient to their masters." The Reverend Nathan Lord, one-time president of Dartmouth

College, said, "Slavery was incorporated into the civil institutions of Moses; it was recognized accordingly by Christ and his apostles. They condemned all intermeddlers with it."

Slavery is not unique with man. The creatures whose policy is the ultimate in stability, harmony, and efficiency, the insects, are notorious slaveholders. Termites and ants carry off slaves, as our ancestors carried off slaves from Africa. Ants subjugate a certain kind of aphis from which they draw milk, and a certain kind of beetle from which they get nourishment in another form. They admit other insects to their nests to act as scavengers. Advanced pre-industrialized human societies, from Ancient Greece and Rome to nineteenth century America, accepted slavery as necessary, natural, moral, and legal.

Blood and iron established the world's national boundaries, not rational deliberations independent of the threat of war. This is perfectly natural for a territorial predator. Violence as an arbiter of territorial borders is unthinkable to a rational creature, but inevitable to an irrational predator. Examine a map of the world! How many of the national boundaries were established by reason, and how many by war? It is difficult to find a single boundary that is not the direct or indirect result of either a recent or past war, or the threat of a war. All the borders of the United States were established under conditions of violence.

The United States border with Canada in the east was established by treaties with Britain which resulted from the American Revolution and the War of 1812 (Treaty of Paris in 1783, and Treaty of Ghent in 1814). It was also the result of the Aroostook War of 1838 and the subsequent Webster-Ashburton Treaty of 1842

The British claimed the Oregon Territory by right of settlements by the Hudson's Bay Company, the North West Company, and discoveries by Francis Drake. The United States claimed it on the basis of the Lewis and Clark expedition and discoveries by Capt. Robert Gray and John Kendrick. Americans flooded into the region over the Oregon Trail beginning in 1843. It was called the "Great Migration."

The threat of war with the British played a major role in establishing the border between the Oregon Territory and Canada in 1846. President James Polk was elected on the platform "All of Oregon or none! Fifty-four forty or fight!" England was in no position to open up new hostilities. She had been fighting the Opium War in China, the British-Afghan War, Maori revolts in New Zealand, Anglo-Sikh War in India, and unrest at home. War with England was finally averted by setting the border at the forty-ninth parallel. The native Indians naturally objected to European predators dividing up their lands. However, their futile uprisings were subdued by superior weaponry, and they were pacified by "turn the other cheek" Christianity.

Alaska was purchased from Russia in 1867 for 7.2 million dollars. This sounds innocent enough, but now for the rest of the story. War was the motivating force behind the deal. At the time of the purchase, many Americans called it "Seward's Folly" and "Seward's Icebox." William H. Seward was Secretary of State. He negotiated the deal. After A.D. 1600, Russia expanded predatorily from Moscow in all directions. By 1815, Russia became the largest country in Europe. She had gobbled up a large empire in Asia as well. In other words, Russia expanded to her eastern frontier, conquering Tartar, Turkish, and Mongolian tribes; exactly as we expanded to our western frontier, conquering Indian tribes in America. The human being, the born predator, has always followed this same mechanistic pattern of territorial conquest.

Russia wanted desperately to annex Constantinople and take control of the Bosporus because she feared that the Turks could close the Straits and bottle up her navy and shipping in the Black Sea. Control of the Bosporus was at least as important to Russia as control of the Strait of Gibraltar was to Britain, and control of the Panama Canal has been to the United States. Russia went to war with Turkey several times to drive the Turks of the Ottoman Empire out of Europe, but Great Britain always intervened. Britain wanted to maintain a balance of power in Europe in order to avoid a threat to her own power from another great power. A powerful Russia could interfere with Britain's communications with her Empire in the East.

The United States had a long history of border disputes with Britain, such as the "Fifty-Four Forty or Fight" dispute over the Oregon Territory border. Russia hoped that by selling Alaska to the United States, the United States would become embroiled in another dispute (preferably war) with Britain, which would divert Britain's attention from the Bosporus and give Russia a free hand in Asia Minor. In addition, the Monroe Doctrine had been heating up tensions between Russia and the United States regarding the Old World's role in the New World. War and the threat of war dictated the Alaska Purchase.

Nor was the Florida Purchase an innocent real estate transaction. It was a territorial acquisition. Spain lost Florida to Britain in the 1763 Treaty of Paris following the Seven Years' War in Europe. American revolutionaries twice invaded Florida during the American Revolution. Florida resisted and remained loyal to the Crown. Florida was returned to Spain in the Treaty of Paris of 1783. The United States and Spain became enmeshed in constant border disputes. Pensacola was captured by General Andrew Jackson in 1814. It had been used as a British base in the War of 1812. Jackson again invaded Florida in 1818 in response to the original owners' (Seminole Indians) refusal to submit to foreign (our) conquest. The pressure was telling on beleaguered Spain, and she realized that she could not defend Florida. As a consequence, she reluctantly ceded it to the United States in 1819 (Adams-Onis Treaty) after the United States agreed to assume the 5 million dollar claim that Americans had made on Spain.

Our borders with Mexico were not established in the manner American Dreamers would prefer to believe. Our guns and our predation decided the borders, not our dollars and a real estate deal. Texas, California, Nevada, Utah, Arizona, and New Mexico were all part of Mexico before the American Empire to the north gobbled them up. It was naked aggression, but American folklore has it otherwise.

When Mexico won her independence from Spain, she offered cheap land to settlers, even to foreign settlers from the United States. Americans, in their lust for the cheap land which had been expropriated from the Indians, flooded Mexico's Texas until thirty thousand had come by A.D. 1835. Mexico, quite naturally, became alarmed because foreigners were greatly outnumbering Mexican nationals; and so, she closed her borders to Americans, which has always been a basic right of sovereign nations. This perfectly legal closure infuriated the foreign Americans from the United States. Tensions built up, and, on March 2, 1836, the foreigners declared their independence from Mexico. It was like inviting your neighbor into your house, and then your neighbor deciding to take possession of your house.

At the time of the Civil War, the South, a part of the United States, was not permitted to declare its freedom and independence from the United States; so why should Mexico permit foreign interlopers to usurp Mexican territory by declaring it independent? Mexican immigrants have flooded into Texas in recent years. If they declare their independence from the United States and ask for admission into Mexico as a state, we will better understand how Texas became a state in the United States. Of course, since the minds of American Dreamers are encapsuled in concrete skulls, they will plead, "THAT'S DIFFERENT!"

Be that as it may, the foreign Americans stirred up war hysteria with the war cry, "Remember the Alamo!" after Santa Anna tried to crush the Texas Revolution of 1835. Sam Houston defeated the Mexicans and captured Santa Anna in the battle of San Jacinto in April of 1836. The Americans took Texas from the Mexicans; who had taken it from Spain; who had taken it from Montezuma's Aztec Empire; who had taken it from other Indian Tribes such as the Comanches and Apaches; who had taken it from yet other Indian tribes going back to the time of man's first arrival in the area. It was always stolen fair and square, according to the rules of human predation which would do honor to Adolf Hitler. The victorious Americans asked for statehood, and, on December 29, 1845, Texas became the largest state in the Empire of the United States.

Mexico's California met much the same fate as Texas, but with England and Russia vying for territory. The American foreigners in California declared their independence from Mexico, under the banner of the Bear Flag Republic, and asked for statehood. Historians generally agree that President Polk wanted to add California to the United States, and that his lust for territory played a large part in his favoring war with Mexico on the rather flimsy grounds of unsettled claims and because of his hurt feelings following his negotiator John Slidell's rejection by the Mexican authorities. The Mexicans moved troops into disputed territory and some bloody skirmishes resulted. The United States then declared war on Mexico. Captain

John C. Fremont and Colonel Stephen W. Kearny invaded California and New Mexico Territory. General Winfield Scott invaded Vera Cruz by sea, captured it, and marched inland to Mexico City, which he captured on September 14, 1847.

The conquest of Mexico rivaled any of Hitler's conquests for speed and efficiency. There was no other power to challenge us and force us to return the annexed territories to Mexico as Germany was forced to return her conquered territories. There is no law so irrevocable as the law of the indomitable predator.

The American Empire expanded with the acquisition of the Mexican territories of Texas, California, Nevada, Utah, Arizona, and New Mexico, while Mexico shrank by the same magnitude. Ah, but we were good guy predators. We paid Mexico 15 million dollars for the rapine. We even allowed the remnants of Mexico to exist and cower in her independence. Genghis Khan and Hitler, the bad guy predators, never paid for their rapines.

The Louisiana Purchase was by no means the peaceful business deal that its title superficially suggests. Considerations of war were decisive ingredients. On October 1, 1800, Napoleon Bonaparte forced King Charles IV of Spain to cede Louisiana back to France. The prospect of Napoleon getting control of New Orleans and control of shipping in the Mississippi caused consternation in the United States. President Thomas Jefferson struck mortal fear into Napoleon when he wrote his minister in Paris, "The day that France takes possession of New Orleans . . . we must marry ourselves to the British fleet and nation."

Britain had been Napoleon's enemy and nemesis. Britain and the United States had been enemies (American Revolution), which was advantageous to Napoleon; but if Britain and the United States were to become friends, especially military allies, it would have been disastrous for Napoleon. Knowing that, the shrewd Tom Jefferson instructed his minister to Paris to negotiate for the purchase of Louisiana. Napoleon was no fool. He knew that he could not defend Louisiana, not with all his problems in Europe, and he was certain to lose the territory to either Britain or the expanding United States Empire; and so, he agreed to sell it. Why not? Like a typical Mafia deal, he had an offer he couldn't refuse. He had the choice of selling, or the gun to his head would go off.

After the sale of Louisiana was completed, Napoleon remarked, "This accession of territory affirms forever the power of the United States, and I have given England a maritime rival that sooner or later will lay low her pride." How right he was! Less than ten years later, the United States slapped England's pride in the face in the War of 1812. Looming violence, war, and predation were the ingredients which gave birth to the Louisiana Purchase, just as war and violence had given birth to the Thirteen Colonies, the United States, and the Empire of the United States. Incredible hubris seemed to shower us with moral dispensations, which allowed us to employ the principle of *Machtpolitik* with impunity, but denied them to Hitler, Mussolini, and Tojo. Had these blustering triplets won World War II, they, too, would have defined morality in their own terms.

The history of the "peace-loving" United States has been one of violence and war. We are a violent society. Four American presidents have been assassinated: Lincoln, Garfield, McKinley, and Kennedy. Many other presidents have been the targets of assassins: Reagan, Ford, Truman, Franklin Roosevelt, Theodore Roosevelt, and Andrew Jackson. We live and breathe violence. THIRTEEN MILLION CRIMES ARE REPORTED ANNUALLY. TV programs, movies, and novels must feature murder and violence in order to succeed. If they featured intellectual themes of philosophy and science, they would fail miserably. Man boasts of being a rational creature, but the facts prove that he is an irrational, predatory animal of violence.

Having engaged in many wars for the alleged purpose of winning freedom from tyranny for ourselves, what should be our attitude towards other people who desire freedom from tyranny for themselves? Reason replies that we should favor them, but our predatory instincts forced us to favor our own predatory (national) interests. We invariably aided the enemies of freedom fighters. We performed exactly like nations all over the world and throughout history. As a nation, we were no longer a band of lawless revolutionaries, and it would not behoove us to link ourselves to revolutionaries. We wanted powerful foreign alliances because they would enhance our power—the natural concern of any predator. Pursuant to this policy, we aided and abetted the most vicious tyrants in history. The only stipulation was that they be OUR vicious tyrants. We sermonized about the evil ways of human rights violators, but, at the same time, we befriended any tyrant or despot who had power and was willing to become our ally.

A few of the most recent tyrants our sacrosanct government embraced include the Shah Mohammed Reza Pahlavi of Iran; President Fulgencio Batista of Cuba; Gen. Rafael Leonidas Trujillo Molina of the Dominican Republic; Gen. Anatasio Somoza-Debayle of Nicaragua; President Papa Doc Francois Duvalier of Haiti; President Ferdinand Edralin Marcos of the Philippines; Gen. Francisco Franco of Spain; Antonio de Oliveira Salazar of Portugal; many South American dictators; and Joseph Stalin of Russia (World War II).

Shah Pahlavi of Iran was showered with encomiums by seven United States presidents. In 1957, the CIA helped him set up the notorious secret police known as the SAVAK. Its mission was to insure loyalty to the Shah. Its method was the use of fiendish torture, which included lashing the victims' feet with electric cables until the flesh was torn apart and bones jutted out; burning parts of the victims' bodies on heated metal grills; insertion of bottles and hot eggs into the anus; mutilating women's breasts; and raping women while the victims were hanging upside down. In 1975, when word of the tortures was leaked out by the political prisoners, the Shah ordered, "Don't take any prisoners! Kill them!" The murder of the victims was covered up with the explanation that they died in gunfights while resisting arrest.

The Shah was steeped in corruption, but, like all despots, he thought that he transcended law and morality. He looted his country of billions of dollars, tortured and killed his countrymen by the tens of thousands, but the United States sponsored, supported, protected, and honored him because he was anti-communistic. And there are people who cannot understand why Iranians hate Americans. And still, throughout the world, the United States supports ignoble tyrants who rise to power on tides of blood from murdered victims, provided they are anti-communists and pro-American. Because the

United States has a fanatical, religious hatred of Communism, a born-again Christian American president may one day plunge the world into a nuclear holocaust by waging a Holy War to defeat the Evil Empire.

Americans are neither evil monsters nor saintly angels. They are simply human beings, like Russians, Englishmen, Japanese, Iranians, Africans, or whoever. A leopard can't change his spots. A human being can't change his predatory nature by becoming an American, but human hypocrisy fosters the belief that he can and does.

Hypocrisy is the product of the human brain and human instincts. We give lip service to the principle of human rights, selectively condemn its violations, as in South Africa, but ignore it, even at home, when we think it is in our predatory interests. Orientals were severely discriminated against by Alien Land Laws and the Chinese Exclusion Act of 1888. Chinese coolies were virtual slaves, used to build the first United States transcontinental railroad.

An executive order signed by President Franklin D. Roosevelt in March of 1942 condemned 110,000 Japanese-Americans to forcible evacuation of their homes on the West Coast and imprisonment in concentration camps, which were euphemistically called RELOCA-TION CENTERS. A penitentiary is a relocation center because it relocates the inmate from society to a prison. The pious devils used the same technique of employing euphemisms to cover up a crime as when they imprisoned the remnants of the slaughtered Indians in concentration camps and called them RESERVATIONS.

The unconstitutional imprisonment of American citizens of Japanese ancestry without a hearing or a trial continued until 1946. The distinguished Earl Warren of the celebrated Warren Supreme Court of the United States urged his constituents to keep Japanese out of California "so long as the flag of Nippon is flying over the Philippines." Yes, THE Earl Warren who made it difficult, if not impossible, to imprison brutal murderers, even with conclusive evidence against them, wanted to imprison decent, law-abiding Japanese-Americans without any evidence against them whatsoever. Even the Supreme Court of the United States upheld the constitutionality of the presidential evacuation order. These persecuted Japanese-Americans suffered at least 400 million dollars in property loss, plus loss of education, civil liberties, business income, and dignity. This national scandal was excused on the grounds that national security made the crime necessary, but not one single Japanese-American was ever accused of sabotage or treason in the continental United States.

Today, our city streets are teeming with hardened criminals and murderers, but they are not removed from society in the interests of public safety. Absolutely guilty vicious killers and sadistic rapists have civil and human rights to keep them out of prison. The innocent Americans of Japanese ancestry had no rights. America displayed barbarism in its drabbest colors. Public safety is jeopardized by freed hardcore criminals stalking the streets, but they cannot be relocated even with irrefutable evidence of guilt because it is excluded from the courtroom due to crackpot technicalities and insane laws. On the other hand, Japanese-Americans who were born in America (Nisei), and the older generation (Issei), who were declared ineligible for naturalization in the Land of the Free, were imprisoned; and EVIDENCE OF INNOCENCE was suppressed by *de facto* exclusionary laws.

The Japanese-Americans (Nisei) were such outstanding soldiers that their regiment in Italy became the most decorated fighting unit in United States history. In spite of the heroism of the Nisei, the American Legion cancelled the charters of all Japanese-American posts. The United States government had always expiated its crimes by payments in cash, as when it annexed Mexican and Spanish territory. It is expected to atone with cash payments to surviving Japanese-Americans.

Franklin D. Roosevelt not only committed an atrocity against citizens of Japanese ancestry, but it appears he may have committed an even greater crime against all American citizens. Churchill told his aides months before Pearl Harbor that Roosevelt was looking for "an incident that would justify him in opening hostilities." William Stephenson fed daily reports of the top-secret Axis messages to FUR. On November 27, 1941, FDR sent Winston Churchill the following message: "Japanese negotiations off. Services expect action within two weeks." Incredibly, FDR did not order a twenty-four hour alert at all major bases. The President had been given advance warning of the sneak attack, but he refused to act on it, knowing it would whip up war hysteria so that he could then come to England's assistance in her war in Europe. It was an apparent, cold-blooded, murderous plot, perpetrated to arouse war fever, but it wasn't the first time, nor will it be the last time. Actually, this technique has been used by hawkish heads of state since the beginning of human history.

The 1898 sinking of the battleship U.S.S. Maine in Havana harbor launched the Spanish-American War. The warmongers had a field day, whipping up war hysteria with the cry "Remember the Maine!" There is some evidence to support the contention of American expansionists' complicity in the sinking for the express purpose of involving us in war with Spain. William Randolph Hearst's "yellow press" which published lurid accounts of alleged Spanish atrocities in Cuba inflamed American passions for war. It also helped to stimulate the sale of his newspapers.

Newspaper tycoon William Randolph Hearst (1863-1951) built a publishing empire of numerous magazines, thirty daily newspapers, and several radio stations. He used the power of his publishing dynasty to control American politics, morals, and manners. He has often been accused of single-handedly provoking the Spanish-American War of 1898. He ordered his artist, Frederic Remington, to go to Cuba and draw pictures of Spanish atrocities for his newspapers. Remington could not uncover any Spanish atrocities; and so, he wired his boss: "Everything is quiet. There is no trouble here. There will be no war. I wish to return." Hearst quickly fired back his infamous reply: "Please remain. You furnish the pictures. I'll furnish the war." Remington remained, furnished his boss with notorious fabrications of Spanish atrocities, and the human robots in America immediately began to scream for revenge.

Actually, most of the American journalists in Cuba at the time faked Spanish atrocity stories. William Francis Mannix of the Washington Star so outraged the Spanish authorities with his fabricated stories that they took a bayonet and frog marched him to a ship bound for the United States. Mannix was a tireless perpetrator of journalistic fraud. He was fired from the Philadelphia Press when it was sued for libel after it published one of his phoney stories. He became so infamous for his fictionalized news stories that he had to change his name to William G. Leonard to get another job. Louis T. Stone (1875-1933) was so well known for his fabricated news that he became known as the "Winstead Liar." The faking of news to instigate war, or just to make money, is not uncommon.

The awesome power of the press was best described by FDR's Secretary of the Interior, Harold LeClaire Ickes: "It has been used to elect and defeat candidates for public office . . . to stampede a nation into prohibition hysteria and to reverse the majorities fourteen years later. The use as well as the misuse of information has made the power of suggestion the decisive force in world affairs. It can cause or prevent war. It can strengthen or destroy a democracy. It can build or wreck a nation."

Propaganda is defined by The New Columbia Encyclopedia as the "systematic manipulation of public opinion, generally by the use of symbols such as flags, monuments, oratory, and publications." It is used to provoke and justify war. Lenin, Hitler, and Mussolini were masters at its use. America is no stranger to it. When it is used to demoralize the enemy, or boost civilian and military morale at home, it is called psychological warfare. America's Office of War Information was established to disseminate wartime propaganda. Our United States Information Agency was established to disseminate peacetime propaganda. Necessary "adjustments" are always made to "information" to make us look like good guys and the other side look like bad guys.

Propaganda even permeates our schools and colleges. In the words of Charles A. Beard, "When teachers take up a text book in civics or economics, they do not know to what extent vital parts of it have been 'doctored' to suit private parties who expect to make profits out of 'educating' the public to take their views of governmental policy." It is impossible to escape propaganda because, as explained by the Institute for Propaganda Analysis, "If one assumes that propaganda is a method utilized for influencing the conduct of others on behalf of predetermined ends, it appears that every articulate person with a purpose is a propagandist."

President Wilson was elected on the platform of keeping us out of World War I; but, upon his election, he quickly moved to bring about our participation in "the war to make the world safe for democracy." He knew how to manipulate the minds of Americans into massive war hysteria. He sent our merchant ships into German blockade areas, knowing that they would be sunk by German U boats and Americans would then clamor for revenge and war. He succeeded in robotizing the American people when they appropriately responded with the war cry, "Remember the Lusitania!" They stumbled over each other in a mad rush to Europe to kill Germans, singing as they went, "We won't come back 'til it's over over there." Mothers were regretting that they had but one son to give to their country.

President Lyndon B. Johnson wanted to legitimatize the unconstitutional, undeclared war in Vietnam. He, like all previous presidents since Harry Truman, stirred up passionate hatred and fear of international communism. He brainwashed many Americans into believing it is better to fight the Communist enemy in Vietnam than in San Francisco or New York. It is almost certain that President Johnson INVENTED the SECOND Gulf of Tonkin incident to secure passage of the Gulf of Tonkin Resolution in Congress so that he could wage an undeclared Holy War against Communism in Vietnam. Holding the dreaded specter of the Domino Theory and the Red Bugbear before the people, the ghost of Mohammed spoke, "Victory or paradise is before you. The devil and hell-fire are behind you. CHARGE!"

Every American president from Truman to Reagan accepted and promulgated the myth of international, monolithic Communism controlled from Moscow. It is certainly true that the COMMUNIST INTERNATIONAL, otherwise known as the COMINTERN, or THIRD INTERNATIONAL, was founded in 1919 in Moscow by Vladimir Lenin with the avowed purpose of promoting world revolution under the direction of the Communist Party in Moscow. Stalin dissolved the Comintern in 1943, but it was mere window dressing. Moscow would certainly love to promote world revolution and dominate the world, and she has certainly given it her best shot, but she cannot even dominate Communist Yugoslavia. Nor can she dominate China. China has a soul all her own. Russia has difficulty enough controlling the weak Communist puppet nations on her borders, and she can do that only with the threat of armed intervention.

Russia cannot control other nations via international Communism for the simple reason that the gregarious, territorial instincts of the human predator unite him in locally centralized territorial tribes and nations, not in international unity by the gravitational attraction of political ideologies. There is no monolithic Christianity, no monolithic Islam, no monolithic Democracy, no monolithic White Man, and no monolithic Black Man. Why should Communism be exempt from all laws governing the human predator?

Moslem Ottoman Turks fought Moslem Arabs. Catholic Spain and her Catholic colonies fought each other. One of the most bitter of wars, the American Civil War, was fought between two democracies, the North and the South. Most wars in Europe, as well as the rest of the world, were nationalistic and imperialistic wars. The most flagitious wars of Europe were religious wars, such as the Huguenot Wars and the Thirty Years' War, which were between Christians and Christians. There is no such thing as a monolithic, international, cohesive bloc. Setting up the ogre of international Communism as the Demogorgon and menace of the world is as childishly naive as most beliefs in gods and devils, but it is this kind of stupidity that hurls millions of human beings into the holocaust of war.

The delusion that Communist countries throughout the world await orders from Moscow, or that countries who receive USSR aid are standing by for orders from Moscow, is not only nonsensical, but the most dangerous threat to world peace. People who rebel against oppressive governments accept aid from whoever will give it. Sun Yat-sen needed arms to fight the warlords in China. Only Lenin would supply him. He took the aid, but he didn't take orders from Lenin. Mustapha Kemal accepted military supplies from Lenin so that he could build an army in central Anatolia and Westernize Turkey, but he took no orders from Lenin. Anwar Sadat accepted aid from the Soviet Union, and then expelled Soviet technicians and advisers from Egypt in 1972.

Communist China split with the USSR in 1963. Border conflicts brought Communist China and Communist Russia to the brink of war many times. Communist Vietnam went to war with Communist Cambodia (Khmer Rouge) in 1978. Red China and Communist Vietnam went to war in 1979. Subliminally, our government actually realized that communism is NOT monolithic. That is why it sent foreign aid to Communist Poland, to Communist Romania, and to Communist Yugoslavia. Even a beginning student of history should know that nationalism supersedes ideology. Ignorant American presidents send the flower of the nation's youth to unnecessary and untimely deaths.

If anyone should have been a Moscow stooge, it was Josip Broz Tito of Yugoslavia. He fought with the Red Army in Russia during the Civil War of 1918 to 1920. He was assigned by the Comintern to reorganize the Yugoslavian Communist Party, and he received direct aid from Stalin in his struggle to seize military and political power from Mihajlovic. In spite of his very close ties with Stalin and the USSR, his deep commitment to Communism, and his being close enough to Russia to face an armed invasion, he quickly curtailed the Russian agents when he gained power. He became completely independent of Moscow, for which he was expelled from the Cominform in 1948. He even led the opposition to the Soviet intervention in Czechoslovakia.

It is unfortunate that our American presidents are either grossly uninformed of history, or incapable of understanding history. It was ignorance that involved us in the Vietnam War, and it is this same ignorance that accounts for our troops being sent to Central America and for millions of dollars of military aid sent to suppress the legitimate struggles of people against repressive governments.

The reason all nations were unified by war and war alone is that local tribal chiefs, warlords, mayors, et cetera are jealous of their power and never surrender it, except by armed force. Even the governors of our fifty states refuse to take orders from Washington, D.C. To say that countries that become Communistic are stooges standing by for orders from a foreign government, whether it be Moscow, Peking, or any other, is to speak childish nonsense. Because of such nonsense fifty-eight thousand of America's youth perished in the Vietnam War, and many more will die in the future because of future nonsense.

Unreasoning obsession with "the Communist menace" has led the United States through an era of McCarthyism in the 1950s. Careers were ruined on the flimsiest of evidence. This sort of obsession prompted the United States to employ Klaus Barbie as her agent to spy on French communists. This "Butcher of Lyon" was the Nazi killer of four thousand French Jews and the deporter of seven thousand five hundred French Jews to Nazi concentration camps between 1942 and 1944. After employing Barbie for four years, the United States Army Intelligence devised an elaborate obstruction of justice scheme which slipped him out of France, and gave him a new identity as Klaus Altmann in Bolivia.

Because of hysteria over Communism, the United States has done business with Mafia killers, Nazi killers, and murderous dictators, colluded with terrorists, and spat defiance at the World Court by rejecting its jurisdiction in the promotion of terrorism in Central America, pursuant to the Reagan administration's secret war against Nicaragua. That the entire world is aware of America's disregard for international law was demonstrated by the United Nations General Assembly's vote of 108 to 9 for deploring the invasion of Grenada. In the Security Council, the United States was the ONLY nation to vote against condemnation of the invasion. This contempt for international law coincided with such scrupulous adherence to domestic law that she was unable to protect herself from vile domestic criminals.

Few people fully appreciate the enormity of our crime in Vietnam. The Vietnamese had been under Chinese rule from 111 B.C. to A.D. 939, at which time Ngo Quyen defeated the Chinese and headed the new state of Vietnam. The Vietnamese resisted several Mongolian invasions, including that of Kublai Khan, but finally succumbed to the power of the Chinese Ming dynasty in A.D. 1407. The Chinese ruthlessly exploited them. By A.D. 1418, and after ten years of struggle, they freed themselves from Chinese domination. Internal struggles divided the country in 1620, but it was reunited again in A.D. 1802 after fourteen years of civil wars and revolutions. Portuguese, Dutch, and English penetrated the country, commencing in 1516, but they withdrew. The French conquered Vietnam in colonial wars from 1858 to 1883. The French mercilessly exploited the Vietnamese for the exportation of rice, tea, and rubber. The Vietnamese were virtual slaves. They tried to rebel, but they had no weapons. The freedom fighters were viciously beaten down.

Woodrow Wilson proclaimed the principle of self-determination as one of his famous "Fourteen Points" to secure peace and justice in the post-World War I world. Ho Chi Minh was sufficiently naive to believe that the allies represented justice and the Central Powers represented injustice, and so he tried to plead for Vietnamese freedom in the Versailles Conference. He was not even allowed entry. The Allies were only interested in splitting up the loot taken from the conquered enemy. In 1930, Ho Chi Minh started a freedom uprising which France suppressed with "an unparalleled wave of terror."

When the Nazis defeated France in World War II, the Japanese took control of Indochina. The Vietnamese at first welcomed the Japanese as liberators, but the Japanese joined with the French to exploit them so savagely that at least two million died of starvation. They learned that Orientals are no more monolithic than communists. Ho Chi Minh collaborated with the Allies by rescuing downed pilots of bombers attacking the Japanese in Vietnam, and by supplying the Allies with vital Japanese troop movement intelligence. Ho Chi Minh was America's good friend and ally during World War II, so much so that he expected the "freedom-loving" United States to help Vietnam win freedom.

Ho Chi Minh actually believed the United Nations' proclamations and propaganda during World War II which blazoned the principle of self-determination for ALL nations. He wrote several letters to President Truman, pleading for help in securing independence for his country, but Harry Truman and Britain were only interested in re-establishing the British and French Empires. Freedom has different meanings for the predator and for the prey. For the predatory imperialistic nations, freedom meant freedom to continue colonial rule. According to the testimony of our own OSS agents who worked directly with Ho Chi Minh in the common struggle to defeat the Japanese, he was first and foremost a nationalist and secondly a Communist. He was a Communist only because he believed that Communism was the best way to relieve the dire poverty of his countrymen. To say that Ho Chi Minh was a stooge of Moscow or Peking is to blather utter infantile nonsense.

Ho Chi Minh struggled against the exploiting French without any help from Russia or China for several years. He wanted and expected help from America, which he ingenuously believed was dedicated to the freedom of all nations. He had read Emma Lazarus's poem graven on the Statue of Liberty: "Give me your tired, your poor, Your huddled masses yearning to breathe free, The wretched refuse of your teeming shore. Send these, the homeless, tempest-tossed to me, I lift my lamp beside the golden door!"

Ho Chi Minh declared Vietnam's independence on September 2nd, 1945, immediately after the defeat of Japan. It was a moving oration, copied almost word for word from the American Declaration of Independence which he held in such high esteem: "We hold these truths to be self-evident: That all men are created equal, *et cetera*." He should have known that it would not impress the Americans. Were not the American Negroes *de jure* slaves for ninety years after that Declaration, and *de facto* slaves nearly two hundred years after that sanctimonious, hypocritical Declaration? Did that Declaration deter the genocidal extermination of the Indian Nations and people?

In March of 1946, France agreed to recognize Ho Chi Minh's government as a free state within the French Union; but, like American treaties with the Indians, France broke her word and became hellbent on re-establishing colonial rule. On November 23rd, 1946, the French shelled and destroyed the Vietnamese section of Haiphong, causing at least six thousand civilian casualties. The vicious war against the Vietnamese freedom fighters was on. The French attacked with blitzkrieg fury and up-to-the-minute science and technology weaponry. The Viet Minh fought back with bamboo spears. The French didn't want to be dominated by the Nazis, but they wanted to dominate and exploit the Vietnamese. The French cried "Attila the Hun" foul to Nazi atrocities; but, typical of the double standards of human predators, they committed these same atrocities against the Vietnamese. French soldiers sent postcards photoengraved with the pictures of severed heads from executed Vietnamese patriots to their sweethearts back home in France.

The one-sided slaughter of Vietnamese went on for over three years. In 1950, Red China recognized the Viet Minh government, closely followed by the USSR. Military aid began to flow to the Viet Minh. The slaughter was not quite so one-sided now. The United States recognized the French puppet government of Bao Dai, the same playboy puppet emperor the French had installed in 1926. He was the son of Khai Dinh, who was the son of Dong Khanh, all of whom were French puppet emperors. Bao Dai also became the puppet emperor for the Japanese when they wrested power from the French. It shouldn't be difficult to see that Bao Dai represented the foreign colonial powers and not the Vietnamese people. Nevertheless, he was the traitorous stooge whom the United States recognized and aided.

In the first Indochina War of 1946 to 1954, THE UNITED STATES HAD ONE INTEREST AND ONE INTEREST ALONE, AND THAT WAS THE RE-ESTABLISHMENT OF FRENCH COLONIAL RULE IN VIETNAM. The historical evidence is clear on this point. The United States had fought her own difficult War of Independence, but once she became a nation, she pursued her own national interests which meant making powerful foreign alliances. This necessitated the suppression of other people in their wars of independence. The United States poured 2.5 BILLION dollars into the French war to suppress the Vietnamese struggle for freedom.

Despite massive American military aid to the French, the awesome power of the French war machine, modern aircraft, paratroopers, bombs, napalm, *et cetera*, the Viet Minh scored a seemingly impossible victory at Dien Bien Phu. It dumbfounded the world. The Viet Minh had drudged heavy artillery over the rugged mountains by footpower and bicycles, reminiscent of Hannibal's feat in crossing the Alps. John Foster Dulles smothered the French with praises for their bravery. It was as ludicrous as a clown showering praises on Goliath for his brave fight against David.

The Geneva Accord signed by the French and the Viet Minh,

following the French defeat, split Vietnam at the seventeenth parallel, but it provided for all Vietnamese elections in July of 1956 to settle the question of unification. The Viet Minh were certain to win the election. The United States did not sign the Accord, but she did promise to respect its provisions. Despotic right-wing Ngo Dinh Diem took over the reins of government from Bao Dai. Diem's brother, Ngo Dinh Nhu, headed the dreaded SAVAK-LIKE secret police. Diem was too independent to make a good American puppet. He and his brother were assassinated following a USA approved coup in 1963.

South Vietnam refused to hold free elections in 1956 as provided for in the Geneva Agreement, and the United States broke her word to respect the Agreement, using the excuse that she never signed the Geneva Agreement in the first place. The truth is that the United States, like Soviet Russia, wants free elections only when they provide the desired results. When free elections brought Marxist Salvador Allende Gossens to the presidency in Chile in 1970, the United States sent its CIA hit squad to Chile to have Allende murdered. The murder of Allende in 1973 was followed by a right-wing military dictatorship, government-sponsored terror, torture, brutality, and murder; but the Land of the Free and the Home of the Brave had achieved her purpose of nullifying the free elections. The plight of the Chilean people did not matter. Right-wing terror is condoned when it suppresses left-wing power because the end justifies the means in the holy war against "evil" Communism.

In 1960, when it became clear that the Geneva Agreement was not going to be honored by the United States and the South Vietnamese government, the Vietnamese opponents of the Saigon regime formed the National Front for the Liberation of the South (NFL). The NFL was also called the Viet Cong. By April of 1969, United States troop strength in Vietnam reached 543,000. A total of 2.5 million Americans fought in Vietnam, of which 303,000 were wounded. The United States bombed Indochina on a scale unprecedented in history. More bombs, 7 MILLION TONS, were dropped on the hapless country than all the bombs in World War II. General Curtis LeMay boasted that America would bomb Vietnam back into the Stone Age. The devastation, suffering, and death inflicted upon innocent people was staggering, but, at that very moment of horror, the lives of our homespun criminal murderers like Charles Manson were spared because we were too civilized to inflict cruel and unusual punishment upon them. *Homo sapiens?* Don't be ridiculous!

Not all of America's fighting men who were sent to Vietnam as robots returned as robots. They arrived in Vietnam programmed to believe they were fighting for America and the freedom of the Vietnamese. Some shook off their programming and began to wonder why the South Vietnamese were unwilling to fight for their own cause, but the Viet Cong and the North Vietnamese were willing to endure unimaginable hardship and agony for their cause. They asked themselves, "Why do the Viet Cong fight with such superb bravery, valor, and endure so many years of brutal punishment for their cause, and why are the South Vietnamese unwilling to show interest in the war? Is the corrupt Saigon regime worth such a terrible sacrifice of human life?" The de-robotized Marines began to feel like unwanted invaders instead of liberators.

At My Lai in 1968, American soldiers under Lt. William L. Calley massacred three hundred forty-seven Vietnamese, including women and children. Every effort was made to cover up the massacre. Lieutenant Calley was convicted of murder in 1971, but a Federal District Court overturned the conviction. Human stupidity is such that the My Lai massacre was looked upon with horror by some, but only because the murders were committed at point-blank range. The 7 MILLION TONS OF BOMBS dropped from aircraft caused infinitely more death and suffering, not on a few hundred but on hundreds of thousands of Vietnamese, and yet the carnage caused by bombings were looked upon with the same moral indifference as natural disasters like hurricanes. Distance not only lends enchantment, it lends moral immunity to guilt for mass murder and barbaric torture.

Only impervious prejudice and blatant chauvinism prevent the recognition of the fact that the Vietnamese Communists won a tremendous victory against not only the overwhelming military power of the French, but also the awesome military power of the United

States, fifty thousand South Koreans, thousands of troops from Thailand, New Zealand, and Australia, combined with the half-hearted assistance of South Vietnamese troops. The Viet Cong and North Vietnam fought with no air force. It was combat between a colossus and a pygmy.

The United States spent 141 BILLION DOLLARS to blast Vietnam back into the Stone Age. Because of military expenditures, social security payments to the needy were cut, the space program was cut, aid to education was reduced; but the interest alone on the 141 billion (10 percent) would provide a million people with an annual income of fourteen thousand one hundred dollars, not for ten, a hundred, or a thousand years, but FOREVER. President Ronald Reagan called the Vietnam War a noble effort. His only apparent regret is that America did not win it. Think about that for a moment! The born-again Christian President of the "civilized" United States did not regret the horrible suffering inflicted upon the Vietnamese, the French, and the American fighting men. He only regretted defeat. In other words, he wished more people had been killed if that were the price of victory. His concern to protect the unborn from abortion did not extend to protection of the born from slaughter. Of course, this is the normal response of a natural predator, even a born-again Christian predator. We must remember that even we Americans are clones of that ancient hominid scourge of Earth.

The Vietnamese were superb in war, but total fizzles in peace. Natural disasters, combined with the natural resistance of people to collectivism, created economic havoc in Indochina. Vietnamese peasants resisted communization no less vehemently than the Russian peasants, and with the same results: famine and starvation. It is a fact of history and a consequence of human nature that human beings will fight courageously for their tribe or nation in times of war, but they will produce efficiently in times of peace only for their own selfish good, not the common good. This is one of the illogical anomalies of human nature. A human being will make selfless personal sacrifices for the common good on the battlefield, but he will sacrifice the common good for his own selfish good when he is not on the battlefield. (Capitalism succeeds where communism fails because it is based on the reality of human nature rather than on unrealistic pipe dreams.)

Vietnamese, like all people, were sometimes the victims of wars of conquest and sometimes the perpetrators of wars of conquest. The era of conquest and expansion for the United States was between the eighteenth and the early twentieth centuries. Japan was a late-comer. For her it was the first half of the twentieth century. Wars of expansion for the Vietnamese extended from the tenth to the nineteenth centuries A.D. In the tenth century, Vietnam was a small area around the Red River Delta with Hanoi near its center. By the fourteenth century, she conquered the territory south to Da Nang. By the sixteenth century, she extended her conquests to Cam-rank. The Saigon area was acquired in the eighteenth and early nineteenth centuries. The French predators conquered the Vietnamese preda-tors in the mid and latter nineteenth century. Vietnam remained a French colony for a hundred years.

So goes the monotonous repetition of human history like the coming and going of seasons. The human predator has always preyed on his neighbors. The American Indians preyed on each other. The Jews and Arabs preyed on each other. European nations preyed on each other. European Empires preyed on each other; for example, World War I. Twentieth century nations preyed on each other to form new empires; that is, World War II. One of the absurdities of the human predator is that he is not cognizant of predation as an evil until he becomes the victim. That is why Americans believe that the Indians were the bad guys, but they were the good guys.

We denigrated our twentieth century victims, the Viet Cong and the North Vietnamese, as bad guys exactly as we had denigrated our earlier victims, the American Indians. The Japanese attack on Pearl Harbor should have given us empathy for the American Indians and later for the Viet Minh, but omnipotent arrogance placed an impen-etrable barrier to identification with victims of our own aggressions.

At one time, the North Vietnamese contended that all captured Americans were war criminals. At the end of World War II we execut-ed several Japanese Generals for being "war criminals," among whom were Yamashita and Homma. The question of who is a war criminal and who is not is resolved by who wins and who loses the war. Bertrand Russell, the noted British philosopher, "tried" the United States for Vietnam war crimes by a tribunal which sat in Stockholm. It was a farce but only because it was not backed up by incontestable military power. Invincible power is the ultimate arbiter of right and wrong. American presidents have sent millions of people, from Indians to Vietnamese, to unnecessary and untimely deaths, but they are gods of power who enjoy absolute impunity.

Indians, blacks, Mexicans, Spaniards, Vietnamese, and workingmen were not the only victims of American predations. Women were also victimized. Many women had taken an active interest in the American antislavery movement when, by 1832, the idea occurred to them that they, themselves, were not exactly free. It also became apparent that if they depended on the intelligence and goodness of males for their liberation, they would have to wait forever.

Elizabeth Cady Stanton and Lucretia Mott became active in the women's rights movement, and in 1848, they issued a call for a women's rights convention. It was the same year that Elizabeth Stanton attended an international antislavery conference in London but was not permitted to speak because the male delegates declared that to do so would be "contrary to the ordinances of the Almighty." It was at that time in history when women had little or no rights, which was most of the time. Their property and their wages legally belonged to their husbands. It was perfectly legal for husbands to whip their wives as well as their children. Medical schools refused to admit women, sometimes on the astounding grounds that "if they are unable to raise a mustache, they are unfit physicians." Oberlin College was the first college to graduate a woman in 1841.

Suffragettes demonstrated in front of the White House in scorching heat and slashing rain with banners reading, "How long must women wait for liberty?" They suffered indignities, insults, and humiliation. Women's rights movements picked up steam with Susan B. Anthony, between 1852 and 1906, but still didn't go very far. After 1906, Anna Howard Shaw and Mrs. Carrie Chapman Catt accelerated the movement, and, gradually, women became enfranchised in some of the states. When this happened, they could elect senators and congressmen of their choice. They were gaining political power, but it took a smash to the nation's head with a two-by-four to do it. Finally, on August 26, 1920, the Nineteenth Amendment was ratified by thirty-six states, and women at long last gained the constitutional right to vote.

During all those many difficult years of tedious waiting and struggling, women suffragists endured insult, ridicule, persecution, and outrages, not only from men but, also, from members of their own sex. Today it seems so right, so proper, and so fair for women to vote, and it certainly follows from the tenets of the Declaration of Independence. Why was the struggle so difficult and so long? If we assume that human beings are intelligent creatures, it would make no sense at all, but if we accept the fact they are predatory animals of colossal stupidity, it makes perfect sense.

Blacks, minorities, women, poor people, and working people did not achieve their civil rights by appealing to reason so much as by appealing to violence. Besides, economic conditions were prerequisites to the enfranchisement of women as well as the emancipation of Negroes. In this modern technological age, a man cannot easily browbeat a woman. When a woman has her finger on the trigger of an equalizer, she has the same power as a man. A woman can push the doomsday button as easily as a man. Male physical superiority, like slavery, has become obsolete. Moral enlightenment and conscience-awakening were merely economic necessities in the technological world following the Industrial Revolution, but it still required a kick in the buttocks to accomplish a full awakening to the new realities. After all, *Homo sapiens* isn't really very sapient.

In human affairs, the irrational power to destroy is more impressive than the intellectual power to create. An arsonist makes the headlines. The builder remains in a limbo of anonymity. Everyone knows Nero burned Rome, but who knows the architect? John Wilkes Booth vies with Abraham Lincoln for fame. A punch in the nose is more persuasive than all the logic in the world. If two men are trying to convince you, one has reason on his side, but the other has a loaded gun in his hand, which man is more persuasive? The American Negro didn't have to invent the airplane, automobile, or TV to get respect. He got far more respect by demonstrating, boycotting, rioting, and burning cities to the ground.

Every society tends to form a tyrannical power structure. Democracies are no exception. To this point, my personal experience as a young college student is apropos. As a youth, I shared the normal patriotic fervor for the great freedoms we Americans purportedly possess. One such freedom is the alleged right to recall corrupt political officeholders by means of the Initiative and Referendum Acts. It happened that corruption flourished in the then little town of San Jose, California, during the 1930s, and it extended from the city clerk to the county sheriff. I had some knowledge of it because a bartender friend of Charley Bigley, the bootlegging political boss, had fixed a traffic ticket for me. As a young idealist, I thought it was time to throw the bums out.

In order to recall the officeholders, it was first necessary to obtain petitions from the city clerk. Before I could get them, I had to sign and give my address. Having received the petitions, I energetically went about collecting signatures for the recall of the corrupt politicians immediately. It was an exhilarating experience, a revel in freedom. I was working my way through college as a part time machinist for the Volmer Butane Company. The following morning, when I appeared for work, Mr. Volmer greeted me with, "Young man, you will have to turn over those petitions you got, if you want to keep your job with me." Upon asking why, I learned that the Standard Oil Company of California refused to renew his butane franchise if I did not comply. I had no choice. I had to either comply or quit college.

My sad disillusionment only began. When I went home that night, my father greeted me with, "Kid, what in the hell have you been up to?" He was frantic. He told me he had a living to make and a family to support. After he calmed down a bit, he told me that his company, the Anderson Barngrover Manufacturing Company (later purchased by FMC), threatened to fire him if I persisted in getting signed petitions to recall the city officials. The corrupt scoundrels even got to my father. It was the termination of my exercise as a free American citizen exercising my theoretical freedoms as an American citizen.

The same story is repeated every day throughout America. Not long ago, Martin Yant became editor of Mansfield, Ohio's Mansfield News Journal. After five months on the job, he directed an eight-part expose of Sheriff Weikel's office which resulted in many indictments against the sheriff and his deputies. As a result, publisher Harry Horvitz fired Martin Yant, but Yant began a crusade on his own. He filed a petition and gathered signatures against the sheriff. The crusader had a five-pound rock hurled through his window, and arson fires were set on his property. He was hit with 45 million dollars libel suits. He lost his life's savings, and his wife and four children left him.

It is one thing to have theoretical freedoms, but if you cannot exercise those freedoms, you are devoid of freedom. Despots have learned that the illusion of freedom is excellent lubricant for robots. The USSR Constitution of 1936 guarantees Russian citizens the same freedoms Americans are guaranteed by the American Constitution, but if Russians try to exercise them, they have to boast about their freedoms in a Siberian salt mine. Americans deplore the USSR's harassment of her nuclear physicist Andrei Sakharov; but the USA's nuclear physicist J. Robert Oppenheimer suffered the same harassment in the Land of the Free for the same reasons. Americans can boast of freedoms, but how many freedoms can they actually exercise? There is only one way to find out. Try to exercise them, and see what happens to you. One thing is certain: the ones you hurt will strike back. If they are a criminal syndicate, you have a good chance of ending up in concrete overcoat on the bottom of a river or mysteriously exterminated like Jimmy Hoffa. If the ones you hurt are less violently inclined, you may be lucky and only lose your livelihood. The Land of the Free and the Home of the Brave may be a great nation, but it is still (like all nations) a nation of human predators, and predators behave much the same all over the world.

A few years ago, the newspapers reported the story of a Greek who had lived in New York City for several years but returned to Greece because he had been mugged fifteen times, sent to the hospital fighting for his life twice, and was forced to the conclusion, "What good is American freedom to me, if I have to remain a prisoner in my own home because criminals will attack me whenever I leave it`?"

Hundreds of elderly people die of heat stroke every year because they are forced to keep their doors and windows locked at all times in fear of criminals breaking into their homes to rob and to kill them. When there is a heat wave, the consequences to the senior citizens are devastating. The Land of the Free is free for criminal predators, not for the quarry.

Hatred and revulsion of al-Qaddafi of Libya is incurred by the civilized world because he is an alleged terrorist who hires assassins to murder enemy heads of states. We are told that he is barbaric, evil and unconscionable, but he is only as guilty as our own government. Our CIA has participated in the assassinations of Allende of Chile, Lumumba of the Republic of the Congo, Mossadegh of Iran, Ngo Dinh Diem of South Vietnam, President Jacobo Arbenz Gusman of Guatemala, Rafael Trujillo of the Dominican Republic, and, presumably, many others. The CIA even enlisted the help of the Mafia for the planned assassination of Castro of Cuba in at least eight separate plots.

The CIA went to such unconscionable extremes as to plot the assassination of columnist Jack Anderson. Meanwhile, ruthless killers like Klaus Barbie, the "Butcher of Lyon," who was given asylum by American Army counterintelligence, are protected. In the 1960s the CIA ran the clandestine operation in Vietnam known as the PHOENIX PROGRAM which was an attack against the civilian leadership of the Viet Cong and resulted in the murder of twenty thousand people. The United States sought the aid of the Mafia during World War II under the code name of "OPERATION UNDERWORLD." Gangster Lucky Luciano was freed from prison as a part of this operation.

The United States government lies to its citizens as a matter of policy. Some of the more notorious lies concerned Gary Powers and the U-2 incident, the secret Cambodian bombings, United States naval vessels furtively carrying nuclear weapons to Japan, and many other lies made known by the revelations of the Daniel Ellsberg papers. However, facts are irrelevant to chauvinists. Like the mother of a murderer proclaiming her son "a good boy," fanatical patriots see no evil, hear no evil, and speak no evil about their beloved fatherland. Human reason is pathetically helpless when it is overpowered by human instinct.

The Almighty Dollar and Almighty God are in a dead heat for universal worship in the United States, where predation is the name of the game. Hospitals refuse dying patients when they cannot show proof of ability to pay their confiscatory fees. To physicians, patients are fair game upon whom they have a natural right to prey. Surgeons sell operations to patients like con men selling refrigerators to Eskimos. Merchants prey on customers, employers prey on workers, and every human being preys on his fellow human being when he possesses predatory power. Success is measured in terms of money, and the possession of excess money is the reward of successful predation.

Young men are drafted to fight and die on far-flung battlefields, but money needed to finance war is sacrosanct. Some wealthy people are multimillionaires, but their wealth is not drafted. It is unthinkable to draft the wealth of the rich, even for the preservation of the fatherland, because the loot of predators is more precious than life. Tycoons like Henry John Kaiser (1882-1967) have become fabulously rich on war contracts, while young men serve their country by bleeding and dying for honor and glory in response to their tribal instincts, aroused by old men who either become rich in response to their acquisitive instincts or macho-intoxicated in response to their vanity.

Essentially, we Americans are no different from other members of the species. We have exterminated Indians, killed for greed, avarice, power, territory, mythological ideals, revenge, and many other reasons. We have rained death, agony, and destruction upon millions of innocent Germans, Japanese, and Vietnamese, with blockbuster bombs, fragmentation bombs, fire bombs, atomic bombs, and many other diabolical instruments of death and torture; but we are too absurdly humane to excise the criminal cancer in our society by executing bestial mass murderers. This is so, because we, as gregarious predators, have a double standard. The in-group must be preserved. The out-group must be destroyed.

Our commitment to war, power, and predation is unquestionable. The Thirteen Colonies were creatures of war. The American Revolution gave us birth as a nation. The War of 1812 quickened American nationalism and expansionism. The Indian Wars, Mexican War, and

Spanish-American War gave us conquest and empire. The Civil War preserved the Union and established the dominance of the North over the South. Two World Wars made us the world's greatest military power which, in turn, fostered hubris, followed by the Vietnam War and global deployment of our troops. Our National Anthem has its setting in "the rocket's red glare, the bomb bursting in air" of the War of 1812. Its theme is war, and its exhortation is, "conquer we must, when our cause it is just." Not surprisingly, all our conquests were just. Fasces symbolize power. They were borne by ancient dictators and emperors. Fascism derived its name and its emblem from fasces. They are also emblems used on American coins. The eagle is the consummate predator. It has been a symbol of war and imperial power since Babylonian times. It was borne on the standards of the Roman armies, Napoleon's troops, and it was a symbol of the Nazi *Wehrmacht*. The bald eagle is appropriately our National Emblem.

Chapter 3

NONSAPIENS, POLITICS, AND ECONOMICS

Communism and socialism, as well as idealistic societies in general, have a long history of failures. Confucius, the Chinese sage who preached the ideal state called GREAT HARMONY, was born in 551 B.C. He believed that the state should be a totally cooperative enterprise, the object of which is the happiness of the subjects and not the rulers. He taught that "Virtue is to love men. And wisdom is to understand men." This was during the Chou Dynasty. The emperors could not contain the Tartar invaders. This circumstance permitted local warlords to become supreme in their own districts. Not surprisingly, they behaved according to the laws prescribed by human instincts and fought constant wars against each other.

Confucius traveled for over ten years, seeking to become prime minister of one of the warlords so that he could establish his ideal, honest and humane government. The closest he came to his goal was a post with an impressive title, but no real authority. It was given him by Duke Ting of Lu. The Duke of Lu became more interested in beautiful girls, horses, and his own happiness than the happiness of his subjects. His hopes having been dashed, the dejected Confucius resigned. Just before his death in 479 B.C., he lamented to his pupil, Tsze-Kung, "No intelligent monarch arises. There is not one in the empire that will make me his master. My time has come to die." This freak human hawk, born with the instincts of a dove, was one of the first visionaries to discover that he could not invert the instincts of his fellow human hawks.

In 387 B.C., Plato, the preeminent philosopher of ancient Greece, was invited by Dionysius I, King of Syracuse, to establish his utopian REPUBLIC in Sicily. When Dionysius learned that he either had to become a philosopher or relinquish his kingdom, his interest turned to revulsion. In fact, he reverted to the more natural human condition of predation. He seized Plato for the slave market. Plato's friend Anniceris of Cyrene rescued him by paying the king a ransom. Plato was invited to Sicily a second time, this time by young Dionysius II after his father had died from overindulgence. The youth was told, as the Duke of Lu was told by Confucius, that he must make himself a model of intelligence and good will if the ideal government were to succeed. The young autocrat's addiction to drink and lechery doomed the ideal state. Plato returned to Athens. He should have learned (but he didn't) that an ideal state has as much chance as a sick hen in a den of weasels.

The nobles in ancient Rome had won control of the land plundered from the vanquished in wars of conquest. In 133 B.C., a gentle soul with abnormal instincts by the name of Tiberius Sempronius Gracchus was elected tribune. He wanted to limit the rich to three hundred acres of public land so that more land would be available to poor farmers. When he proposed and managed to pass the Sempronius Law which called for a redistribution of public lands, he stepped on the toes of the rich and powerful senate. No predator will tolerate the loss of his spoils. It is one thing to preach land reform, but quite another thing to enact it (our Founding Fathers didn't make the same mistake; they only gave lip service to their ideals). The senators incited a riot and murdered Tiberius. His brother Caius Sempronius Gracchus also tried to redistribute public lands for the benefit of the poor, but he met his brother's fate. Communism's ideal of land redistribution has always been resisted, like a vicious dog resisting the taking away of his bone.

Sir Thomas More, the author of Utopia, proposed one of the best known of ideal states. It was based on reason and unselfishness. Its *esprit de corps* was humanitarianism and the common good of all. It, too, was basically a Communist state. Sir Thomas More, too, was destined to learn a practical lesson about the snowball's chances of doves surviving in a society of hawks. He sided with the Pope of Rome in the power struggle between the Pope and Henry VIII for control of the Church of England. Henry VIII had proclaimed himself the head of the Church of England by the Act of Supremacy. The king considered Sir Thomas More a traitor because of his support of the Pope; and so, in London's Tower Hill in A.D. 1535, More's lifeless head dropped into a basket, which made him a member of the illustrious club of Henry's beheaded subjects, among whom were Anne Boleyn, Lord Chamberlain, Thomas Cromwell, and several others. Neither the kings, the Church, the popes, or the nobles were interested in any ideal system which would vitiate their power and wealth.

We constantly hear of GODLESS Communism, but at the end of the sixteenth century, a GODLY COMMUNIST utopia was established in Paraguay. The Jesuit rulers placed dress, work, and worship under rational order. However, predatory instincts were not to be repressed. Power struggles soon surfaced between the secular and clerical factions, just as they had in Europe for hundreds of years. Power struggles and revolts became continuing features of the Ideal State. Paraguay became involved in a major war with Brazil, Argentina, and Uruguay between 1865 and 1870. Strife was continuous. The Gran Chaco War, from 1932 to 1935, was devastating. Once again, human greed and lust for power and profit spelled finis to the Ideal State.

Francois Babeuf, the first modern Communist, advocated an equal distribution of land and income. He sought political AND economic equality. His egalitarian doctrines proclaimed the people's fundamental right to an equal share of the fruits of production. The American Declaration of Independence addressed itself to political equality, not economic equality. Like Karl Marx, Babeuf recognized the necessary role of force in dispossessing the entrenched Establishment, which naturally resists any change in the status quo. His organization became known as the Conspiracy of the Equals. His theory of equality was subversive to the ensconced power structure; and so, in 1797, he was guillotined.

Human rapacity has usually aborted Communism's inception, but even when it was given a chance it failed miserably. One of the best examples of the dismal failures of communism can be found in the early history of the United States. A band of Englishmen under the Charter of the London Company founded a colony at Jamestown, Virginia, in 1607. The company owned the land, but the colonists worked under a communistic system of putting all grown foodstuff into the public granary to be divided among the settlers on a share and share alike basis. It was a disaster. The lazy tried to live as parasites on the labors of the hard workers, just as modern welfare recipients live off the labors of taxpayers. Captain John Smith decreed that those who did not work could not eat. The system did nothing to satisfy natural predatory aspirations. By 1610, because of famine and ruin largely induced by the natural inefficiency of the communist system, only a few starving remnants were left.

Jamestown was abandoned. Then it was resettled under a new charter. Sir Thomas Dale instituted the private enterprise system. Those who were lazy and unproductive under the communist system suddenly became industrious when working for their own self-interests. Prosperity began, and the colony became a towering success.

Robert Owen was a rare breed of English capitalist. He was the wealthy owner of the New Lanark mills in Scotland in 1813 and the employer of two thousand workers. While most capitalists were consumed with a selfish passion to wallow in luxury by exploiting their workers, he had an altruistic passion to make his workers happy by allowing them to share his profits. He was convinced that the capitalism of his day was evil. He raised wages, established free schools, sold food at cost, and built homes for his workers. He spent a fortune on a cooperative community in Indiana which was called NEW HARMONY. It was the "perfect" communist community in which everyone did what he could do best, and each was paid according to his needs. It was based on rational, humane, non-predatory principles. It was obviously not compatible with human predatory instincts. It failed as did all other such communities. Owen spent the last twenty five years of his life writing and lecturing on education, marriage, and religion.

Charles Fourier founded another of the many utopian societies in which work was apportioned among people according to their natural abilities, and minimum income was guaranteed to all workers. Surplus produce was shared equitably. His followers established many colonies in France. They all failed. Fourier attracted many American advocates, among whom were Horace Greeley,

Hawthorne, Emerson, Thoreau, and Henry James. George Ripley's Brook Farm survived from 1841 to 1847. Originally an outgrowth of Unitarianism, it converted to Fourierism in 1844. The burning of the uncompleted central building was the death knell of this ideal community.

Many intellectuals dreamed of the day when all men would share like brothers in the economic wealth of the world. They rebelled against the capitalistic system because it seemed to them to be the embodiment of the jungle system of predatory exploitation of the weak. They regarded excessive profits, gouging rents, and usurious interests as the unacceptable exploitation of man by man. They denounced the profit motive as "an inhuman concentration on one's own pecuniary interest, unsoftened by any tincture of public spirit or private charity." It was seen as a "lust of gain." Money-lenders were looked upon as "monsters of iniquity." Capitalism was condemned as "congeries of possessors and pursuers."

Socialists taught that economic freedom, defined as the freedom from exploitation of man by man, is the foundation of all other freedoms, and that the most essential freedom is the freedom from want. They exposed the stupidity of a technological society, with the capacity to overproduce and to eliminate poverty, actually causing want, poverty, depressions, unemployment, and hunger. Socialists offered salvation and redemption to oppressed workers, but workers rejected it. The ideal of the greatest good for the greatest number is an inspiring ideal, but only when it is recognized that the greatest number is NUMBER ONE.

A scientific, rational politico-economic system for the "Technate of America" was proposed by Howard Scott in New York City in 1931. It was known as Technocracy. It was critical of the distribution of goods and services by means of the price system as used in the capitalistic system. In a nutshell, Technocracy taught that the price system is based on scarcity, which is an anachronism in an industrial-technological society whose very essence is the capacity for the production of abundance. The result of the price system is the inevitable paradox of poverty in the midst of plenty. If anyone has any doubts about poverty in the midst of plenty in modern America, he has but to visit the teeming slums of our ghettos and then visit the mansions of Beverly Hills.

Consider the problem of farmers under the price system, for example. The more they produce, the cheaper their commodity becomes because of the law of supply and demand. The cheaper their commodity, the less the profits. In fact, when the farmer overproduces, he depresses the price so much that he must sell at a loss. Consequently, he must cut back on production or burn his crops in order to create an artificial scarcity. When his commodity is in short supply, the price goes up and so do his profits. Poor people cannot afford high prices, and so they must go hungry. To an intelligent person, it seems insane to operate a high-tech, modern, industrial society under a system based on SCARCITY when, in fact, it should he operated under a system structured for abundance. Actually, it is like operating a Boeing 747 as a Greyhound bus by taxiing it on the highways.

Our modern industrial, technological world can easily produce an abundance for everyone, but full production is deliberately stifled because our modern world of industry and business is run by the principles of medieval economics. Abundance is suppressed under the economic pressures of the price system, which is based on scarcity. Scarcity commands high prices and huge profits. Abundance triggers low prices and crippling losses. Technocrats would substitute Energy Certificates for money because production and distribution based on energy units would elevate medieval economic systems into a computer age, scientific society, directed by able engineers for the benefit of ALL members of society. Money-grabbing without money would become impossible. Extreme poverty and extreme wealth could not exist in a system based on scientific production and distribution rather than on exploitation for profit.

Under Technocracy, each person's income would be determined scientifically by his energy contribution to production and his energy needs in society. The Energy Units would he time-expiring to prevent hoarding. Governmental organization would recognize natural inequalities and place only qualified engineers and technocrats in office, but they would he denied the weapon of exploitation; that is, the price system. The price tag of a greedy merchant is as effective a predatory weapon as a gun in the hand of a robber, and it has the added advantage that it is sanctified by legality. The exploitation of the workingman becomes impossible when wages are a function of energy contribution rather than predation. Technocracy was the craze for a few short years, but it faded by 1936. Human predators cannot stomach an economic system that castrates them.

The day-to-day functioning of the price system, and the artificial limiting of supply, for the purpose of enriching the greedy and impoverishing the victims, are best seen by the operation of international cartels and monopolies. Like a gluttonous ogre awakening to its power to devour, OPEC increased the price of crude oil from two dollars a barrel to almost forty dollars a barrel in a few short years. The production costs were less than a dollar a barrel. The price system permitted an incredible transfer of wealth from the industrial nations to the oil-producing nations. In 1975, 113 BILLION DOLLARS flowed out of consumers' pockets into the coffers of the OPEC countries. The balance of payments deficit of industrial nations rose from 16 to 40 BILLION DOLLARS in 1980. Third World countries had another 60 BILLION DOLLARS added to their foreign debts.

The sheep made the lion purr for his gasoline. The wealth which OPEC countries confiscated put the Barbary Pirates of the sixteenth century through the eighteenth century to shame. The high prices were maintained by cutbacks on oil production (artificial scarcity). Arab sheiks swam in oceans of confiscated wealth. This idle mammon prompted a Los Angeles judge to award one of the wives of Sheik Mohammad Al-Fassi 81.5 million dollars. The Arab tycoons multiply their pelf by making high-yield investments with their booty. The Koran forbids the use of interest, but this hurdle is surmounted by the use of euphemisms. They redefine interest as "service fee" or "return on investment." Price-fixing is one of the attractions of the price system, and it is a more effective weapon for plundering wealth than guns in the hands of bandits.

Diamonds would be relatively cheap but for one thing! THE DE BEERS CONSOLIDATED MINES LTD. MONOPOLY, which owns 90 percent of the world's production of diamonds. It was established by British imperialist and business magnate Cecil Rhodes

(1853-1902) in South Africa, 1888. This monopoly maintains a rigid control of Kimberley diamond production to ensure the scarcity of diamonds; otherwise, the market would be flooded, which would depress the price and reduce the profits as determined by that inexorable law: the law of supply and demand.

The most prominent figure in the history of Communism is Karl Marx. He reacted to the ruthless exploitation of labor by the capitalists of his day by not only proposing the remedy which he believed was the establishment of a socialist society, but also by proclaiming the inevitability of the triumph of the working class in the historical process. He recognized that the history of mankind is a history of warfare, but he narrowed the fundamental struggle to the class struggle. It is undoubtedly ONE of the causes of eternal human strife. In ancient Rome, the class struggle was between the Patricians and the Plebeians. In medieval times, it was between the serfs and the nobles, and between the nobles and the kings. In Marx's time it was between the proletariat and the bourgeoisie.

Philosophically, Marx turned idealistic Hegelian dialectic upside down and called it Dialectical Materialism. Hegel was concerned with SPIRIT. Marx was concerned with MATTER—the body, if you will. He borrowed the Hegelian dialectic of thesis, antithesis, and synthesis in order to lend intellectual authority to the doctrine of the philosophical inevitability of Communism in the historical process. Put simply, according to Hegel, every concept implies its opposite, and both become synthesized into a new concept, repeating the previous triadic process in an on-going, upward development. Thus, according to the Marxian interpretation, the existence of the exploitable class (proletariat), i.e. the thesis, begets the exploiting class (bourgeoisie or capitalists), i.e. the antithesis, and this generates world revolution and the inevitable proletarian victory and the Ideal Communist State, i.e. the synthesis. The dictatorship of the proletariat, which is required to expropriate the expropriators, is supposed to wither away, and a classless society emerges because there is no longer an economic base for the survival of exploiting capitalists. The dialectic process is now arrested, and eternal paradise and tranquility arrives. So goes the dream. It is Grimm's Fairy Tale written for adults, and as naive as religion's Heavens and Hells of the hereafter.

According to Marx, violent revolution is necessary to expropriate the expropriators because history proves that no person, no class, no nation, and no empire has ever relinquished its abusive power or its territory without a bitter struggle. Socialism is an heretical sect of Communism. It believes that it can achieve the same ends by peaceful means. Marx identified the power of capitalists to exploit labor as residing in their ownership of the tools of production. This ownership makes the workingman completely dependent upon them. It enables capitalists to enrich themselves on "surplus value." Value of goods and services lies in the labor necessary to produce them, but the worker receives only a small portion of the total value he creates. The lion's share of value is confiscated by the employing capitalist, and it is called "surplus value." It exists in profit, rent, and interest. Greed for profits induces capitalists to overproduce, said Marx. Overproduction leads to unemployment and continuing crises. Eventually, workers are displaced by machines, whereupon the class struggle is exacerbated.

Marx attacked religion as "the opiate of the people" because he claimed that "collusion" of the church with capitalists is a conspiracy to lull exploited workers into believing that the existing capitalistic social and economic system is the will of God, just as exploiting kings lulled their subjects into acceptance of the status quo with the doctrine of "divine right of kings." Workers, said Marx, are taught to tolerate an abusive system by the church and by capitalists by promising them that they, the poor exploited favorites of God, will be rewarded for their earthly suffering in the heaven of the next world; but the capitalists, the rich for whom God makes passage into heaven as difficult as a camel passing through the eye of a needle, will suffer the gnarling and gnashing of teeth in eternal hellfire and brimstone.

In other words, Marx believed that religion is a conspiratorial pacification plot designed to protect the wealth of the rich from seizure by the poor exactly as Christianity has pacified some conquered American Indians. (According to an Indian proverb, "At first we had the land and the white man had the Bible; now we have the Bible and the white man has the land.") Marx wanted working people to share the same mundane heaven of luxury as the capitalists and clergymen. He was of the same mind as Omar Khayyam: "Some for the Glories of this World; and some sigh for the Prophet's Paradise to come; Ah, take the Cash, and let the Credit go, Nor Heed the rumble of a distant Drum!"

Marx's shibboleth was, "Workingmen of the world, unite! You have nothing to lose but your chains. You have a world to win." Workingmen did not heed the rumble to any significant extent. When oppression exceeds human endurance man will revolt against the oppressor, as we have seen in the French and Russian Revolutions, but it was never a coordinated revolution under the banner of Communism. The Romanov czars starved and oppressed the Russian people until they were driven to revolution in 1905 and 1917. The palace guards refused to obey Czar Nicholas II's order to fire upon the demonstrating, starved, tattered masses. In fact, they joined the Revolution. The Civil War of 1918-1920 between the Reds and the Whites followed the Revolution. The Reds executed the entire imperial family (1918). The reign of the czars was drowned in a sea of human blood and replaced by a new tyranny.

The Russian Revolution was NOT a Communist revolution. The first provisional government was headed by Prince Georgi Lvov, an advocate of constitutional democracy, but he was a lamb amid a pack of wolves; when pressure forced his resignation, Aleksander Kerensky, a moderate socialist, took over. He was certainly NOT a Marxist Communist. World War I was raging, and Kerensky wanted to continue the war on the side of the Allies. Germany made a brilliant strategic move by rushing Lenin from his exile in Switzerland back to Russia, knowing he would take Russia out of the war and give her a free hand on the Western Front. Nicholas Lenin and Leon Trotsky soon seized power from Kerensky, and Russia's chance for democracy was lost for the indefinite future. The Bolsheviks made peace with Germany in 1918. Russian capitalists, nobles, and clergy had a great deal of wealth to lose from the advent of Communism, and so, flying the white flag, they started a counterrevolution. Allied capitalist countries feared eventual assault on the wealth of their plutocrats; and so, they sent troops to aid the White Army. The White Army nearly won; but Trotsky and his Red Army, plus brilliant military tactics, crushed the Whites in 1920. The Reds gave Russia its present oppressive Communist government.

Communism has never been successful, and it wasn't successful in Russia. Communism drove farm production into chaos. Peasants refused to provide food for the cities. Lenin sent his army to take the farm produce from the farmers by force whereupon the peasants began growing only enough food for their own needs. Russian farmers were now producing only 5 percent of what they produced under the czars. In 1921, it was necessary for Lenin to permit limited capitalism under the NEP (New Economic Policy) in order to save the nation from collapse. This limited capitalism aroused the predatory instincts of businessmen and farmers sufficiently to produce surplus goods for profit. The peasants on the collective farms were allowed to share in the profits. Rewards were offered to everyone who made outstanding contributions to the two Five Year Plans designed to transform Russia from a farming to a manufacturing country. Amazingly, Lenin was an eyewitness to the superiority of capitalism over Communism, but man's capacity for fanaticism totally nullifies his ability to learn.

Lenin died in 1924. Joseph Vissarionovich Stalin won control after an acrid power struggle. He banished Trotsky because of policy differences; for example, Trotsky wanted to promote world revolution, but Stalin wanted to industrialize Russia first. Trotsky was exiled to Turkestan in 1928. He soon fled to various countries, and finally settled in a suburb of Mexico City; but Stalin caught up with him in 1940, when one of his agents split Trotsky's head open with an alpenstock. Lenin and Stalin were as cruel and murderous as the czars. Lenin presided over a reign of terror and, with the help of the dreaded Cheka, executed all Russians suspected of trying to overthrow the Communist regime.

Stalin displayed even more ruthlessness in enforcing Communism upon an uncooperative people. Troops, assisted by the OGPU, exiled, shot, or sent to Siberia's arctic hell tens of thousands of kulaks. It is thought that Stalin was responsible for the death of some 10 MILLION peasants during the twenties. His great purges of the thirties renewed an orgy of bloodbaths, and, according to the *Encyclopaedia Britannica,* his "political victims were numbered in tens of millions." According to *Time* magazine, 25 years of Stalin's government-by-bloodbath left a toll of some 20 million dead, including victims of famines. The Russian people were obviously not very ecstatic over the Workers' Paradise. This situation has never changed. East Germany had to build a wall contrary to all historical precedent: not to keep invaders out, but to prevent her own people from fleeing paradise.

Why has Communism invariably failed? Why is it that Communism must be forced on people by murderous dictators and by brutal methods? No Communist country dares to have free elections because it knows that the majority of the people would vote Communism into oblivion. Communism can normally assume power only by coups sponsored by militant minorities, by assassinations, by murders, plots, and violence—seldom by free elections. Chile was an exception, but it would not have maintained power for long without assuming a harsh dictatorship. There can never be an enduring democratic Communist state because human beings take to Communism like the plague. Democracy and Communism are incompatible.

Hypocrisy is a human idiosyncrasy. Communist governments assuming the name of "People's Democracies" are like the IRS assuming the name SERVICE. Even under the dictatorships of Lenin and Stalin, Soviet Russia maintained a respectable facade of democracy. The trappings included the Supreme Council, made up of the Council of the Union and Council of Nationalities, which were supposedly subject to the Supreme Court, and the Council of People's Commissars. The Communist party consisted of party cells, the All-Union Congress, and the Politburo. It was a farce. With no title other than Secretary General of the Communist party, Stalin was absolute dictator of Russia. Because Communism is a secular religion, it lends itself to personality cults.

Democratic countries that vote the socialist party into office continue to be basically capitalistic. Sweden is vaunted as a socialist country, but over 90 percent of her industry is private enterprise capitalism. England's Labour Party nationalized the Bank of England, coal, electrical power, and inland transport, but no private interest was confiscated. Besides, England is no exemplar. She declined from the world's greatest power to a very mediocre country. Even Russia is a greater power, but she is primarily a military power built at the expense of reducing the populace to a ghetto-type standard of living. She built up her Space Age, nuclear military machine by kidnapping German space experts and scientists after World War II and stealing American nuclear and technological secrets.

The USSR has made every effort to stimulate economic productivity by appeals to patriotic duty. In spite of everything, she could not induce Communist workers to be productive workers. Even little capitalistic Japan outproduces "mighty" Russia. The Russian soldier gave his all for Mother Russia in the wars against Hitler and Napoleon, but he gives his very least for the common good as an economic producer. The performance of the Russian farmer is pathetic. Approximately 23 percent of Russian workers are on farms which cannot supply the country's food needs. The 2 percent of Russia's farm land that is privately owned produces 25 percent of all Soviet agricultural output. Russia is dependent upon capitalistic countries like the United States, Canada and Argentina for grain to feed her people.

Small capitalistic countries like Hong Kong and Singapore are showcases for productive miracles. After 1959, when Singapore abandoned communism for capitalism, its industries burgeoned. It became a financial center and the world's third largest oil refining center. Socialist countries are showcases of dismal failures. The evidence is clear. Why do Communist die-hards refuse to accept the evidence? For the same reason religious fanatics believe ludicrous fables and refuse to accept evidence, and the same reason American presidents insist upon viewing all Third World struggles against oppression as an EAST-WEST CONFRONTATION. In two words: HUMAN STUPIDITY!

There is a simple reason why Communism and socialism are always failures, and capitalism is successful in producing a viable economy. If the human being were a rational creature, Communism would be an outstanding success. Intelligent people like Einstein always seem to favor a socialist state. Socialism makes good sense from an intellectual standpoint. A planned economy is rational. An unplanned economy run by whim, hit-and-miss, boom and bust, is not befitting an intelligent creature. However, the economic system of an animal must be adapted to the nature of the animal. The animal cannot be adapted to the economic system. A wolf cannot adapt to the grazing ways of a lamb. MAN IS NOT A RATIONAL ANIMAL. ANY ECONOMIC SYSTEM THAT DOES NOT RECOGNIZE THE FUNDAMENTAL TRUTH THAT MAN IS A TERRITORIAL PREDATOR MOTIVATED BY PREDA-TORY INSTINCTS RATHER THAN REASON IS DOOMED TO FAILURE.

Capitalism is the ideal economic system for a territorial predator. It is based on the predatory acquisition of wealth, and the selfish, greedy exploitation of man by man. That is to say, it is based on man's basic nature. The instincts of a predator require that he preys upon others. The dog does its thing when it chases rabbits. The hawk does its thing when it swoops down on doves. Man likewise does his thing when he performs as a predator, which he has throughout history by preying on other animals, other tribesmen, other kingdoms, and other nations. When a human being puts over a slick business deal which makes him richer but his victim poorer, he is in ecstasy because he has succeeded as a predator.

The business deal is the sublimation of bloody, territorial preda-tion. Communism deprives human beings of their natural right to exploit their fellow man. It dooms man to a life of frustration and discontent. It is like extracting the teeth and claws of a lion and turn-ing it out to pasture. Capitalism permits the entrepreneur to profit from the labors of his employees. The word "profit" is a euphemism for booty. It is Karl Marx's surplus value which is plundered from the worker. It is the basic human right of the capitalist to make a profit because it is the basic right of the predator to prey upon its quarry. Speculators who make huge profits on real estate, stocks, bonds, and securities are pirates in the purest form. They acquire wealth, but per-form no constructive work to produce the wealth which they seize by virtue of their profits.

Curiously, everyone is supposed to be of equal worth in America, but the labors of all people are not of equal worth. American incomes are on an aristocratic scale unprecedented in history. The labor of one prehistoric-type hard rock singer is worth the labors of two thousand five hundred college educated school teachers, as deduced from the fact that Michael Jackson has an annual income of up to 50 million dollars and a school teacher's income averages twenty thousand dollars a year. Democratic capitalism promotes the political equality of unequals; but, at the same time, it promotes incredible economic elitism of primitive types, which results from economic predatory power rather than intellectual ability. Communism promotes economic equality, but political elitism. The Declaration of Independence was really a declaration of predatory rights. It declared the right of the colonists to assume what had been the Crown's exclusive predatory rights.

If a capitalist makes 2 million dollars in profit a year, he can use it to hire three hundred people to work for him all year every year at the minimum wage. This is to say, he has the equivalent of three hundred permanent slaves working for him, and he doesn't have to provide them with food and shelter. His "slaves" must fend for themselves, but they do not object because they experience the illusion of being free. Naturally, the capitalist does not see himself as a predator. He sees himself as a legitimate businessman: a benefactor, in fact, who provides employment for the unemployed. The wolf doesn't see itself as the murderer of a fellow creature when it captures its prey and devours it. It merely does the natural thing of eating a meal in order to survive. Our heroes who dropped two atomic bombs on Japan and slaughtered tens of thousands of their fellow human beings didn't think of themselves as murderers, even though they caused the horrible deaths and inhuman torture of two or more hundred thousand fellow human beings at one blow. Our heroes merely did their duty. It is the function of predators to kill. Even Hitler was a hero to millions of Germans. They didn't think of Hitler as an evil person so long as his predations were successful.

Philosopher Friedrich Nietzsche recognized the logical contradiction in capitalistic democracy because it proclaims the democratic justice in equal political power—that is, one man, one vote—but, at the same time, it sponsors the justice of economic predation, which results in the unequal concentration of wealth in the hands of a few superpredators—for example, capitalists, entertainers, primitive musicians, and athletes—while others merely subsist, or go hungry, laboring at less than a minimum wage, or because they are denied employment. Logical contradictions are natural for a non-rational predatory creature.

Workers in a capitalist society are pacified in their subservient role with the dream that they, too, can become capitalists, and they, too, can participate in the ecstasies of predation. It is possible. It happens every day. Many people with humble beginnings enter the capitalistic jungle (business) and become rich predators. Even a football player with an IQ of 80 can loot the economic pie to the tune of millions a year. Being rich is a relative condition. In order to be rich, it is necessary that others be poor. It is necessary to confiscate wealth from other people in some way, shape, or form. This is accomplished, rather adroitly, by utilizing the price and wage system of capitalism, which is the superb sublimation of violent, bloody predation. The exploitation is so surreptitious and insidious that the expropriated workers don't even realize that they are victims of predation, and if they do realize it, the knowledge that capitalism permits them equal privileges for predation buoys up their spirit and loyalty to the system. It gratifies their natural instincts, and they join the chorus singing the praises of capitalism.

We have previously alluded to the inexorable law of supply and demand, the most fundamental operational law of free enterprise economics. Economists build the capitalistic edifice upon this law, but they do not penetrate the surface to peer into its soul. When supply is low, and demand is high, this law stipulates that the price MUST be high. But WHY must it be high? Is it like the law of gravity by which the sun captures the Earth in eternal orbit? The price must be high because the preemptive law of human avarice demands that every human predator must exploit to the fullest any and all opportunities available for the exploitation of his fellow man. THE LAW OF SUPPLY AND DEMAND IS SIMPLY THE LAW OF

HUMAN GREED. IT IS THE LAW OF THE PREDATOR.

As an example of the law of supply and demand in action, let us examine rentals. When rental property is in short supply, the landlord inevitably gouges the tenant to the limits of his ability. He does this because the renter is made an offer he can't refuse. Either pay the extortionary rent or be homeless. It does not matter whether the tenant is impoverished or the landlord is wealthy. It does not matter whether the renter is in destitute decrepitude or the landlord is in opulent robustness. What does matter is that the landlord is in a circumstance of predatory power which permits him to exploit his fellow man, and the law of human predation (supply and demand) decrees that he must. If man were a rational, humanitarian, non-predatory, intelligent being, he would not be subject to this law. People in fortunate circumstances would not be instinctively driven to profit from the misfortunes of others. THE LAW OF EQUITABLE DISTRIBUTION WOULD GOVERN HUMAN ECONOMIC BEHAVIOR RATHER THAN THE LAW OF SUPPLY AND DEMAND. BUT MAN IS A PREDATOR. CONSEQUENTLY, THE LAW OF SUPPLY AND DEMAND IS AS INEXORABLE AS THE LAW OF GRAVITY. Capitalism realistically accepts predation as the guiding economic principle. Communism has its head in the clouds and is guided by will-o'-the-wisps.

Capitalist societies set up rules for predation, just as all societies set up rules for killing. Killing is not only permitted in war: it is glorified. The greater the enemy body count for a soldier, the greater the honor bestowed upon him. In like manner, the rules of capitalism not only permit predation, they glorify it, but it is euphemized as profit. People boast about doubling or tripling their money from investments, which enables them to plunder from the economic pie as freeloaders without performing gainful labor to produce it. Criminal robbers are subject to violence committed on their person plus prison terms and fines. Speculators and businessmen rob even more effectively with price tags, fees, rents, interest, and miscellaneous charges, but they are honored and respected pillars of society.

Under capitalism, everyone is a potential victim of predation via the mechanism of the wage-price system. Potential victims in the jungle of economic predators must be vigilant. They are forewarned by the maxim *caveat emptor*. Stupid members of a capitalist society plunder with knives and guns like primitive Neanderthals or Viking raiders. With so many effective and perfectly legal ways that man can prey on his fellow man in a capitalist society, it is sheer stupidity to resort to crude, illegal methods.

As a personal note, and for purposes of illustration, my experience as a young man in San Jose, California, is pertinent. I had the concession for radio repairing in one of the leading appliance stores, and learned firsthand the lessons of free enterprise predation from the owner of the store and most respected leader in the community. One day in my absence, a large console radio was left in the store for repairs. The complaint was that no broadcast station could be received. When I returned to the store and looked at the set, I quickly discovered that the only trouble was someone (perhaps a child) had turned a normally inaccessible service switch the wrong way. I flipped the switch back, and the radio worked beautifully.

The store owner asked me what I was going to charge for "repairing" the set. "Twenty five cents," I replied. This naive reply prompted him to chuckle and to instruct me on the intricacies of the capitalist system. He telephoned the customer, told him that he owned a top model radio such as "they don't make like that anymore," but it required considerable work to restore it to perfect working condition. The customer was told that it would ONLY cost the modern equivalent of eighty dollars, and the set would be ready for pick-up in two days. The customer agreed. I pushed the set off in a corner. A few days later, the customer picked up his radio. He was delighted because it worked well, and I was delighted to make eighty dollars for simply turning a switch. If I had mugged the customer and gotten five dollars, he would have called the police and had me arrested. I acquired SIXTEEN TIMES THAT AMOUNT OF LOOT the smart, sophisticated way via the capitalist price system. I had been inclined toward socialism, but this experience was like a religious conversion. I became a born-again capitalist.

What I did was essentially no different from normal business procedure. For example, union electricians, union plumbers, and other union tradesmen and contractors have sweetheart deals. A customer has a furnace installed. First, the customer pays brain surgeon's wages for the installation, which would put any mugger to shame. Then, a special licensed electrician is called to make a simple electrical connection. He must be called because the electricians had a city ordinance passed which requires a licensed electrician to make the connection. The license legitimizes predation. It is a license to steal. The customer may have to pay over a thousand dollars for a length of conductors and a simple connection worth about twenty dollars, depending upon how unscrupulous the electrician happens to be. A mugger may have to work a full week or more to make that kind of money, and take the risk of getting his head knocked off to boot. Minimum charges, markups, high prices, overcharges, and extortionary labor charges are all excellent means of predation. Even this little glimpse at capitalism in action should convince the most skeptical that it is the system par excellence for a predatory animal.

Returning to my early tutoring in the operating procedures of capitalism: My appliance company owner associate had me accompany him in the company pickup to see about a washing machine repair one day when his repairman was out sick. We arrived at the destination. It was the rectory of a church, and the occupants were an elderly clergyman and his wife, probably in their nineties. We inspected the washing machine. Then my proprietor mentor told the clergyman that we had to take the machine to the shop for repairs because the needed work was too complicated to be done there.

I helped him load the machine on the pickup, and on the way back to the store I asked, "Why in the hell didn't you fix the machine there? All it needed was a tightening of the set screw on the pulley." "Son," he replied in disgust at my young innocence, "that is not the way to conduct a successful business. We take the machine to the shop, take it apart, then call the customer to the shop and explain that most of the parts are worn and have to be replaced. We tell the customer it would cost more to fix the machine than to buy a new one, and, fortunately, we are running a sale on washing machines this week. The customer buys a new machine. We put the old one back together and sell it, and we make a profit on both machines."

The way my guru's sale worked was that he added a hundred dollars to the list price, and then gave a seventy-five dollar discount. It sickened my heart to see what was happening, but I was assured that it constituted the legitimate functioning of the free enterprise system, and that it was as American as apple pie, and I wanted to be a good American. When people are old, feeble, and poor, a successful businessman charges them more because it is easier to get more money out of simple, trusting people than it is to get it out of rich, savvy, sophisticated people. Prices are frequently higher in ghetto markets than in markets that cater to the more affluent. That is how successful predation works. The predator seeks the easiest prey. The weak are natural targets of predators. It is the way capitalism works. Capitalism is tailor-made for a predatory animal. Communist societies execute economic predators. Capitalist societies honor them.

A tender-hearted person not fully endowed with predatory instincts may be inclined to feel sorry for the elderly clergyman and his wife, as, indeed, I did. However, as I learned later when I had my own store, some people positively demand to be exploited. There were times when a tender spot in my heart caused me to do a TV repair job at cost because I felt that the poor person couldn't afford more. I learned that many people equate value with price, and if the charge is low, they feel cheated because they think that they were given an inferior job. By tripling the price on a job, some customers feel that the job is three times better; in which case, the customer is happy because he is convinced he received greater value, and the businessman is happy because he received more profit.

There was a coffee shop in Japan that charged customers forty dollars for a cup of coffee. Tourists loved to patronize it so that they could boast about the forty-dollar-a-cup coffee they drank. Strange animal, the human creature. Predatory animal that he is, yet many get a masochistic thrill from being the victim of predation.

There are many artifices at the disposal of a businessman in the pursuit of successful predation. For example, some stores use large signs reading "OUR LOW PRICE" plastered on items all over the store. Actually, the prices may be higher. This technique operates on the principle of the big lie. When the customer sees the sign often enough he becomes hypnotized into believing that the prices really are low. Another effectively used way of ensnaring the prey is by operating under the name of DISCOUNT STORE and requiring membership cards to enter the store, but charging more than the general retail store. The customer believes that the prices must be discounted, if a membership card is required to patronize the store. He is not bright enough to shop around and compare prices. Capitalism encourages the use of every wile, trick, and cunning conceivable to a resourceful predator. Small wonder free enterprise capitalism is the perfect system for the human being.

Early Christianity recognized the predatory nature of capitalism. The Church Fathers denounced commercialism. Saint Jerome held that all profit is unjust. Saint Augustine looked upon all business as evil. Church councils forbade the use of interest, and the Church tried to control the profit motive. The city of Piacenza denied the sacraments and Christian burial to those who charged interest. The Koran forbids the charging of interest. Bishop Grosseteste lamented the "extortions of merchants and exchangers." Medieval Jews branded monopoly and "corners" as sins. They regulated profit, fixed maximum prices and minimum wages in order to prevent predation. Christians turned the "sinful" practice of money-lending over to the Jews, but the lure of profit caused them to change their minds by the thirteenth century. There was no way religion was going to curb the predatory nature of man any more than the Volstead Act was going to stop people from imbibing, or the Commandment "Thou Shalt Not Kill!" was going to stop born killers from slaughtering each other.

Men have always itched for money and anesthetized their consciences at the call of gold as had Cortes and Pizarro. I learned something about the modern conquistadors in the world of money-lenders as a young man when I borrowed money to buy a used car. I wisely asked the interest rate. When told it was 6 percent (1936), I thought it was a pretty good deal. I signed the loan papers. When I started to make the payments, I had the strange feeling that they were rather high for 6 percent. I went storming back to my friendly moneylender and demanded an explanation for the high payments which I computed to include 25 percent interest. He gave me a few more lessons about capitalism in action. I learned that the interest rate is MERELY ONE weapon of predation for money lenders. There is the loan fee, the credit check charge, the accounting fee, the assignment fee, the prepayment penalty, the late payment penalty, the surcharge, the tax, the surtax, *et cetera, ad infinitum*. It is easy for a loan shark to masquerade as a respectable moneylender by the simple use of euphemisms known as FEES.

What a superb weapon of predation is that innocent appearing instrument called FEE! It is so good that other predators have expanded it into user's fees, consultation fees, referral fees, finder's fees, access fees, service fees, escrow fees, assumption fees, transfer fees, credit fees, assignment fees, recording fees, handling fees, *et cetera, ad infinitum*. Legitimate moneylenders have come up with a better weapon than fees. It is called the point system. The seller or buyer of a mortgaged house pays points, and paying points is the same as paying one-shot interest charges, but it is an euphemism which circumvents usury laws. It is such an incredible weapon because the victim doesn't feel victimized by paying points. If points were called "penalty assessments," he would feel robbed. Paying points is like a man having his pockets picked by a beautiful girl while she is fondling him.

There are so many delightful ways of painless predation in a capitalistic society! Several people have become multimillionaires by buying and selling property. They do not develop property. They do not manufacture products. They do not provide a service. They merely buy property at one price, sell it at a higher price, and the difference is profit, which is plunder even the Barbary Pirates would have envied. Some predators rake in millions by buying large tracts of land, subdividing them, making no improvements, and marking the lots up several hundred times. They can buy undreamed-of luxuries and comforts with their unearned loot, which must be provided for by the labors of other people. No slave owner was a greater parasite on his fellow creatures, and yet the real estate speculator is a respected member of capitalist society. He is a barbarian raider of the gross national product. He loots the wealth of the nation without contributing to it, but he is honored and respected. He obeys the rules and regulations of legitimate predation.

Realtors charge 6 percent of the selling price of a home as commission. Commission is an excellent weapon of predation, especially when it is based on percentage. A million dollar home may not require any more work to sell than a ten thousand dollar home, but the million dollar home will yield sixty thousand dollars in loot while the ten thousand dollar home will yield only six hundred dollars. Percentage is such a good weapon for predation that lawyers use it to loot estates and trusts. It may only require typing in a few more digits on legal papers, but lawyers can extract many thousands more dollars on large probates and trusts by charging a percentage rather than a flat fee or by the hour. Truly, capitalism is a paradise for human predators. Communism is hell for them.

Government contracts are a lucrative field for predation. It was widely reported, for example, that the Air Force paid $221 for a pair of needle-nose pliers and $269 for a socket wrench extension, both of which are available in hardware stores for less than $10. This form of predation is extremely popular. It certainly beats armed robbery.

The AMWAY (American Way) Corporation has been the subject of the CBS "60 Minutes" program. According to it, the founders of AMWAY made two hundred million dollars on the bright idea. High-pressure distributors, using evangelistic-type mesmerization of the congregation, reap fortunes. The fortunes are made in the super distributorships because a percentage is raked off from other distributors. Many workers who sell the products make meager incomes. Some make only "starvation" commissions. The spiel is that anyone can make it big, but only one out of a hundred actually makes out. Only the superpredator can become wealthy. Nevertheless, the dream of becoming a superpredator has tremendous appeal to the human animal. The dream and the fulfillment constitute the American Way.

Organized charities are good sources of plunder. Sometimes they return as little as 3 percent of donations to the actual charity; 97 percent enriches the promoters. United Charities took in more than a million dollars a year from bingo, but paid out less than twenty-five thousand dollars to its three sponsoring charities. Dayton, Ohio's Aid the American People First fundraiser took in seven hundred and twenty-five thousand dollars in its first year, but paid out less than four thousand dollars to charity. In 1977, Americans contributed thirty-five billion dollars to charities, but only a small portion reached the needy.

Evangelists and faith healers get wealthy promoting eternal salvation and miracle healing. Medical doctors get rich on unnecessary laboratory tests and unnecessary operations. They make millions on fraud and abuse in Medicare and Medicaid. The health bill in America jumps up to twice the rate of inflation, and burial costs rise apace because of ghoulish predators in the medical and undertaking professions plundering from the sick, the dying, and the dead. Predation in government agencies is rampant. According to former GSA administrator Jay Solomon, "fraud, waste and outright thievery are a way of life" in the GSA.

Because people are predators who constantly look for something for nothing, they become easy victims of other predators. As one example, Ronald Rewald founded the fraudulent "international investment company" called Bishop, Baldwin, Rewald, Dillingham and Wong of Honolulu. Bishop, Baldwin, and Dillingham are to Honolulu what Rockefeller, Harriman, and Roosevelt are to New York, but they were in no way associated with Rewald and Wong. Their names were used in the confidence racket to lure four hundred investors to pour thirteen million dollars into the flimflam firm with the promise of a high return on their money. Rewald used the investors' money not to reinvest, but to purchase a million dollar home for himself, two Hawaiian ranches, seventeen polo ponies, luxurious living, and exotic travels.

Rewald paid high dividends to earlier investors out of funds forked over by later ones. Those payments enticed more investments from the earlier investors plus many new ones. Rewald falsely claimed that the invested money was FDIC-insured. His easy success, soaring greed, and overconfidence tripped him up. At this writing, he is in prison in Honolulu in lieu of ten million dollars bail. Rewald used the old Charles Ponzi racket of 1919. Ponzi offered to pay investors $1.50 in forty-five days for every dollar invested. When the word got out, crowds of suckers grew so large outside his Boston office that they blocked traffic. Ponzi eventually went to prison.

Unique means of exploitation exist in Hawaii. Choice land is owned by wealthy estates such as Bishop Estate, Campbell Estate, and Harold Castle Estate. The reader should not be surprised that these are European names rather than Polynesian names. The tactic of marrying into wealth is a proven method of predation as old as civilization. In 1479, Ferdinand, King of Aragon, united the Spanish peninsula with his marriage to Isabella, Queen of Castile. Louis VII of France married Eleanor of Aquitaine in A.D. 1137. The marriage united a good deal of France; but the marriage was annulled, and she married Henry II of England circa 1152, which gave England a claim on much of France and centuries of war between England and France. Napoleon divorced his beloved Josephine, and married Marie Louise, daughter of the Emperor of Austria, for predatory reasons. It is smarter to build an empire or unite a country by marriage than by bloody conquest, just as it is smarter to acquire wealth by legal capitalistic predation than by illegal mugging or robbing at the point of a gun.

Having married the Polynesian princess landowners, Bishop, Campbell, and Castle not only made out well for themselves, but also were instrumental in setting up trusts and endless lines of heirs and trustees to enjoy the fruits of predation. To build a home near Sandy Beach Park in Hawaii Kai, a section of Honolulu, the home builder must pay the KACOR Development Company one hundred twenty thousand dollars for the mere right to LEASE an eight thousand square foot lot, and he must pay LEASE RENT of two thousand dollars a year which periodically increases at the CPI rate. These payments are shared with Bishop Estate. After some few years, the lease rent must be renegotiated, and the homeowner is placed in a life-death struggle to keep financially afloat. Even though the homeowner doesn't own the land, he must pay the property tax. While the mere right to just LEASE the lot on which the home rests costs one hundred twenty thousand dollars, the median cost of OWNING BOTH A HOME AND LOT on the mainland is forty-seven thousand two hundred dollars.

The trustees of the estates receive fabulous fees. Their salaries are nearly a quarter of a million dollars a year. Of course, capitalistic predation is always concealed by hypocrisies. The predation is hidden as a charitable trust to help support the Kamehameha schools, and it has tax-exempt status. We are reminded of organized charities which disperse 3 percent of income to the needy and 97 percent to administrative expenses (huge salaries). The Mafia never had it so good. The estates are racist and discriminatory. The Princess Bernice Pauahi Bishop's will favored boys over girls, the Protestant religion over all others, and the aboriginal Hawaiian race over all other races.

Few people have had business training, but everyone has a natural talent for capitalistic exploitation because everyone is a natural predator. The average man in the street will buy a home, use it for years, make no improvements on it, and believe that he was endowed by his creator with the inalienable right to make a profit on it over and above any inflationary increase when he sells it. If anyone thinks that a used car dealer will give him a screwing, he ought to try buying a car in a place like WHEELS AND DEALS, where the car owner sells his own car. The average person who sells his own home or car will use every trick, cunning, and deception to conceal defects. His sales pitch even makes a used car salesman seem honest by comparison.

People expect to make a profit when they buy stocks, bonds, or any other investment, for doing no useful work or for performing no service to society. If a person has to work hard for several years to save ten thousand dollars for the purchase price of a new car, he takes possession of his car only at the cost of years of sweat, toil, and sacrifice which had contributed to the nation's economic wealth. If another person makes ten thousand dollars on an investment, he can purchase the same new car without working at all or without returning productivity for the productivity he receives. Others do his productive work for him. He couldn't do better if he owned slaves. Profit on investment is successful predation, but it is not thought of as predation. It is "return on investment," the same euphemism Mohammedans use to circumvent the Koran's proscription against charging interest.

Slavery is a predatory relationship between human beings by which the master can live in idle comfort while others (slaves) do his work for him. The exploited workingman is, effectively, the capitalist's slave. Investment profit enables the investor to receive the benefits of productive work without performing any productive work himself. This is a master/slave relationship. Put another way, when one creature lives off the labors of another, it is the parasite/host relationship. Put yet another way, when one creature captures or plunders the wealth or goods of another creature whether legally or illegally, it is the predator/prey relationship. Capitalism permits predatory man to prey and parasitize, but it sanitizes the predation and narcotizes the victims. Capitalism is the opiate of the exploited victims. They are blissfully unaware and indifferent to their own victimization.

Capitalism is sublimated jungle predation, codified by economic laws and principles. Advertising and salesmanship are the lures of economic predators. Advertisers use every legal or illegal device conceivable to snare customers and to sell unneeded products and services. False, misleading, deceptive, and exaggerated claims are constantly made in sales pitches, the purpose of which is the transfer of wealth from the prey to the predator. Dangerous or useless drugs are sold over-the-counter on the basis of unsubstantiated claims. Prescription drugs are marked up two or three times the cost of over-the-counter drugs. Vanity publishers get rich luring aspiring authors into their clutches by arousing false hopes. I learned about this one the hard way. I was a victim of a vanity publisher.

Some fifteen years ago, I submitted my manuscript, *Voyage 69*, to vanity publisher Carlton Press, Inc., of New York City. They gave it a glowing appraisal that would make William Shakespeare envious. My original manuscript contained seven hundred fifty pages. Carlton Press agreed to edit it to three hundred pages. I sent the company more thousands of dollars than I care to remember. When I read the galley proofs of the edited copy, it was evident even to an idiot (which I was for getting suckered) that Carlton Press had no intention of marketing my novel. They deleted pages from the manuscript indiscriminately and at random. The novel became a disjointed, incoherent jumble of words worthy of a lunatic. It became abundantly clear that vanity publishers make their money on gullible authors, not on the sale of books. After I had lost my money, I learned that there were thirty-three complaints lodged against Carlton Press with the Federal Trade Commission, plus local complaints with the New York City Better Business Bureau. Carlton Press is still in the business of preying on authors. If all economic predators were put out of business, capitalism and the free enterprise system would collapse like a house of cards.

Capitalism utilizes the fundamental principle nature uses in her evolutionary process. No human being would exist today were it not for genetic drift, variation, and mutation acted upon by natural selection. The essence of natural selection is survival of the fittest. Fitness has nothing to do with morality. More often than not, the fit are completely unscrupulous. Man survived because lesser predators were selected out. This same principle is the essence of capitalism. Under the free enterprise system, many businesses enter the arena of business competition. The inefficient are weeded out. Almost 85 percent of all new businesses go bankrupt, usually in the first year. Only the fit survive. This guarantees efficiency and maximum productivity. Communism protects the unfit, which makes for inefficiency and minimum productivity. This is why capitalism is a howling success, and communism is a crying failure.

We don't have to go to Russia to see inefficiency and the survival of the unfit. We merely have to go to our local post offices. The post office does not permit any competition that could put it out of business. The unfit are protected by civil service, the American Postal Workers Union, and the National Association of Letter Carriers. The United States Post Office is a standing joke. United Parcel Service, a private enterprise postal service, is cheaper, faster, and parcels arrive all in one piece. A recent check showed that UPS charged $1.04 for one-pound packages vs. $2.96 by the Post Office. Even the IRS has been switching to UPS. Post Office money orders are far more expensive than private bank money orders.

Communists berate the greed of capitalists. Union workers denounce the greed of the employer. They all forget one thing: capitalists and employers are not greedy because they are capitalists and employers. They are greedy because they are human beings. They are born predators, and if they exploit, it is because they have the opportunity to exploit. Modern democratic capitalism has made organized labor a partner in predation. It, too, now enjoys the legal prerogative of preying on other members of society.

We have touched on the ruthless exploitation of labor by the early capitalists. They made extensive use of gunmen, spies, frame-ups, anti-labor injunctions, yellow-dog contracts, goon squads, state and federal troops, and every possible tyrannical device to suppress labor organization. The abuses of child labor, long working hours under inhumane working conditions, starvation wages, and cruelty were a national scandal. Labor unions arose to protect the workers against such abuses. It was a fierce fight against terrible odds, but labor union recognition was finally won. With this victory came power, and with power came greed and inevitable abuse and corruption. Once in a position of power, organized labor, itself, used every device at its disposal to exploit and to gain ever greater wealth. It betrayed its original cause just as the United States betrayed its original cause of fighting tyranny by supporting tyrants. Philosopher Herbert Spencer predicted in the nineteenth century: "We shall presently see the injustices once inflicted by the employing classes paralleled by the injustices inflicted by the employed classes. "

The magnitude of labor union exploitation in the Western World is in direct proportion to the power it wields. Unions profiteer and plunder under the same veiled mechanism of wages and prices as is used by capitalists. The method of union predation is not a great deal different from the method used by our barbarian ancestors who conducted raids on wealth, kidnappings for ransom, and extortions by threats of violence and vandalism. Labor's big gun is the STRIKE, but it is often reinforced with threats to the lives of "scabs," business owners, and customers who cross picket lines. Vandalism is also frequently resorted to. Union labor uses the same methods human predators used throughout history. The news media slant the news in favor of labor unions because the reporters and cameramen are union men, and they want to protect their own right to exploit. Cameras focus on the strikers and their grievances, but scant attention is given to management's views, which are restrained by intimidation.

Labor's predatory weapons are neatly couched in euphemisms.

Collective bargaining is an euphemism for extortion which is accomplished by kidnappers (strikers) taking a business hostage, and releasing the victim (business) only upon payment of the ransom demands of high wages and benefits. When big labor calls a strike, business is halted, and it must bargain for its life as it suffers an increasingly crippling financial loss. The loss to the striking employees is not nearly so devastating. They tap their strike fund. Some states even pay strikers unemployment insurance. The company is given a Mafia-like offer it can't refuse: either pay the ransom or die (go bankrupt). If the wage demands are met, the company must increase the prices of its products to survive, but even if survival is not at stake, human greed for profit demands price increases. (When OPEC multiplied its price, the oil companies increased their prices well beyond the increase in the cost of crude oil to them.)

Many people have difficulty understanding a very simple but fundamental fact: CORPORATIONS AND BUSINESSES DO NOT PAY WAGES. CONSUMERS (OTHER WORKERS) PAY WAGES. The consumer provides the wages by buying the employer's goods or services. The employer merely takes the money given him by the consumer and redistributes it to his employees. All salaries are paid either by consumers or by taxpayers. Every time a union worker gets a pay increase, other workers must pay more for his product. They take an effective pay cut because their incomes no longer go as far. Companies are often driven into bankruptcy by exorbitant wage demands which cannot be passed on to the consumer.

It is good PR psychology to promote the myth that you get what you pay for because price can then be jacked up, and more profit can be extracted, provided the customer can be programmed to equate value and price. However, any shrewd shopper knows that he can go from store to store and sometimes pay anywhere from 10 percent to 100 percent or more for the identical product made by the same manufacturer. If a product costs five dollars in one store, and the identical product costs ten dollars in another store, the ten dollar product is not twice as good, but the buyer is twice as stupid for paying the higher price because he believes that he gets what he pays for.

Doubling a worker's wages does not make him twice as good, but it may make him twice as greedy. The great inventors, artists, poets, writers, and scientists often chose poverty rather than wealth for the privilege of working at that which they enjoyed. Actually, the facts seem to indicate that as wages go up, the quality of work goes down. When construction workers were making seventy-five cents an hour in the thirties, they did excellent work. If we index wages using the 1934 CPI index of 40 and the 1983 index of 301, construction workers should be earning not over eight dollars an hour today, but they get twenty-five dollars an hour, and more in many areas, plus fringe benefits unheard of in the thirties, all of which drive up the cost of homes beyond the reach of many Americans. Is the quality of construction better today? It was never worse! Anyone who doubts this should compare the construction of a house built in the thirties with one built today. Japanese workers produce superior cars to those of American workers, even though their wages and benefits are less than half. Wages are profits on labor, and union labor is as greedy for profits as the most avaricious capitalist.

Labor unions use PR very effectively. For themselves, they project an image of the downtrodden, exploited, overworked victims of the greed of their wealthy employers, even though they may be unconscionable leeches on the GNP and wealthier than their employers. When air traffic controllers and airline employees go on strike, for example, they promote the fiction of being the good guys who are interested in public safety and want to protect the lives of the airline passengers from "victimization by the avarice of greedy employers"— the bad guys. They are very careful to conceal the facts of their own greed, which include featherbedding, wages that are several times higher than the national average, and generous fringe benefits, all of which deprive poor people of the opportunity to fly because the consequent high fares make flying prohibitive for them.

Labor union PR and propaganda are so effective that people— radio talk show host, Ray Breim, for example—are automated to declare that they want their airline pilot to make one hundred thousand dollars or even two hundred thousand dollars a year because they want their lives protected by the expertise of the best man possible when they fly. Actually, when pay exceeds the basic needs of the pilot, it becomes irrelevant to the quality of the pilot. Some people have a passionate love of piloting planes. Danger to passengers exists when the man in the cockpit is there for the fast and easy buck instead of the love of flying. Pilots need good wages, but they don't need huge confiscatory wages that supply them with surplus wealth for large-scale business investments. An airline pilot is interested in flying safely to protect his own life. If he enjoys flying more than personal wealth, he is more likely to be a good pilot, and he will fly safely and well. Besides, airlines are interested in protecting their investments and will hire the best qualified pilots they can, if they are not restricted by labor unions that often protect incompetent members.

Unionized government workers have managed to exploit their fellow Americans to an alarming degree. When they secured a cost of living increase with kicker clauses in their pension contracts, they put themselves in the enviable predatory position of receiving more money as nonworking retirees than they received as workers. Other pensioners who are in near poverty have to pay income tax on their meager incomes, which forces them to subsidize the high incomes of the government pensioners. Capitalistic societies consist of never ending predatory contests between all classes of competing predators.

Labor unions appeal to patriotism by asking Americans to BUY AMERICAN UNION-MADE PRODUCTS. However, they, themselves, are patriotic only to their own bank accounts, not their country. They want higher wages, more vacations, higher pensions, more sick benefits, shorter hours, more holidays, and work rules that reduce their productivity. By contributing less to the gross national product but gobbling up more of the gross national product, they become luxuriating parasites and looters of other workers' productivity in the same fashion as the nineteenth century capitalist exploiters. This is the key point. This is why labor unions are as anti-communistic as any dyed-in-the-wool capitalist. With union labor in the position of sharing the carcasses of expropriated labor with capitalists, union labor is not about to promote its own emasculation.

The predation process of labor unions is sufficiently disguised in the wage-price system that it is undetectable by the dim-witted. It is really quite simple. The gross national product is the nation's total economic pie. The more big business and big labor hog from the pie, the smaller the crumbs left for the expropriated workers (non-union). Every pay increase that is not accompanied by a corresponding increase in productivity is an effective pay decrease for all other workers because the drain on their incomes from the purchase of goods and services of overpaid workers leaves them with less money for other necessities. When productivity increases as a result of technology, workers demand higher wages, even though they did not and could not create the technology. They want to prey on the creativity of others.

Some economists insist that ONLY the printing of money causes inflation. They insist that high wages do not cause inflation. They seem incapable of understanding that even by their definition of inflation, high wages cause inflation because confiscatory wages put a demand on the money supply, the end result of which is the printing of more money. Printing money is the material cause of inflation, but greed, confiscatory wages, and exorbitant profits are the efficient causes of inflation. It is easy to see that if we take every dime in circulation and double them by cutting them in half, and then imprint each with the inscription "TEN CENTS," we are only trying to deceive someone because the real value of each half of the dime is only five cents. The dimes cut in half are the material causes of inflation, but the greedy person trying to double his wealth is the efficient cause of inflation. Printing twice as much paper money is the same as doubling the dimes by cutting them in half and still calling them dimes. It merely creates the illusion of doubling wealth, while, actually, it creates 100 percent inflation.

The cost of goods and services is labor. Eighty-five percent of the cost of running the United States Post Office is labor cost. If postal workers get a 100 percent wage and benefit increase, everyone who uses the services of the post office must pay at least 70 percent more than before the pay hike. If we have to pay 70 percent more for something, we obviously have less money left than before the wage increase. Whether the reduction to our purchasing power is due to inflation or union wage increases, the net result to all workers not participating in the wage increase is exactly the same—they become poorer. The fact remains that wage increases without productivity increases inevitably inflate prices, and it is not very relevant to the consumer whether or not the inflated price conforms to the classic definition of inflation decreed by professional economists.

Labor unions advertise, "LOOK FOR THE UNION LABEL— AMERICANS HELPING AMERICANS!" Truth in advertising would require it to read, "LOOK FOR THE UNION LABEL— AMERICANS EXPLOITING AMERICANS!" Labor unions have progressed from a movement to protect labor against predation by capitalists to an economic power bloc with predatory power rivaling that of capitalists. If labor unions really believed in Americans helping Americans, they would harness their greed, and keep their wage demands down so that other American workers could afford to share in the same good life they demand for themselves. But sharing is communistic, and they are certainly not Communists. They are good Americans who subscribe to capitalism. Therefore, they are disciples of the religion of predators which is dedicated to the principle of Americans exploiting Americans.

Union people rebut the argument that they diminish the standard of living of non-union workers with, "Why don't they organize, and then they, too, can enjoy high wages?" If wages increased for everyone, but the gross national product remains the same, the standard of living would remain exactly the same as before the wage increases. All prices would rise in accordance with raised wages, and the situation would be unchanged. The ONLY time a wage increase is beneficial to anyone is when other workers DO NOT get the increase because then the exploitation situation exists, and one group of workers can parasitize the other.

Many working people suffer economic loss because of gains made by labor unions. Many cannot see beyond employers handing out paychecks, and are blind to the fact that they, not the employers, pay for the gains. Their intelligence is such that they cannot penetrate behind the wage-price scenes to see that paychecks are monies acquired from them. They seem to think that employer funds are self-generating entities, unrelated to external factors. Their thinking is on the same level as that of the cargo cultists.

Cargo cults are religious movements found chiefly in Melanesia. The primitive natives had seen airplanes and ships land at their islands and unload cargoes of modern European products and supplies, but they had no idea that the supplies were manufactured in European shops and factories. They thought the "cargo" of goods came from supernatural sources, that they were created instantly by magical means, much as the Bible states that God created the Heavens and the Earth by divine fiat. "Let there be Adam," and PRESTO! Adam was created! The natives expected the spirits of the dead to answer their prayers and return with cargoes. They built wharves and landing strips, destroyed their own food stocks, and awaited airplanes and ships laden with cargo; much as Christian Adventists have sold all their possessions and awaited the end of the world and the Second Coming of Christ.

When union labor asks for the support of non-union workers in their demands for higher wages, they ask for that support on the grounds that both union and non-union workers belong to the same class of people known as workers, and, therefore, have a common cause. It is like the wolf asking the lamb not to flee, but to yield to its hunger on the grounds they are both animals and have a common cause (staying alive); in fact, both are quadrupeds and both are mammals; and with all that in common, simple fairness should dictate that the lamb ought not to resist while the wolf's taste buds are being titillated. They may have millions of things in common, but the singular fact that the wolf is a predator and the lamb is the quarry overrides the million facts of commonage.

It is absurd, yet, incredibly, millions of non-union workers accept the argument that ALL WORKERS MUST STICK TOGETHER, even while they are being eaten up alive by high prices. They, thinking like cargo cultists, are unable to associate high prices with high labor costs. Capitalism's disguise of exploitation under the camouflage of wages and prices is perfect. Actually, the significant class distinction in this age is not between worker and capitalist. It is between the class of the exploiters and the class of the exploited. When a worker drives up prices in his greed for profit (high wages), like merchants raising prices in their greed for profit, he becomes a member of the same class as the exploiting capitalists. He is an exploiter in the same sense that a pacifist who wages PREVENTIVE war is really a militarist. What the exploited must fear is not corporations, capitalists, or employers *per se*, but whoever exploits them.

Some union workers have extracted phenomenal wages from the system. Many union plumbers get ten times the minimum wage, and that's not counting pensions, vacations, holidays, and so forth. Some sheet metal workers get TWENTY TIMES the minimum wage. Each of their annual wage increases is more than the total minimum wage. When one worker must work twenty times longer, produce much more because his inefficiency is not protected by a labor union, and receives no fringe benefits, he is being ruthlessly exploited by his "brother" workers because the union worker confiscates from twenty to forty man-hours of labor production for only one man-hour of his own. The union worker has the equivalent of twenty to forty slaves working for him, and he is spared the responsibility of housing and feeding them. He can procure the fruit of the labors of others as surely as a master does from a slave; that is, he can "buy" new homes, take expensive vacations, own expensive sport cars, and enjoy exquisite luxuries for one reason and one reason alone: the confiscatory power of his union allows him to plunder inordinate loot from the economic pie with the expedient of high wages, while his non-union "brothers" must scramble for crumbs and struggle to exist on low wages.

WAGES ARE PROFITS FROM LABOR. The profits from labor can be as staggering as corporate profits. High wages and reduced productivity of union workers are as oppressive for the masses as low wages and high profits of employers and high prices of merchants. Fringe benefits and featherbedding are frequently used tools of union exploitation, and it's the public that's exploited, not business. If the employer cannot pass the exploitation on to the public, he goes out of business. Organized labor has predatory tooth and claw in modern democratic societies. Workers in Poland sought tooth and claw, but they were defanged before their weapons could grow. The Polish government saw the FREE LABOR MOVEMENT as a FREEDOM TO EXPLOIT MOVEMENT.

Quite naturally, organized labor and capitalists are equally venomous in their hatred of Communism.

The greed of union workers—as displayed by their demands for high wages, huge fringe benefits, and guaranteed pay whether they work or not—is sometimes so great that they bankrupt their employers because there is a limit to the exploitation that employers can pass on to consumers. Eastern Airlines lost 128.9 MILLION dollars in the first three quarters of 1983. Because of competition resulting from deregulation, the airline could no longer charge the high fares necessary to sustain the obscenely high union wages. Pilots were making ninety thousand dollars a year for working twenty hours a week (overseas union pilots make up to one hundred fifty thousand dollars a year). Flight attendants made up to forty-three thousand dollars a year and luxuriated under featherbedding rules. The union struck the dying company rather than have any part of its booty taken away. The unions demanded re-regulation. In other words, they wanted their predatory wages subsidized by fixing high fares. It did not matter that poor people could not afford the high fares. Americans helping Americans? Please!

Greyhound Lines ran an operating loss of 16.3 MILLION dollars for 1982. Bus drivers received an AVERAGE annual pay of 35,474 dollars including benefits. Deregulation and consequent competition made it impossible for Greyhound Lines to mollycoddle their drivers with salaries more than twice as high as the wages of college-graduated school teachers. Rather than lose part of their booty, which was gotten by the usual extortionary process of striking and threatening the company with financial murder, the union employees struck the ailing company. When the company struggled for survival in November of 1983 by hiring non-union employees, the striking employees resorted to violence. Strikebreakers and passengers crossing the picket lines were assaulted and threatened with death. Strikers pelted buses with bottles and smashed their headlights. Passengers were so intimidated by gangster tactics that they were afraid to board the buses. People who are not beneficiaries of labor union predations, but still cheer unions on to greater effort should realize that they are lambs applauding the wolves as they are being devoured.

As union labor drives up prices, it uses the very increase in prices it causes as an excuse for further wage increases. The spiral of wages chasing prices and prices chasing wages accelerates at an ever increasing rate. The public is the victim of the resulting inflation. Powerful unions profit from inflation because of the cost of living escalator clauses in their contracts. From 1967 to 1978, steelworkers gained 32 percent over inflation. Autoworkers gained 24 percent, and they want to limit Japanese imports so that they can maintain their predatory advantage. Petrochemical workers gained 22 percent. Truck drivers gained 14 percent. Fangless workers who had brain but little brawn lost heavily from inflation during the 1967 to 1978 period. University professors lost 18 percent. Librarians lost 11 percent, and accountants lost 9 percent. The most devastating loss was suffered by the millions of weaponless people who work for wages at or below the minimum wage. They are modern America's serfs and peons who feed the gorge of Big Business and Big Labor. Another great profiteer from inflation is the federal government. A 10 percent rise in inflation produces a 16 percent increase in federal revenue, as more taxpayers are pushed into higher income brackets.

It was a national scandal some years ago when it was reported that the elevator operator at Cape Canaveral made more money than the astronaut he lifted to the spacecraft. It is well known that some janitors make more money than the school principal. Garbage collectors sometimes make more money than engineers and scientists. From a rational point of view, this is insane. It is like paying a monkey a thousand dollars a day for loading computers into a truck, but feeding bananas to the Einstein who created them. It doesn't make much sense to a rational animal; but, AH, man is NOT a rational animal! He is a non-rational predator, and when this is fully understood, it all makes perfect sense.

Human labor is compensated according to power factors, not intellectual factors. If a union garbage collector can strike and threaten the health and well-being of the community with the stench and pollution of tons of uncollected garbage, he has the same power Vandals had when they raided the Roman Empire and collected large ransoms. The union garbage collector has vandal power, and this entitles him to high predatory wages. The engineer, scientist, or school teacher, if he is not organized, if he cannot destroy the community, and if he only possesses non-predatory intelligence, is valued less and paid less in a society of predators. After all, Nero is immortal for having burnt Rome, not for building Rome. Who knows and who cares who built Rome?

The American grain farmer is the most efficient producer in the world. Because he is efficient, he overproduces, drives the price down due to the law of supply and demand, and produces himself into bankruptcy. Because he can feed the world, he cannot feed himself. He succeeded as a scientific farmer, but he failed as a predator. Therefore, he must pay the price of relative poverty. Food is vital to the world, certainly as vital as oil. If he formed a cartel like OPEC, or withheld his labor like powerful labor unions, or limited the supply of food like the diamond monopoly, he could be as rich as the billionaire Arab sheiks. Money, not accomplishment, commands respect. At one time, a truck driver was looked down upon. Today, he is highly paid and has the respect of a brain surgeon; but first, his teamsters' union had to teach him lessons on predation.

Labor unions have secured a massive transfer of the nation's wealth to their leaders, to pension funds, and to their members by means of their weapon, the strike, which permitted the "extortion" of money from employers; and employers passed the costs of the extortion on to the consumers, much as OPEC caused the transfer of huge wealth to their members by extorting money from the oil companies via crude oil prices; and the oil companies passed the cost on to the gas pumps, along with an additional bonus for themselves.

In 1982, UAW members received $19.65 per hour in wages and fringe benefits as compared to $8.16 for the average industrial worker. They also drove productivity down by such fringe benefits as forty-three paid days off a year and early retirement. This drove the average price of a car to ten thousand dollars. Non-union workers who had no clout were practically driven out of the new car market. For them, it was a used car or nothing. Others were put in hock for four years, paying for the new American car AND LUXURIES FOR UAW MEMBERS.

Steelworkers (USW) drove their wages and benefits to $23.40 per hour, which also drove the price of domestic products sky-high and American steel off the world market. In 1982, the USW members were offered a generous profit-sharing contract in return for a less than 10 percent cut in pay for the first year, so as to make American steel more competitive on the world market, and protect jobs for the USW workers; but the union chieftains turned it down. They were not about to surrender any "hard-won" loot. The spoils of predation are inviolable.

Inadequate company investment in new plants and modern machinery has been blamed for loss of productivity of the American worker; but union looting of profits, and union contracts which prohibited the installation of robotic equipment that would reduce the work force and dues-paying membership did not encourage such investments. In 1950, it took seven Japanese or three German workers to match the industrial output of one American, but by 1982, the gap closed, and foreign workers are now surpassing American worker productivity. The American union workers' answer is to stop foreign imports. A poll conducted by the National Enquirer showed that 74 percent of the voters urged a ban on imported cars. This 74 percent did not understand that without competition from foreign manufacturers to check the greed of the American manufacturers and the American labor unions, the price of a new car would be driven up to the price of a home (it actually has in some cases), and those who could still afford a new car would be in hock closer to ten years than four years in order to feed the greed of their fellow Americans. Protectionism protects predation.

A typical example of labor union greed and tactics is the American Air Traffic Controller's strike of 1981. They complained that they were overworked, needed shorter hours, more money, and more controllers. The fact was, they worked only about 50 percent of their eight-hour day. The General Accounting Office had made a study before the strike which showed that 66 low-use control towers and hundreds of air controllers could be eliminated. After the strike, the FAA eliminated 8,506 controller positions and closed 58 towers; and, still, the nation's airports operated smoothly. It was as Richard

Suter, executive vice president of the National Taxpayers United of Illinois said: "It's very clear that controllers who were on the job before the strike were not working very hard. They were spending half their working day doing nothing. It's just extortion that they want more money and fewer hours." Fortunately, President Reagan aborted their attempted predations, which was an unconscionable assault on the taxpayers. Unfortunately, labor unions often do get away with robbing taxpayers and consumers while the victims submit like euphoric zombies or brainless robots.

I obtained first-hand knowledge of labor union predation when I worked in the merchant marine. In 1982, some men on tankers made over four thousand dollars A WEEK. At the same time, some people ashore had to work a full YEAR to equal two weeks wages of these latter day pirates. Work rules, overtime, and other gimmicks accounted for the legal looting. If that sounds like Happy Hunting Grounds for predators, think about the six months paid vacation per year the tanker men get. Vacation pay includes "in lieu of overtime pay." In other words, they get paid overtime not only for not working overtime but for not working at all. Bank robbers are in the wrong racket.

Union members belong to the same species of predators as capitalists. Consequently, they use the same methods of terror, violence, threats, and vandalism that capitalists had used in their heyday of the nineteenth century. Strikebreaking teamsters have been shot at and beaten, and their property vandalized. When the International Ladies' Garment Workers' Union tried to unionize Mike Matthew's Electro-Harmonix, Inc., employees were warned, "Sign up or you'll go to a hospital!" Mike Matthews was severely beaten by five union goons. Employees who tried to go to work were shoved, kicked, punched, and screamed at. Unions now have political muscle, and NOW the law protects THEM. Seven union goons were arrested on charges of assault, disorderly conduct, and harassment, but the charges were dismissed. The same pattern is repeated time and time again as, for example, with Coor's Brewery, trucking companies, and construction companies.

When Deanna Ussery crossed a United Steelworkers' Union

picket line in Hot Springs, Arkansas, her house was shot up, and her daughter narrowly escaped death. Other employees were threatened, and after sixty-four days of terror, the company, National Rejectors, faced with financial ruin, caved in to union terror. Even then, the violence continued because the union wanted to get even with the "scabs." Similarly, a rampage of bombings, shootings and arson against nonstriking workers at the Jarl Extrusions Company was carried on by the striking union. When Teamsters struck the Redman Moving Company in Thousand Oaks, California, they damaged twelve of its fourteen trucks. Vandalism, looting, and barbarism is a way of life today in "civilized" societies, as it had been thousands of years ago. The human animal, the king of predators, must always prey, and he must always justify his predations. No matter how much loot unions plunder from the economy, they will always feel justified, and nothing can convince them to the contrary.

Walter Mungovan and his wife opened the C & W (Cher & Walter) Construction Company in Hawaii. He paid his help union wages or better, but he could not join the carpenters' union because it promoted inefficiency by restricting carpenters to a narrow field of carpentry work. Such "featherbedding" would destroy his business. His wife, Cher, said, "This is America. No one can force you to sign." For one thing, she suffered the same delusions most Americans suffer. She was ignorant of the American labor movement's history, which was among the most violent in the world. From the Know-Nothings of the last century; the bloody battles between strikers and company cops or state militia; the murderous Pennsylvania miners known as the Molly Maguires, who assassinated fellow workers and bosses; the Wobblies (Industrial Workers of the World); to the present—violence dominated the labor scene.

Mungovan's cars were vandalized and "scab" was scrawled on them. Tools and materials were stolen. "Sign or be torched!" he was warned. Every kind of intimidation and coercion was employed. He got little help from police because the police themselves were union members. If he was low bidder on a project, he didn't get the contract anyway because of the bid-taker's fear of reprisals from labor unions. The loss of the contracts was euphemized as due to "political reasons."

Walter Mungovan was put out of business by violence. He testified against two carpenters' union business agents in a perjury trial. The government recognized that his life wasn't worth a plug nickel after that; and so, he was put on the identity relocation program on the mainland. It was designed to protect Mafia informants. The union agents were sentenced to six months in jail. Mungovan's life and marriage were destroyed. Walter and Cher now have grave doubts about freedom and justice in the Land of the Free, but this doesn't even put a crackle in the voices of some two hundred million automatons singing in the chorus praising AMERICA THE BEAUTIFUL AND AMERICA THE FREE.

The wealth pirated by labor unions is staggering. It naturally invites corruption. Three nearly consecutive International Brotherhood of Teamsters bosses were charged and convicted of crime: Dave Beck, Jimmy Hoffa, and Roy Williams. Frank Fitzsimmons bluntly told his teamster members who wanted to clean up the union to "Go to hell!" Only a small fraction of the crooks are even charged, and an even smaller fraction are convicted.

Union wealth has attracted the Mafia. According to Lester Velie, Mafia infiltration has affected transportation, construction, hotels, tourism, and Eastern Seaboard shipping. Fortunes are made by selling labor peace and by sweetheart contracts. Union pension funds exceed 25 BILLION DOLLARS. Union bosses loot it legally and illegally, and then use the money to finance criminals. In 1974, labor union czar, Bernard Rubin, took for himself one hundred eighty thousand dollars a year in salaries alone. Unauthorized salary increases netted him three hundred twenty-nine thousand dollars. While he was on appeal for an embezzlement conviction, he was alleged by lawyer Marty Steinberg to have embezzled an additional 2 MILLION DOLLARS. The law is of little assistance. Miami strike-force chief, Atlee Wampler, asserts that twenty-two mobsters and mobster fronts "continue their pillage immune from investigation."

Figures available at the U.S. Dept. of Labor show that Cleveland labor boss Harold Friedman got $352,330 in salary and expenses in 1976. William Joyce of the Chicago Teamsters took $174,214. Jackie Presser took $201,721 (nearly $500,000 in 1983). Presser's father got

$136,541, *et cetera, et cetera*. THESE ARE ONLY THE REPORT-ED FIGURES, AND THEY ARE RAPIDLY INCREASING. Actual figures are unknown.

Some of the most successful predators in the modern American capitalistic system are not capitalists, Mafia godfathers, or labor leaders, but actors, primitive singers, dancers, and athletes. Alfred Hitchcock looked upon actors as intellectual children because, like children, they love to "fantasize." They enjoy pretending to be that which they are not, like little children playing daddy, mommy, doctor, Indian, or cowboy. Some actors with intellectual endowments no greater than a child's ability to play-act can extort more loot from the economic larder in one day than many hard-working non-union workers can earn in a lifetime. Their predatory euphemism of "residuals" guarantees them perennial booty from a single performance. In return for their play-acting, and by means of the wage-price confiscatory mechanism, they can expropriate palaces, Rolls Royces, luxury cruisers, and the ultimate in comforts such as would make kings and emperors look like ghetto paupers.

The palaces and luxuries the emperors of old enjoyed were produced by slaves. Actors do not build palaces, Rolls Royces, or any such things by their own labors. Other people whose labors they purchase do the construction work for them. When an actor can get two hundred thousand dollars in one day, and then take that money to buy several homes, for example, which required the labors of perhaps a hundred people over a period of months, he has command of slaves in the same sense the pharaohs of Egypt commanded slaves. Actors are among the most successful predators in history. They fantasize about living for their art, but, if that were true, why do they strike for more millions when they already have so many millions that they could not spend it in several lifetimes? The fact is, the richer they get, the greedier they get. Greed feeds on itself. With the help of shrewd agents, they syphon off wealth from the nation like Arab sheiks syphoning wealth via the OPEC cartel. Most actors don't make a living wage, but the dream that they, as actors, can someday become superpredators spurs them on.

The peculiar thing about American capitalism is that the victims of economic predation cheer on the predators with "MORE POWER TO THEM!" They are cognizant of no oppression. They are pacified with food stamps, a little public welfare, and the pipe dream that they, too, have the freedom to become history's most successful predators. But that's what it's all about: predators preying on each other, and the fallen victim exhilarating himself with the impossible dream. If this dream doesn't mollify the victims, the dream of the Christian paradise in the life to come does.

Here is a brief accounting of thespian predation: Carroll O'Connor gets $275,000 a show. Cindy Williams and Penny Marshall get $90,000. Alan Alda creams $225,000 a performance. Henry Winkler rakes in $175,000 per show. It is said that Michael Landon makes 8 million dollars a year from *Little House*. Bob Hope admits to being worth 75 million dollars "give or take a few digits." Johnny Carson snatches 5 million dollars a year for a few nights a week. James Coburn received $500,000 for saying two words on a TV commercial. Wayne Newton was paid 40 million dollars for five years of thirty weeks per year. Ed Asner pulls down 2 million dollars a season, and he picketed for more money during the actors' strike. Suzanne Summers was in the million dollar club, and she struck for yet more money. Think of all the millions and millions of hungry people these plundered millions of dollars would feed if they were used rationally instead of to appease predatory greed.

Top stars dropped out of the Las Vegas circuit because their huge salary demands were not met. Diana Ross made three hundred thousand dollars a week, which is more than some people make in an entire lifetime. Frank Sinatra, Ann Margaret, and Kenny Rogers each made two hundred fifty thousand dollars a week. Dolly Parton topped the list with three hundred fifty thousand dollars a week. Dean Martin and Sammy Davis, Jr. ONLY made two hundred twenty-five thousand dollars a week. Kenny Rogers had so much money, he paid 21.5 million dollars for a home he never lived in; some people have to live in abandoned box cars and scrounge garbage cans for food. At the very moment of these obscene predations, more and more people are slipping below the poverty level every year in America. Ours is not a predatory society? PLEASE!

Greed and madness run amuck in this, the human predators' paradise. Marion Brando got two hundred and fifty thousand dollars A DAY for eleven days acting in the movie *The Formula*. For contributing absolutely nothing to science and technology that took us out of the Stone Age, but for singing semi-primitive jungle music apropos to 50,000 B.C., Willie Nelson and Paul McCartney tapped the economic depository for 15 million dollars a year. This could easily feed three thousand hungry people a year. Rod Stewart made 10 million dollars a year. Kenny Rogers' 20 million dollars a year could easily feed over four thousand hungry people a year. Some people in America would have to work over six thousand years to earn what the Rolling Stones get in one year.

Michael Jackson's unbelievable 50 million dollars a year confiscatory income from performing prehistoric music would feed ten thousand poor people a year. Some hard-working Americans would have to work ten thousand years doing useful work to equal Jackson's yearly income for prehistoric jungle performances. No plundering pirate or barbarian invader in the history of the world could seize, by terror or violence, what primitive jungle music performers can plunder legally from the industrial wealth of the United States by means of the price-wage-profit system of modern American capitalism. If the loot pirated from America's economy by our anachronistic primitive types were distributed to the needy, poverty would be abolished in America.

The greed, exploitation, and insanity in the Predators' Paradise is so outrageous that those who simply read the news on TV expropriate more loot from the economy than those who make the news. News reporters who cover the White House make far more money than the President of the United States, whose awesome responsibilities influence world history and the lives of billions of people. As far hack as 1976, Barbara Waiters was pulling down a million dollars a year. Dan Rather contracted for 8 million dollars over a five year period, which is thirty times more than Huntley and Brinkley made in their prime. Howard Cosell takes in a million a year. Meanwhile, more people are slipping below the poverty level every year. The irrational, predatory distribution of wealth in the United States is an irrefutable fact.

While the wealth of the successful predators is growing by leaps and bounds, the poverty of the economic prey is increasing. The Census Bureau reports that more people are constantly slipping into the poverty level. The wage gap is the greatest in all recorded time, but no pressure is applied to the successful predators to reduce their greed and plunder. Incredibly, the pressure is on the poor to reduce their minimum wage "as incentive for more employers to hire them." At this very time, day, and in this "civilised" age, the pressure is on the poor to make them even poorer, not to make the filthy rich a little less filthy rich so as to make dire poverty less dire. Reduction in the greed and plunder of the successful predators would increase the economic share of the poor and eliminate all poverty. but the loot of the predator is sacrosanct. The Predators' Paradise will brook no impediment to the predators' avarice.

Athletes are in the front lines when it comes to successful looting of the economic ambry. A Neanderthal type whose only claim to greatness is that he can knock another human being unconscious can sequester millions of dollars in a single boxing match. We would all be primitive cannibals if this were the limit of our superiority, and yet, in a few minutes, a missing link out of the pre-Stone Age can loot more goods and services out of a twentieth century technological society which he is totally incapable of creating than the scientists who created this technological society can in a lifetime. Dave Parker makes 1.5 million dollars a year. Nolan Ryan and J.R. Richards get 1.1 million dollars a year. Kareem Abdul-Jabbar makes over a million a year as a reward for his skill of dropping a ball in a basket. This is grim testimony to the basic irrational, primitive essence of the world's most advanced society surfaced with the veneer of advanced civilization. The plundered millions of dollars from our society could be fed into medical science and eliminate diseases like cancer, advance our Space Age technology, and feed the hungry.

The nineteenth century saw white plantation owners commanding the labors of black slaves. The twentieth century sees black athletes, black actors, and black rock musicians commanding the labor of millions of white workers. A black boxing champion can get up to 10 million dollars for a single fight. This money permits him to hire one thousand five hundred men for a full year (at the minimum wage). This is reverse slavery, made possible by the legerdemain of modern American capitalism. He can purchase, for example, two hundred homes from the proceeds of one fight at the current median price. Thus, he has hundreds of "slaves" toiling away building homes, automobiles, and modern technological miracles for him in return for his prehistoric skill in pummeling a fellow human being into unconsciousness. His "slaves" must provide their own food and lodging with whatever wage they must work for. What slave-owner in history ever had it better?

The uniqueness of modern capitalism is that it places a mask on slavery, and no one can recognize the demon behind the mask, but it is humane slavery. It confines the body only eight hours a day, and the slave has some choice in the selection of his master. The price-wage-profit system destroys the appearance of slavery without destroying its essence. It has appeal to the vast majority of human beings. The communist ideal of eliminating exploitation of man by man is so repugnant to the instincts of the masses who enjoy capitalistic exploitation that they are willing to wage suicidal war to extirpate it from the Earth. Poverty is a natural consequence of exploitation, and exploitation is the natural function of predators. It can never be eliminated in a predatory society.

Capitalism is founded on private ownership, that is, the individual possession of territory (property). It appeases the human instinct to possess, protect, defend, and acquire territory. A territorial animal without territory to defend is like a fish without water. That is why Russians fought bravely against the Germans in World War II. They were defending territory. It is also why they lack great enthusiasm for Communism. Communism gives them no private property to defend or acquire. Only territorial creatures can experience patriotism and be willing to die for their country.

Man will die for his countrymen in war; but in peace, he lives to exploit his countrymen, and he "dies" if he can't. This is the paradoxical dual nature of man. In peace, he is self-seeking, self-centered, and greedy. In war, the same person is a self-sacrificing, generous, philanthropic, altruistic creature to his countrymen, but a vile beast to the enemy. Human beings will give their all for their comrades on the battlefield, but they will exploit those same comrades on the economic battlefield. The food they share in the foxhole, they snatch away in the marketplace. Survival instincts are aroused on the battlefield. Predatory instincts are aroused in the marketplace. Man's nature changes as different circumstances bring different instincts into play. A male having sex with his lover behaves differently from when he is in predatory competition with her.

All our ancestors were marauding plunderers whether they were Goths, Vandals, Norsemen, Hungarians, Germans, or African tribesmen. The Goths delighted in plundering the wealth of cities in the Roman Empire. Danes, Norwegians, and Swedes made regular coastal attacks to plunder and burn the towns of Europe and sack the churches. Normandy was a base for the Norsemen (Norman plunderers). The Viking raids were notorious in history. Plundering and vandalizing is a natural instinct which emerges early in the life of a human being. Children enjoy destructiveness. They mark clean walls, break windows of vacant buildings, and destroy property for kicks. It is sheer instinctive pleasure for them. Constructive behavior, such as cleaning dirty walls and repairing damage, is sheer torture for them. Civilization suppresses our true natures and masks them with facades, hypocrisies, and euphemisms.

History clearly proves that man is a plunderer, a killer, and a hypocrite. He cannot face the reality of his own despicable nature. Even when he kills, he fancies that he performs a service to God or country. Capitalism satisfies all the predatory instincts natural to man in the economic purlieu; that is, satisfies his need to plunder, prey, defend, and to mask his predations with euphemisms and hypocorisms. We did not think of ourselves as plunderers stealing territory from Mexico, and Mexico did not think of itself as stealing from the Indians, nor those Indians from other Indians. Predation is normal and natural for the human species. Capitalists, actors, athletes, and rock musicians do not think of themselves as plunderers of the fruits of the labors of working people, nor do union workers think of themselves as plundering from nonunion workers. Plundering has always been perfectly natural and ethical for the human animal; only the rules governing predation change. For example, excess profits of corporations are now considered unethical, but excess profits of labor (wages) are perfectly ethical.

Modern science has introduced new techniques for economic predation; namely, mind control. The tobacco industry controlled the minds of Californians at least twice by preventing the passage of non-smokers' rights propositions. The straw polls originally indicated that the voters favored by a substantial majority the proposition protecting the breathing space of non-smokers from invasion by the pollution of smokers. The tobacco industry, employing techniques of mind control through psyching public opinion and the appropriate use of propaganda, managed to reverse public opinion and protect its rich profits at the expense of public health.

The tobacco industry posed as "Californians Against Government Intrusion," but neither were they Californians nor were they against government intrusion. They were for government intrusion when they were the recipients of large tobacco subsidies. According to the Surgeon General, there are three hundred twenty thousand smoking-related deaths in the United States each year; but these deaths didn't deter the tobacco industry from spending over 5 million dollars to robotize sufficient numbers of people to go to the polls and suicidally vote against their own health interests; nor do these deaths stop the smoking robots from filling three hundred twenty thousand annual vacancies in the nation's cemeteries.

Behavioral control is the whole idea behind advertising, the purpose of which is to robotize people into marching down to the nearest store to purchase the product which will increase the wealth of the advertising agency and its clients. This is accomplished by creating an urge in the customer to purchase products and services, whether he needs them or not. The subject is robotized by hypnotic suggestion. He is made to feel the urge or desire to become a willing victim of economic predation.

Computer software is available for salesmen to psychoanalyze their customers on a one-to-one basis. Psychological profiles of the customers and the salesman are computerized from the input to the answers to eighty questions relating to the personality and psychological traits of each subject. The psychological profiles of the salesman and the individual customers are paired, and the computer then instructs the operator how to manipulate his customer in order to robotize him: in other words, how to clinch the sale. The future will see computers used more and more in the attempts of people to prey on other people. The consequences of computer software to control human behavior are frightening, so much so that a minister was prompted to say, "It is the work of the devil." But he hastened to add, "Where can I buy it?"

Governments exploit their citizens by "TAXING" them. Tax is a euphemism for the confiscation of wealth no less than "profit" is a euphemism for corporate confiscation of wealth, or "wages" and "fringe benefits" are euphemisms for labor union exploitation (when excessive). Inflation has been an effective method of government exploitation. Under the graduated tax system, inflation pushes low-income people into higher tax brackets, even though their real incomes have either remained the same or were reduced. The tax bite automatically increases with inflation. According to one study, if the 1948 six hundred dollar tax exemption were indexed for inflation, it should have been five thousand eight hundred dollars in 1982, or about six times the actual exemption.

Some elderly people whose only income was interest from bank savings deposits at the low rate of 4 percent had their real principal shrink at the rate of more than 8 percent a year because of inflation, but they were taxed on the 4 percent loss as if it were income. The tax money was used to fund confiscatory government workers' pensions, prodigious waste, and right-wing oppression and slaughter in foreign countries. It is difficult to understand how any government claiming to be humane could be so insensitive to the plight of poor people by taxing them to feed the greed and corruption of the unscrupulous, and oppressive foreign governments.

The income gap between the rich and the poor is greater today in the United States than it was in Europe during the French and Russian Revolutions. However, because of the Industrial Revolution, there is usually enough disposable "cake" to placate the exploited masses. Nevertheless, many elderly people are reduced to scavenging garbage cans for food in order to stay alive. Many Americans are forced to huddle in cold flats because they cannot afford heat after they have been depredated by big government, big business, and big labor. Many Americans are homeless. They live in their automobiles, or abandoned sheds or boxcars, and suffer hunger pangs while other Americans, like primitive rock musicians, Neanderthaloid athletes, and sub-sapient thespians, loot the economy out of billions of dollars and live in regal splendor like mindless wastrels gorging themselves on the nation's cornucopia.

The United States appropriately chose the American bald eagle for its national emblem by an act of Congress in 1782. The eagle is the world's most inspiring predator. It was called the "winged wolf" by the Aztecs, and has been used as a symbol of imperial power by most human superpredators, including Hitler, since Babylonian times. Predation gave birth and transcontinental expansion to our nation. Our nation's economic system, capitalism, is predicated on predation. The city, county, state, and federal governments prey on the wealth of its citizens with income tax, sales tax, property tax, excise tax, inheritance tax, corporation tax, excess profits tax, windfall profits tax, gift tax, gasoline tax, liquor tax, cigarette tax, *et cetera*, *et cetera*.

Merchants prey on customers by means of the price system, high-pressure salesmanship, deceptive advertising, and psychological coercion. Employers prey on employees with low wages and employee dependence. Union workers prey on employers with strikes and violence, and employers, in turn, prey on customers—the public, that is. The home seller preys on the home buyer, and the more the buyer is exploited, the more he is again preyed on by the city and county because he is taxed not on the true value of his home but on the inflated price which the seller managed to gouge out of the buyer. Religious predators prey on naive believers by peddling salvation and healing. Quacks prey on the sick and the dying with phony cures. And, of course, we have the Mafia, conmen, bunko artists, dope peddlers, muggers, burglars, plus a thousand and one other predators enriching themselves on their quarry. Yes, the eagle is a fitting national emblem for the American Dream, i.e., the dream of the human predator to have the good life. The good life for any predator is the life of unrestricted predation. This is what the American Dream is all about.

Chapter 4

NONSAPIENS AND LAW

To say, "We are a nation of laws and not of men," is sheer nonsense. Human laws are creations of man. They are interpreted by man, and they are either enforced or not enforced by man. The Supreme Court justices are people, not abstractions, and they can, and do, rule that black is white. Just as there are thousands of different Christian sects based on the same Bible, there are thousands of different legal interpretations based on the same Constitution. Human laws foster the same absurdities, cruelties, and irrationalities as man himself. However, there are certain similarities in human law throughout the world and throughout history.

Hammurabi's Code of ancient Babylonia (circa 1680 B.C.) was one of the earliest codifications of custom and precedent. Like the Commandments of Moses, Hammurabi's Code was looked upon as a gift from God. In this case, a gift from Shamash the Sun-God, rather than Yahweh, the Hebrew all-purpose God. Shamash's gift preceded Yahweh's gift by several hundred years. Historians consider Hammurabi's Code as a major achievement in the social development of man. Hammurabi considered himself to be a father to his people and a giver of pure government. Few of us would want such a father. Here are some of the provisions of Hammurabi's Code:

If a man knocked out an eye or tooth of a nobleman, his own eye or tooth was knocked out in retaliation. If he knocked out a commoner's eye, he was fined one mina of silver. If he knocked out the eye of a slave, he was fined the price of the slave. If a house collapsed and killed the owner, the builder of the house was executed. If the collapsed house killed the owner's son, the builder's son was executed. If a man struck a girl and killed her, there was no penalty for the killer, but his daughter suffered the death penalty. A man who struck his father was punished by having his fingers amputated. A nurse who willfully substituted one child for another was punished by having her breasts amputated. The death penalty was inflicted for such crimes as rape, kidnapping, burglary, incest, harboring a fugitive slave, malpractice in selling beer, uneconomical housewifery, and malfeasance in office. Essentially, the Code was based on the time-honored principle of *Lex Talionis* (an eye for an eye), and it was the product of the identical human brain we all possess.

The law of the Assyrians (circa 740-700 B.C.) was severe. Punishment for such crimes as adultery, theft, and rape included cutting off the ears and nose, pulling out the tongue, castration, gouging out the eyes, decapitation, and impalement. Islamic Law in some modern Arab countries retains much of this brutality. Sargon II added the punishment of burning the offender's son or daughter alive on the altar of the gods. Trial by Ordeal often determined guilt or innocence. The accused was bound and thrown into the river. If the river accepted him, that is, he went to the bottom and drowned, he was adjudged innocent. If the river rejected him, that is, he floated, he was adjudged guilty and executed. Trial by Ordeal was an inspired innovation of the human brain, that same infamous organ of human stupidity which inspired 70 million contemporary human beings to slaughter each other in this century alone.

The Hebrew legend of Moses receiving the Decalogue from Jehovah atop Mount Sinai amid thunder, lightning, and earthquakes was copied from legends common to most ancient people. The Law-Codes were gifts from the various gods. The god Thoth gave Egypt its laws. The Sun God Shamash presented Hammurabi the Law-Code. Ancient Crete received its laws as a gift from its deity to King Minos on Mount Dicta. The Greek lawgiver was the god Dionysus. According to Persian Legend, The Book of the Law was presented by Ahura Mazda to Zoroaster on a high mountain amid thunder and lightning. The Mosaic Code was a latecomer in the ancient world, and it was retrogressive to religious control in which priests were judges, and the temples were the courts.

The Old Testament is our source for the study of Hebrew Law. The Hebrew God was insensate, and His laws were draconian. Anyone refusing to accept the rulings of the priests was executed (Deuteronomy 17:9-12). Oaths were taken by placing one's hand on the genitals of the person to whom the oath was made (Genesis 24:2-3). In some cases, trial was held by the ordeal of drinking poisonous water. If the accused died, he was pronounced guilty. If he lived, he was innocent (Numbers 5:27-29). The death penalty was decreed for striking or for cursing one's parent, for idolatry, adultery, and stealing a slave, but there was no death penalty for killing a slave. If an ox gored a man or woman to death, both the ox and its owner were condemned to death. Anyone copulating with an animal faced the death penalty (Exodus 21:15-31, Exodus 22:19). "If the daughter of a priest be taken in whoredom and dishonor the name of her father, she shall be burnt with fire" (Leviticus 21:9).

Blood feuds like the famous Hatfields and McCoys feud were sanctified by biblical law (Numbers 35:19-21). To quote: "The kinsman of him that was slain shall kill the murderer: as soon as he apprehendeth him, he shall kill him. If through hatred anyone push a man, or fling anything at him with ill design, or being his enemy, strike him with his hand, and he die, the striker shall be guilty of murder; the kinsman of him that was slain, as soon as he findeth him, shall kill him." Hebrew law was an exercise in vindictive brutality and religious intolerance. Death was decreed for witches (Exodus 22:18). "He that sacrificeth to gods, shall he put to death, save only to the Lord" (Exodus: 22:20).

Hebrew law was considered ordinance of God, and the Hebrew God was a predator's God. The proof is in the Bible, and it is incontrovertible. Deuteronomy 20:10—18 clearly bestows upon the Jews the divine right and DUTY of military conquest. It even COMMANDS the infliction of inhuman cruelty upon prey who do not yield to predation by opening its city's gates to the predator, in that when victory comes at such time that "the Lord thy God shall deliver it unto thy hands, thou shalt slay all that are therein of the male sex, with the edge of the sword, excepting women and children, cattle and other things, that are in the city. And thou shalt divide all the prey to the army, and thou shalt eat the spoils of thy enemies, which the Lord thy God shall give thee. So shalt thou do to all cities that are at a great distance from thee, and are not of these cities which thou shall receive in possession. But of those cities that shalt be given thee, thou shalt suffer none at all to live, but shalt kill them with the edge of the sword, to wit." This mandate in the "HOLY" Bible lends religious authority to the Judaic-Christian tradition of predation: from the Hebrew conquest of the Canaanite Promised Land to the European conquest of the American Indian and the founding of the American Dream.

Man makes his gods in his own image. It is, therefore, natural that the god of a predator is the Supreme Predator. The Sixth Commandment, "Thou Shall Not Kill," did not apply to members of the out-group, just as the equality enunciated in the Declaration of Independence did not apply to Negroes, Indians, or women. In the words of Will Durant in his Our Oriental Heritage, "The Sixth Commandment was a counsel of perfection; nowhere is there so much killing as in the Old Testament; its chapters oscillate between slaughter and compensatory reproduction. Tribal quarrels, internal factions, and hereditary vendettas broke the monotony of intermittent peace."

Double standard hypocrisy reached the pinnacle of absurdity when Christians transmogrified the Hebrew God of predators into a loving God of peace, gentleness, and charity, but maintained the predatory, murderous ways of predators. The Christian Promised Land (The AMERICAN DREAM, that is) is blood-drenched land, plundered from Indians exactly as the Hebrew Promised Land was plundered by King David from the Canaanites. But the Hebrews were more straightforward: they conquered in the name of the God of predators, not in the name of the Prince of Peace. Nevertheless, God of predators or God of Love, the Indians and the Canaanites became victims of human predation which was hallowed by human gods and legalized by human laws.

India was a land of many contradictory laws. Law in Moslem India was whatever the sultan or emperor decreed. In Hindu India, law was a strange combination of caste rules, tradition, and royal orders. Torture was often used to extract confessions, as in much of today's world. Minor theft, damage to royal property, and breaking and entering were punished by death. Those who were executed were the lucky ones. Punishments included such refinements as death under the hooves of trampling elephants, or by being devoured alive by wild and hungry dogs; amputation of nose, ears, feet or hands; gouging-out of eyes; molten lead poured down the throat; sawing the body apart; impaling; quartering; burning and roasting alive; driving nails into the feet; and severing the sinews.

The Hindu Code of Manu was the gift of the God Brahma. This code of law decreed trial by ordeal. The accused was required to plunge his arm into boiling oil mixed with cow dung. If his arm was not scalded, he was proven innocent. If scalded, he was as guilty as sin. Another method of trial by ordeal consisted in blindfolding the suspect and having him select a coin or ring from a basket which also contained a deadly poisonous snake. If the accused retrieved the coin or ring without being bitten, he was innocent; but if he was bitten, he was found guilty.

Trial by ordeal was a product of the same vaunted human intelligence we all possess. These trials were as rational as most modern human concepts. The validity of trial by ordeal was based on the belief that the gods would certainly protect the innocent in the trial. The logic was flawless, but the belief was absurd; and yet the belief was not a whit more absurd than most modern beliefs. The fact that human reason is subordinate to human belief and that belief is lackey to human instincts reduce the human brain to an organ of outlandish stupidity.

According to the Code of Manu, Hindu law applied differently to the five castes. The top caste was the Brahman (priest and learned class). The second caste was the Kshatriya (warrior and ruler class). Third was the Vaishya (farmers and merchants). The fourth was the Sudra (peasants and laborers). The fifth and lowest class, the Panchamas (untouchables), were the servants. The Code of Manu warned kings against taxing the Brahman Caste because the priests could place curses and hexes on them. Superstition is the traditional predatory weaponry of priests. The Brahmans became rich from fees paid them in sacrifices to the gods, for working "miracles," and from capitalizing on thousands of superstitions, much as many charismatic Christian preachers become rich in today's "enlightened" America.

According to the Laws of Manu, the Brahmans are at the head of all creatures, and the entire universe is their property. It isn't difficult to figure out that Brahmans wrote the Laws of Manu. If a person in a lower caste attempted to strike a Brahman, he was condemned to hell for one hundred years. If he actually hit the Brahman, he was condemned to suffer in hell for one thousand years. If a Sudra committed adultery with a Brahman's wife, his property was forfeited, and Manu mandated the cutting-off of his genitals. If a Sudra killed a Sudra, the law required the killer to give ten cows to a Brahman. If he killed a Vaishya, he was required to give a Brahman one hundred cows. If he killed a Brahman, he was executed. The predatory power of priests is always directly proportional to the ignorance and superstition of the people.

The Laws of Manu set low caste for life. One of low caste could not change his caste until his next reincarnation. Brahmans could not marry out of their class, and if one married a Sudra, his children were outcasts (pariahs). A Brahman could not associate with the lower caste because he would become low by association; much as in the McCarthy era, non-Communists became Communists by association. Punishment for theft was more severe on the higher castes because they were expected to toe the moral line. A Sudra thief was fined eight times the value of the theft; a Vaishya, sixteen times the value; a Kshatriya, thirty-two times; and a Brahman, sixty-four times the value.

The caste system tended to be eugenic because it prevented diluting the finer strains in society. Because of a religiously fanatic fixation on the irrational belief in equality, eugenic breeding is taboo in modern America. The mere mention of ethnic purity nearly lost Jimmy Carter the presidential election. Modern culture, like primitive cultures, is steeped in superstition, absurd beliefs and taboos.

In India, temple prostitutes had the same high social status as nuns. Highly respectable ladies dedicated their daughters to temple prostitution with as much pride as a son entering the priesthood. In the nineteenth century, some temples were actually whorehouses, but they radiated the same aura of holiness as cathedrals. The prostitutes ceremonially sang and danced lasciviously twice a day, honoring the history of the gods. Like ancient Greek gods, the Hindu gods were subject to the same venality and lasciviousness as mortals. The holy prostitutes, a la modern America's Happy Hookers for Christ, were "servants of the gods" who served the gods by servicing the priests, but they could also extend their services to the general public PROVIDED they shared their earnings with the priests. The venerated prostitutes were called devadasi. The Chola King Rajarja Temple of Tanjore housed four hundred devadasis.

The social esteem of whores in world history varied with the times and the society. In ancient Greece, the hetaerae were women of high social status; but in ancient Rome, they were called meretrices, and they were so low in the social strata that they had to wear wigs and special dress for identification purposes. The enormous diversity of human stupidity, as displayed by innumerable contradictory concepts and countless ridiculous beliefs and customs, defies rationality. Human values are relative to the species, society, and the individual.

The law as set forth in the Code of Manu placed women under the guardianship of their fathers; next in the hegemony were their husbands; and if fathers and husbands were dead, women were under the guardianship of their sons. A wife was required to serve her husband as if he were a god, even if he were the vilest of beasts. She addressed him as either "My Master," "My Lord," or "My God." The husband seldom deigned to speak to her in public, and she was required to walk with sufficient distance behind him to reflect her lowly status. (Almost the same situation existed in Japan until recently. The status of women in the Islamic world is equally low.) Only women of high social status, like temple prostitutes, were educated.

Brahmans' wives were forbidden to learn philosophy because knowledge was thought to render them depraved. In other words, knowledge would corrupt their morals with heretical views of equality; and the next thing, they would be screaming for civil and human rights as they have in the modern Western World. A wife could not own property. She could be divorced for unchastity, but she could not divorce her husband for any reason whatsoever. In today's Islamic World, a husband can repudiate his marriage to any of his wives at will by repeating three times, "I divorce thee." This constitutes the final, irrevocable dissolution of the marriage.

Hindus practiced a ceremony known as suttee (meaning "faithful wife"). Suttee is the burning-alive of widows on their husbands' funeral pyres. It has been practiced throughout the world by such people as the Scythians, Egyptians, Scandinavians, Africans, and Chinese. It originated in the world-wide custom of immolating wives and concubines on the funereal pyres of royalty so that they would be immediately available in the afterlife to serve their masters. One might look at this practice in horror, but actually, the immolated wives and concubines looked at it as a great honor and privilege. Thracian wives fought for the honor of being killed on their husbands' graves. It was coveted glory, like dying for one's God or for one's country.

The human brain is a stupendous organ of stupidity. No other animal seeks its own death for such vacuous reasons; but, of course, other animals are spared the fountainhead of asininity—the human brain. Hindu law prescribed the rule that a chaste widow must not want to live after her husband dies but must proudly walk into the fire and to death by being roasted alive. Yes, wives often fought violently against anyone who would deny them the honor and privilege of dying in the funeral rite. Can anyone imagine a dog being stupid enough to do this? When a Rajput expected to die in battle, he burned his wives to death before going to battle.

The British tried to abolish suttee by law in 1829, but voluntary suttee persisted well into the twentieth century. Even today, Japanese commit hara-kari (seppuku) as expiation for defeat or as means of self-sacrifice. Because it is an extremely slow and painful death, it is supposed to demonstrate courage and self-control; but what significance do courage and self-control have for a corpse?

Thirteenth century Mongols looked upon acts of kindness as criminal acts. Their law imposed the death penalty on anyone showing undue kindness to a captive, or anyone harboring a runaway slave. Stepping on the threshold of a commanding officer's tent without permission was an automatic death sentence. Execution was the penalty for an officer seeking favors from anyone except the great Khan himself. Human life was not precious then, and it isn't now.

Human life has always been as cheap as dirt. The 70 million people slaughtered in this century's violence makes 8.5 BILLION pounds of carrion. If we Americans were to lay end to end all the bodies of the people we killed in Vietnam, Cambodia, Europe, and the Pacific in this century, they would extend from New York to San Francisco. If all the people slaughtered by war during the first three quarters of this century alone were laid end to end, they would encircle the Earth THREE TIMES. There are 2 million aborted human fetuses thrown into the garbage dump like dead rats every year in the United States alone. Every Russian woman averages FIVE abortions in her lifetime. Countless millions of human fetuses are flushed down toilet bowls along with human excrement every year. Human life is precious? Is human feces precious?

According to Old German law, anyone who did not obey a court order was proclaimed an outlaw, whereupon the king confiscated his property and anyone was free to kill him on sight. The penal code authorized the amputation of the nose, ear, feet, hands, upper lip; decapitation; drowning; stoning; castration; enslavement; flogging; or throwing the convict into an abyss. German intellectual superiority has been demonstrated by innovative and ingenious methods of torture and execution. In ninth century England, men were enslaved for debt and minor crimes. Any man could legally sell his wife and children into slavery if he needed the money. He could kill his slaves for any whim. The German courts provided whipping boys who were playmates of young princes and were vicariously whipped, instead of whipping royal children, when the royal children misbehaved. It was based on the same principle the majority of Americans accept in their belief that Christ could atone for the sins of man by vicariously suffering and dying on the cross.

In Islam, as in Judaism, law and religion were one. Jurisprudence was part of theology. Every sin was a crime, and every crime was a sin. Women were required to wear a purdah (veil) because it was unlawful for a Moslem to see the face of a woman other than his wife, relative, or slave. Women were secluded because of the taboo of menstruation and childbirth. They were excluded from mosques, and forbidden to go out shopping. They were legal prisoners of their husbands. If they were surprised while nude, they would cover their faces rather than their sexual parts. They were nonplussed that God did not strike European women dead for dancing with men indiscriminately and exposing a part of their bosoms. Infidelity by a wife was punished by death.

Traditional shari'ah law of Islam punishes apostasy by death. It may seem severe, but it was the usual punishment. The Jews punished heresy and blasphemy with death. The Roman Catholic Church punished heretics with inhuman tortures, and death by burning them at the stake until the nineteenth century. Suspects of heresy were tried by the Church and turned over to the secular authorities for punishment. Shari'ah law punishes adultery by stoning the culprits to death. Drinking any intoxicant is punished with eighty lashes. Offenses against persons are punished by retaliation: that is, an eye for an eye, a life for a life. There is considerable diversity in penal codes among human cultures, but diversity is NOT indicative of "richness", as so many sociologists and anthropologists are fond of repeating. It is indicative of the DIRE POVERTY of the human intellect, the relativity of human values, and the kaleidoscopic variability of human stupidity.

Trial by ordeal was an honored adjudicative procedure in Asia and Africa until recent times. It was widely used in Western Europe during the Middle Ages. Trial by ordeal determines the guilt or innocence of the accused by dangerous or painful physical tests rather than by factual evidence. There were many tests devised by human ingenuity. Ordeal by Fire was common. The accused walked through fire, or put his hand in fire or molten metal. If the accused received severe burns, he was proven guilty. If he received no injury, he was proven innocent. Absurd? Not a whit more than the modern American adversary system of justice. Trial by ordeal was as rational and logical as most human reasoning. It followed from the belief that God, in His infinite justice, must spare the innocent. If the belief is valid, the conclusion is valid. The absurdity of the human animal lies in his propensity to believe the most ridiculous nonsense and his use of "reason" to rationalize this nonsense.

There are many variations of trial by ordeal. A woman accused of being a witch underwent trial by water. The accused woman was bound and thrown into water that was blessed by a priest. If the blessed water rejected her (she floated), she was presumed to have been rejected and pronounced guilty by God Himself and was, therefore, burned at the stake. If the blessed water accepted her (she sank and drowned), she was adjudged innocent by God. Accused perjurers were tried by the ordeal of blessed bread. If the accused could swallow bread blessed by the priest, he was "obviously innocent" because it was believed impossible for the guilty to swallow Holy Food. Accused murderers in medieval Europe underwent ordeal of the bier. The accused was required to touch the corpse, and if it appeared that blood was made to flow in the corpse, the accused was proved guilty beyond question.

In the Middle Ages, trial by combat was used to determine guilt or innocence in disputes between two adversaries. Both disputants took an oath of truthfulness, and then they fought a duel. The judicial system worked on the principle that God, in His infinite justice, would favor the cause of the righteous in combats, a logical conclusion in the Age of Faith. It was believed that the victor in combat was pronounced RIGHT by none other than God, Himself. To the faithful, this system was superior to trail by jury or by human judges because everyone knows that the Omniscient Deity is a judge who is superior to venal man. Women, children, and disabled men were represented in combat by a "champion." Eventually, a class of professional champions arose out of necessity because omnipotent God always showed favoritism for the strong, even though they needed no favoritism. If God only helps those who help themselves, He is partial for predators and discriminates against the prey.

Even religious fanatics finally realized that God was derelict, and so, trial by ordeal is now thought absurd because it doesn't determine the guilt or innocence of the accused. This is precisely why modern American justice is equally absurd. It does NOT determine the guilt or innocence of the accused. It is based on the adversary system. It does not matter who is right or wrong, innocent or guilty, but who wins and who loses. A good flimflam defense attorney can secure the freedom of a proven guilty man, and a good flimflam prosecuting attorney can jail an innocent man. A cunning defense attorney can turn a proven killer loose on society by resorting to technicalities, by invoking exclusionary rules which invalidate conclusive evidence, or with the plea of not guilty by reason of insanity. A good actor can feign insanity. Modern justice is based on the amount of money one can afford for a clever lawyer. The madness of modern man is identical to the madness of medieval and ancient man. Only the method to his madness has changed.

Modern American justice by the adversary system is exactly like medieval trial by combat. Instead of PHYSICAL COMBAT, it is now FORENSIC COMBAT between defense and prosecuting attorneys. It is a battle of wits, cunning, and deception. In neither medieval nor modern trials by combat is guilt or innocence the paramount issue. When conclusive evidence of guilt is thrown out of American courts by successfully invoking one of the various exclusionary rules, it is touché for the defense attorney. When this thrust is successfully parried, it is touché for the prosecuting attorney. There is no progress—only change. Trial by physical combat has become trial by mental combat with the judge or jury being the referees to determine the winning combatant.

Sometimes, the guilty escaped punishment during their lifetime, but this presented no problem in the past: their corpses were exhumed, put on trial, and punished. In A.D. 1661, the bodies of Cromwell and his two associates were exhumed from their graves and punished for beheading Charles I. The rotted corpses were hanged, beheaded, and buried under the scaffold. In 1589, Jacques Clement's corpse was put on trial, and found guilty of murdering Henry II. The sentence read, "His Majesty, on being advised by the Judicial Council, ordered that the above named Clement's above mentioned corpse should be quartered by attaching four horses to his four limbs. Thereafter burned and its ashes to be scattered in the river in order to remove every atom of his memory."

Animals were put on trial for various offenses. It was often trial by torture. If the accused animal emitted sounds of pain, it was tantamount to a confession of guilt. The "guilty" animal was then placed in human prisons and executed, but the majesty of the law required that the sentence be pronounced to the animal in full formality. Some of us should envy the "lower" animals for having been spared the consequences of our organ of human stupidity, the human brain. In 1705, while the English and the French were enthusiastically slaughtering each other in one of their interminable wars, an ape washed ashore on the English coast. The English thought it was a French spy, and its ape-chatter was the French language. It was put on trial, convicted of espionage, and duly executed with the full pomp and circumstance of the law.

In 1972, a crow was arrested in Tokyo for using obscene language in public and for pecking children. The police read the crow its rights. In Salem, Massachusetts, and most of Europe, cats were considered demonical accomplices of witches. Thousands were burned at the stake like human heretics. In 1922, a Pennsylvania judge condemned a dog to die because its master entered the United States illegally. President Warren G. Harding asked Gov. William Sproul to pardon the dog. He did.

The famous French lawyer Bartholomew Chassenee defended a pack of rats which were charged with destroying a barley field. He managed to delay a judicial decision by arguing that if his clients appeared in court, they would be endangered by "evilly disposed cats" in the area. He also employed the legal technicality that each rat should be issued an individual summons instead of being jointly summoned. His tactics finally won a dismissal of the case, and the rats were spared execution. A chicken was burned at the stake in Basel, Switzerland, in 1471, upon being convicted of being a devil in disguise. The evidence that convicted the chicken was the oddly-colored, bright egg which it laid. In 1963, seventy-five pigeons were given the death sentence by an Italian court upon conviction for smuggling money into Libya.

The history of human law is a history of cruelty, insanity, and absurdity. Charles Dickens dramatized the injustices of the law and the gruesomeness of debtors' prison in his nineteenth century novels. His own father was imprisoned for debt. Imprisonment for debt has theoretically been abolished in England and the United States, but for every law there is a loophole. The courts can now order the payment of a debt, and if the debtor does not pay, he can be imprisoned for contempt of court. A debtor can be imprisoned for concealment of assets, and on many other collateral charges. Not so very long ago, many men in the United States were serving *de facto* life imprisonment for nonpayment of alimony (Alimony Row) while, at the same time, vicious killers were freed from prison.

Theocratic blue laws (Sabbatarian laws), so-called because they were written on blue paper, were enforceable until recently. Some are still on the books in America and even enforced. These laws wrote Puritanic religious morality into the civil and criminal codes in New England. They regulated dress, enforced family discipline, and prohibited the breaking of the Sabbath. All games and entertainment on the Sabbath were illegal. The law required the closing of all stores on the Sabbath. All merrymaking on Christmas was forbidden because it was considered a solemn day of fasting and atonement. Many states enacted laws against unnecessary work and all secular amusements on Sunday.

There were many priggish absurdities to the blue laws such as forbidding a husband to kiss his wife on Sunday, whistling on Sunday, the use of cosmetics, card-playing, and cigarette-smoking on Sunday, and so forth. Those who broke the blue laws suffered punishments such as the stocks, pillory, public whippings, and tarring and feathering. Blue laws are forms of sumptuary laws, which are derived from religious and moral beliefs concerning diet, drink, dress, and mode of living. Laws relating to dress prevented a lower class person from assuming the appearance of a superior class person in the same spirit that our modern laws make the donning of police or military uniforms by civilians a criminal act.

Louis XIV of France, like most monarchs, believed that he was ordained by God to govern with absolute power. He is reputed to have said, "L'etat, c'est moi!" (I am the State!) He was the law. Bishop Jacques Bossuet, the prelate who orated on the sublime dignity of being poor but preferred to be one of the depraved rich, obsequiously backed up his claim with biblical quotations. Ecclesiasticus 17:14 reads, "God has given every people its ruler." The New Testament reinforces this concept in Romans 13:1-2, "Let everyone be subject to the higher authorities, for there exists no authority except from God, and those who exist have been appointed by God. Therefore, he who resists the authority resists the ordinances of God; and they that resist bring on themselves condemnation. "

Actually, it is impossible for any Christian or Jew to justify democracy on the basis of the Bible, or for any Mohammedan to justify it on the basis of the Koran. Louis XIV, exercising his Biblically justified divine right, pronounced Protestants "criminals" and decreed the death penalty for Protestant clergymen. Acting on this same divine right from the same God, English monarchs made Catholicism a crime, and Catholic priests were hanged for crimes such as "seducing the people."

Kings—Henry VIII, for example—beheaded their subjects with the insouciance of swatting a fly, for theirs was the majesty, pomp, power, and law. Ivan the Terrible murdered his own son and several of his wives with impunity because he was the law. He built a monument of great beauty and then had the architect's eyes gouged out so that he could never duplicate the structure of beauty for anyone else. Lower animals do not commit such insane atrocities because their brains are not overlaid with a cancerous growth of cerebral cortex like human beings. Modern despots commit the same enormities as were committed in ancient times. Modern American justice commits the same atrocities by proxy in turning its surrogates—the fiends, sadists, the criminally insane, murderers, rapists, and every sort of brutal criminal—loose on society.

The citizen who lives in dread of left or right-wing autocrats' secret police has his counterpart who lives in dread of brutal criminals in the United States. In a dictatorship, the citizen is spared the atrocities of criminals but not the atrocities of the dictator. In modern democracies, the citizen is spared the atrocities of the state (except when he must die in a president's undeclared, holy wars against Communism) but not the atrocities of the criminals. Lenient courts and autocratic liberal judges make society a jungle of lurking killers, sadists, muggers, and rapists, always poised to pounce out of the shadows.

Modern law has its rationalizations not unlike the insane laws of Ivan the Terrible which were rationalized as the divine right of kings. Modern America's insane laws are rationalized under the umbrella of civil rights; but, ironically, they protect the criminal, not the victim. They make as much sense as preventive war. The same insane rationale which held that it was better to fight the Communists in

Vietnam than in New York also holds that if criminals are denied civil rights, it is only a matter of time before everyone will be denied civil rights. It is as stupid as saying that if drunks are denied the right to drive a car, it is only a question of time when everyone will be denied the right to drive.

Human beings enact stupid laws. Americans are no exception. In 1692, twenty people were legally executed upon conviction of witchcraft in Salem, Massachusetts. Article IV, Section 2, Paragraph 3 of our revered Constitution forbade a slave from fleeing captivity and seeking freedom, and it provided for his permanent status as a slave. The Eighteenth Amendment to the Constitution forbade the manufacture, sale, or transportation of intoxicating liquors within the United States and all its territories. The Land of the Free denied everyone the freedom to drink a schooner of beer or a glass of wine. Catholic priests needed special dispensation to drink wine to celebrate Mass. The Volstead Act was responsible for the proliferation of crime and the birth of vicious mobs, gang wars, and general lawlessness. Thousands died as a result of scofflaw predators bootlegging denatured alcohol and improperly cured whiskey. The logic that "anyone old enough to fight and die is old enough to drink" inspired laws that enabled teenaged drunks to litter the highways with victims of mayhem.

Nothing has changed in the modern human being. He is the same killer, and his laws are as half-witted as at any time in the past. Innocent people suffer the same cruelty the ancients suffered. Liberal judges and ridiculous laws foster brutality and atrocities by opening the floodgates for known murderers, rapists, sadists, and hardened criminals. In New York City, Angel Claudio confessed to killing a high school honor student. Judge Kenneth Browne threw his confession out on the grounds that the defendant's lawyer showed such poor judgment in allowing his client to confess that the defendant had been effectively denied the right to counsel. This ruling was based on the 1949 opinion of the United States Supreme Court Justice Jackson that "any lawyer worth his salt will tell the suspect in no uncertain terms to make no statement to police under any circumstances." Ivan the Terrible couldn't have said it better or protected a murderer better.

Bobby Joe Maxwell was released from the Tennessee State Prison after serving only half of his ten year armed robbery sentence. Authorities paroled Maxwell in spite of several violent incidents. He was caught with a concealed weapon, sentenced to sixty days, but the judge put him on probation the next day. Upon being turned loose, eleven people were murdered, and the police allege that he was the "Skid Row Stabber." James McClain was found guilty and sentenced to life for hurling his girlfriend's infant son down an eleven-story garbage chute and killing him. The Maryland's Court of Appeals threw out his conviction because the police were twelve minutes late in getting him to a court commissioner.

Robert Keith stabbed his friend Phyllis Rank to death in 1964. He was found not guilty by reason of insanity, and Judge Harold Holden ordered him to the Atascadero State Hospital for the criminally insane. In 1967, Keith stabbed another patient to death. Despite District Attorney Jack Cardinale's warning that Keith "has the potential for great harm," he was paroled. The killer now brushes elbows with the unsuspecting populace, ready to strike at any time of his choosing. A jury in Hawaii convicted Lange Hashizume of murdering his neighbor and attempted murder of the victim's fleeing brother. Judge Acoba overturned the conviction and found Hashizume innocent by reason of insanity. The killer can go totally free upon duping the hospital's psychiatrist into believing he is sane.

Spencer Snell was charged with murdering a man during an argument. Florida Circuit Court Judge Joseph Durant freed him on two thousand five hundred dollar bond. While free on bond, police charged him with murdering another man near a poolroom in an argument over who had the next game. Snell pleaded no contest, and Judge Durant sentenced him to three years. This same judge ruled that pistols were excluded from the definition of firearms due to a technicality in the State law. Therefore, Snell could legally carry a pistol. Similar logic deprived Negroes and women of civil rights because they were excluded from the definition of human beings.

Paul Miskimen bludgeoned his sleeping wife, and then strangled her with her own pantyhose. California Superior Court Judge Sheldon Grossfeld ruled that he was not guilty of murdering his wife because one of his multiple personalities, Jack Kelly, committed the murder. Paul was sent to Napa State Mental Hospital for the murder "Jack Kelly" committed. If he is clever enough to con the psychiatrists into believing that Miskimen and Kelly have become amalgamated, he will be free to again ply his exciting trade of criminal attacks on the unwary.

In 1977, Willie Edward Level bludgeoned to death a female student in the parking lot of Bakersfield College in California while her husband watched in frozen horror. The killer was apprehended shortly thereafter with blood on his hands and shoes, and his fingerprints were on an object near the body. Level waived his rights, but he asked for his mother. While waiting for his mother, he made a detailed confession. A jury found him guilty of second degree murder. The Appeals Court overturned his conviction because it ruled that when an adult suspect wishes to see his mother, police must stop all questioning. Willie could go free again not because he was innocent, but because he asked to see his mother, and he confessed before seeing her. An outraged attorney fumed that the decision made him disgusted with his profession. Medieval trials by ordeal made as much sense. They were irrelevant to guilt or innocence; and so are American Trials, which are Contests of wit and oratory. American law is a mockery of justice, and it made America a Happy Hunting Grounds for criminals—the Criminal's Dreamland.

Rochester, New York police brought in Irving Jerome Dunaway for questioning about an attempted robbery and murder of a pizza parlor owner. Dunaway voluntarily made incriminating statements the same day. He was convicted of the murder, but the United States Supreme Court overturned the conviction by six to two because "there was not enough evidence to make an arrest" at the time he was picked up for questioning. Police had advised him in advance that he had the Fifth Amendment right to remain silent and to have a lawyer. The high court's decision was based on the "exclusionary rule" which prohibits the use of any evidence obtained by an unconstitutional search or seizure. The detention of Irving was considered an illegal seizure. The Supreme Court effectively ruled that rights of murderers supersede the rights of the citizenry to be protected from murderers.

It was the logical decision expected of a session of novenary predators higher in age than IQ.

When police break the law by making illegal searches and seizures they become criminals, but they are not punished. The police commit the crime, but the public is punished because the courts declare open season on victims for marauding killers, rapists, and burglars when incontrovertible evidence of vicious crimes is thrown out of court. In the Criminals' Paradise, otherwise known as the American Dream, society is punished for the crimes of the police as whipping boys were punished in Medieval Europe for the misbehavior of the princes. France displays more intelligence. There the police are punished, but the evidence is used so that future innocent victims can be spared inhuman outrages.

Philosopher Sidney Hook wrote, "When we read that a man whose speeding car had been stopped by a motorcycle policeman, who without a search warrant forced him to open his trunk that contained . . . corpses . . . walks out of court scot-free because the evidence is ruled inadmissible, we can only conclude that the law is an ass." Philosopher Hook was probably thinking of the California case in which police stopped a speeding car and routinely searched it; upon opening the trunk of the car, the police discovered the brutally murdered bodies of a young woman and her three children; the court ruled that the car was illegally searched because the police had not obtained a proper search warrant; as a result, the case was dismissed, and the car's driver was freed. To say American law is an ass is to insult the dignity of an ass.

The California case was a clear affirmation of predator rights in a society of predators. It was madness beyond rational redemption and doublethink insanity at its worst for victims of criminal predation. The letter of the law was finically adhered to in releasing murderers, but international law was callously winked at in the Grenada invasion which violated the U.N. Charter (vote one hundred and eight to nine against), the O.A.S. Charter, and even the Caribbean Alliance Charter (vote was not unanimous). The apologists for the double standard defended the release of murderers on the grounds that if the civil rights of criminals are not protected, we will all soon live in dread of the midnight knock; but criminals were not so absurdly pampered before the assaults on victims by the Warren Court, and law-abiding citizens didn't live in terror of the police. The apologists had no difficulty euphemizing the illegal Grenada invasion as a rescue mission. However, we must not forget that the behavior of a predatory animal toward the out-group and the in-group is programmed to be schizoid.

A federal court in Massachusetts freed a man and returned a million dollars that was confiscated from him because a police typist accidentally transposed the digits in the address on the search warrant. According to Wayne Schmidt of the Americans for Effective Law Enforcement, thousands of criminals have their convictions overturned because of technicalities. We can diligently search through the pages of ancient and medieval history, but we cannot find more juristic stupidity than exists in modern America. The stupidity is rationalized by the maestro of human stupidity, the human brain.

More often than not, the victim of a rape is on trial rather than the rapist. She is subjected to humiliation and dehumanizing inquisitions which victimize her for the second time. She becomes a victim of American justice. The courts presume that the victim of rape is guilty of seductively luring the rapist, and she must prove her innocence. The rapist is presumed to he innocent. The victim's sexual life from the time of her birth is made an open book for the scrutiny of the court and the world. The rapist's previous history of crime and rape is buried in secrecy lest the court be "prejudiced" against the criminal, but it is openly prejudiced against the victim. The courts have ruled that if a beautiful girl wears a bikini in a public place, she stimulates the erotic impulses in the male and is responsible for her rape. The rapist is exonerated because he merely reacts normally to external stimulation. The victim is the criminal in our society of predators.

Women have always been victims because they are the physically weaker of the sexes in the human animal; hence, prey for predators. In the ancient world, the rape of women of conquered nations was the legitimate perquisite of conquering soldiers. Some American Indian tribes punished adulterous wives by subjecting them to gang rapes by twenty or more men. Throughout history, and in many parts of the modern world, women are legally nonpersons. Rape is not a crime against women as persons, but a crime against the property of a father or a husband; frequently, not even against property if the victim is not a virgin because only the defilement of PURE property is a crime. British and American justice has applied the subjective test of guilt to the rapist; that is, he is only guilty if he, the rapist, thinks he is guilty of rape. An appeals court threw out the rape conviction in the 1975 British Morgan rape case because the jury was not advised to vote for acquittal if they thought that the accused believed that the victim wanted sexual intercourse.

Again and again, we see that the predator is given the legal advantage in American society. Typical of this is the case of Mark Alexander. He was convicted of forcibly raping a Michigan woman in her mid-twenties. Kalamazoo's Judge William Beer postponed sentencing for one year to see whether Alexander "could lead an exemplary life and stay out of trouble." The victim fled in terror to Louisiana when she learned that her attacker was again loose and on the prowl. The agony of the trial itself, which was postponed four times, drove her to attempt suicide. Said the victim, "My whole life has been changed—and his hasn't. That's what gets me. "

The judges, who should protect the public, endanger the public by releasing inhuman beasts to stalk its victims in freedoms guaranteed by the Constitution. In the economic jungle of the predators' paradise, the prey is warned, "Let the buyer beware!" In the jungle of criminal predators, the situation is similar, "LET THE VICTIM BEWARE!" A potential victim of murder cannot call the police until a crime is committed, but after he is murdered, it is too late—at least for him. Criminals soon learn that the only crime in America is the crime of getting caught.

Anthony Pannell dragged a woman pedestrian into a car, and his accomplice drove them to a deserted area where the woman was brutally assaulted, raped, and robbed at knifepoint. Pannell was apprehended. Prosecutors pleaded with Bucks County, Pennsylvania, Judge William Hart Rufe III not to release Pannell on bail. The pleas were ignored. Less than a month later, and while free on bail, he savagely attacked an eighteen-year old who was four months pregnant. She was raped, robbed, and her right arm and nose were broken. Time and time again, judges release convicted violent criminals, effectively giving them a license to repeat their crimes while they await sentencing for previous crimes.

In Chicago, a rapist broke into Angela Window's fifteenth floor apartment and sexually assaulted her friend, who was waiting for her return to the apartment, and then threw her out the window. Angela returned to her apartment, discovered what had transpired, and managed to fire her gun at the rapist as he fled. She was arrested for firing a gun inside the city limits and for not having registered the gun with the city and state. The law proudly wore blinders for the Grenada invasion, but it used a microscope to punish a victim of domestic crime. The law is the law except when hubris declares that it is not the law.

In New York City, a fist-swinging masher molested Raven Novie in a bar. In an attempt to protect herself, she sprayed him with tear gas from her tear gas gun. She was arrested and convicted of third degree assault charges and violation of the Sullivan Law. She now has a permanent criminal record. Her attacker was neither arrested nor charged with any crime. One night, Arlene Delfava was attacked by a rapist on a New York street. She bravely fought him off with a switchblade knife. She was charged with assault and violation of the Sullivan Act. This should not surprise us. A society of wolves is not likely to protect the sheep with its laws.

In Benson, Minnesota, Michael Clemens fired a warning shot toward Francis Rakowski, a successful small-time burglar, after he burglarized the Clemenses' family car of one hundred fifty dollars worth of goods. The burglar was accidentally shot in the foot. Rakowski pleaded guilty to the crime and was given probation. Six years later, he sued Clemens for damages because he claimed that the shot in his foot crippled him. The jury agreed, and awarded him seventy-five thousand dollars without even deducting one hundred fifty dollars for the property he burglarized. Medieval trial by ordeal wasn't so ridiculous after all.

The outlandish absurdity of American law is so pervasive it

would require volumes to truly expose it. We can only briefly touch on it here. Seventeen-year-old Clifford Smith had an argument with nineteen-year-old Robert Loftman in a New York high school playground. Three times, Smith squeezed the trigger of his gun which was aimed point-blank at Robert. The first two misfired; the third shot Robert dead. New York State Supreme Court Justice Kenneth Browne voided Smith's confession of murder, and even acquitted him of a gun possession charge while chastising his attorney for incompetence because he allowed his client to even make a confession. This conclusively proves that the law favors the predator, not the victim.

Yuba City, California, mass murderer Juan Corona, had his first conviction overturned on the grounds he was not adequately defended. The proof rested not so much in the preponderance of evidence against him, but on the fact of conviction. Perhaps every convicted murderer should demand a new trial on the grounds that his conviction is proof of incompetent legal representation because, in our system of trial by forensic combat, a lawyer with superior cunning CAN ALWAYS defeat the inferior prosecuting attorney because cunning is more important than evidence. When the criminal beats the rap, he praises the system "because it works" (for him). When it doesn't work for the predator, he screams that he didn't get a fair trial and didn't have competent legal representation. He is often assisted by candlelight vigils chanting sympathy for him while the nation is in nepenthean apathy for the agonies of victims and victims' relatives.

Mrs. Udine Harp's scorched body was recovered from the living room of her Boise City, Oklahoma home after a gasoline fire had been extinguished. Her body had been punctured by numerous bullet holes, indicating that she was the victim of murder. During the course of the investigation in which the Assistant District Attorney asked the dead woman's sons about possible suspects, one of them, teenager Bruce, confessed to the murder. Since the prosecutor did not suspect any of the sons, it never occurred to him to warn them of their right to remain silent, and their right to counsel, a requirement flowing from a Supreme Court ruling. Because of this technicality, Judge Lansden barred the confession, and found the murderer not guilty. Bruce cannot be tried for murder again. The prosecutor fumed, "This is ridiculous. It means we have open season on mothers up here." He finally awakened to the fact that the law of the predator prevails in America.

Charles Kenney confessed to his complicity in the robbery and cold-blooded murder of a filling station attendant. He was dutifully informed of his right to remain silent and his right to counsel. However, he was not told that the state would provide him with a lawyer if he couldn't afford one, and the reason he was not told was that the United States Supreme Court's ruling on this requirement was not handed down until after Kenney's confession. Because of this technicality alone, Charles Kenney was acquitted by a California court, and he is now a free man—free to rejoin his fellow predators and make America unsafe for decent society.

Charles Wesley Furnish confessed to infanticide seven different times; but his murder confession was overturned in California because of the Supreme Court's ruling on informing the accused of his right to remain silent and right to counsel. Dan Clifton Robinson was convicted of murdering a Los Angeles bartender. A Supreme Court ruling won him a new trial and acquittal which prompted the judge to chide the jury with, "You have been induced to let a killer go." In Ohio, Arthur Lee Davis blurted out a confession of murder while he was being questioned about a burglary. His confession even led police to the conclusive evidence of the murder weapon and empty shotgun shell, but the confession and evidence were ruled inadmissible. Hence, another murderer was turned loose on society with all his predatory options open.

When a New York mother was acquitted of the self-confessed, cold-blooded murder of her four-year-old son, and she thanked the judge, he replied, "Don't thank me! Thank the Supreme Court of the United States. You murdered the boy and ought to be jailed!" Fausto Flores was acquitted of murdering his pregnant mistress because the murder evidence was obtained by a "bug," which was ruled inadmissible by a United States Supreme Court decision. The High Court's Escobedo and Miranda rulings were landmarks and the greatest boon to crime since Cain.

As Charles Silberman, author of Criminal Violence, Criminal

Justice observed, "Crime is as American as Jesse James." Despite the ridiculous myth that America is a peace-loving nation, its entire history has been of countless aggressive wars against native Indians; wars against Spain and Mexico; two wars against England; many other foreign wars such as Korea, Vietnam, and two World Wars; a bloody Civil War; extreme violence of the Wild West; a long history of crime, violence, gangsterism, mobs, Mafia; and vigilantes who represented mob violence rather than law and order.

It is an obvious fact that America's vicious killers are greater heroes than its scientists and intellectual benefactors. Movies, TV, books, songs, dances, and ballads honor such rapacious criminals and desperadoes as Butch Cassidy and the Wild Bunch; Johnny Ringo; the Sundance Kid (Harry Lonabaugh); Frank and George Coe; the Apache Kid; Joaquin Murrieta; Doolin Gang; Belle Stan; Billy the Kid (William Bonney); Jesse James; "Legs" Diamond; "Scarface" Al Capone; Dutch Schultz; "Babyface" Nelson; "Machine Gun" Kelly; "Pretty Boy" Floyd; John Dillinger; Bonnie Parker and Clyde Barrow; Louis "Lepke" Buchalter; "Lucky" Luciano; "Mad Dog" Coll; "Bugsy" Siegel; *et cetera*; *et cetera*.

A predatory, nonrational animal would naturally make a killer-predator a hero before it would make a philosopher or a scientist a hero. ONLY AN INTELLECTUAL CREATURE WOULD GLORIFY INTELLECT OVER VIOLENCE. The violent nature of society in the United States, which is the hallmark of predators, is indicated by the facts that three murders are committed every hour, that a woman is raped every seven minutes, that a house is burglarized every ten seconds, and that a violent crime is committed every twenty-seven seconds. In 1980, one out of every three households was affected by serious crime. At this writing, the profit from crime is at least 125 BILLION dollars a year and growing. Simple automobile accidents often escalate into gun fights, reminiscent of the Wild West days.

One study in Washington, D.C., showed that 24 percent of all serious crime was committed by 7 percent of the criminals who had been arrested on the average of four times in a little over four years. The fact that these recidivists are repeatedly released to again prey on society says a lot about the predilection and sufferance of our laws and the society which makes the laws. Of one hundred thirty thousand felony arrests in New York State each year, only about eight thousand go to prison. According to New York Police Commissioner Robert McGuire, "The criminal justice system almost creates incentives for street criminals." Youths are given a license to commit murder. In many states, a youth can commit murder and not spend a day in jail. At the age of eighteen, youthful murderers with long histories of crime can walk the streets with unblemished records. This is reverse *lex talionis* inhumanity.

A New York teenaged thug flippantly bragged of shooting a "dude" because, "It wuzn't nudd'n. I jess had to kill 'em. Dat's de way I looks at it, cuz I wuz young. De most I cud've got den is 18 monts." Fifteen-year-old Edward Robinson of Miami laughed at the accusation that he raped a housewife at knifepoint and sneered, "What you gonna do to me? Send me to youth hall? I'll be out in a few hours." Andrew Vogt of Colorado's District Attorney's Association pointed out that because juvenile criminals are precluded from punishment, we have effectively created a privileged class in society.

No child is too young to display the savage nature inherent in the human animal. A six-year-old boy in Washington, D.C., siphoned gasoline from an automobile, poured it on a sleeping neighbor, threw a lighted match on him, and amused himself by watching his victim thrashing about suffering throes of agony in the flaming inferno.

Typical of predators, youthful criminals seek the easiest and most defenseless prey. They prey on the old, the sick, the blind, the lame, and the very young. One eighty-four-year-old New York City woman described how she was choked and beaten by two young punks: "The big one hollered, 'Hit her!' and the little one would come over and hit me again. And I looked at the little one and said, 'Shame on you!' I saw death and I was dead, and I started to call the Lord. I was thinking to myself. 'What a nightmare. Oh, what a nightmare!'"

Yes, it's a free country for the predator, but the old, the sick, and the blind must cower in their homes in fear that, if they leave the relative safety of their homes, they will be robbed, beaten, and murdered. Citizens of totalitarian countries must fear the tyranny of the secret police, but we must fear the tyranny of the criminals who thrive under the privileged sanctuary of the law.

A few years ago, an Alabama deputy sheriff had to transport a juvenile criminal to Louisiana. When the sheriff saw that his deputy was going to let the boy ride unhandcuffed in the front seat, he advised him that he should confine the youth to the caged rear of the police car, but the deputy rebuked him with, "There is no such thing as a bad boy. Any boy who is treated with kindness will respond with kindness." When the deputy did not show up in Louisiana, an APB was put out for him. The deputy's police car was located in a deserted area, abandoned but containing the body of the deputy with a .3H slug in his head. If an abandoned dog is rescued, fed, and treated with kindness, it will more than likely sacrifice its life for its loving master. If an abandoned human being is given the same kindness, his benefactor stands a good chance of being beaten, robbed, or murdered—if the value of the loot is deemed worth the effort. Man is not only the king of predators, he is the paragon of treachery.

There are some forty thousand people in the United States who have an absolute right to commit crime with complete impunity. They can murder anyone, and the murder isn't even a crime. This special privilege is known as diplomatic immunity. If a murder is committed and the killer is apprehended, the moment the killer is found to have diplomatic immunity, the police blotter is erased. Murder under the sanctuary of diplomatic immunity is no crime. The dead person is not a victim of murder. He is a victim of diplomatic immunity. The worst possible scenario is that the killer would be required to return to his native country. Predation enjoys international blessing.

Law in the United States is always biased in favor of the criminal. The criminal is often not even blamed for his crimes. Victims are blamed on the insane reasoning that the crime would not have been committed if the victim had not been at the scene of the crime. The criminal has the right to be at the scene of the crime, but the victim does not. "Underlying social causes" are blamed, not the criminal. Racism, poverty, lack of education, junk food, stress, disintegration of the family, and other environmental factors are to blame—never the predatory nature of the beast. The majority of people are incapable of establishing valid cause and effect relationships. This is why the human genus, Homo, was on Earth 2 million years before a very small, superior minority in a small area of the world was able to develop modern science and technology, and it is why man is certain to destroy himself in a holocaust of nuclear explosions in the indefinite future.

Criminals are released on bail, only to commit more crimes while they are free on bail. If they are rearrested for other crimes, they are released on bail again to commit more crimes. It is revolving door justice. Criminals use their freedom while they are on bail to intimidate or even murder the witnesses. With the murder of the witnesses goes the case, and they are freed for lack of evidence. Some prisons give their prisoners nearly unlimited telephone privileges which are used to phone and intimidate the witnesses. The exclusion of evidence under exclusionary rules guarantees an untruthful verdict. We suffered centuries of total ignorance during the Dark Ages because scientific evidence was excluded from society for religious reasons. Exclusion of evidence is the exclusion of truth, and it is the greatest of crimes.

Our courts ruled that the Haitians who entered the United States illegally had their civil rights violated because they were NOT GIVEN A SPEEDY TRIAL, but when the trials were speeded up, the Appeals Court held that their civil rights were violated because they were not given ENOUGH TIME to prepare an adequate defense.

Top drug queen Martha Gaviria ran a 30 million dollar a year drug ring in Florida. She was arrested after some difficult police work, but Judge Clyde Atkins freed her on bail after she posted one hundred fifty thousand dollars in cash and an eighty thousand dollar bond, which were petty cash to her. She promptly jumped bail and skipped back to her mansion in Columbia, free to continue her drug operations.

Civil rights are extended to outlaws who are contemptuous of the civil rights of others. The mercy of the courts subjects the innocent to those who are without mercy. We endorsed the ancient legal principle of *lex talionis* when we tried to bomb Germany and Japan into the Stone Age not too many years ago. We made the blood of millions of innocent people flow like raging rivers in Europe, Asia, Vietnam, Cambodia, and other parts of the world as we proudly bragged about our revenge, vengeance, and reprisals; but we think it is barbaric for a man to want the murderers of his wife and children executed for reasons of revenge. We think his desire for revenge is unbecoming civilized people. And so we protect the savage murderers in our society with every resource at our disposal. Madness? Of course! But whoever said human beings are sane except self-serving human beings?

Henry Lee Lucas was convicted of murdering his mother. He went on trial for the murder of Frieda "Becky" Powell, whom he confessed to stabbing to death, having sex with the corpse, and dismembering the remains with a ten inch knife. He admitted to killing more than one hundred and fifty women. If he had been executed after his first murder, at least one hundred and forty-nine innocent women would be alive today. But capital punishment is uncivilized. However, the burning alive of one hundred thousand Japanese by means of two diabolical atomic bombs was civilized. Misguided liberals cannot see that the execution of dangerous criminals is the humane surgical removal of malignant cancer cells from the body of society.

There are many career criminals in our society. They live the same natural life of predators that all of our barbarian ancestors lived for thousands of years whether in Europe, Asia, Africa, or any other place. Civilization is the superficial taming of man's natural predatory instincts. Civilization is to man what domestication is to animals. In war, violence, and crime, man finds his true freedom and greatest pleasures because he then expresses his true nature. That is why violence on TV, in the movies, and in novels is so popular. People who lack the guts for personal contact with violence must enjoy it vicariously. Liberals make society a scapegoat for crime, but a predatory people cannot disavow their predatory nature. Society is made up of people, and it must reflect the nature of its constituents.

Former Attorney General Griffin Bell observed, "The truth is that there are a lot of bad people out there who ought to be locked up to protect the rest of us. Unless we're willing to face that, we don't really deserve a safe society." Hundreds of experimental studies on the rehabilitation of criminals show that no form of rehabilitation works, whether it be vocational or academic training, individual or group counselings, long or short sentences, probation or parole. To prevent gregarious predators from completely destroying each other, physical violence and aggression must be suppressed and sublimated in the in-group by acting out their predatory natures as capitalists, labor leaders, actors, athletes, or rock musicians. Human predators who are incorrigibly antisocial must be either permanently locked up or permanently eliminated.

It is impossible to deal with crime when society is dedicated to the protection of criminals. A psychopathic axe killer attacked several people in Springfield, Illinois' Lauterbach's Cottage Hardware store. John Ewing's head was split open. The wife of the store's owner was partially paralyzed and blinded as a result of the attack. Another victim was seriously injured. The police had evidence which linked the killer to a patient in the psychiatric ward of the city's Saint John's Hospital, but his identity is protected by a confidentiality law passed by the Illinois Legislature in 1979. In a similar manner, the investigation of the murder of William Kennedy near a Washington, D.C. drug store treatment center was hampered because Superior Court Judge Frank E. Schwelb protected the identity of the addicts treated at the center at the time of the murder.

The fact that the legal system in the United States protects killers and punishes victims can be documented by tomes of evidence, but we must confine ourselves to only a very few cases. Elmer Wayne Henley Jr. confessed and was convicted of the gruesome sex-and-torture murders of twenty-seven young boys. The trial had been moved from Houston to San Antonio for the benefit of the defense, but the Texas Court of Criminal Appeals overturned the conviction on the grounds that more consideration should have been given to the defense's request for yet another change of venue in the interests of a "fair trial." Meanwhile, the parents of the murdered boys have to suffer the tortures of hell all over again by facing the ordeal of a new trial. Actually, the last thing a killer wants is a fair trial. He wants to be acquitted, which means he demands an unfair trial, and the courts often oblige. Justice in the Old West gave the killers a "fair trial," and then hanged them. It was open season on criminals. Now it is open season on victims.

Proof that law in the United States protects the criminal is also conclusive in the case of Barry Braeseke who confessed four times (once on national TV with Mike Wallace on "60 Minutes") to shooting his father in the head three times, and his mother in the head and stomach to collect an inheritance; but the California Supreme Court threw out his murder conviction because when he made his first confession to the police, he asked to speak "off the record," and in so doing "revealed a marked lack of understanding of his legal rights." The killer's former attorney, James Crew, grumbled, "Legal procedures today favor the obviously guilty person—the one we know did it. Violent criminals are going free, and innocent, law-abiding citizens can no longer count on protection . . . When we know a person is not innocent, then the system becomes deaf, dumb, and blind." If it is ruled that the publicity generated by Crew's comments prevents Braeseke from getting a "fair trial," he will be freed and get the two hundred thousand dollar inheritance from the three people he murdered.

Think about it for a moment! We send our armed forces all over the world to dispense massive death and torture to political opponents in the out-group. We pour death-dealing arms and ammunition into foreign countries so that right-wing people can murder and torture left-wing people. We are prepared to wipe all life from the face of the world with our arsenal of nuclear weapons, but we coddle our fiendish, brutal murderers at home with kindness and solicitude. Our ill-advised liberals insist that capital punishment is no deterrent to crime, but no one has ever seen an executed murderer commit another murder. It is the one and only perfect deterrent. Thousands of innocent people would be alive today if the mass murderers had been executed after their first murder. Liberals decry capital punishment as an uncivilized lust for revenge, but when asked whether Hitler should have been executed, their mouths drool at the very thought of revenge.

Our legal system of predators, by predators and for predators, provides many safeguards and loopholes for criminals. John Ray

Johnson was charged with the brutal axe murder of his grandmother near Seattle. He beat the rap by sneaking the prosecution's star witness into jail and marrying her. The case had to be dropped because Washington State law provides that one spouse cannot testify against the other without the accused person's consent.

The pretext of racial discrimination is a very effective loophole. A Mr F., a black, was rejected for a job with the Department of Housing and Urban Development because he was on probation for assault. He complained to the Equal Employment Opportunity Office that he was a victim of racial discrimination, and he was upheld. The reasoning was: blacks are arrested more often than whites. This proves discrimination. Whether they commit more crimes is irrelevant. If ten blacks and one white commit murder, juristic affirmative action limits the law to the arrest of one black, and requires the impunity of nine. The logic of insanity decreed that Mr F was discriminated against because of his race, and he received one year's retroactive pay for not working. *Homo sapiens*? Nature's supreme joke perhaps, but not *Homo sapiens*!

The Navy and Air Force frequently observe drug-smuggling operations at sea, but they are forbidden to do anything about it because the law bars the military from active involvement in domestic law enforcement. Dan White murdered San Francisco Mayor George Moscone and supervisor Harvey Milk in cold blood, but he was only convicted of voluntary manslaughter because of the M'naghten rule under which a defendant can use a "Twinkie Defense" of "diminished capacity to know right from wrong." Vietnam vets plead post-traumatic stress syndrome for obtaining acquittals on criminal charges. One judge gave a criminal a suspended sentence because he "suffered from vitamin deficiency. "

Senator Orrin Hatch spoke out against the legal loophole of the insanity plea which sends the criminal to a hospital instead of a prison, and the hospital turns the criminal free when the doctors decide he is better. Not guilty by reason of insanity is insane nonsense. If a person commits a crime, he is obviously guilty. If he is insane at the time of the crime, he is guilty by reason of insanity. American law provides ample loopholes for cunning predators, whether they be economic predators, religious faith predators, or criminal predators.

Some of our "intellectuals" cannot understand that many born killers in our society are beyond rehabilitation. William F. Buckley Jr. helped set free convicted killer Edgar Smith who again attempted to commit murder when he was freed. Buckley later admitted how easily conned and naive he had been. Norman Mailer was instrumental in freeing convicted "belly of the beast" killer Jack Abbott. Shortly after his release, he murdered Richard Adam. Abbott was convicted of manslaughter only. Norman Mailer appeared more defiant than penitent for having sponsored the needless murder, but then Norman Mailer was no stranger to violence himself. He stabbed his second wife in 1960 and got off with a suspended sentence.

If one has a choice, he had better elect to be the criminal rather than the victim. As a victim, he must suffer the frightful consequences of being the prey. Not only is he victimized by the criminal, but he is also victimized by the law. A victim has no constitutional rights which will improve his status as a victim, but the criminal has the full power, pomp, and majesty of the law at his disposal to mitigate and improve his circumstances. To say the law is an ass is to insult an ass. The rational quality of the law is depicted by the old Indiana law which decrees that if two trains approach each other, they must both come to a complete stop, and neither may proceed again until the other has departed.

Do-gooders rally to the defense of hardened criminals, demonstrate for their release, and make heroes out of them as, indeed, they had for Caryl Chessman. Thousands of people from writers to housewives fought to save him from capital punishment. They actually wept for him. No one wept for the destroyed lives, psychological torture or lifelong anguish of his many victims. The news media and cameras did not focus on the pains and sufferings of his forgotten victims. The news media induce sympathy for the criminal and oblivion for the victims; but, then, of course, it is perfectly natural for a race of predators to be more impassioned by the fate of glamorous predators than the fate of lackluster prey.

The Orlando, Florida *Sentinel* reported that nineteen-year-old babysitter Christine Falling confessed to killing five children in her care during a two-year period. Almost immediately, many people sprang to her defense. The chief concern of most people was to invalidate her confession. No one seemed to give a hoot or holler in hell about the victims except the victims' families. When Black Panther Eldridge Cleaver guested on TV talk shows, he was shown more dignity and respect by the women in the audience than they would deign for the technological architects of the Space Age. Cleaver's victims were forgotten, but the man of glamour, the charismatic predator, was in the limelight, and he was the hero.

The news media glamorize criminals. Even history spotlights criminals. The more vicious the crime, the more fame and notoriety the criminal receives. John Wilkes Booth is almost as famous as the man he assassinated, Abe Lincoln, but even Lincoln's fame is contingent on his glorious victory in the Civil War in which tens of thousands of Americans slaughtered tens of thousands of other Americans. One of the most famous men in history is Jack the Ripper Everyone has heard of him. But the greatest intellects of history like Immanuel Kant, Georg Hegel, and Baruch Spinoza are unknown by the public. Jack the Ripper's victims were anonymous nobodies, but he will live forever, even though his true identity is unknown.

The news media attend vicious killers right to the death chamber (when they are not released to prey on society). Reporters hang on to their every word and emotion. They vividly describe the terror in the killer's eyes, but equal time is not given to the terror that was in his victim's eyes. The victims' families may be haunted with nightmares and terror for fifty years or more, but the plight of prey is not newsworthy to predators. Intelligently balanced news would demand that the predicament of the victims and their families be given equal time because the one-sided exposure of the suffering of the criminal is bound to create misplaced sympathy. If executing criminals seems barbaric to do-gooders, there's a simple solution: round up all hardcore criminals, relocate them in hutches in a Nevada desert, and then drop bombs and napalm on them. If it was civilized for the United States to drop bombs and napalm on millions of innocent Vietnamese and Cambodians, it is certainly civilized to drop bombs and napalm on vicious murderers, cruel sadists, and brutal rapists.

We often hear people complaining about violence and sex on TV. It is ridiculous and futile to complain about the very substance of the human species. Anything other than sex and violence bores a natural predator to tears. Violence, crime, and vandalism are exciting, exhilarating, and thrilling for the human predator. The human instinct for predation manifests itself early in life. Children get a big thrill out of mischief and violence like breaking windows, damaging property, smearing walls and buildings with paint, setting fires, stealing, and gang fights. If you make a child clean a dirty wall, it is cruel and unusual punishment. When the child smears or defaces clean walls or breaks windows in abandoned buildings, he is in ecstasy.

Few people watch the construction of a building. It is dull. However, when the building is torched and blazes away in conflagration, people stumble all over each other to be first at the exciting scene. Sex and violence sell because they constitute the fundamental fabric of the human animal. The Bible is one of the most popular of books. If anyone says it is not ridden with sex and violence, he simply has not read the Old Testament.

Many very intelligent people choose the life of crime for the sole reason of excitement. Meyer Lansky was a financial genius, but he chose crime. Arnold Rothstein and Willie "The Actor" Sutton were extremely intelligent, but a nine-to-five job was too tedious for them. Said Sutton, "I was more alive when I was inside a bank, robbing it, than at any other time in my life." Henry Starr (1881-1921) who started out as a horseback outlaw and became the first American criminal to use an automobile in a bank robbery described the excitement in his profession thusly, "There's the robbery: thrill of dashing into a town after an all-night ride, guns blazing . . . from every window across the street, rifles and shotguns are spiriting lead at you. The boys who had gone into the bank come running out with a grain sack bulging with loot. You vault into the saddle and roar out of town, guns bucking."

Henry Starr was describing the same excitement all our barbarian European ancestors experienced when they raided and looted the

Roman Empire. He was describing the thrill of being human. The thrill we all enjoy vicariously when we see a violent movie or TV production—the thrill children experience when they vandalize property—the thrill many of us would like to enjoy but don't have the "stomach" required to experience the real thing.

Sex is obviously vital for the replenishment of the supply of human predators so that they can keep one step ahead of the prodigious losses due to war, crime, disease, and natural disasters. Sex is as popular as violence. Every movie must contain some sex. Because of the female's reproductive importance, she has enjoyed traditional perquisites. The law protected the married woman with alimony, child support, survivor rights, and chivalrous succors, most of which have eroded in the modern America of the "liberated" woman. Modern woman has liberated the male penis rather than herself. Her shack-ups, euphemized as "relationships," deprive her of the law's munificence, and even threaten the survival of the ancient profession of prostitution. The male partner shies away from commitment when circumstances permit because it is uneconomical to buy a cow when all he wants is the milk.

What a deal the liberated penis has today! The female lives with the male and shares expenses. When he tires of her, he simply kicks her out and finds himself another "liberated" female to feed his lust. It's the male's dream and the prostitute's nightmare come true. It is the sexual predator's paradise. If he keeps his shack-ups short termed, he can escape all legal entanglements. She stands a fair chance of becoming a single parent and having a life of struggle to be both the caring mother and provider for her child. The liberated woman has liberated herself from the protection of the law and lost her predatory advantage. She has become the slave of male concupiscence, but, like a brainwashed cultist, fancies herself supremely free.

The Constitution of the United States is like the Bible in that it can be interpreted any way anyone wants to interpret it. The fact that the Bible lends itself to infinite interpretations is evinced by the thousands of warring Christian sects, all contradicting each other, some killing each other, but all based on the same Bible. Justices on the State and Federal Supreme Courts seldom agree on Constitutional questions. That organ of human stupidity, the human brain, can twist the meaning of anything to suit the instincts of its host. The Fourteenth Amendment declared that no state shall deprive any person of equal protection or due process under the law, but judges used it to protect property and not people. Justices rule that black is white and rationalize their rulings with "learned" opinions. In the past, the courts favored business leaders over labor leaders. They struck down minimum wage laws, maximum working hour laws, and child labor laws. President Franklin Roosevelt packed the Supreme Court with liberals and got most of the pro-New Deal decisions he wanted.

The Warren Court began to legislate social reform, and it usurped the prerogatives of Congress by unwarranted interpretations of the Fourteenth Amendment. President Eisenhower remarked that the greatest mistake he ever made was the appointment of Earl Warren to the Supreme Court. The Supreme Court has recently ruled that so-called legislative vetoes limiting actions by the Executive Branch are unconstitutional. This ruling reshapes the powers of Congress and the President.

The High Court's 1954 Brown vs. Board of Education decision ruled that separate is not equal in public schools. This ruling effectively usurped the powers of Congress and wrote integration and bussing laws. The 1966 Miranda decision liberated crime and criminals as the Nineteenth Amendment to the Constitution liberated women. The Burger Court effectively wrote an abortion law with its 1973 Roe vs. Wade decision.

Chief Justice Earl Warren read his own narrow moral views into the law. He was not concerned with the Constitution as is. He rewrote the Constitution by interpreting it to suit himself. His pet questions were, "Yes, yes, yes! But is it right? Is it good?" This proves, of course, that we are not a nation of laws. We are a nation of dimwitted judges and justices who spew out new laws by revamping old laws. We are an oligarchy, not a democracy, because nine aging men can overturn the vote of the people and Congress as they see fit. The wisdom of Justice Louis Brandeis is lost. Said he, "The most important thing we do is not doing."

Our Imperial Judiciary rules by divine right like ancient monarchs. Chief Justice John Marshall decreed that a justice is responsible "only to God and his own conscience." In 1978, the Supreme Court ruled, five to three, that a judge could exceed his authority, act maliciously, commit grave procedural errors, and yet be immune to personal damage suits. The Supreme Court has given itself dictatorial powers denied it by Article III of the Constitution. It did this by its 1803 Marbury vs. Madison decision which grants the judiciary the right "and duty" to strike down acts of Congress which it deems unconstitutional. The 1857 Dred Scott decision struck down the Missouri Compromise, and declared that slaves are not human beings—they are property with no claim to civil rights. It required an amendment to the Constitution to reverse the 1857 Court decision that blacks are not human beings and have no legal rights.

In 1946, the Hobbs Act was passed by Congress to outlaw extortion in all aspects of interstate commerce. In 1970, striking labor union members and officials were convicted on charges of conspiring to sabotage a Louisiana utility company's equipment by blowing up a transformer substation. In the 1973 appeal to the United States Supreme Court, the conviction was overturned five to four on the grounds that the Hobbs Act did not cover violence or threats used to achieve "legitimate" union objectives. What is legitimate? The grasping of a million dollars a day by avaricious movie actors, athletes, and rock 'n' roll missing links? Is unlimited predation legitimate for superpredators? That ruling legally condones violence when predation is in the name of profits on labor. If the Supreme Court were abolished, and Constitutional decisions were based on the flip of a coin, sanity would at least have a fifty-fifty chance.

As we mentioned, the United States is actually an oligarchy of harebrained judges and justices, many of whom hold power for life just like monarchs of ancient times. The people do not make the laws. Laws are made by judges and justices who twist and subvert the law to their own will. In 1964, the people of California voted two to one in favor of Proposition 14 which became Section 26 of the California Constitution, but the State Supreme Court declared it unconstitutional. The United States Supreme Court upheld the California

Court decision five to four. Speaking for the four dissenters, Justice John M. Harlan sharply accused the majority of unfairness.

Supreme Court justices have the power to rule that two plus two equals six. The Warren Burger Court made integration laws, bussing laws, voided abortion laws of forty-six states, and overturned death penalty statutes. An "activist" court is not a court at all. It is a legislative body and an executive body rolled into one. A Parma, Ohio Federal Judge ordered the community to provide low income housing. In 1961, the Supreme Court ordered state and federal courts to strike conclusive evidence from the record when obtained in violation of the Fourth Amendment (Mapp vs. Ohio) whereupon crime immediately proliferated and the number of unsolved murders tripled. In 1971, the Supreme Court ruled that local Federal judges have dictatorial power to enforce racial balance. The Supreme Court has displayed every judicial hubris short of declaring the law of gravity unconstitutional.

Just what is the United States Supreme Court? It was created by the Federal Judiciary Act of September 24, 1789 after having been established by the United States Constitution in Article III. The Authority of the Court is set forth in Section 2 of Article III which reads, "The judicial power shall extend to all cases in law and equity arising under this Constitution, the laws of the United States, and treaties made, or which shall be made, under their authority; to all cases affecting ambassadors, other public ministers and consuls; to all cases of admiralty and maritime jurisdictions . . . ."

Generally speaking, the Supreme Court does not hear original cases but acts on appeal or writ of certiorari. It rules on the constitutionality of Congressional enactments, Federal and State laws, and executive, legislative, and electoral actions. The Constitution does not prescribe the size of the Supreme Court. It started off with six members which was unsatisfactory because the Court was perennially bogged down in hopeless three to three deadlocks. In 1869, the Court was increased to nine members which is its present size. It consists of one Chief Justice and eight Associate Justices. Appointments to this high tribunal are for life, and they are made by the President with the advice and consent of the Senate.

Because Supreme Court appointments are for life, incompetence due to senility is not uncommon. The effects of senility are not always as obvious as when a Supreme Court Justice once voted one way on a decision, but wrote a judicial opinion which spiritedly contradicted his own vote. Had he simply voted and remained silent, his doddering senility would never have become evident. Dotage is protected for the mutual benefit of all the justices. Nowhere is stupidity, absurdity, and incompetence better protected or more respected.

Everyone agrees that two plus two equals four regardless of how poorly he is educated, but regardless of how many university degrees in jurisprudence the justices possess, no two of them can read the Constitution and agree to what they had read. Judicial opinions are as relative and varied as tastes in food. Upon tabulating seventeen major decisions by the United States Supreme Court during one year, it was determined that ten of them were by a five to four vote. Strange as it may seem, by taking nine pennies and considering heads a constitutional vote and tails an unconstitutional vote and tossing them seventeen times, the 'vote" of the coins almost exactly coincided with the actual vote of the Supreme Court. This indicates that the Supreme Court decisions obey the law of chance rather than the law of precise rationality and mathematical invariance as contained in the equation two plus two equals four.

It should come as no surprise that the Supreme Court decisions obey the law of chance because chance is the predominating factor in its decisions. Its decisions depend upon the accident of a particular president of a particular political persuasion being elected; the accident of his moods and prejudices in appointing justices; the accident of the predispositions of the justices as derived from genetic and environmental factors; the accident of their educational influences; the appellant attorney's persuasive powers; and a thousand and one other accidents which culminate in a Supreme Court ruling. Since the rulings are not so much related to the letter of the Constitution as to the relativity of the justices' moral concepts—and moral concepts are relative to the individual—it would make more sense to eliminate the Supreme Court entirely and substitute a machine of chance.

We suggest that this Supreme Court Eliminator be called the AU-TOMATED SUPREME COURT ADJUDICATOR, or ASCA. It would look like a slot machine except it would have nine revolving wheels to represent the nine justices. Each wheel would have CON and UNCON alternately written on the peripheries. A technician would give the machine's arm a hefty yank, let the revolving wheels whirl and settle to a complete stop, and simply read off the decision of ASCA. Most of the decisions would be five to four as they are now, and they all would follow the same law of chance they now follow. The advantages of ASCA are impressive: it would save the high cost of the salaries, benefits, vacations, and pensions of the justices, and provide swift and honest decisions. The rich and the poor, blacks and whites, men and women, and the weak and the strong would all have an equal chance, with no fear of conflicts of interest. Best of all, sanity would finally be given an even break. The nonsensical, interminable legal briefs, lengthy argumentation, posturing pomposity, and astronomical expenses incurred by nine supercilious dotards would be eliminated.

ASCA really makes more sense than the present system. Under the present system, the Appellate Division reverses the Lower Court's decision. The State Court of Appeals reverses this decision. The State Supreme Court reverses this decision. The United States Supreme Court reverses that decision. If there were a Super United States Supreme Court, it would reverse this decision, and if there were an Ultra Super United States Supreme Court, it would reverse that decision. Why go through all this time-consuming, expensive, nonsensical claptrap and ridiculous ostentation, when ASCA could make the one, the only, and irrevocable decision in a matter of seconds? ASCA makes more sense, but it will never happen. The human animal's instincts demand a show of ceremony and a display of rationalizations. The illusion of rationality is all-important. The reality is unimportant. "Reasons" must be invented, no matter how inane, childish, idiotic, or insane. No rationale is so absurd that some human being doesn't or hasn't proclaimed it at some time or in some place as intellectual excellence personified. The diversity displayed by human stupidity is truly astounding.

We must accept the fact that chance subjective rulings of the Supreme Court will never be carried to their logical conclusion and streamlined with the use of ASCA. However, here is even a better idea: the state of the art in computer technology is such that a computer can now make a mathematically certain decision based on the Constitution, free of human error and prejudice. A computer can be programmed with the Constitution and its Amendments. A questionable law can then be put to the computer which would make a search to see whether or not it falls within the parameters of the Constitution. Within seconds, a computer would make precise decisions based on the law and not on human prejudices.

Neither the computer nor ASCA would ask, "Yes, yes, yes! But is it right? Is it good?" It would ask only the pertinent question: "Is it Constitutional?" It would not be subject to the venality of man, the persuasive power of clever but devious attorneys, the prejudices, biases and bigotry of man, bribery, conflict of interest, and many other human frailties. It would make the United States a nation of laws and not of men for the first time. But, of course, the computer will never be used. It would deny man the luxury of hypocrisy, the delusion that he is a rational animal, the instinctive pleasure of ignorance strutting in regal pomp and impressive ceremony. It would eliminate vested interests enjoyed by the holders of thousands of superfluous jobs, and it would displace an entrenched oligarchy, which would fight for its territory like the Viet Cong. Man must always remain an absurd, murderous predator, and his swaggering ceremonies, majestic laws and legal ostentations must reflect and guarantee it in the manner prescribed by his animal instincts.

Chapter 5

NONSAPIENS AND RELIGION

Taboo is a Polynesian word meaning "THOU SHALT NOT." It implies a system of strict prohibitions, the violations of which carry severe, automatic punishments of a supernatural nature. Unlike the Decalogue, taboos are implicit rather than explicit. There are two great taboos in modern America. The first is the critical, rational, scientific analysis of religion. The reason it is taboo is that it exposes the froth upon which religion is based, and this invokes the fury of fanatics, bigots, and irrational fideists, who are dedicated to telling people what to think, rather than how to think. Knowing this, we will be foolhardy and rush in where angels fear to tread.

Religion is as instinctive in man as nesting is in birds. It is found in all cultures and in all eras. Along with war, the leitmotifs of history are prayer and sacrifice to appease the angry gods, ceremony and prayer to wheedle special favors from the gods, and ceremony and prayer to thank the generous gods—usually for victory in war. At the moment of this writing, millions of Americans are not content to pray in their churches, homes, and the wide open spaces. They are demanding the Constitutional right to inject prayer in public schools.

What are the gods? They are the repositories of man's ignorance and the fountainheads of his hopes and aspirations. That which man cannot understand is assigned to the realm of religion; as he becomes enlightened, religion's dominion dwindles, and the scope of science expands. Fear is the mother of the gods, and man has always been beset by a myriad of fears, ranging from fear of natural disasters to fear of personal injury, sickness, and death. In the words of Philosopher George Santayana, "The gods are demonstrable only as hypotheses, but as hypotheses they are not gods."

When a person known to be dead appeared in the dreams of primitive man, he was terrified. He thought it was the return of the dead person's spirit. In attempts to forestall the return of the dead to haunt or curse him, he devised tricks such as rushing the corpse out of a hole in the wall rather than through the doorway, and running around the dwelling several times with the body so as to confuse the spirit of the cadaver and make it difficult for the ghost to find its way back to haunt the dwelling. These stratagems to outwit spirits were among the greatest achievements of human intelligence for hundreds of thousands of years.

The ancient Greeks placed a coin in the sarcophagus to provide the corpse with fare to ferry his soul to Hades across the river Styx. Some Welsh tribes buried their dead upright to make it easier for their souls to ascend into heaven. Vikings buried their dead with weapons so that they could continue their favorite sport of fighting in Valhalla. Until 1823, the English buried suicides at crossroads with stakes through their hearts. The stake was supposed to anchor the soul in one spot, but if the spirit broke loose anyway, the crossroads were supposed to confuse it and make it less likely for the ghost to return and haunt the living.

Primitive man imagined that numerous spirits were lurking in the world about him. These spirits were his gods. He had his wind god, mountain god, ocean god, moon god, sun god, and every planet was a god or goddess. He could not conceive of inanimate objects moving without a conscious force making them move in the manner he, himself, either moved or caused other objects to move. All gods were naturally anthropomorphic. They were figments of his imagination. During the 4.5 billion years before the emergence of man on Earth, there were no gods, nor was there any need for gods. Because of the importance of the Sun to man, it usually became a major god. The ancient Greeks knew the Sun god as Helios, and the Romans knew this god as Sol. We still honor the Sun god by naming the best day in the week SUNDAY. The halo around the heads of Christian saints is a relic of Sun-worship.

North American Indians believed that even trees have souls, and when the white man cut them down, they thought they had lost the protection of these spirits. They blamed deforestation for their defeats in wars with the white man. Some primitive people prohibited any noise near a tree in blossom because the tree was considered pregnant, and it could drop its fruit before its time like a pregnant woman. In some societies, people had sexual intercourse in the planted fields so as to encourage the spirits to respond in kind and produce fertile crops. Sex was worshiped in various ways from fertility cults to the worship of Priapus who was a small Greek god with a huge phallus. Snakes were worshiped as a phallic symbol. The biblical serpent symbolizes the evil aspects of sex and its temptations. Phallic worship is one of the oldest and most universal of religious practices. The ancient Greeks had their Orphic and Dionysian cults. The Romans had their cult of Cybele and Attis. The American Indians had their phallic buffalo dance.

The quality of human reason can be best appreciated by observing its contributions to religion. One such contribution was the "ingenious" method of transmitting messages to the spirits of the dead. When a tribal chief or a king wanted to send a message to a dead relative, he simply read it to a slave and then chopped off his head. The spirit of the dead slave was expected to deliver the message personally. If the chief forgot to say something in the original message, he simply sent a postscript via another slave, who was read the postscript and then summarily dispatched to the next life in the interests of expeditious delivery service. Resourceful kings arranged to kill their slaves and servants at or about the time of their own deaths so that they could serve them uninterruptedly in the next world. Scores of wives, slaves, and horses were buried alive with the corpse of ancient Scythian kings (Darius, for example) so that they could serve their masters in the afterlife.

Many religions taught that every enemy slain by the faithful in a Holy War would be their servant in the afterlife. Therefore, that "noble and most sovereign reason" concluded that it was logical to maximize human slaughter. In other religions, people feared that the slaughtered enemy might return to haunt them. Reasoning from this premise, the Bantu shaved their heads and painted them with goat dung to discourage the slain enemy spirits from approaching them.

Nearly every animal, from the Egyptian scarab to the Hindu elephant, has been worshiped as a god. Unfortunately, one man's god is another man's devil. Snakes are gods in eastern Mysore, and temples have been erected in their honor. Hebrews looked upon snakes as devils, one of which tempted Eve. The Moslems, like the Jews, have a taboo on eating pork, but they eat beef. To many Hindus, the cow is sacred: it is the mother of life and akin to the Christian Mary, mother of God, and its urine is a sacred wine that cleanses the soul. The killing and eating of cows is a sacrilege and an unutterable defilement according to many Hindus.

Those religious beliefs laid the groundwork for disaster in India. Hundreds of "cow riots" arose in which many people died because Moslems desecrated their sacred cows. Mohandas Gandhi wanted a total ban on the killing of cows. The Indian Constitution included a bill of rights for cows. In 1966, a mob of one hundred twenty thousand Hindus, led by naked holy men, smeared themselves with cow dung ash and then demonstrated and rioted in front of the Indian House of Parliament. Many people were killed and injured. The sacred status of the cow was a factor in the partition of India into Hindu and Moslem countries.

Human sacrifice to the gods has been a ritual in nearly every society. The Hebrews practiced it religiously. Exodus 22:29-30, reads, "Thou shalt give the firstborn of thy sons to me. Thou shaft do the same with the firstborn of thy oxen also and sheep." The Canaanites sacrificed children to Moloch. The Carthaginians sacrificed children to Baal. Human sacrifice has been practiced in modern times in Rhodesia and India. The Indian Express reported at least eleven ritual murders in India during 1980. A twelve-year-old boy was sacrificed in Rajasthan to insure the success of a canal about to be dug. The throats of three children were slashed by a Hindu mystic, and their blood was offered to the goddess during a full Moon to provide the swamis with supernatural powers. The Indian Express wrote, "There are people who still believe that blood from a newborn baby will please the goddess and cure infertility in women."

According to Aztec religion, the Sun came into existence when the gods gathered in the twilight, and one of the gods threw himself into a huge brazier as a sacrifice. He arose from the furnace transformed into the Sun, but the Sun could not move through the heavens until other gods sacrificed their blood to give it life. Nothing could move without life. The Sun, born of blood and sacrifice, had to be vitalized by blood and sacrifice. Twenty thousand human beings were slaughtered and sacrificed to the gods every year to insure the morning sunrise. The priests stretched the human sacrificial victim out on a sacrificial stone atop the Hill of the Stars. A priest plunged the sacred knife into the victim's chest and twirled the sacred firestick in the wound. The heart was ripped out of each body with a skillful twist of the holy knife, and offered to the gods.

The observed fact that the Sun did rise each morning after the sacrifices were performed was proof that the human sacrifices worked, and it was a mandate for their continuation. If the Sun appeared not to rise, or to die as in an eclipse of the Sun, human sacrifices were hurriedly increased. With the restoration of the Sun, the Aztecs had positive proof of the effectiveness of human sacrifices. If the Aztecs had been blessed with the brains of monkeys, they would not have behaved so stupidly.

The Aztecs sacrificed children to the rain god by drowning them. There was a special sacrifice to the god of spring: the sacrificial victims were peppered by a shower of arrows, whereupon their spouting blood rained upon the earth. They were then skinned, and their skins were dyed yellow. The priests wore the human skins as a symbol for the change in the Earth's vegetation mantle in the dry season. The goddess of young maize was appeased by bestowing a young maiden with the honorary title of a goddess for an hour or two. The honorary goddess was escorted to the temple by a throng of singing and dancing worshippers. The ceremony was culminated when the officiating priest lopped off her head with the ceremonial knife. Children were thrown into fire and burned alive in devotion to the god of fire. The victims usually died proudly as for the call of duty to God and country. They died happily in the "knowledge" that their sacrifices made it possible for the world to survive.

The wives of Fijian chiefs accepted death by strangulation as a sacred duty upon the deaths of their husbands. One day, a European with humanitarian sentiments rescued a widow from ritual execution, but she fled her rescuer that very night, swam across the river, and presented herself to her people insisting upon the completion of the sacrifice which she had in a moment of weakness reluctantly consented to forego. Another rescued widow heaped abuse on her rescuer, and, thereafter, "manifested the most deadly hatred towards him."

There is a cult in India which worships the goddess of fertility Bahuchar Amata by ritual emasculation. The voluntary members are called hijras. They are all male, and there are an estimated one hundred thousand of them in India. The mutilation rite calls for bathing the candidate in scented oil and covering him with garlands as he sits in a chair; other hijras sing and dance around him in the nude; and when the frenzy reaches a crescendo, the priest amputates the neophyte's sex organs with a swipe of a razor as he is held down. The hijras are supposed to possess holy powers. They earn money by giving blessings at births and weddings.

Emasculation is an ancient religious rite. It was self-performed in the worship of Cybele in many areas of the Mediterranean. Even the New Testament honored the rite. Matthew 19:12, reads, "And there are eunuchs who have made themselves so for the sake of the kingdom of heaven. Let him accept it who can." In the festival of the Syrian Astarte at Hierapolis, wailing women, clamorous flutes, and drums created a cacophonic maelstrom while eunuch priests danced wildly as they slashed themselves with knives. Spectators became engulfed in the frenzy, flung off their clothing, emasculated themselves, and swore eternal service to the goddess.

The Skoptsi sect believed that Christ was a eunuch who had originally taught the doctrine of castration. They believed that the New Testament was falsified in later centuries. To them, "baptism of fire" meant castration. Their forerunners, the Valerians, not only castrated their own members but anyone they could find. Some years, they castrated up to seven hundred victims. They believed they were doing God's will by excising the sinful sex organs. The Skoptsi expanded their doctrine to include the sexual parts of women, which also had to be excised for the greater glory of God.

The modern world is equally replete with bizarre religious behavior. In the Indian village of Deshnoke, there is a Hindu temple where several thousand rats are fed and worshipped. The reason they are worshipped is that they are believed to be the reincarnations of the villagers' families and friends. According to the head priest, "These rats are proof that our life will go on. They are proof that the miracles of Shri Karni Mata are continuing today." Mata is a Hindu goddess who promised to be reincarnated as a rat. The worshippers kneel in front of an altar with their heads contacting the floor while rats lick at their hands and heads. Food and money are offered to the sacred rats. The stench is overwhelming, but the worshippers haven't minded it for four hundred years. Whoever designated man "*Homo sapiens*" had better rethink his position.

Reincarnation is a commonly held religious concept in the world. Fijians believe that if they misbehave, they will be reborn as animals. Some American Indians think reincarnation proceeds in progressive stages, from rocks, vegetables, fish, birds, mammals, and finally, to humans. Australian aborigines believe they will be reborn as white people. One of them who was about to be executed shouted with joy, "Very good! Me jump up white fellow!" The Tibetans read the *Tibetan Book of the Dead* to the corpse to instruct it on the mysteries of reincarnation, and as an aid to its return to Earth in a new life.

The Brahman priests devised a curious way of punishing the Rajput kings for taxing them. The priests stabbed themselves to death in the presence of the kings. There was no greater or more terrifying curse than the curse of a dying priest. The priests complied with Brahman law requiring aspiring suicides to fast for three days prior to suicide. An unsuccessful suicide attempt required severe penances from the bungling priests. The laws of Akbar allowed anyone to sacrifice himself to the gods. Some made the sacrifice by allowing themselves to he eaten alive by crocodiles, and others covered themselves with cow dung and immolated themselves.

The English word "thug" comes from the Hindu religious sect of murderers and robbers called "Thugs" (literally, 'cheats'). They disguised themselves as religious mendicants or merchants and ingratiated themselves to wealthy travelers. They awaited the opportunity to strangle their victims with a sacred scarf, as a sacrifice to the goddess Kali, and then rob them. The loot was divided with local officials. Thugs originated in the thirteenth century and were active until the mid-nineteenth century, when the British repressed them by means of mass executions.

Cannibalism and headhunting can be found in the early history of every human culture, and it was almost always a religious service. Evidence for it in the form of cranial mutations dates back over a million years to the time of *Homo erectus*. Similar mutations are made by modern headhunters of Borneo and New Guinea. The brains of the deceased are extracted from the skulls, often by sucking them out through the nose of the corpse or roof of the mouth, and ceremonially eaten by the sons so they can acquire their fathers' wisdom. June 16, 1980, *Time* magazine reported a New Guinea tribe being threatened with extinction because of a nerve disease transmitted by eating human flesh and organs.

The purpose of cannibalism is to preserve the spirit of dead relatives in a kind of immortality. It "enables" the cannibal to absorb magical powers from the dead. One uncommonly intelligent cannibal stated his position in convincing terms by asking the rhetorical question, "When you die wouldn't you rather be eaten by your own kinsmen than by worms and maggots?" Putting it that way, perhaps we should all reconsider our modern prejudices against cannibalism.

Cannibalism is so pervasive to human experience that symbolic cannibalism is practiced by millions upon millions of people in Europe and the Americas this very day. Roman Catholics perform the cannibalistic ceremony of Holy Communion, and Catholic priests perform the ancient cannibalistic ritual of the Holy Sacrifice of the Mass. Thomas Jefferson alluded to "cannibal priests." He was thinking of Catholics who believe that they actually eat the body of Christ in Holy Communion. Catholic priests believe they actually drink the blood of Christ. If they did not believe it, they would be excommunicated because it is essential to the official dogma of the Church. The substance of bread and wine are supposed to be changed into the substance of the body and blood of Christ by the miracle of Transubstantiation during the ritual of the Holy Mass. Dogma decrees that only the appearance and taste of bread and wine remain, but that this is an illusion. There is ample Biblical justification for the dogma: Matthew 26; Mark 14; Luke 22:1; and 1 Corinthians 11.

There has been no fundamental change in the human animal in the million or two years he has inhabited the Earth as the genus *Homo*. Ancient man ate his tribal leaders (and gods) so that he could assimilate their noble or divine attributes, just as he ate the hearts of lions to obtain the courage of lions. Modern man ceremonially eats his God to assimilate divine grace. Holy Communion is symbolic cannibalism to the outside observer but ACTUAL CANNIBAL-ISM to the faithful. Ancient absurdities are transmogrified into modern sophisticated absurdities.

From the most ancient of times, man thought it necessary to appease the wrath of his gods in order to avert natural disasters, sickness, death, and to gain military victory. The most primitive form of appeasement was human sacrifice. Millions of human beings, including children, virgins, and holy men, were slaughtered to placate the gods. The same basic belief that human sacrifice is necessary to appease the gods persists to this very day. It results from the fact that man is a bloodthirsty predator. Millions upon millions of Americans, as well as people throughout the world, believe that Christ, the son of God, died as a human sacrifice to appease the wrath of God the Father, just as sons had always been sacrificed to the gods. Instead of sacrificing millions of human sons by slitting their throats or ripping out their hearts upon the altar of the gods, ONE SON, Jesus Christ, substitutes for the mass slaughter in a single suffering and death.

Christianity is a sophistication and refinement of a very primitive belief. The basics are identical, whether ten thousand years ago or today. The concept of one God, or Three Divine Persons in one God (a mystical merger of many gods into one), is a consolidation of the gods of ancient superstitions. If the belief in many gods, such as the rain god, the fertility god, the Sun god, *et cetera* is puerile, the belief in the merger of these gods into one God does not become less puerile: only more streamlined.

At least it must be said that ritual cannibalism as practiced by Catholics and Anglicans is humane. The real thing can be very brutal. Jaggar, a Methodist missionary of the nineteenth century, described cannibalism as practiced in Fiji. The victims were forced to dig a hole to make an earthen oven, and then they had to cut the firewood needed for the roasting of their own bodies. They were required to bathe, and then make banana leaf cups which were filled with their own blood. The victims watched the cannibals drink their blood. Next, the victims' arms and legs were hacked off and roasted. Some of the meat was offered to the limbless victims. Fish hooks were then put in their tongues. They were pulled out as far as possible, cut off, roasted and eaten while the cannibals taunted, "We are eating your tongues. We are eating your tongues." The victims were then split open, and their guts scooped out. Sometimes, the human meat was sold in the meat markets along with the meat of animals. Symbolic cannibalism removes the brutal aspects from the ancient religious practice of cannibalism.

There are common denominators to all religions because they are all responses to the same basic human instincts and needs, just as there are common denominators to all human behavior all over the world and in all periods of history. All nations have had the same history of conquering their territory from previous owners with the approbation of their gods. All nations create myths to justify their murderous ventures, as typified by Americans, who conquered the aboriginal Indians, the English, the Mexicans, the Spanish, and African tribesmen for slaves, and promptly created the myth of being a peace-loving, justice-seeking nation of God-fearing saints. It was the same with the ancient Hebrews, who tried to emulate the Egyptians, Persians, Assyrians, *et cetera* in building an empire. All peoples had, or attempted to have, an empire of plundered territory, whether they were Romans, English, Americans, Germans, Japanese, Negroes, or anyone else.

The ancient Hebrews were but another of history's hungry nomadic hordes besieging a settled community. Their god, Yahweh, commanded them to slaughter the victims of their aggressions and win plundered empire exactly like other ancient gods. Kings David and Solomon conquered a small empire, but it was short-lived. An Assyrian captain once taunted the besieged Hebrews with, "Our god Assur will prove stronger than your god Yahweh!" He was right. Assur, Ahura Mazda, Astarte, Shamash, Osiris, Mars, Allah, Christ, and many other gods proved stronger than Yahweh.

The Hebrews were the vanquished in the endless contests for empire in the Middle East more often than they were victors. However, they learned a great deal from the more advanced peoples who conquered them. When they were in Egyptian captivity, they acquired the concept of one god for the entire world from the fourteenth century B.C. pharaoh Iknaton, who originated a new religion which proclaimed ATEN the one and only true god. This idea did not survive in Egypt because it clashed with the rackets of the many priests whose existence and wealth were dependent upon the existence of MANY gods.

While in Babylonian captivity, the Hebrew prophets received their inspiration from Babylonian legends which now appear in the Bible as the inspired Word of God. The Babylonian legends were accepted as the word of the Babylonian gods by the Babylonians, but they have now been relegated to the realm of mythology because there are not enough believers around to defend them as eternal truths. One religion's eternal truths is another religion's mythology. Infidel Christians look upon ancient Greek religion as Greek mythology. Unbiased, educated people with a scientific orientation rather than a religious orientation look upon Christian religion as Christian mythology.

The story of Noah and the Flood was inspired by the Babylonian legend that the gods became dissatisfied with the humans they created and decided to destroy them with a deluge. But as they sent the raging, destructive flood, they suddenly realized that if they destroyed all mankind, there would be no one to offer them prayers, sacrifices, and libations. This would devastate their egos—an unthinkable calamity for a god. The gods wept bitterly over their rashness. Ea, the god of wisdom, decided to save one man, Shamash-napishtim, and his wife. Shamash-napishtim built an ark which became perched on Mount Nisir when the flood subsided. He sent out a reconnoitering dove. Shamash-napishtim sacrificed to the gods in gratitude, and the gods were delighted. Flattery is the lifeblood of the gods.

Babylonian legends also inspired the Biblical story of creation. The Bible says, "The earth was void and empty, and darkness was upon the face of the deep." The older Babylonian legend says, "In the time when nothing which was called heaven existed above, and when nothing below had yet received the name earth." The Biblical story of Lucifer revolting against God and fighting against Archangel Michael was inspired by the Babylonian legend of the goddess Tiamat revolting against all the other gods; but the god Marduk vanquished Tiamat by throwing a spear into her enlarged belly, after he had created a typhoon in her mouth when she opened it to devour him. The Virgin Mary has her counterpart in the Babylonian goddess Ishtar, who was referred to as "The Virgin Mother," and "The Holy Virgin." It is certainly true that the Hebrew prophets were inspired, but they were inspired by the legends of their more advanced captors, not by God.

The repeated defeats of the Hebrews gave birth to the dream of a Messiah—A MILITARY MESSIAH. They dreamed of the coming of a military prince like David to destroy enemy nations in a holocaust of clashing armies and falling cities. It was this Prince of War whom Christians converted into a Prince of Peace and spiritual Saviour. The Hebrews expected Yahweh to reward them for their long sufferings and many defeats with complete victory. Jeremiah promised that the avenging sword will be made drunk with enemy blood, and "all the inhabitants . . . shall howl." Ammon will become "a desolate heap, and her daughters shall be burned in fire." The Book of Daniel prophesied a military-messianic redemption and a great Jewish empire.

Jesus spent most of his life in an era of fierce guerrilla uprisings. The crucifixion of Jesus was a Roman attempt to destroy the military-messianic consciousness of Jewish revolutionaries. It certainly succeeded because the Jewish heresy was transformed into Gentile Christianity. There were many Jewish military claimants to the title of the Messiah, some of whom persuaded the Jews to attack the invincible power of Rome. In A.D. 132, Bar Kochba (Son of a Star) organized a Jewish state with a force of two hundred thousand men, but it was routed by Roman military might after three years. A thousand villages were destroyed, a half million people were killed, and thousands were sold into slavery. Bar Kochba was then denounced as a "Son of a Lie." For somewhat similar reasons, Jesus Christ had been repudiated by His countrymen. Jews had good reason to reject him.

Moses of Crete was another of the many claimants to the title of Messiah. He promised his followers that he would lead them to the Promised Land by smiting the waters with his staff, whereupon the waters were supposed to part, as legend had it that the Red Sea had parted for Moses and allowed the Jews to walk victoriously to the Promised Land. Moses of Crete and his faithful followers boldly leaped into the Mediterranean from a promontory. Everything went wrong. The waters did not part. All who could not swim drowned, including the Messiah, Moses of Crete, himself. Jews continued to await the coming of the Messiah as Christians await the Second Coming of Christ and Judgment Day. They will await the Coming in joyous hope while they are alive. When they are dead, it will no longer matter.

In Matthew 10:34, we read, "Do not think that I have come to send peace upon the earth; I have come to bring a sword, not peace." In Luke 12:51 we read, "Do you think that I came to give peace upon the earth? No, I tell you, but division." Luke 22:36 reads, "Let him who has no sword sell his tunic and buy one." John 2:15 says, "And making a kind of whip of cords, he drove them all out of the temple." These quotations do not depict a Prince of Peace, especially when we realize that the Jewish Messiah was expected to be a politico-military figure who would reunite the twelve tribes of Israel into an empire by military conquest. The Jews were chiefly interested in a glorious kingdom on Earth. The Kingdom of Heaven in the skies was a kingdom of last resort. The Christian spiritual Messiah and Prince of Peace was an invention of Saint Paul and the Evangelists.

Christ had only a small following at his crucifixion because it was evident to his one-time disciples that only a phony Messiah would allow himself to be crucified. The two "thieves" crucified on either side of Him were two fellow insurrectionists. Saint Paul created a cult of peaceful messianism. The image of Jesus as a peaceful Messiah was not established until after Rome destroyed Jerusalem. Having forfeited any status as a Jewish Messiah by His utter failure to free the Jews from Roman domination, he became the peaceful Gentile Messiah. The mundane Kingdom ascended into Heaven and became the Kingdom of Righteousness. Having convinced Rome that their

Messiah was a harmless pacifist and no threat to the Roman Empire, Christians were grudgingly tolerated. They were persecuted for refusing to give the Emperor divine homage.

Julius Caesar was the first Roman to claim the honors of a god. He traced his ancestry to the goddess Venus. Thereafter, emperor-worship became a continuing religious phenomenon in the Roman Empire. Japan practiced emperor-worship until World War IL The Japanese Emperor traced his ancestry to the Sun goddess. Japanese regularly prayed all day on their hands and knees outside the palace gates. In bitter cold winter, when foreign visitors shivered by the palace gates, they were told to remove their overcoats because they were "in the presence of the Sun."

The Roman persecution of the Christians was relatively subdued—certainly not a persecution of extermination. If Jesus had remained a traditional Messiah like Bar Kochba, his sect would have been equally annihilated. Saint Paul's Christian pacifism changed into Christian militarism after Constantine became a Christian in A.D. 312, following his victory at Mulvian Bridge when his soldiers placed the Christian cross on their shields. After this victory, the cross of the peaceful Messiah became the banner of military conquest and the banner of the Roman Empire. Christianity had come full circle. The contradictions remain to this day. Christians talk peace out of one side of their mouths, and war out of the other side. Millions upon millions of Christians perished in Christian wars of conquest, Christian wars of liberation, and Christian religious wars.

The concept of a messiah is as old as history. It reflects a universal psychological need even as religion, itself, reflects a deep psychological need. Buddhists, Zoroastrians, and Confucians believe in the redemption of mankind by the coming of a saviour-king or Holy One. The American Indian prophets in the eighteenth and nineteenth centuries foretold the regeneration of the red man and the recapture of their lands from the white man, provided their people followed prescribed religious practices. The similarity to the Hebrew prophets is astounding. But all human behavior is mechanized by the same basic instincts. Consequently, it follows a common, predetermined pattern. Only the fine details differ.

Nowhere is the profound absurdity and stupidity of the human race more evident than in the field of religion. The nonsense that grown, adult human beings accept as gospel truth should make a child blush with shame. The Dalai Lama's disciples, for example, kept him in wealth buying medicinal pills made from his excrement. What is even more remarkable, students of history read about the various incredible religious beliefs of man without batting an eye. They never ask the simple question of how can creatures who claim to have the power of reason be so utterly and completely stupid? Only an absurd creature can be oblivious to the glaring absurdities of religious belief. Either people are incapable of recognizing nonsense for what it is, or they cannot admit to it because they belong to the same species of animal, and it puts them, too, in the same category of a ludicrous, comic creature which is distinguished from all other animals not for intelligence but for stupidity. Man is, indeed, unique. No other creature is so insanely ludicrous or viciously destructive.

For hundreds of thousands of years, if not for millions, the human genus, *Homo*, dealt with the world of nature in the belief that he could manipulate it by magic, ceremony, prayer, and petitions to the gods. Nature was thought to be animated by beings similar to himself. These beings were anthropomorphic spirits he called gods. Eventually, the gods were consolidated into one Super God. When ancient man planted seeds, he employed ceremony, magic, and prayer to induce the gods to give him good crops. After many thousands of years, a very small minority of the more intelligent human beings discovered that chemical fertilizers, crop rotation, and other scientific agricultural methods could succeed where the gods, and even Super God, had failed.

It required eons of failure under the hypothesis that nature is governed by gods or God before one out of billions of the human species would speculate that perhaps, just perhaps, he was barking up the wrong tree, and had better try another hypothesis. This rare freak among billions of dimwits was finally able to develop a science which could achieve success in an instant where prayer sustained failure for a million years or more. But a million years of ludicrous failures do not deter the faithful. They have unwavering and abiding faith. In a word, nothing can shake them loose from the shackles of ignorance. In the words of Hegel, "What experience and history teach is this: that people and governments never have learned anything from history."

In the pious days of my pristine youth when we had droughts in California, my parish priest always read a special prayer for rain at the end of Mass. Yes, the Dark Ages cast their shadows of ignorance on our modern age of science. The faithful have been praying for rain in the Lima, Peru, area for hundreds of years, but it never came. Why should it? The millions of people who died from the Black Plague were not cured by prayer. Only penicillin or a similar antibiotic affected the cure. The prayers of ephemeral pismires, wise only in their own conceits, are not likely to alter the dynamics of the Cosmos. How can anyone have the effrontery to call man an intelligent animal when even a million and more years of religious failures and instant scientific success cannot shake him from his dogmatic paralysis? He is obviously a stupid creature of blind religious instinct—not a creature of intelligence.

Human beings have always been extremely slow to learn. For a million or more years, they roamed the face of Earth engaging in their most popular sport of slaughtering their fellow animals, and each other, before a rare freak, a person of uncommon genius, discovered that transportation could be improved by simply jumping on the back of a horse, camel, or other beast of burden. It required even more centuries before another genius chanced to appear on Earth who got the bright idea that it is much more effective to have oxen pull plows than to have human beings pull them. After a few thousand additional years, another unlikely genius came along who made the remarkable discovery that a collar placed on the driven animal would place the strain on its shoulders rather than on its neck, and not strangle the poor creature to death.

The collar is acclaimed as one of the great discoveries of man, and rightly so. It is surprising that he ever made the discovery. Actually, MAN DID NOT DISCOVER IT. The freakish ONE-IN-MILLIONS genius discovered it, and others copied like apes. The average man could discover nothing. He was bogged down in ancient superstitions and confronted nature at an intellectual level lower than the lowest ape. Man, *Homo*, was on earth 2 million years before he could invent or discover the simple wheel. The ancient Egyptians, for all their ability to build pyramids with slave labor, did not have the simple intelligence to move their heavy stones with wheels, even though the wheel was used by the peoples surrounding them. They had to drag their heavy weights.

Natural disasters were always thought to be God's punishments of wayward man. In Hawaii, the Polynesians prayed to Pele, the goddess of the volcano, to appease her anger and prevent eruptions. The Greeks prayed to Zeus for good weather and fertility and to forestall thunderbolt attacks. The Romans sought protection by giving homage and sacrifice to Jupiter. The Hebrews feared the vengeance of Yahweh. In Genesis 6:12-13 we read, "And when God had seen that the earth was corrupted, he said to Noah: The end of all flesh is come to me, the earth is filled with iniquity through them, and I will destroy them with the earth." Because all mankind is subject to the same basic instincts, the same emotions of anger and desire for revenge, it is natural that all peoples created similar gods with similar attributes.

Disease was always thought to be caused by evil spirits taking possession of the human body and by punishment from God. During the eleventh, twelfth, and thirteenth centuries, decimating plagues were carried to Europe by the Crusaders. Epidemics wiped out populations by the hundreds of thousands, even millions. The dying populations prayed for divine relief. The bishops and priests prayed. The Pope prayed. But the more they prayed, the more they died. Black Death and plagues ravaged most of Europe during the sixteenth and seventeenth centuries. Priests offered Holy Sacrifices of the Mass, benedictions, novenas, prayers, rituals, and every ceremony human intelligence could devise, but God was not impressed. The plagues and Black Death raged on. Epidemics and pandemics were eventually conquered NOT BY GODS OR BY PRAYER, but by a rare, gifted 56/100 of 1 percent of human freaks, who developed medical science in face of brutal Church opposition.

Religion and science are natural enemies because religion is based on blind faith in the dogmatic pronouncements of pretenders to truth, whereas science is based on the critical analysis of nature and the experimental method of ferreting out truth. Science is as destructive to religion as light is to darkness. Therefore, religion, in its struggle for survival, must combat science not by knowledge but by fanaticism, ignorance, and superstition. The Church naturally dealt harshly with men of science when it was in a position of strength. Michael Servetus, whom Victor Robinson, in *Pathfinders in Medicine*, describes as "the greatest man of his age. His brain was the torch that burned to enlighten the world . . . the discoverer of the pulmonic circulation of the blood," was bound to the stake by iron chains with the book "that should have made an epoch" bound to his side. Flames were made to burn him to an agonizing, shrieking death by order of the Church. Why? For heresy! He was a devout believer in God, but he rejected the dogma of the Trinity.

The Church inflicted torture and death on men of learning and science, in order to preserve religious ignorance, just as Communist countries today inflict punishments on political heretics. Men of science never tortured or executed men of religion because tolerance and inquiry are the essence of science—intolerance and dogmatism are the essence of religion. French scholar Étienne Dolet was burned at the stake in A.D. 1546. In 1619, philosopher Lucilio Vanini, in the words of Robinson, "was condemned to have his tongue cut out, to be strangled at the stake, and then burnt to ashes—and not a jot of this sentence was abated by the gentle lambs of organized theology." In 1600, Bernard Palissy was burned at the stake for the heresy of asserting that fossils were once living animals. Philosopher, astronomer, and mathematician Giordano Bruno was burned at the stake by order of the Church in 1600 for the heresy of seeking truth through individual inquiry.

When the Church was in the saddle, it persecuted science as heresy. It thought it was doing God's work and it was saving souls. It imprisoned, tortured, and burned scientists at the stake. Today, after centuries of trying to eradicate science, and from a position of relative weakness, the Church has the audacity to insist there is no conflict between religion and science. No other animal tortures and slaughters its brothers and sisters in the name of God, Truth, and Goodness; but no other animal possesses man's cerebral organ of infinite stupidity.

The great scientist Galileo was convicted of heresy in A.D. 1633 for advancing the theory that the Earth revolves around the Sun rather than vice versa. He managed to save his life by denying what every schoolchild now knows is true. Galileo advanced the cause of truth; the Church advanced the cause of ignorance and superstition. In his pathetic pleas to save his life, he said, "I am not of this opinion, and have not been of the opinion of Copernicus (Earth revolves about the Sun) since I was ordered to abandon it. Besides, I am in your hands. You may do as you please."

During the million or more years before the advent of medical science, witch doctors and priests "cured" sickness and disease. The usual method was the exorcism of devils and demons. It was accomplished by magic, witchcraft, and sorcery. The New Testament makes many references to Christ's ability to cast out devils. Two such references are: Matthew 12:28, when after denying that he casts out devils by the power of Beelzebub, Christ argues that he does it by the power of God: "But if I cast out devils by the Spirit of God, then the Kingdom of God has come upon you." In Act of the Apostles 19:15-16, after explaining that exorcism must be performed in the name of Jesus, it reads, "The evil spirit answered them and said to them, 'Jesus I acknowledge, and Paul I know, but who are you?' and the man in whom the evil spirit was sprang at them and overpowered them both with such violence that they fled from the house tattered and bruised."

The Roman Catholic Church even today believes in devils and exorcism. Each May 1, in the Harz mountains of Germany, witches and demons are exorcised from the town through the use of holy water, incense, and loud noises. The basic primitive, superstitious nature of man has never changed. Ignorance merely changes its raiments.

Incredibly, in this modern age of medical science, people readily and eagerly believe in evil spirits and exorcism. A few years ago, William Peter Blatty wrote a novel called *The Exorcist*. The heroine,

Regan, was supposed to be a victim of demonic possession. She was exorcised of the demon by Catholic priests. Father Karras sprinkled the patient with holy water and followed the Roman Ritual, while Father Merrin recited prayer. The novel was a bestseller, and the movie was a smash hit. Millions of people believe that the little girl, Regan, was really possessed by a demon and that the only appropriate treatment was exorcism.

The primitive belief that sickness is caused by evil spirits is as readily believed today as it was at any time in the dim past of abysmal ignorance. Exorcism is still the therapy of choice in many backward countries. The fact is that Regan was not possessed by a demon, and she did not require a priest or a witch doctor. She needed a medical doctor because she suffered from Gilles de la Tourette's syndrome. The recommended treatment according to the *Merck Manual* is 2 mg/day of haloperidol taken orally and increased to 50 or 100 mg/day. Only in a novel could the priests have effected a cure for Gilles de la Tourette's syndrome. In the world of the real, the priests would have been no more effective with their prayers and ceremonies than they were during the Dark Ages, when they combatted Black Death with prayer, and yet at least one third of the world's population was wiped out, half of the population of England perished, and Europe was decimated anyway.

British clergyman Dr. Donald Omand is one of England's most famous current exorcists. He performs exorcisms on highways, danger spots where motorists lose control of their cars. He says that he has "exorcised roads all over the world, and evidence shows that many of them have remained accident-free." A leading American newspaper credits his ancient ritual with "stunning success" in banishing evil spirits from dangerous stretches of highways. Second exorcisms have been so effective that "there have been no accidents on the spot." These are not quotations from 2,000 B.C. They are quotations from today's newspapers.

Why do human ignorance, stupidity, and ferocity persist even in modern times? Voltaire suggested an answer in his eighteenth century novel *Candide*:

> *"Do you believe,"* said Candide, *"That men have always massacred one another as they do today, that they have always been liars, cheats, traitors, ingrates, brigands, idiots, thieves, scoundrels, gluttons, drunkards, misers, envious, ambitious, bloody-minded, calumniators, debauchees, fanatics, hypocrites, and fools?"*
>
> *"Do you believe,"* said Martin, *"That hawks have always eaten pigeons when they have found them?"*
>
> *"Without a doubt,"* said Candide.
>
> *"Well, then,"* said Martin, *"if hawks have always had the same character, why should you imagine that men have changed theirs?"*

Candide rebutted with the commonly believed myth that man is unique among all animals, and that he can detach himself from his nature by a magic wand which invokes free will. Hawks can never become pigeons, but man is free to become anything. But man, like hawks, is a product of his birth. The mechanical combination of two X chromosomes makes us female. One X and one Y chromosome make us male. A chance extra chromosome makes us mongoloid idiots. Slightly different mechanical combinations of chromosomes and genes make us apes, birds, or cockroaches, each with a mechanistically determined nature. Our genes program us like data on computer chips. The fortuitous concourse of an infinitude of improbable accidents culminated in our phylogenetic identity. Having been born as human beings only because of the dint of DNA strands in the double helix, why should we suppose that we are magically released from the control of DNA merely because of the illusion of experience? We are conscious of our desires and wants but unconscious of the mechanical, genetic determination of our desires and wants. Herein lies the plot of the human comedy.

The stupidity of man results from his biophysicochemical dependency. His mind is dependent upon his brain, and his brain is subject to chemistry rather than logic. He believes every conceivable absurdity because of the compulsion of his chemistry. Think of an absurdity! You can be certain that some man, somewhere, at some time believed it to be an eternal truth. Some people believe that the human nose was designed to bear spectacles; that pigs were created so than man can eat pork; that stars were created to beautify the firmament; that Communism is the solution to man's economic problems; that man was created to worship God; and that prayer has the power to suspend the laws of nature. Millions of people believed that the burning of heretics at the stake was a loving service to God. Mohammedans believed that killing infidel Christians was the will of Allah, and Christians believed that killing infidel Mohammedans was the will of their God of Love. Human stupidity is not a matter of choice. It is a matter of physics and chemistry.

There are no-win situations. The faithful put themselves in a no-lose situation. They pray for an event. If it occurs, they thank God. If it does not, they rationalize that the infinite wisdom of God determined that it is best for it NOT to occur. They appear incapable of realizing that if they prayed to bull manure, the exact same scenario would exist except that bull manure would join the endless liturgies of man-made gods. If this sounds silly, remember that cows, cow urine, and cow manure are sacred to Hindus.

Faith can lead to strange behavior. In A.D. 1823, Holy Margaret founded a religious sect at Wildisbuch, Switzerland. At her own behest, her followers tortured her and crucified her by driving iron nails through her arms, feet, and breasts, thus pinning her to the cross. She displayed ecstatic joy in the proceedings of her martyrdom. Her faithful followers fulfilled her final request by splitting her head open with an iron wedge. Her disciples were stunned to discover that Holy Margaret failed to rise from her death on the third day as per her prophesy. She did not resurrect on the third week, the third month, or the third year, and it is doubtful whether she will even rise from the dead in the third century or millennium.

Moses Botarel believed that he was the Messiah. He wanted to convince the King of Spain of his sincerity. At his own insistence, he was cast into a burning furnace. He promised that he would resurrect from the ashes like a phoenix. Such proof would certainly convince even the most hard-nosed skeptic. Unfortunately, the world is still awaiting his resurrection. In A.D. 1172, a self-professed Messiah was arrested and hauled before the King of Yemen who asked for proof that he was the Son of God. The Holy One unhesitantly replied, "Cut off my head, and I will return to life immediately." The king agreed that this test would constitute adequate proof and performed his part of the test. As of this writing, some eight hundred years later, the Messiah has still failed to comply with his part of the test.

Nearly every year, some cult somewhere determines from Biblical calculations or from "divine inspiration" that the end of the world is at hand. The members of the cult sell off their worldly possessions and await, with full confidence, the Second Coming of Christ at the appointed time and at the designated place. The Advent invariably fails to take place, and recalculations must always be made. However, the faith of the believers remains unwavering. Christ had said to Saint Thomas, "Because thou hast seen me Thomas, thou hast believed: Blessed are they that have not seen me, and have believed." Blind faith is virtue, and doubt is sin in religion. Doubt is virtue, and blind faith is sin in science. Blind faith keeps con men, bunko artists, and religious leaders well-heeled. It enables predatory seduction.

Cyrus Reed Teed announced his astronomical revelations in his book *The Cellular Cosmogony*. In it, he says that we live on the inner concave surface of an egg-like hollow shell, inside which are the Sun, Moon, planets, and stars. Outside the shell, there is absolutely nothing. The Earth seems convex, but it is an illusion of optics. Astronomers and geologists are correct except that they have everything inside-out. Teed used impeccable human logic to support his views. His truths came from an unassailable source, God, Himself. God spoke his truths in the Bible. What is not in the Bible is illusion. Isaiah 40:12 says that God "hath measured the waters in the HOLLOW of his hand." Hollow means concave. Consequently, Teed deduced and taught, "To know of the Earth's concavity . . . is to know God, while to believe in the Earth's convexity is to deny Him and all His works." He condemned all who did not accept his views as Antichrists.

In the 1890s, Teed, going by the name of Koresh (Hebrew for Cyrus), bought a tract of land near Fort Meyers, Florida, which he called "THE NEW JERUSALEM," and which he prophesied would become the capital of the world. In his book *The Immortal Manhood*, he taught that after his physical death, he would rise and take all his faithful followers into heaven with him. When he died in 1908, the true believers prepared for both his and their own ascension into heaven. They kept constant prayer vigil over his body; but as time went on, the stench, flies, and corruption from his decaying body forced the County Health Officer to order his burial. His disciples buried the badly decomposed body on Estero Island, but a 1921 hurricane pounded the island, and huge waves carried the tomb into an unknown, watery grave. Another holy man went the way of all flesh, and the animal world was given additional proof of its good fortune in being spared that organ of human stupidity, the human brain.

John Alexander Dowie, a Scottish faith healer, founded the Christian Apostolic Church in Zion, Illinois, in 1895. In 1905, Wilbur Glenn Voliva became the ruler of Zion, population six thousand. He was one of the many believers in the flat Earth theory who proceeded from the logical premise that the intellectual authority of God is greater than the intellectual authority of lowly, mortal man. God made it abundantly clear that the Earth is flat in His Biblical revelations. Voliva offered five thousand dollars to anyone who could prove to him that the Earth is round. He made several lecture trips around the Earth, but he believed that he merely traced a circle on the Earth's flat surface. He taught that the stars, Moon, and Sun are small bodies which revolve around the flat Earth, and that the Moon is self-luminous.

Voliva, appealing to common sense and reason, wrote, "The idea of a Sun millions of miles in diameter and 91 million miles away is silly. The Sun is only thirty-two miles across, and not more than three thousand miles from the earth. It stands to reason it must be so. God made the Sun to light the Earth, and therefore must have placed it close to the task it was designed to do. What would you think of a man who built a house in Zion and put the lamp to light it in Kenosha, Wisconsin?" Thus we see the paradigm of human reason in normal operation. We should now understand better how it had the potential to persuade five American presidents to preach the Vietnam Crusade.

Voliva claimed he could "whip to smithereens any man in the world in a mental battle." This is the tragedy of human reason. It can make absurd rubbish appear as logically sound as the most profound truth. In fact, 99 and 44/100 percent of humanity are incapable of recognizing logical fallacies such as *post hoc ergo propter hoc*, broad and hasty generalizations, emotional appeals, irrelevant evidence, *et cetera* which prompt man to accept absurd nonsense as immutable truth. In the words of logician Professor Roger Holmes, "It is just not human nature to think clearly." Hence, Voliva's disciples readily accepted his teachings and predictions that "God Almighty will smite them" (his 'Antichrist' opponents). He predicted the end of the world in 1923, 1927, 1930, and 1935. The fact that the end did not come did not detract from his disciples' faith in his infallibility. Faith and "reason" set man apart from all other animals: lower, not higher, that is.

Reason persuaded some theologians to conclude that the Earth cannot be spherical because people who live on the other side would be deprived of the sight of Christ when he descends from Heaven at his Second Coming. Besides, how could the Earth be round? People on the bottom side would fall off. Not only that, but if the Earth were rotating at the surface rate of one thousand miles per hour, we, and everything else would be flung out into space by centrifugal force. The same human brain that gave us concepts like Newton's Laws of Motion less than 56/100 of 1 percent of the time, gave us concepts like "the angry gods cause natural disasters and illnesses," 99 and 44/100 percent of the time.

When astronomers proved that the planets are large bodies, like the Earth, revolving around the Sun, theologians argued that they must contain life, otherwise "God would have wasted His energy if He had not populated them." Some even argued that extraterrestrial beings must exist on the Sun for the same reason. We now know there is little evidence of life on any of the solar system's planets. Orville and Wilbur Wright were criticized by the clergy because "if God wanted man to fly, He would have given him wings." Physicists "proved" with mathematical precision that heavier than air flight is impossible—before they were embarrassed by the Wright brothers.

Religious cults originate in the minds of men like autisms with the difference they are taken dead seriously. There are literally endless numbers of religious cults. One Russian sect preached the bliss of death through strangulation; another preached the bliss of being buried alive. Cultist Feodor Kowalew buried twenty-one of his followers alive, but he deprived himself of that bliss. Thousands of cultists voluntarily die in ritual fires. In Olonetz, three thousand died in the ritual of a village fire. A preacher by the name of Chadkin led his flock into a forest in 1917 to die by starvation for the glory of God. One member defected from the flock. Fearful that the defector would report him to the police, he massacred them all, a la the Jim Jones cult, except that Chadkin remained alive.

During 99 and 44/100 percent of historical time, the human brain rationalized incredibly stupid and cruel behavior such as the waging of religious wars, wars of extermination, Vietnam type wars; and the creation of religious cults, ridiculous laws, and absurd beliefs. Less than 56/100 of 1 percent of humanity had the intelligence to beget modern science and technology. At least 99 and 44/100 percent of historical time is consumed by man approaching nature from a religious reference and producing nothing but ignorance and superstition—FOR 2 MILLION YEARS, IN FACT. Only 56/100 of 1 percent of historical time shows man approaching nature from a scientific reference and producing the technology of the modern world in which 99 and 44/100 percent of the people are still steeped in superstition and ignorance not unlike that of ancient times. Some surveys indicate that 85 percent of Americans want prayer in public schools, but they seem unconcerned about science in public schools. They should try going to the moon, curing cancer, designing aircraft, producing TVs, computers, *et cetera* with prayer, a proven failure, vis-à-vis science, a proven success.

The intellectual caliber of modern America is clearly illustrated by its values and its heroes. A Neanderthal subhuman type whose only contribution to the human race is he can flip a basketball into a basket, or he can reproduce the music of 50,000 B.C., is entitled to the rewards of fame, glory, prestige, and a million to 50 million dollars a year income; but the intelligent scientist who bestows the world with the miracles of modern science and technology is rewarded with scant notice and a relative pittance. Space flight is ballyhooed, but the scientists who made it possible are unsung whiffets. Anthropoid missing links are glorified, memorialized, and enrichened like royalty. Einsteins are ignored, unknown, and unappreciated. Any self-respecting ape should resent any theory which links him with man.

Religious cult leaders range from ridiculous crackpots to scheming scoundrels. Perhaps Jim Jones was a bit of both, but faith in him by his followers was unflinching. He was addicted to drugs. He would force a child to eat his own vomit. He was both kind and fiendishly cruel. He milked the poor of everything they owned and became rich on his gullible disciples, but he also helped the poor. According to one disabused disciple, "The only difference between him and a gangster is that he used a *Bible* instead of a gun." His silver-tongued eloquence enabled him to mesmerize thousands and fleece them out of millions of dollars and, eventually, their own lives.

Jim Jones prohibited sexual activity between People's Temple members, but he, himself, engaged in bisexual behavior voraciously. He constantly bragged about the size of his penis and the number of his male and female conquests: up to fourteen women and two men, the same day. He said he detested homosexual activity but engaged in it only for the male Temple members' own good. He thought he was the reincarnation of Lenin and predicted he would die with a bullet in his body like Lenin. Nine hundred eleven people died in the People's Temple massacres and suicides, but this is a small fraction of the millions upon millions of people who have accepted crackpot credos and died for or with their crackpot leaders.

I was personally acquainted with "Father" W.E. Riker. He founded a cult in the Santa Cruz mountains during the pre-World War II era. He called his settlement Holy City. It was a tourist stop between San Jose and Santa Cruz on the old highway. He ran for governor of California one time and made the headlines with his twenty-five thousand dollar offer of reward to anyone who could find a flaw in his system of perfect government, which advocated white supremacy. His disciples considered him a prophet possessing supernatural powers. They believed they would live as long as Methuselah, or about one thousand years, on Father Riker's promise. Even though the prophet was getting crippled with age and infirmity, the faith of his disciples remained unshaken. They worked at the filling station, garage, and restaurant for nothing more than their basic necessities. The Great White Father controlled all finances. It was just another of the many absurd cults which passed away with its founder. Barnum was right. There's a believer born every minute.

The Hermanos Penitentes was a cult in New Mexico. It was a flagellant cult. Flagellation is a ritual as old as Christianity. Ceremonial whippings in rites of purification occurred among primitive peoples. About A.D. 1260, flagellants grew into large organized bodies throughout Europe. They marched from town to town, baring their backs in public, whipping each other and themselves as they exhorted the spectators to join them and repent. Flagellant orders were approved by the Church at first, but they were repressed when they were seen to impinge on the Church's sacramental monopoly.

Flagellant cults were revived at the time of the Black Death in A.D. 1348. The members thought that the plague was sent as divine punishment, and only by being penitent through whipping, beating, and mutilating each other could they save the human race from being destroyed. Only self-punishment, they thought, could placate the wrath of Almighty God. They gradually came to believe that flagellation was the ONLY way to salvation rather than the Sacrament of Penance as administered by the Church and priests. Obviously, if this belief caught on, it would put the Church out of business. Salvation was the principal service the Church was selling. No thriving business will sit still while competition destroys it. So, naturally, Pope Clement VI condemned flagellation, as did the Council of Constance. The flagellants were declared heretics and burned at the stake. The monopoly of the Church was restored once the flagellants saw the error of their ways after the application of the convincing logic of searing flames. There is no better way to eliminate competition than to eliminate the competitors. Ask any Mafia Godfather!

Christians considered choir singing to be an integral part of divine worship. The Christian God never tired of flattery and adulation in any form. Women were historically banned from choirs and from the stage. Men played the parts of women on the stage and sang in choirs in place of women. The substitution in the choir was achieved by castrating young male children before the age of puberty. They were known as the castrati. They developed powerful soprano or contralto voices due to their greater lung capacity and physical size. The sexual organs of a castrato-to-be were mutilated primarily to accommodate the church choir in the sixteenth century, but the castrati came in great demand for operas during the seventeenth and eighteenth centuries. Farinelli was the most famous of the castrati opera singers. He became wealthy as the official singer to Philip V of Spain. Most the the castrati were proud of their soporano voices and did not resent having been sexually mutilated, either for the glory of God, for the opera, or for money.

Taxas Maxim, the Shemenov peasant who founded the Russian religious sect called the Chisleniki, taught that "men must be saved from sin, but if they do not sin, they cannot be saved. Therefore, sin is the first step on the road to salvation." This sect taught that "in sin alone, real salvation of the soul can be found. The more you sin, the more glorious the merit of the Saviour becomes." Sin was the gateway to the glory of Heaven. It isn't difficult to guess that the cult members wallowed in crime and corruption. The reasoning behind the philosophy of this sect, like all reasoning, is as cogent as one's predilection to accept it. It is the same with any religious, political, economic, or moral belief. This is why both Hitler and Christ were heroes to some but rogues to others. To a hawk, the arguments of a dove are nonsense, and vice versa.

The Carpocratians were a second century A.D. sect of Gnostic heretics founded by Carpocrates of Alexandria. They believed man was once united with the Absolute, but became separated through corruption. Salvation was attainable only by having every possible experience both sinful and unsinful. No one could have all possible experience in one lifetime. Therefore, reincarnation was a logical necessity. They thought that matter is the realm of evil spirits, but their ability to communicate with demons made them superior to the material world.

The Lothardi sect believed that any person sanctified by faith is beyond evil. No crime or outrage committed by a true believer could soil his soul. The related Euchites made sexual orgies part of their religious ritual. The children born of these orgies were murdered. The drained blood and ashes from their burned bodies were mixed for a ceremonial concoction. They reasoned that the murder of the children broke the devil's seal in their souls and permitted them to consort freely with the evil spirits. The Bogomils ceremonially tossed the children born of sexual orgies from hand to hand until they died. The Multiplicant sect was devoted to sexual pleasures exclusively. The versatility and diversity of human debauchery and stupidity is flabbergasting.

The Devil Hunters of America sometimes beat children to death in the performance of their holy service of driving Satan from their young bodies. The Sect of the Holy Mother performed similar services in devotion to God. The Crusaders slaughtered Moslems and heretics in service to God. Some sectarians even kill themselves in the belief that God demands the supreme sacrifice from them. There is a seemingly endless array of Christian splinter groups, such as Anabaptists who believe that infant baptism is not authorized in Scripture and should be administered to believers only; and splinter groups from them, such as the Mennonites, Hutterian Brethren, Trembleurs, or Holy Rollers (they serve God by dancing and rolling down aisles), et cetera. It is incomprehensible that people who know history can speak of human beings and intelligence in the same breath.

Charles Taze Russell founded Jehovah's Witnesses. He promoted miracle wheat, which he sold for a small fortune. Judge Rutherford took over in 1916, when Russell died. This cult believes that only Jehovah's Witnesses will be saved, and it will be after the Battle of Armageddon in which the hordes of Satan, including Catholics and Protestants, will be defeated. Christ is not God. All human governments and civil authority are of the devil. Hence, they will salute no flag, refuse conscription into the armed forces, and will not vote. They refuse blood transfusions to save the lives of their own children. Court orders requiring the transfusions are necessary to usher them into the twentieth century and to save the lives of children.

There are endless religious sects, including Christian sects. The Copts are native Christians in Egypt who were not converted to Islam after the Mohammedan conquest. The patriarch of Alexandria is the titular head of this church. The Church of Ethiopia declared its independence of the Coptic Patriarch in 1961; reminiscent of Henry VIII declaring the Church of England independent of Rome in A.D. 1534; and the Greek Church becoming independent of the Roman Catholic Church in A.D. 1054. Diversity programmed into human nature makes revolts and differences inevitable in "inspired" religious matters as well as in prosaic secular matters. Time and space limitations don't permit us to even scratch the surface of this subject; suffice it to list but a few of the independent movements among Christians: the Roman Catholic Church, the Orthodox Eastern Church, the Armenian Church, Congregationalists, Methodists, Unitarians, Presbyterians, Baptists, *et cetera*, *et cetera*, all claiming a monopoly on truth and accusing all others of gross error.

We cannot leave this subject without at least summarizing a few of the other major Christian sects...

Joseph Smith founded the Mormon faith in 1830. He claimed that Jesus Christ and God the Father came to him in the flesh to reveal the TRUTH that all churches are in error. It is interesting to note that in his early revelations, as contained in *Doctrine and Covenants*, he warned against polygamy, but when it became known that he was married to at least twenty-seven women, the sin of polygamy suddenly became the virtue of "Holy Polygamy." He claimed he had a revelation which made polygamy a special gift of God. According to Jimmy Swaggart, in his book *Cults*, "One could write volumes on the misdeeds and character weaknesses of this individual, Joseph Smith, who is supposed to have a vision of an angel called Moroni who revealed to him where some golden plates were hidden, and how that he would be given spectacles (glasses) that would enable him to miraculously read these golden plates and to translate them into what is now the *Book of Mormon*."

Joseph Smith revealed to his followers how God came to be God, and how they, themselves, could learn to be gods. He then said in *Times and Seasons*, "No man can learn you more than what I have told you." Divine revelations of eternal truths did not encompass revelations on simple English grammar. Jimmy Swaggart says that Mormonism teaches that Christ and the devil are brothers, that people raise children after they leave Earth, and that no Negro can become a priest or go through the secret Mormon Temple. Says Swaggart, he wants "you to have faith in the world of Joseph Smith, a leader whose writings revealed amazing ignorance and undisciplined imagination and whose reputation for drunkenness, adultery, and gambling is a embarrassment to his own followers."

Seventh Day Adventists, like Seventh Day Baptists, believe Saturday, not Sunday, is the Sabbath. It is a very important issue because Biblical law does not say to keep Saturday or Sunday holy specifically. It says to keep the Sabbath holy. Sabbath is the Hebrew word for "rest," not "seven." Because the day of rest is one day in seven, "sabbath" has sometimes acquired the meaning of "one in seven," or "seventh" day. To the faithful, keeping the correct day holy spells the difference between eternal salvation and eternal damnation.

William Miller had been a Vermont farmer, deputy sheriff, Justice of the Peace, and captain in the War of 1812. After a comprehensive study of the *Book of Daniel*, he concluded, and warned in 1831, that the world would end "by fire" on April 3rd, 1843. He claimed that the meteoric shower of 1833 was proof his prediction was reliable. It convinced his followers. When he declared that the dead would be taken into heaven before the living, hundreds of people murdered their beloved families and committed suicide so that they would be first in line in that long queue waiting to pass the Pearly Gates. On the appointed day, thousands of his followers gathered and prayed on the hilltops all over New England. When a prankster blew his bugle in a comical imitation of the angel Gabriel, the multitude shrieked and screamed for divine mercy. Some of the faithful attempted to soar into heaven from hilltops on makeshift wings, but they ended up with broken limbs on the bottom of the hills.

When the fiery end did not take place, Miller rescheduled it for July 7th, 1843. In the meanwhile, he made a fortune selling "ascension robes," Bibles, paraphernalia useful for the Day of Judgment, and giving lectures. On July 7th, 1843, thousands of his followers sat in dug-out graves awaiting the end. It was another false alarm, and the Advent was rescheduled for March 21st, 1844. Meanwhile, the believers GREW to OVER ONE HALF MILLION members. Another false alarm and another rescheduling—this time for October 22nd, 1844. The inordinate frequency of false alarms caused the faithful to break up into scores of different sub-sects, the largest of which was the Seventh Day Adventists. William Miller died on December 29th, 1849, predicting that the end of the world would closely follow his own end. The Seventh Day Adventists now number over 1.6 million members. Offshoots such as the Church of God have seventy-five thousand members, and the Advent Christian Church has thirty-one thousand members. Can anyone question the fact that man is unique among all other animals?

Christian Science, which critics claim is neither Christian nor science, was founded by thrice married Mary Baker Eddy, after Phineas Parkhurst Quimby cured her of hysterical paralysis by means of hypnosis therapy in 1862. Having been "inspired" by the power of mind over matter because of her own "mental" cure, she founded a religion which proclaimed mind as the only reality, and denounced matter as an illusion. However, she substituted God for Quimby as the source of her inspiration, not unlike the Hebrew prophets who substituted Jehovah for Babylonian legends as the source of their inspiration.

Quimby was the father of the New Thought Movement, a religio-metaphysical mental healing cult, the principles of which became the major feature of Mrs. Eddy's divine healing. Mrs. Eddy had a turbulent, neurotic early life. Spirited differences with her first disciples and lieutenants often ended in lawsuits and excommunications. She was terrorized by the devil of her own creation: "Malicious Animal Magnetism." Christian Scientists deny the reality of the material world, and insist that illness and sin are illusions to be overcome by the mind. They refuse medical treatment for sickness. Thousands of the faithful have died prematurely as a result, but the Inspired One writes, "In the illusion of death, mortals wake to the knowledge of two facts: (1) That they are not dead; and (2) that they have but passed the portals of a new belief." This and the "final revelation of the absolute divine Principle of scientific mental healing" are in her book *Science and Health with Key to the Scriptures*. Many people find it difficult to look at a corpse and call it an illusion; but, oddly enough, many do not. The success of Mary Baker Eddy is certainly no illusion.

If we were to pose the question, "What is the relationship between current, voltage and resistance in an electrical circuit?" and we got thousands of different answers—each with a rationale to prove its solution is the only correct one and all others are in error—instead of the precise equation $E = IR$, we would have to conclude that physics is useless lunacy, and we live in a universe run by capricious gods and mad devils instead of an orderly Cosmos. However, this whimsical insanity exists in religion. There is one *Bible* and one *Koran*, but there are endless contradictory religious cults based on the same *Bible* and the same *Koran*. The Great Taboo discourages critical analysis of religious lunacy; ensconces it in a privileged sanctuary, safe from rational attack; and protects it as religious freedom, in the manner rogues are protected by the Constitutional right of religious freedom. Reason runs amok when it becomes intoxicated with fanaticism. *Homo sapiens*? Really?

Thrice-married Aimee Semple McPherson achieved great success in the religious healing business. Her disciples built the famous Angelus Temple for her in Los Angeles, where she employed highly successful theatrics like dressing in a policeman's uniform when sermonizing on "God's Law." She built a radio station, founded a Bible school, wrote books, and spread her gospel throughout some two hundred missions. She became phenomenally successful. There's no biz like showbiz. In May of 1926, she disappeared while swimming at a California beach and reappeared in June of the same year with a bizarre tale of having been kidnapped, instead of the likely fact of having been in a love tryst. She was tried for fraud but was acquitted. Her questionable financial activities led to numerous legal actions: as many as forty-five at one time. Religion is an excellent Constitutional shield for fraud, extortion, and embezzlement in the United States because they are protected under the umbrella of religious freedom.

Her membership peaked at nearly ninety thousand. She died at age fifty-four from an overdose of sleeping pills.

There are many extant faith healers and evangelists vying for fame and fortune, such as Oral Roberts, Pat Robinson, Jerry Falwell, Billy Graham, Rex Humbard, Jim Bakker, *et cetera, et cetera*. There are many strange cults, such as incest cults based on the implicit biblical incest of the children of Adam and Eve. Others include the Happy Hookers for Jesus, the Children of God (the Family of Love), Hare Krishnas, the Divine Light Mission, *et cetera*. According to the Citizens Freedom Foundation Information Services, there are over three thousand destructive cults operating in the United States alone. There are many controversial, wealthy religious cults like Herbert Armstrong's Worldwide Church, L. Ron Hubbard's Church of Scientology, Rev. Sun Myung Moon's Unification Church, *et cetera, et cetera*. Many are out-and-out frauds which are exempt from governmental scrutiny under Constitutional guarantees of religious freedom. With religion being a 20 BILLION DOLLAR (with a "B") business (1980), and an exploitable human foible, fraud is inevitable. The religious instinct makes human beings quarry of incredible gullibility. Gullibility invites predation.

We can but skim the surface concerning black Messiahs in America. Father Divine (1877-1965) was accepted by his disciples as God, Dean of the Universe, and Harnesser of Atomic Energy. At age seventy, he married a twenty-one-year old white disciple who became Mother Divine. Another black Messiah began as a cook on a Southern railway. In 1926, he "received a call from God to preach." He ordained himself Bishop Grace and soon gave himself the ultimate promotion by declaring himself God. He was worshipped as Daddy Grace. He died in 1960, but the faithful still genuflect and pray before his picture. Marcus Garvey preached that God is black, Jesus is black, and subservience will not end until blacks start worshipping a black God instead of a white God. He was entangled in a mail fraud charge and deported from the United States in 1927.

Prophet F.S. Cherry and his followers identified themselves as black Jews and claimed that black people originated with Jacob. The Church of God and the Saints of Christ, under the leaderships of

Prophet William S. Crowdy and Bishop William Plummer, taught that all Jews were originally black, and that Negroes descended from the "lost tribes of Israel." Bishop Plummer proclaimed himself "Grand Father Abraham." Prophet William Lewis heads the House of Judah, a black sect which claims to be the only true Jews because THEY belong to the "lost tribes of Israel." They were recently accused of beating a twelve-year-old to death with a large club, but they defended their brutality as the will of God, sanctioned by the Bible.

Timothy Drew founded the Moorish Science Temple of America in 1913. He preached that he had been ordained as Prophet Noble Drew Ali by Allah, Himself, and salvation for the blacks will never come until they discover and identify with their national origin as Moors. He was the forerunner of the Black Muslims, also called the Nation of Islam, founded in 1930 at Detroit by W. D. Fard whom his disciples believe to be "Allah in person." This made him even greater than Mohammed, Himself, who merely claimed to be the Messenger of Allah. Fard, or Farad, mysteriously disappeared in 1934, and Elijah Muhammad assumed leadership. Malcolm X began a power struggle with Mohammed which led to his suspension in 1963, and his assassination in 1964.

An extremist group of black Muslims were responsible for the Zebra killings of 1973-74. They murdered or maimed twenty-three white San Franciscans. These cultists shoot or stab from behind to the cry of "KILL! KILL! KILL!" much like Charles Manson's "family" of fanatical followers who spouted "Peace! Love! Death!" and murdered in ceremonial service to the DEVIL. The Zebra splinter of black Muslims preaches fanatical hatred of whites and imposes the duty on each neophyte to kill nine white men, five white women, or four white children. More points are given for murdering children because it requires more "heart." They learn to kill with a single blow to the larynx, chest, or neck while in prison, but prison authorities cannot stop the training because it is protected as freedom of religion. American Civil Liberties Union and various black groups indignantly denounced police surveillance and police Operation Zebra which called for stopping and searching suspects who bore likenesses to sketches of the killers. Operation Zebra was declared unconstitutional because it was "racist" and interfered with religious freedom. Meanwhile, Clark Howard, in his book *Zebra*, estimates that the Death Angels have murdered about two hundred seventy white men, women, and children in California, but very few killers have been apprehended.

Fundamental identity pervades human behavior at all times and in all places. Common instincts compel common behavior. Differences are more apparent than substantive. Genetic and environmental variations decree the splintering of all creeds, beliefs, and religions. There is no monolithic Communism, Christianity, Mohammedanism, or anything else. Nevertheless, naive American presidents have been committed to belief in monolithic Communism like fanatical cultists. Muslims, like Christians, split into many sects. The main split was into the Sunni and Shiite faiths. Minor splits include the Druze who have recently been engaged in mutual massacres in Lebanon with Christian Phalangists. The Sunni split into the Hanafites, Malikites, Shafites, and Hanbalites. The Shiites split into the Ismailis, Fatimids, and Assassins or Nizaris.

The English word "assassin" comes from the religious order of Assassins, founded by Nizar ibn al-Mustansir and Hasan ibn al-Sabbah. The devotees to the cult of Assassins were given hashish so they could get a foretaste of Paradise, which was promised them as a reward for murdering the cult's enemies and for dying in their murderous cause. The religious order of Assassins splayed terror throughout the Moslem world. Other splinters of Islam are Bábísm and Baha'ism. Human brutality and stupidity have no geographical or racial barriers.

Islam, the religious faith of Moslems, was founded by a simple camel driver who married into wealth: his rich Mecca employer who was a widow. His name was Mohammed. He was inspired with the idea of one god by the Jewish traders passing through Arabia. The Jews, in turn, had gotten the idea of one god from an Egyptian pharaoh. Mohammed liked the idea so well that he decided to make the god of his own tribe, Allah, the one god of the entire universe. Like most religious leaders, he had visions (or hallucinations) purportedly from God. His visions included "communications with the angel

Gabriel. " The priests of Mecca did not take lightly to an upstart who threatened their lucrative business by denouncing their gods, the source of their power and wealth. Hence, they resorted to a proven remedy: namely, elimination of the competitor.

Fortunately for Mohammed, his camel outran those of his would-be murderers all the way to Medina where he found sanctuary. This flight to Medina is called the Hegira. It ended on a Friday in A.D. 622. Thenceforth, Friday became the Sabbath of the new religion. Mohammed became so successful in Medina that his followers were able to defeat an army sent by the priests of Mecca; and he was even able to lead an army of conquest and force the priests of Mecca to swear obedience to his god, Allah. He destroyed all the pagan idols except the large black stone (probably a meteorite) thought to have magical powers. It was housed in the famous pagan shrine known as the Kaaba. He had to spare it because pilgrimage to Mecca meant big business for the Arab merchants, and he could not afford to alienate them.

Mohammed was illiterate. Even the omnipotent power of Allah could not make him literate. His disciples jotted down his teachings and collected them in the *Koran*, the *Bible* of the Mohammedan world. Koran means "the law." Islam means "submission (to Allah)." At first, Mohammed expected the Jews and Christians to convert to his religion. He even had his followers face Jerusalem when they prayed. After it became clear that the Jews would not convert, he ordered the faithful to change directions and face Mecca. Having been piqued by the Jews, he began to persecute them. The Prophet was more modest than Christ. He did not claim to be God, only the Messenger of Allah. As with Christians, heretics quickly sprang up, such as the Wahhabis, Alawis, and Sufis.

The ancient, annual pilgrimage to Mecca was extremely profitable to the merchants. The religious ceremony at the Kaaba Shrine in the Great Mosque of Mecca consists in kissing the Kaaba stone, circling the shrine three times running and four times walking, and then running to a nearby hill seven times. Upon doing all this, the pilgrim earns the coveted privilege of wearing a green sash around his fez. The true believer is rewarded with eternal Paradise, otherwise known as the Garden of Delights, in which he reclines in robes of shimmering silk on couches of exquisite design while being attended by beautiful girls. The unbeliever (infidel) is punished by being hurled into eternal Hell, where he wears a cloak of fire and drinks scalding water. The advantages of being a believer are very attractive (for a man). The disadvantages of being an infidel are obviously very dissuasive.

A shortcut to Paradise was available, and that was by dying in a holy war for Islam. The Japanese kamikazes "enjoyed" a similar honor in dying for their Divine Emperor during World War II, but the emperor lost his godship. He was downgraded to a mere man by the victorious Americans. Mohammed was both a religious and a military leader. He spread Islam by the sword, which gave his believers many opportunities for rapid transit into paradise. United by religious zeal, the Arabs became bold conquerors. Their motto was: "*The Koran*, tribute, or the sword!" Tribute became more important than the *Koran*. They rapidly built an empire which included the Holy Land, Armenia, Egypt, and the New Persian Empire to the frontiers of India. They conquered the entire coast of North Africa to the Atlantic Ocean; then crossed into Spain in A.D. 711 and conquered it; then pushed into France where they were halted by Charles Martel in the Battle of Tours in A.D. 732.

A large part of Spain became a Moorish kingdom until 1492. The victory at Tours enabled the Catholic Church and the Holy See to continue building up wealth in Europe by means of simony; tithing; charging Peter's Pence; and by receiving rich inheritances from believers who wanted their salvation assured by "willing their property to God," in other words, to the Church. Best of all, the victory at Tours made almost all of modern European and American nations Christian instead of Mohammedan. Thus it was that Europeans killed American Indians and each other, as well as enslaved black Africans, in the name of Jesus Christ instead of Allah. Millions upon millions of Europeans and Americans go to church every Sunday, praying and worshipping Jesus Christ, the only TRUE GOD, as they pity the lost souls of the infidel Moslems, not realizing that if the Battle of Tours had gone the other way, they would now be worshipping the only TRUE GOD, ALLAH, in a MOSQUE every

Friday and pitying the lost souls of the infidel Christians. *Homo sapiens*? Are you kidding?

We cannot even scratch the surface on the subject matter of religion here. There are endless religious cults, including tribal and shamanist religions, Buddhism, Confucianism, Shintoism, Bhagwan Shree Rajneesh (Antelope, Oregon) cult, *et cetera, et cetera*. At least 80 percent of the present world's population have a religion, and most of the remaining 20 percent have some sort of faith. The Gallup Poll indicates that 94 percent of Americans believe in God; 50 percent of them believe the biblical legend of Adam and Eve. Even the atheistic Communists have made a religion of Communism. Karl Marx is Christ, the Messiah. *Das Kapital* and the *Manifesto* are the Bible and Scripture. Lenin and Stalin are the Apostles. The revisionists and deviationists are the heretics. The Communist state is heaven, and the capitalist state is hell. Sinners are sent to Purgatory and Limbo (Siberia). Missionaries are sent to the four corners of Earth to proselytize the infidels. When religion is kicked out the door, it sneaks back through the window. Man's animal instincts will not be denied.

Any person capable of using at least a modicum of intelligence must surely ask himself: "With all the thousands and thousands of religions, religious sects, and cults claiming to possess the sole truth, and denouncing all others as frauds, how can I determine which is the true faith and which is false?" One thing is absolutely certain: they cannot all be true, but they can all be false. Actually, the answer is rather simple, and it is not an oversimplification. Any other would be an overcomplication. From a psychological, subjective frame of reference, they are all true so long as they satisfy the instincts of the individual concerned. From a rational, objective frame of reference, they are all utter nonsense. Because man is not a rational animal, he does not and cannot view religion objectively.

To a rational person, it is incomprehensible that grown adults in this day and age can take Biblical myths seriously. But the fact remains: as religions supplant each other, the displaced "Bible" is relegated to the realm of mythology, and the new one is elevated to the realm of Absolute Truth. Loftiest intelligence becomes utter madness when it is drunk with subjectivity and driven by irrational instincts.

Most Christians accept their faith so blindly that they do not ask themselves exigent questions like: "Do I really want to spend eternity bloating the ego of a super-egomaniacal God? After a few million years of groveling at the feet of the Almighty Ego, would I not explode with infernal boredom and shriek in desperation, 'The hell with it!'?" If a man created robots for the express purpose of singing his praises, it would be off to the booby hatch with him, but he creates gods who are even more insane. An omniscient God KNOWS He is the greatest. He doesn't need some addle-pated born killer like the human absurdity to constantly remind Him of His greatness. Besides, why should anyone want to behold God's face for all eternity? What is so attractive about a deity who created a murderous world in which half of all creatures can survive only by devouring the other half; who shapes innocent human infants into hideous monsters; plagues his hapless creatures with crippling diseases and terrifying natural disasters; and destroys them by the millions, even while they are in the act of divine worship? A little sanity, if you please! But whoever claimed that human beings are sane except human beings themselves?

There is far more incentive for man (the male, that is) to accept the revelations of the *Koran* than the *Bible*. What a Paradise for the male Moslem believer! The Blessed will luxuriate in one vast Garden of pleasant rivers shaded with spreading trees while reclining on soft couches, dressed in silk brocades and adorned with gems as handsome youths serve them. The limbs of fruit trees will bow down to fill the hands of the Blessed with delicious fruits. Rivers of milk, honey, and wine will flow freely. The wine, forbidden to the faithful on Earth, will be served them from silver goblets in the Garden, and the wine will cause no hangovers. Best of all, the believer will have virgins "never yet touched by man or jinn . . . in beauty like the jacinth and coral stone . . . with swelling bosoms but modest gaze, with eyes as fair and pure as sheltered eggs," and bodies of musk, free from any imperfection. Each believer (male) will have seventy-two of these gorgeous maidens. His eternal pleasures will not be marred either by exhaustion or by diminution of the houris' beauty. This is Mohammed's promised paradise, and one I, personally, could enjoy for two or three eternities.

What a world of difference between the Christian and the Moslem Heaven. Why would a virile man want to stare an egotistical, cruel monster in the face for all eternity when he could be having a ball in Mohammed's hedonistic Garden? Small wonder Mohammed's followers killed to the chant "Allahu Akbar!" (Allah is Great!) and died happily in wars of conquest. The Moslem faith inspired Baber to behead entire regiments of soldiers after battle and build minarets dedicated to the worship of Allah from their skulls as a symbol of Islamic superiority over the infidel Hindus. While instantaneous Paradise was guaranteed those who died in battle for Islam, the rich, for example, were required to cool their heels for a five-hundred-year waiting period.

Unflinching faith in absurdities distinguishes man from all other animals, and it debases him. It certainly does NOT ennoble him. People can be easily conned when they are told what they want to hear. Old ladies are conned out of their life savings by swinging gigolos who shower them with counterfeit love. People are swindled out of their life savings by con artists who promise to make them rich from phony investment schemes. People dying of cancer are cheated out of fortunes by quacks who promise their victims sure cures. Religious leaders and preachers swindle gullible believers out of everything they own by promising them the only true route to eternal salvation, or by claiming healing powers as intermediaries of God, and sometimes even as God.

People seem incapable of asking themselves simple, rational questions. For example: "Why does Almighty God reveal His Truths to illiterate rascals, and depend upon THEM to disseminate His Truths to the entire world?" An Omnipotent Power should have the capability of revealing His Truths DIRECTLY to each of His creatures in unmistakable terms. With tens of thousands of messiahs, prophets, messengers of God, gods, holy men, goddesses, monks, priests, ministers, parsons, popes, bishops, and clergymen, all of different faiths, sweeping the Earth, clamoring for acceptance as the ONLY AUTHENTIC voice of God, a rational God would expect His creatures to also be rational and demand rational proof of authenticity.

Phony miracles prove nothing. For example, some terminal

cancer patients will recover whether they do nothing, take a patent medicine, pray to Allah, Christ, Buddha, Mithra, or a clump of feces. Many will die regardless of what they do or to whom they pray. The ones who recover will attribute their "cure" to whatever they did prior to the "cure. " Thus, the patent medicine, Scientology, Allah, Christ, Buddha, or Mithra will be credited with the "miraculous cure." Most of the 99 and 44/100 percent of the people are unable to establish valid cause and effect relationships. They are victims of the *post hoc, ergo propter hoc* fallacy.

At 9:40 A.M. on All Saints' Day, Nov. 1, 1755, a frightful earthquake struck Lisbon, Portugal, at the very moment when churches were crowded with worshippers. Thirty thousand people died. Why did the Great Inscrutable select a Catholic city, and the very hour His pious worshippers were offering Him homage at the Holy Sacrifice of the Mass? Why, amid all the ruin, did He spare the house of Marques de Pombal, the enemy of the church? One priest blamed the destruction on God's punishment for the sins of Lisbon. But why did He slaughter so many priests and nuns in His fit of anger and revenge? Why should a loving God have such despicable emotions of anger and such a lust for revenge? Some Protestants blamed the disaster on divine punishment for Catholic atrocities against humanity, but a few days later the Great Inscrutable struck the Puritans with an earthquake at Boston, Massachusetts. One clergyman debauched human reason by arguing that the Lisbon disaster "displayed God's glory in its fairest colors."

In a sermon given by John Wesley entitled "The Cause and Cure of Earthquakes," he reasoned that sin and the curse of Adam and Eve cause earthquakes, and they can be prevented only by prayer and piety. Geologists formulated a different theory, but they were held in contempt by theologians. Even today, people insist that sin is the cause of disease, not germs; and sin is the cause of earthquakes, not shifting tectonic plates. Many people still believe that prayer is more effective for producing good crops than fertilizer, that prayer can influence the weather, and that Eve was created from the rib of Adam rather than gradual evolutionary processes.

Stone Age laws are on the books in the United States which

dignify biblical legends with the title of "Creation Science," and give them equal time in education with the scientific fact of biological evolution. It is as ridiculous as giving equal time to both the sin theory of disease and the germ theory of disease, or the sin theory of earthquakes and the shifting tectonic plates theory. The human mind is still undaunted by a million years of continuous religious fiascoes, nor is it impressed by the fantastic success of the scientific method. Schools in America still propagate ignorance rather than knowledge. If *Homo sapiens* (WISE MAN) were nature's intent instead of man's delusion, she had better go back to the drawing board.

Human beings have died like rats and cockroaches by countless millions because of natural disasters throughout history. In the one year of 1976 alone, nine hundred thousand people around the world died as the result of earthquakes, not to mention the thousands of deaths from other natural disasters. Religion and prayer never inhibited the Great Inscrutable one iota. Earthquakes killed eight hundred thirty thousand people in China during A.D. 1556, and three hundred thousand in India in A.D. 1737. Tidal waves killed nine hundred thousand in China in 1887, and NEARLY 4 MILLION in 1931. Between A.D. 1330 and 1350, the Black Plague ravaged Asia and Europe, killing from a quarter to a third of the human population of the world. OVER 25 MILLION HUMAN BEINGS DIED IN THE 1918-1919 SPANISH INFLUENZA PANDEMIC. Millions have died in recent famines in Africa and Asia. It made not a whit of difference whether they were saints or sinners, prayed to God or cursed God. Nevertheless, the faith of believers remains unwavering. This is solid evidence of man's total incapacity to learn in areas where his behavior is under the tyrannical control of instincts.

According to Catholics, missing Mass on Sunday is a mortal sin. The truant is doomed to eternal Hell if he does not receive absolution from the priest. A saint could live an exemplary life for a hundred years, doing nothing but good all his life, but if he misses one Mass on the Sunday before his death, he must suffer the pangs of hellfire and brimstone for all eternity. On the other hand, a heinous scoundrel could live a hundred years doing nothing but committing murders, rapes, mayhem, robberies, and every fiendish crime conceivable to venal man, but if he is given absolution by the priest and is granted plenary indulgence, his soul ejects straight up to Heaven and eternal bliss. Such a transparent absurdity and monstrous outrage should give pause to even the most substandard intellect, but they don't. They are rationalized as facets in the Grand Design, which is beyond the ken of mortal man. It will all become clear in the undiscover'd country when we have shuffled off our mortal coil.

Christians believe that forty days after Christ's resurrection, He led His apostles to Mount Olivet where He lifted up His hands, blessed His apostles, and slowly rose from the surface of the Earth, passed a cloud which concealed Him from sight, and ascended into heaven where He sits, and will forever sit, at the right hand of His Father. This fable might not have seemed preposterous to the ancients, who believed that the stars are nearby pinpoints of light created to beautify the firmament; but today, we know that the stars are distant suns, some of which are millions of times larger than our own Sun, which, itself, is over a million and a quarter times the size of Earth by volume. There are 100 billion stars (suns) in our own galaxy alone, but there are over 100 billion other galaxies each of which contains an average of 100 billion stars (suns). There are probably as many planets as there are suns.

Knowledge of astronomy makes childish nonsense of the Bible. Traveling at the speed of light (one hundred eighty-six thousand miles per second), it would require light billions of years to traverse the depths of the universe. The entire Solar System could be obliterated, and the loss would be as one grain of sand lost from all the shores of all the seas and oceans. If Heaven is "up" with reference to the Earth, and Hell is "down," and if Jesus had waited twelve hours, the rotation of the Earth would have made him descend into Hell instead of ascend into Heaven. The absurdities of creation by divine fiat, Noah's Ark, the passage of the Red Sea, Jehovah's command "that the sun stood still in the mid-sky, and hastened not to set for about a full day" (Joshua 10:13-14) to give the Jews more daylight to facilitate conquest, plunder, and human slaughter don't faze true believers one tiny bit.

Why should this fatuous clown, this rabid killer, the scourge of the animal kingdom, and the king of predators, man, have an immortal soul? Hasn't he done enough killing, looting, polluting, torturing, swindling, raping; and hasn't he committed enough assorted abominations in one lifetime that he should require eternity? If man is immortal, when does he acquire his immortal soul? When he passed through the birth canal? What happens when birth is via Caesarian section? At what point is he mortal, and at what point is he immortal? When an infant is born with two heads, and it happens, does he have two souls? Do mentally retarded people with less intelligence than apes have immortal souls? How can a soul see without eyes, or think without brains, when most people can't even think with brains? How can an infant which has less intelligence than a mature dog suddenly awaken in paradise fully conscious? Conscious of what? Why was man (*Homo*) on Earth 2 million years before Religion's contradictory Eternal Truths (as contained in the *Bible*, the *Koran*, and other such sources) were revealed to him?

Immediately after a Catholic receives absolution and is granted plenary indulgence, he is eligible for eternal paradise. Why doesn't his intelligence urge him to die at that point rather than live a few more measly years in this vale of tears and place his chances of gaining eternal Paradise in jeopardy again? Why shouldn't every believer want to depart for eternal Paradise when salvation is assured? Is it not written, "What does it profit a man, if he gain the whole world, but suffers the loss of his own soul?" Apparently the human instinct for survival tells human intelligence to go back to sleep.

Why should an innocent child be held responsible for original sin, be condemned to eternal Limbo, and be denied heaven because of someone else's sin: namely, the sin of Adam and Eve? Where, today, is there a sane person who would advocate the punishing of children for the crimes of their parents? The doctrine of original sin contradicts the Christian doctrine of freedom of choice and personal responsibility for one's own actions. Why should some ridiculous ceremony like baptism spell the difference between eternal Limbo and eternal Paradise? How can anyone reconcile the absurdities of religion with reason? Why should we accept any religion or any prophet on faith? Isn't the first thing every con artist says to his intended victim, "Believe me! Would I lie to you?" Would a hungry wolf eat a tender lamb? In the words of Voltaire, "The first divine was the first rogue who met the first fool."

The value of religion is derived not from gods, but from one's own mind: that is, the power of suggestion. Suggestion is the tendency in people to accept a proposition as true without any logical basis for its acceptance. Hypnosis is a state of heightened susceptibility in which the subject accepts nearly every suggestion. If a subject is told he looks well, he feels well. If he is told he looks ill, he feels ill. Religious healing is not accomplished by the gods. It is accomplished by one's faith—by suggestion and hypnosis, that is. Christ spoke the truth when He said, "Take up they bed! Thy FAITH hath made thee whole." Hypnosis has effected many cures, but usually when the illness was due to neurotic causes: that is, the illness was mental in the first place.

The power of suggestion is clearly seen in voodoo and black magic. A doll or wax image is made and then given the name of the person about to suffer telepathic death. Either pins are stuck in the doll, or the wax image is burned to the chants of the priest or witch doctor. The most important part of the proceedings is that the intended victim must know about it, and he must believe in the power of black magic and the witch doctor. The victim often dies, but only because of his faith. The power the witch doctor wields over his victim rests solely and entirely on the victim's belief in his power. To paraphrase Christ, "Lie in thy grave! Thy faith hath done thee in!" Witch doctors rescind their curses when the price is right. Money speaks with miraculous tongue.

There is no mystery to sympathetic black magic. People die from fear regularly. After the 1981 Athens earthquake, the death rate from heart attacks jumped 50 percent. It is thought that some people die in their sleep from fear induced by a nightmare. Most of us have awakened from sleep at some time or other with our hearts pounding because of a nightmare. If a mad dog charges us, our hearts will pound and adrenaline will flow to prepare us for the fight-or-flight response. This same response will take place in us whether the objective event actually happens, whether we dream it is happening to us, or whether we merely believe it is happening to us. This is the power of the mind. It is the power of mental rehearsal and imagination which makes the unreal real, so far as our bodies are concerned. Our bodies respond to mental, subjective states in the same manner as to real, objective experience. Our conscious world is a mental world. Thinking makes everything so. Beauty AND reality are in the eye of the beholder.

Physicians know that placebos (sugar pills) often effect the same cures as authentic medicine. Experimental evidence has proved that chemicals produced in the brain (endorphins), which resemble opiate drugs like heroin, are released by the placebo effect; that is, by psychological stimulation. Marijuana smokers experience a "high" even when not smoking marijuana—by merely being led to believe they are smoking it. The placebo effect is powerful because suggestion is powerful. Experiments show that if a subject inhales hot air through tubing, and he is told it is cigarette smoke, he believes it is cigarette smoke—provided he is blindfolded. The sensation of smoking a cigar is lost when it is done in the dark. One subject of an experiment was told by several people that he looked ghastly. He was in perfect health, but the power of suggestion made him feel ill, and he sought a physician. Suggestion is a useful weapon of predation. It is the insidiously inconspicuous hidden persuader used in advertising. In the service of Svengalis and Rasputins, it can adversely alter the course of history.

The power of prayer is the power of autosuggestion and self-hypnosis. It is easy to set up a scientific experiment to determine the objective value of prayer, but the faithful cry "FOUL," because religion and prayer cannot abide rational, scientific analysis. Science utterly demolishes religious faith. We know that prayer and religious ceremony did not prevent hundreds of millions of people from dying of diseases or from natural disasters. Millions died in World Wars I and II whether they prayed or not. The praying survivors thought they were singled out by divine favoritism, but they were selfishly oblivious of the millions who also prayed but died. If pressed for an explanation, they simply say, "It's God's will."

All one needs to do is open his eyes, and he will discover that the prayers and the non-prayers have equal longevity. The prayers and the non-prayers suffer the same illnesses and recover at the same rate. The prayers and the non-prayers die in equal numbers during natural disasters. But man has prayed, does pray, and will continue to pray. LOGIC AND REASON CANNOT TALK INSTINCT OUT OF ANY ANIMAL, INCLUDING MAN.

Prayer has immense psychological value. Subjective religious experience can give one a better "high" than LSD, angel dust, or any drug. Marx was not all wrong. Religion IS the opiate of the people. Prayer has no objective power. It cannot make the mountain come to the Prophet, but it can impel him with the psychological energy needed to drudge to the mountain. To pure reason, it may seem silly for a penis to plunge into a malodorous vagina and take off into frenzied reciprocation; but, frankly, instinct doesn't give a damn. Compulsion is not dissuaded by logic. Besides, how can anyone argue with anything that feels as good as sex? To reason, religion and prayer are silly; but instinct doesn't care. You can't argue people out of religion any more than you can argue them out of sex. You can take primitive man out of the 50,000 B.C. jungle, and put him in a twentieth century technological society, but you can't take the primitive mind out of twentieth century man.

Glaring hypocrisy, as displayed by the gap between Christian ethics and Christian practice, doesn't perturb the faithful at all. The faithful worship the Gentle Lamb but emulate the predacious wolf, and they are proud of their predations. Christians have preached the Beatitudes ("Blessed are the meek, for they shall possess the land. Blessed are the merciful, for they shall obtain mercy. Blessed are the peacemakers, for they shall be called the children of God. Blessed are they that suffer persecution for justice's sake, for theirs is the kingdom of God..."), but the peaceful Messiah has presided over the slaughter and massacre of uncounted millions of human beings through centuries of religious and political wars, including the dumping of two atomic bombs on Japan and seven million tons of death and destruction upon the tortured people of Vietnam. G.I.s unashamedly printed "KILL A GOOK FOR GOD" on their helmets. This very day, Catholics and Anglicans, Christians and Druze, Mohammedans and Hindus, *et cetera*, are slaughtering each other for the glory of God.

Religion has always inspired killings and cruelty. It inspired the ancient Hebrews, and it is now inspiring the warring Moslem sects in Iran, and the Moslems and Christians in Lebanon. It inflames Hindus and Mohammedans with killer fanaticism in India. Buddhist Singhalese and Hindu Tamils are driven with deep passion to kill each other in Sri Lanka, *et cetera*. The Crusades saw Christians killing infidel Moslems, and Moslems killing infidel Christians. The People's Crusade of three hundred thousand fanatics, led by Peter the Hermit in A.D. 1096, marched to the Holy Land, murdering Jewish men and children and ravishing women en route. It left a trail of smoldering Christian villages and raped Christian women. The Hungarians retaliated by massacring two hundred thousand of Peter the Hermit's followers. The remnants of the Crusaders marched into a Turkish trap where they were butchered, sold into slavery, and used as targets for archery practice.

Godfrey of Bouillon led a six hundred thousand man Crusade of Princes in a trek of plunder and butchery to the Holy Land. Most of them were killed en route by Christians, who avenged the inhuman outrages of their predecessors. Twenty-five thousand reached Jerusalem in A.D. 1099 where they gave the inhabitants a sample of Christian love and mercy by massacring seventy thousand Moslem civilians. Included in the carnage was the bashing of the heads of infants, raping of the women, and herding of all Jews into a synagogue where they were burned alive. The Crusaders then went to the Holy Sepulchre to thank Christ for their righteous and glorious victory. One diary reported, "The horses waded in blood up to their knees, nay up to their bridle. It was a just and wonderful judgment of God." Perhaps nature made a mistake when she selected dinosaurs for extinction to make room for man.

When the Fourth Crusade was victorious at Constantinople, the Crusaders expressed their Christian love by brutally slaughtering a million Greek Catholics. In 1208, Pope Innocent III launched the nefarious Albigensian Crusade against a million heretics, 99 percent of which were exterminated. In 1212, the same pope launched the Children's Crusade of fifty thousand boys and girls, most of whom were kidnapped by Christians and auctioned off in Algiers and Cairo as girl prostitutes and pleasure boys for the Saracens. The Fifth and Sixth Crusades were failures, but they added to the carnage. The Crusaders in the Seventh Crusade were massacred. The Eighth and final Crusade also failed. The last Christian bastion in Palestine fell to Sultan Khalil in A.D. 1291. Sixty thousand prisoners were either massacred or enslaved. The long wars of the Cross against the Crescent, Christ against Allah, left the landscape strewn with human carnage. Christ was evicted from the Holy Land until after World War I.

Christian intolerance and cruelty were egregious from the moment Christianity attained power in the Roman Empire. Free inquiry became strangled by fanaticism. For example, Hypatia was born in Alexandria in A.D. 370. She was a mathematician, astronomer, physicist, and head of the Neoplatonic school of philosophy, and a woman of great beauty. The Church identified learning and science with paganism. Therefore, Hypatia was an enemy of the Church. The followers of Cyril, the archbishop of Alexandria, dealt with her the way the Church dealt with science and learning for the one thousand five hundred years it wielded political power. They waylaid her in A.D. 415, tore off her clothes and flayed the flesh from her bones with abalone shells. Her remains were burned. Cyril's other contribution to Christ was the expelling of the Jews from Alexandria. The Church rewarded Cyril. It canonized him a saint. Christianity scored a fateful victory over science. The world center of learning, the Alexandrian Library, was destroyed. Superstition and ignorance dominated Europe for the next one thousand five hundred years. Science did not dare to peek from under the murky darkness of religious fanaticism until the seventeenth century.

The Dark Ages were a triumph of human stupidity presided over by religious faith. Piety, prayer, superstition, and hypocrisy were the rages of the day. Science and rationality were driven underground. Any deviation from rigid dogma was ruthlessly suppressed. The St. Bartholomew's Day massacre in 1572, when Catholics slaughtered thirty thousand Huguenots within twelve hours, is an example. In one town in southern France alone, twenty thousand Albigensian heretics were slain under the guise of religious piety. The murderers sanctimoniously went by the letter of the Bible (Deuteronomy 17:2-5): "If there be found . . . man or woman . . . (who) has gone and served other gods . . . thou shalt stone them with stones that they die." The long history of Catholics slaughtering Protestants and Protestants slaughtering Catholics, such as in Ireland today, is too extensive to pursue here.

Jews were persecuted by Christians because Christians resented Jewish rejection of the divinity of Christ, the killing of Christ (God), their clannishness, and their different customs such as observing the Sabbath on Saturday instead of Sunday. The Christians trumped up charges accusing Jews of kidnapping Christian children for sacrifice to Yaweh, and using their blood as medicine and in the making of unleavened bread for the feast of the Passover. Hatred for Jews was stirred up during Holy Weeks when thousands of priests recounted the story of the Passion, i.e., the story of their God being tortured and crucified at the behest of the Jews. During Holy Week, Jews had to barricade themselves in their homes in fear of their lives.

The Jews were expelled from Christian England in 1290, from Christian France in 1392, from Christian Spain in 1492, and from Christian Portugal in 1497. Jews were scapegoats for all Christian misfortunes. Jews suffered terrible pogroms in Russia and Poland. The God of Love failed to instill any semblance of love in His believers. Even the sacraments, benedictions, grace, prayer, holy water, papal blessings, indulgences, and all the holy rites and sacred ceremonies of the Church—including the cannibalistic rite of eating His body in Holy Communion—failed to instill one iota of love in the faithful. As Christians slaughtered each other, along with Jews, pagans, and Moslems, they prayed, "Forgive us our trespasses as we forgive those who trespass against us." If that prayer wouldn't assure them of eternal damnation, nothing would.

Now we come to that monstrous HORROR OF THE AGES, and savage outrage to reason: the infamous Inquisition. Philosopher/ historian Will Durant writes, "Making every allowance required of an historian and permitted to a Christian, we must rank the Inquisition, along with the wars and persecutions of our time, as among the darkest blots on the record of mankind, revealing a ferocity unknown in any beast." And this is the understatement of the ages. No wild beast or mad dog displays more viciousness, savagery, insanity, or cruelty than "true believers" displayed in doing the will of their God of Love. They burned their victims at the stake rather than chop their heads off because their twisted logic told them that blood-letting is abhorrent. Today, burning at the stake is abhorrent, but dropping napalm on civilians, blowing people to smithereens with bombs, roasting a million people alive with incendiary and atom bombs as we did not long ago in Germany, Japan, and Vietnam, is not considered abhorrent. Slaughtering people in the name of democracy and in the name of Christian values is twentieth century America's Inquisition.

In A.D. 1000, a French sect denied the value of baptism, miracles, and the doctrine of transubstantiation, for which they were burned at the stake as heretics in 1023. Many Christian sects arose which taught that priests should live in poverty like Christ. They were persecuted as heretics for their impertinence in exposing the Church's hypocrisy. In 1170, Peter Waldo, a wealthy merchant in France, formed a religious society dedicated to poverty called the "Poor Men of Lyons." Believing that Christians should live like the apostles, he gave his wealth to the poor. His followers, the Waldenses, rejected the authority of the priests in administering the sacraments. The Church protected its franchise on salvation by burning thousands of Waldenses at the stake.

Among the larger heretical sects were the Cathari (Greek for "pure"), Bulgari (Balkan heretics), and Albigenses (French town of Albi). The Cathari wished to return to the early Christian principles of peace, love, and charity. They refused to kill animals for food. They were basically vegetarians. They cared for the sick and the poor, taught to love one's enemies and never use force. They denied that popes were successors to Saint Peter, noting that popes were really successors to the Roman Emperors and that they were living in palaces (Vatican), and Christian prelates were wealthy. Christ had no place to lay his head, but popes had sumptuous, regal palaces from which they ruled as dictators and emperors. The Cathari considered the reigning pope to be an antichrist. They denounced as murderers those who preached the Crusades. In short, they wanted to practice what Christians preached. Unfortunately, a lamb has little chance trying to preach love and coexistence to a pack of wolves programmed for predation.

Pope Innocent III bore down hard on the Cathari, and naturally so: impostors cannot brook exposure. He summoned Christians from all countries to crusade against the heretics, promising them eternal paradise the easy way via plenary indulgence. The call to arms was known as the Albigensian Crusade. These pious Killers for God and Pope captured Beziers and massacred twenty thousand men, women, and children. Even those who fled to the church for asylum were murdered sans a morsel of pity. When the papal legate, Arnaud, asked the monk, Caesarius, if Catholics should be spared massacre, he replied, fearing heretics would escape the massacre by feigning orthodoxy, "Kill them all, for God knows His own!" He had no difficulty combining piety with murder. The rapines, massacres, and atrocities not only continued—they exacerbated.

The organ of human stupidity, the human brain, was of great service to Pope Innocent III. He used it to rationalize religious barbarity: "The civil law punishes traitors with confiscation of their property, and death . . . All the more, then, should we excommunicate, and confiscate the property of, those who are traitors to the faith of Jesus Christ; for it is an infinitely greater sin to offend the divine majesty than to attack the majesty of the sovereign." In 1215, the Pope demanded that all civil authorities "exterminate from the lands subject to their obedience, all heretics who have been marked out by the Church for due punishment" or be indicted for heresy themselves. Church and state collaborated. Impenitent heresy was treason—a sin and a crime punishable by death.

After A.D. 1227, the pursuit of heretics by "inquisitors" went into high year. Dominicans were such avid hunters of heretics that they were called "*Dumini canes*" (dogs of the Lord). They were pious, religious, possessed puritanic morals, but they had not one drop of the milk of human kindness in them. One day alone, "Robert the Dominican" burned one hundred eighty benign people at the stake in 1239 for trying to divert humanity from its usual course of vicious predation to the unnatural course of peace and love. One of his victims was a bishop who had extended excessive love to heretics.

In 1252, Pope Innocent IV authorized the use of torture in extracting confessions from suspected heretics. Later popes also condoned torture. The popes advised that torture should be applied only once; but the Inquisitors were human beings not unlike United States Supreme Court justices, and so they interpreted "only once" in ways that appealed to their own foibles. Only once to them meant only once per each examination. By conducting several examinations a day, they could enjoy the sadistic delights of watching their fellow human beings writhe in excruciating agony several times a day.

Inquisitorial tortures featured roasting the suspected heretic's feet over burning coals; pulling his arms and legs out of their sockets with cords wound on a windlass; hanging heavy weights on his testicles; floggings; and mutilations. Manacled heretics were heaved into filthy, dark, undersized dungeons in solitary confinement, where they weltered in the stench of their own urine and excrement. Some were forced to endure the days of their lives lying on their backs on the cold earth and in their own feces. Many died from unendurable pain induced by inhuman tortures. All of these inhuman tortures and unspeakable atrocities were conducted for the greater glory of the God of Love in the atmosphere of piety, and to the intonation of solemn prayers. *Homo sapiens*? *Homo stupido*, perhaps, but definitely not *Homo sapiens*!

In Spain, the Inquisition was called an Act of Faith (Auto-da-Fe) for reaffirming the Church's faith. Tomas de Torquemada (1420-1498) was a devout Dominican and Inquisitor General of Spain. He burned heretics while quoting Jesus. His name will live in infamy forever. In 1492, he persuaded the King and Queen to expel from Spain all Jews who refused to convert to Christianity, the number being about one hundred seventy thousand. He devised twenty-eight harsh rules for judging heresy, apostasy, and other religious crimes. He authorized diabolical tortures for obtaining confessions of heresy. He was responsible for the murder of some two thousand people. They were roasted alive at the stake for the crime of believing a ridiculously childish fable which did not conform to his own ridiculously childish fable. Heretics were tortured and slaughtered over picayune quibbles on matters of absolute inconsequence. The most horrible of the inquisitorial atrocities were concealed in dank dungeons, and were never exposed by the light of flames licking at the limbs and torsos of the hapless victims in public squares.

Henry Charles Lea wrote the three volume *History of the Inquisition of the Middle Ages*. It was first published in 1888, and reissued in 1955 by Russell and Russell. No student of history can truly understand his own species until he reads the three volumes. One passage describes how the burnt corpses of heretics were disposed of: "After it had burned away, there followed the revolting process requisite to utterly destroy the half-burned body: separating it in pieces, breaking up the bones and throwing the fragments and the viscera on the fresh fire of logs. When, as in the case of Arnaldo of Brescia, some of the spiritual Franciscans, Huss, Savonarola, and others, it was feared that the relics of the martyr would be preserved, special care was taken, after the fire was extinguished, to gather up the ashes and cast them in a running stream."

Even the dead were desecrated. The rotting corpses of heretics who escaped burning at the stake were exhumed from their graves and dragged through the streets to the shouting of, "Who does so shall perish so. They shall burn in honor of God and of the blessed Mary His mother, and the blessed Dominic His servant." One champion of the Inquisition boasted that from the beginning of the fifteenth century and for the next one hundred fifty years, the Inquisition burned at least thirty thousand witches, and thus "the world must thank the Holy Office, for had those witches been permitted to live, they would have destroyed the world." We heard the same idiotic refrain from five American presidents: "If the Communists are permitted to take over Vietnam, they will soon control Southeast Asia, then the world, and we, will be destroyed." The human brain has remained static during the last quarter of a million years.

In A.D. 1437, Eugenius IV urged the inquisitors throughout Europe to show greater zeal in bringing witches to judgment. Another infallible, Pope Innocent VII, in his Bull of 1484, declared that witches abounded which sought to seduce the faithful into following their malignant lead. Popes Calixtus III, Pius II, Alexander VI, Julius II, Leo X, Adrian VI, and Clement VII all declared it was the duty of the Church to EXTERMINATE witches. Why? Because it was the accepted belief that witches dug up corpses and ate them at their Sabbath feasts, that they drank the blood of children, and that they killed newborn infants in order to use their bones for spells and potions. The faithful were instructed to wear a holy relic as protection from malignant spirits. Witches were supposed to grow pale and flee if they were exposed to the sign of the Cross. Anyone who is impressed with human intelligence ought to bear in mind that witchcraft, human sacrifices, torture and killing of heretics, senseless wars, and religious insanity comprise 99 and 44/100 percent of human history.

A dissident is adjudged insane in the USSR and sent to an asylum because "anyone without the mental capacity to understand that Communism is the messianic salvation from the evils of the capitalistic world is obviously insane." The reasoning of the inquisitors was identical: A heretic who tried to escape the horrible tortures of the dungeons was considered insane because he lacked the sanity to underhand that his punishment was for his own good—to cleanse sin from his erring soul. Torture was salutary medicine offered in good faith to heal and save the soul of the misguided heretic. It was thought that only a lunatic would shun brutal punishment inflicted upon him for the good of his immortal soul. *Homo sapiens*? Not really!

Here are some of the Inquisitorial edicts: Suspects of heresy were required to prove their innocence within one year or be condemned as heretics. The Church delivered them to the secular arm for death by burning. If they recanted through fear of death, they were imprisoned for life and made to do perennial penance. All property of heretics was confiscated and their heirs disinherited. Their children, to the second generation, were denied employment unless they betrayed their parents, friends, or other heretics. The Nazi Gestapo stole a page out of the history of the Inquisition. All defenders and advocates of heresy were banished forever, and their property confiscated. The houses of heretics were destroyed, never to be rebuilt. The

Church, informers, and the state got rich on property confiscated from heretics.

The great intellects of the Middle Ages such as leading philosophers and theologians justified the Inquisition. This certainly says something about the quality of the human intellect. Thomas Aquinas, the intellectual giant of Scholasticism, reached the apex of theological profundity when he "proved" that the sin of heresy is more divisive from God than any other sin including murder and rape. Therefore, because it is the greatest of sins, it must be punished with more severity than any abomination or heinous crime. Surely the gods gave man reason so they could frolic over his insane antics.

Philip IV (The Fair) of France secured the election of a French archbishop as Pope, and the papacy was moved from Rome to Avignon, France. He, Pope Clement V, and his French successors, lived in a luxurious palace at Avignon for sixty years. When the popes returned to Rome, the Romans demanded an Italian pope. The cardinals elected Urban VI, but they had a dispute with him because he wanted reforms, so they held a second election, and elected Clement VII who reestablished the papacy at Avignon. From A.D. 1378 to 1415, there were two popes; each claimed to be the true Pope, and each excommunicated the other; each taxed all of Christendom, and each commanded the allegiance of separate kings.

It is a strain, even on human intellect, to understand how there can be two infallible popes at one time, excommunicating and contradicting each other and calling the other "Antichrist." An even more hilarious comedy of infallibles occurred in 1409 when THREE popes—Pope Benedict XIII, Pope Gregory XII, and Pope Alexander V—each claimed to be the infallible pope at the same time; and each excommunicated the other two. However, absurdity is no impediment to faith. If the believer wishes to accept one hundred infallible popes reigning at the same time with each contradicting the other, there really are one hundred such popes. It is consistent with George Orwell's doublethink. War is peace. Freedom is slavery. Stupidity is intelligence. Human intellect is not disturbed by contradictions, whether in 1984 B.C. OR A.D. 1984. Faith conquers all, especially good sense.

Papal farces have a long and inglorious history. In A.D. 897, Pope Stephen VII dug up the body of his predecessor, Pope Formosus; had it dragged by its feet, and seated it in the Synod which condemned the corpse for heresy; and punished it by cutting off two fingers of the right hand and then throwing it into the Tiber; but it was rescued by fishermen and reburied. The next pope, John IX, annulled the proceedings; but Pope Sergius III again exhumed the body, clothed it in pontifical robes, seated it on a throne, and after solemnly condemning it again, beheaded the corpse, cut off three more fingers, and once again consigned the body to the Tiber. The contest of contradicting infallibles is like an irresistible force meeting an immovable object. Something has to give, and it seems to be sanity.

Is there any correlation between religious belief and IQ? Apparently not! People of high IQ are both believers and nonbelievers. People of low IQ are also both believers and nonbelievers. The determining factor in belief is WILL, not intelligence. If a person wants to believe in nonsense, he will, regardless of the facts and regardless of his intelligence. If one is more interested in truth than its personal effects on him, he has a fighting chance to be objective even if he isn't a super-intellect. The super-intellects who WANT to believe in God devised ponderous metaphysical arguments to reconcile faith and reason, impossible though it is. Here are some of the "proofs" the great intellects offered to convince themselves and others that the God in their minds also exists in the external world...

The Ontological Proof: If you define God as the being none greater than which can be conceived, and you agree that you can conceive of a being none greater than which can be conceived, God must logically and necessarily exist because a being none greater than which can be conceived (God) which merely exists as an idea is not as great as one which exists in reality as well as just an idea. The fact of your conception of such a being establishes HIS existence, otherwise you would contradict your conception of the greatest being. This "Proof" is intellectual nonsense. You can't infer existence from conception. No sophistication of metaphysical legerdemain can transpose the idea of a hundred dollars in your pocket into the reality of its being there.

You cannot infer existence from conception. If you could, we would really live in a mad, mad world. From conception, I can prove that I can walk away from a bullet aimed directly at me. The proof is simple. When the bullet arrives at the point where I was when the gun was fired, I will have moved a distance however small away from it. When the bullet arrives at my new position, I will have again moved another distance however small away from it. And so on to infinity. Infinity requires infinite time. Therefore, the bullet can never catch up to me.

Another proof: I don't even have to walk away from the bullet. It still can't touch me. Before the bullet can strike me, it must first move half the distance to me. Before it can traverse the remaining half distance, it must traverse its half distance. Every time the bullet arrives at the half-way mark, there is yet another half distance, however small, remaining. There is an infinite number of half distances always getting infinitesimally smaller but ALWAYS another half distance remains before the bullet can reach me; i.e., the distances become one half, one fourth, one eighth, one sixteenth, *et cetera* to infinity. Therefore, it can never reach me because there is always a half distance remaining which must be again halved throughout eternity. It is this kind of intellectual nonsense that "proves" the existence of God.

The Teleological Proof: This is the argument from design and purpose. If a person "finds" a watch, he must conclude that it didn't come out of nowhere from nothing. It had to be designed by an intelligence, a watchmaker. By the same token, the order in the universe forces one to infer a Grand Designer. God must have given order and uniformity to the Cosmos. Extensive knowledge removes the luster from the beauty of this argument. Nature is savage and wasteful. The evolution of man, himself, was a chance accident which occurred after several billion years of erratic, discontinuous evolution. Millions of species have become extinct after many millions of years of existence, dinosaurs, for example, which doesn't speak well for intelligent design. Huge suns explode in the Universe and form supernovae spilling into areas larger than our solar system. Collisions of astral bodies occur throughout the Universe. Much of the evidence has eroded away on Earth, but the evidence of collisions on the moon in the form of craters is clearly evident. Besides, the conception of a Grand Designer is no guarantee of His existence. And who designed the Grand Designer? Chimeras of gods exist only in the mind.

The Cosmological Proof: This argument states that every effect must have a cause, and the long causal chain must start at the primordial First Cause or Prime Mover, which is God. This specious argument proves nothing because even the First Cause must, itself, have a cause. To stop looking for causes at any arbitrary point, and substitute the word "God," is merely making God an euphemism (or synonym) for ignorance.

The Moral Proof: This is Immanuel Kant's argument that the sense of duty, the sense of conscience, and the sense of morality implies a moral cause stemming from a cosmic moral lawgiver, or God. Because many people are obviously not rewarded for obeying the moral law in this life, there must be an afterlife which fulfills the requirements of moral law. A study of the history of man, his wars, his massacres, his beliefs, his Inquisitions, *et cetera, et cetera*, should dispel the nonsense of any connection between mankind and morality. Besides, morality is not absolute. It is an invention of man, relative to each religion, each society, and each individual. Abortion, for example, is moral to some, immoral to others. When man becomes extinct, morality and gods will share extinction with him.

The Mental Proof: This argument holds that the cause of man's power of reason can only be caused by an all-intelligent being—God, that is. As stated by C. S. Lewis, "If any thought is valid, an eternal, self-existent REASON must exist and must be the source of my own imperfection and intermittent rationality." This is like the arguments which prove a speeding bullet can never strike me. Mind cannot impose existence on its conceptions. Such reasoning gave the world its devils, evil spirits, witches, centaurs, and gods. It gave the world the concept that disease and natural disasters are due to punishment by God for the sins of man. Besides, human reason has been the source of man's phenomenal ignorance and colossal stupidity for from one to two million years. Science and technology are the fruits of but 56/100 of 1 percent of the human race. The billions of the world's humanity copy and imitate the technology of the intellectual elite like monkeys and apes.

The Experimental Proof *(experimental in this instance means empirical, or based on experience)*: This argument reasons that because religious experiences are universal, there must be a God inspiring them. But sexual experiences are universal. Therefore, there must be an Almighty Sex Spirit inspiring them. RELIGIOUS EXPERIENCES ARE UNIVERSAL BECAUSE THEY ARE INSTINCTIVE IN MAN. Laying eggs is a universal experience for birds. Is there an EGG GOD inspiring them? Man will grasp at any straw to rationalize what he desperately wants (or needs) to believe.

The Pragmatic Proof: This is the best argument. It is difficult to refute. It states that if believing in God makes us feel better, it is true for us. Whatever is useful (pragmatic) is also true. Truth is a function of utility. Objective reality has nothing to do with truth. If the belief in Santa Claus makes children feel good, they should accept Santa Claus as real. If we believe in the value and dignity of human life, and the concept has pragmatic value, we should accept it as true. The objective reality that human life is as cheap as dirt is irrelevant. Pragmatic value is the criterion of truth.

It is certainly true that religious experience is universal and has considerable pragmatic value. Christianity helped to tame the savage German, Viking, Vandal, and other barbarian tribes to the point that they could live in civilized societies; but it did not stop them from slaughtering each other in political and religious wars. The taming effect of religion on the born killer has some pragmatic value. Anything that can in any way diminish however little the ferocity and viciousness of man should not be slighted. Unfortunately, religion has also intensified man's ferocity as in religious wars, crusades, inquisitions, *et cetera*.

Why did religion—belief in gods and prayer—become an instinctive, universal experience? Simply because it has survival value for man in his struggle for existence. The psychological value of belief in gods and prayer is inestimable. Everyone knows that he can fight better if he has moral support. Weak animals can often defend their territory against stronger opponents because of the moral value in fighting for what they instinctively believe is rightfully theirs.

In a rush of superhuman strength, one hundred eighteen pound Martha Weiss lifted a four thousand six hundred pound Cadillac to free a child pinned under its wheels. The mental image of the pitiable face of the child being crushed under the car stimulated her maternal instincts which caused a surge of adrenaline in Martha's body, resulting in the "miraculous" feat of strength. The state of her mind more than tripled the normal strength of her body. Imagine the moral boost and the surge of adrenaline in one's body if he is convinced that all the powers of nature and the Cosmos are aligned on his side. It would constitute the ultimate in psychological stimulation. Obviously, nature and the Cosmos must be anthropomorphized for the desired results; that is, nature must be transmogrified into gods or God who possess human attributes.

History clearly proves that religious faith has made man a superior predator. At one point during the First Crusade, the Christian army was being decimated. Disastrous defeat was suddenly changed into overwhelming victory when a peasant soldier claimed he had a vision that the lance which pierced Christ's side as he hung upon the cross was buried at a nearby church. When the lance was found on the spot indicated, the Crusaders interpreted it as a miracle and as a sign of divine favor. Using the lance as a standard, the psychological shot in the arm enabled them to nearly wipe out the Moslems; but the reality was that the lance was a plant, and the story of a vision was a hoax.

Joan of Arc imagined she heard heavenly voices which bade her go forth and save France. She and the French warriors fought fiercely because they thought that God was on their side. It enabled them to win at Orleans. Though Joan was captured and burned at the stake by the English in A.D. 1431, the French became convinced that God favored their cause. The psychological stimulation spurred the French to expel the English from France.

Oliver Cromwell (1599-1658), lord protector of England, was totally imbued with the religious fervor of Puritanism. He and his soldiers were certain that God was their right hand. They fought with the doggedness that earned them the nickname of "Ironsides" by their enemies. Cromwell's motto was "Fear God and keep your powder dry!" The ferocity induced by religious zeal catapulted the Puritans to victory in England's civil war, whereupon Cromwell set up a military dictatorship in 1653. The religious exuberance was lost when Cromwell died. The Puritans were driven from power in 1660.

Religious stimulation enabled the Hebrews to conquer the Promised Land. The sign of the cross gave Constantine the psychological stimulation needed for victory, whereupon he made Christianity the official religion of the Roman Empire, which, in turn, made the Western world Christian. Religious fanaticism enabled Mohammedans to conquer a huge empire. Their belief that they fought in the service of Allah, and that He would reward them with an eternal paradise of voluptuous pleasures if they died for Islam, suffused them with ferocity few foes could resist. In the competition among human predators for survival, those who were impassioned by religious fervor were selected for survival over those who were not inflamed. Natural selection eliminated the less motivated nonbelievers. Religious instincts joined with sexual, maternal, and gregarious instincts for the survival and perpetuation of the human species. The basis for universal religious experience, therefore, is natural, not supernatural. Religion has survival value, like the tooth and claw of predators.

In the evolution of man, natural selection favored the most ferocious killers. They survived and became the breeders of the race. Those who were supercharged by religious myths had the evolutionary edge. They had superior morale and staying power. Had our forefathers not believed that they were exterminating the native Indians in service to Christ or some other God, we, today, would probably not be here to participate in the fruits of their predations. We would not be here to expatiate on the glories of our American Dream. How could the great plunderers and predators of history have endured the hardships and sufferings concomitant with bloody conquest if they had no gods to give them solace, stimulation, and a promise of heavenly reward? Religion and belief in God empowered the human predator with the floods of adrenaline and consequent superhuman strength required to make him the king of predators. Religion was the greatest innovative accessory to predators since the evolution of tooth and claw.

It should be of no surprise that religious experience is universal. The psychological energy derived from faith in gods and faith in prayer is fabulous. It matters not at all that prayer has absolutely no objective value. Prayer cannot suspend natural law. What matters is whether one believes his myths are true. The god of war served the Scythians well; and, in return, they honored him by bleeding one out of every hundred prisoners to death. Mars and Bellona served the Romans well; and they were honored with bestial sacrifices. Christ and Allah have served their devotees better than all the gods; and they were honored accordingly with human sacrifices whose numbers defy the imagination.

Religion also serves man well for his sublimated predations in the economic and sports ambience. It charges him up with surplus killer energy. Additionally, it serves man's deep psychological needs. It carries his instinct for survival to the ultimate, that is, eternal survival, by assuring him of an immortal soul. Religion fulfills man's need for purpose to life. The fact that this purpose is fictional nonsense does not detract from its psychological value. Religion satisfies the prey as well as the predator. Man's need for dignity, love, and affection is gratified by the ultimate of love-givers: the fabled Heavenly Father and the legendary Heavenly Mother. The frustrated predator is consoled with dreams of eternal paradise for himself, and his envy is allayed by the belief that his successful rivals will find it as difficult to enter heaven as for a camel to pass through the eye of a needle.

If we scan the Cosmos in search for God, we will never find Him. We can discover God only in our own minds, and He resembles Proteus. All religions are equally true and equally false. To say that any particular religion is the one, true religion is like saying that English is the one, true language.

RELIGION IS AS INSEPARABLE FROM HUMAN NATURE AS VIOLENCE, SEX, HYPOCRISY, AND PREDATION. RELIGION WILL SURVIVE SO LONG AS THE HUMAN RACE SURVIVES.

Chapter 6
NONSAPIENS, SCIENCE, AND ART

In one field of human endeavor, man has transcended the possible. The landing of man on the moon, interplanetary and extra-solar probes, genetic engineering, computer science, medical science, and high technology are such incredible marvels that their mere mention as possibilities would have made one a candidate for an insane asylum a hundred years ago. Any one of a thousand commonly used technological devices in today's world placed in the hands of a medieval man would have qualified him for worship as a god. However, it was NOT MAN as typified by 99 and 44/100 percent of the featherless bipeds who gave the world the marvels and wonders of science and technology. We enjoy the boons of our modern Space Age not because of the run-of-the-mill human being but in spite of him.

The source of nuclear energy is not uranium as such. Most uranium is non fissionable uranium-238. The natural source of nuclear energy is in the rare isotope of uranium—fissionable uranium-235. In like manner, the source of uncommon human intelligence required to create science and technology does not reside in the common breed of man. It is sparsely distributed in the species. It exists only in the atypical, rare breed of human genius—a breed apart. The average, normal, everyday man is apathetic, if not hostile, towards science. He is normally predisposed towards the primitive and the irrational. This is why America's heroes are rock 'n' roll throwbacks to the jungle music of 50,000 B.C.; Neanderthals who are proficient in knocking a fellow human being unconscious with a haymaker to the head; missing links who are adept in flipping a ball in a hoop; and mental midgets who delight in the infantile fantasies of playacting. Americans honor, worship, and enrich sub-intellects who perform on TV and on the silver screen, but they are totally oblivious of the super-intellects who gave them TV, transistors, microchips, *et cetera*.

Millions of people derive intense enjoyment from memorizing the names and athletic records of all the team members in all the sports; the names and biographies of all rock 'n' roll performers; the tedious gossip and trivia about Hollywood stars; but they have no idea who invented the transistor, one of the greatest inventions in the history of the human race, and they couldn't care less. Hundreds of thousands of shrieking, whirling, flipping, flaming youths joyfully congregate to listen to the prehistoric sounds of rock 'n' rollers; but a lecture explaining the intricacies of quantum physics attracts almost no one. The basic primitiveness and non-rational preferences of the normal human being are demonstrated a zillion times a day, every day. Exhibitions of the lowest animal instincts thrill him beyond words. Cinema and TV productions featuring sex and violence are smash hits. No movie producer in his right mind would attempt to wow the public with science and philosophy.

Millions upon millions of people throughout historical times were turned on by religion, but turned off by science. There's a Bible in nearly every home, but in how many homes are there science textbooks? Today, Billy Graham is known by everyone, but John Bardeen is known by no one. There were great intellects in ancient Greece; but, like today, the tenor of the masses was ignorance and superstition. The father of medicine, that fabulous ancient Greek of the fifth century B.C., Hippocrates, observed, "Science and faith are two things; the first begets knowledge, the second ignorance." The masses preferred ignorance. Medicine, health, and healing were in the hands of the priests who served Asclepius, the god of health, and his daughters Iaso, Panacea, Aegle, and Hygeia, the goddesses of health and healing. Patients observed purification rites, fasted, and sacrificed. Then they spent a night in the temple of Asclepius, sleeping on the skin of the sacrificed animal or on a couch near the statue of the god. When they were cured, and nature cures 90 percent of all patients without them doing anything, they thanked Asclepius by tossing gold into the sacred fountain, and by hanging *ex-votos* on the walls of the temple.

The next great figure in the history of medicine was Galen (A.D. 130-200), court physician to Marcus Aurelius. He was hampered in his medical research because there was a taboo on the mutilation of the dead, at the very time that the mutilation of the living in gladiatorial contests was in full vogue. The progress in science and medicine made by Hippocrates and Galen degenerated into magic and sorcery during the Age of Faith. Where the Greeks looked to Asclepius for healing, Christians looked to Christ. To Christians, it was not a theory that demons, devils, and evil spirits cause disease—it was an obvious fact. Only prayer and exorcisms could cure disease, but the bona fide fact that millions and millions of the faithful died, prayer or no prayer, exorcism or no exorcism, did not suggest to them that perhaps they could be mistaken.

Louis Pasteur emerged from the morass of 99 and 44/100 percent of *Homo nonsapiens* in France in the year A.D. 1822. The scientific community at this time believed that the imbalance of humors (blood, phlegm, choler, and melancholy) was the cause of disease. As a result of Pasteur's experiments, he proposed and became the father of the germ theory of disease. However, when he presented his evidence to the physicians of his day, they only ridiculed him. Their response to his evidence was: "Monsieur, where is your M.D.?" Pasteur was only a chemist. What could a chemist know about medicine?

Pasteur's studies of fermentation revolutionized the manufacture of beer and wine. He saved the silk industry by developing a cure for silkworm disease. He developed a means for preventing the dreaded anthrax in cattle with an inoculation. He reduced the nearly 100 percent death rate among human beings who contracted hydrophobia to less than 1 percent. His germ theory made it possible to attack the true cause of disease, *a la* modern medical science. The result was the practical elimination of smallpox, Black Death, and many other epidemics. He saved countless millions of human lives by the application of medical science. The religious healers destroyed countless millions of human lives by adhering to ancient superstitions. Pasteur did more for the health of the human race than all the holy men who ever lived or ever will live put together. Louis Pasteur was that rare subspecies of *Homo sapiens*: one of the 56/100 of 1 percent of the human race; but Saint Bernadette of Lourdes is better known and better honored than he.

Now that Pasteur opened man's eyes to the true cause of disease, surely man would abandon the futile ways of religious superstition? Not so! Devils are exorcised this very day and in the United States. Prayers and ceremonies are still thought to have power to cajole and wheedle the gods into infracting the laws of nature for the indulgence of the faithful. Even though medical science weakened religion's grip on natural philosophy, science could not break its hold on the supernatural or the parapsychological. Religion maintains undisputed sway in the bogus world of the supernatural.

A German professor, Justus von Liebig, published a work in 1840 which explained that plants grow because of food supplied them from the soil in the form of chemicals. His experiments showed that three essential chemicals are required by plants: phosphorus, potash, and nitrogen. A few people were learning that the world of nature is a world governed by the inexorable laws of physics and chemistry rather than by the whims of bribable gods. The development of scientific farming made it possible for 3 percent of Americans to supply not only the entire food needs of their own country but much of the rest of the world besides. The phenomenal success of scientific agriculture, and the dismal failure of religion (prayers, magic, and ceremony offered for good crops), did not make much impression on many people. People still pray for good crops and good weather. A creature of instinct is unresponsive to the persuasions of reason.

Oddly enough, it was the predatory instincts in man that serendipitously honed his intellect for the acumen needed to develop science. Catching prey is intellectually more challenging than escaping capture. Hence, keener intelligence evolved in carnivores than in herbivores. However, there is a giant gap in the intelligence needed to capture prey, and the intelligence needed to create science. Obviously, few were able to bridge this gap because man was on Earth as Homo for 2 million years before the idea of agriculture even occurred to him. It required over ten thousand years for man to evolve from primitive agriculture to scientific agriculture. His eventual development of science and technology was never a foregone conclusion.

Of all the numerous civilizations which independently created art, literature, philosophy, architecture, and primitive science, ONLY WESTERN CIVILIZATION CONTINUED ON TO ADVANCED SCIENCE AND TECHNOLOGY. ALL OTHERS EITHER STAGNATED OR RETROGRESSED.

Between the years 3000 B.C. and 2300 B.C., the Sumerians invented the plow, sailing ships, carts with wheels, the potter's wheel and written language (cuneiform) which survived for two thousand years. Progress then ceased and regressed for two thousand years following a series of foreign conquests. The Egyptian civilization of 3000 B.C. became static. The same thing occurred in India from 2300 B.C. to 1750 B.C. There was some improvement after the Aryan invasion during the fifth century B.C., but it stagnated again for two thousand years. The same can be said of China. Nineteenth century China was little improved over third century B.C. China, in spite of inventions like gunpowder, the printing press, and paper. Hellenistic science declined after the Roman conquest, and it did not recover the same level until one thousand six hundred years later. Rational science and high technology were always alien to the human mind

If science were natural to man, ALL civilizations would have developed science and technology, just as they all developed a spoken language and a religion. The only reason Western civilization did not continue in utter ignorance and superstition was that it became the recipient of an improbable series of lucky accidents, not the least of which was the birth of several bona fide *Homo sapiens*. Human beings have always associated the way of things with the way of the gods. For thousands and thousands of years, the building of military empires and the authoritarian control of the masses were the normal and natural functions of the human being. The creation of advanced science and technology couldn't have been more unnatural for him.

If evolution on Earth were to be repeated, man probably never would again develop modern science and technology. He would probably go through his entire cycle of evolution and extinction without having developed anything remotely similar to modern science. The 2 million year history of Homo should make this abundantly clear. The flowering of the scientific-technological revolution was made possible in the West because of fortuitous circumstances, and accidents of history, which assured the unusual situation of an extended period in which a competitive international system existed. Any possibility of an open and innovative society would have been strangled, had not Britain prevented France, Russia, Prussia, and Austria from establishing an autocratic multinational empire, which, as history proves, would have been death to free inquiry and science. Throughout past history, any slight improvement in technology facilitated the creation of military empires because of superior weaponry, but the resulting autocratic, authoritarian empires immediately brought free scientific inquiry, and any further progress, to a grinding halt. Science would always self-destruct.

"History," in the words of Thomas Carlyle, "is the essence of innumerable biographies." Were it not for genetic sports and lucky mutations, which created the freakish human intelligences capable of thinking in terms of inductive logic rather than in terms of non sequiturs burgeoning from a priori assumptions, the modern world of science and technology would never have come into being. A free society is a prerequisite for free inquiry and science; but first, there must exist people capable of incisive thought processes. Science and technology are the fruit of rare intellects. No society is better than its greatest intellects. Can you imagine a Computer Age society emerging from a race of mongoloid idiots?

Even great men are surprisingly stupid. The great Aristotle believed that women have fewer teeth than men. This absurdity would have been avoided if he had used the inductive method of inquiry and condescended to look into the mouths of men and women and count their teeth. Even the greatest of human intellects were unable to completely shake themselves loose from myths and superstitions. William Harvey associated the circulation of the blood with planetary movements. Charles Darwin thought that women's sexual cycles were influenced by the tides of the ocean. Johannes Kepler, who formulated the laws of planetary motion, believed in witchcraft. He was employed as an astrologer and he cast horoscopes. He envisioned the day when man would navigate the universe by "celestial ships with sails adapted to the winds of heaven."

The 56/100 of 1 percent of mankind who were capable of partially lifting mankind (*Homo*) out of over 2 million years of stupidity, ignorance, and superstition found only partial liberation for themselves. The fabulous Sir Isaac Newton—who was credited with "prodigious intellectual powers" because he discovered the laws of inertia, formulated the laws of motion, and invented differential and integral calculus—blotched his A.D. 1687 *magnum opus, Philosophiae Naturalis Principia Mathematica*, with mystical nonsense. When his equations showed that the orbit of the moon was shrinking and the moon would one day plunge catastrophically into the Earth, and when irregularities such as comets apparently disturbed his conceptions of the perfect harmony of the solar system, he concluded that God personally intervened with miracles to preserve the solar harmony. Pierre Laplace proved that the irregularities correct themselves and no miracle is required.

Newton had a lifelong interest in the pseudoscience of alchemy. He accepted every word of the Bible as the word of God. Newton encouraged his friend John Craig to write *Theologia Christianae Principia Mathematica*, which professed to determine the exact date of the Second Coming of Christ by mathematical computations, and to determine the mathematical ratio of maximum Earthly happiness to heavenly bliss awaiting the faithful in the afterlife. Sir Isaac Newton wrote a commentary on the Apocalypse in which he argued that the Pope of Rome is the predicted Antichrist. He praised William Whiston's *New Theory of the Earth*, published in 1696, which argued that the original orbit of the Earth was a perfect circle; that the year was exactly three hundred sixty days long; and that the length of the day equaled the length of the year, but God punished the wicked world by striking it with two comets which threw the Earth into an elliptical orbit and increased the length of the year to its present three hundred sixty-five and one-quarter days.

As we have seen with geniuses like Newton, regardless of how intelligent they seem to be, it is almost impossible for them to escape absurdity and stupidity. The great Thomas Edison—who held over one thousand three hundred patents, invented the phonograph, the movie camera, the microphone, the mimeograph, the stock ticker, the incandescent lamp, and discovered the "Edison effect", which launched the Electronic Age—believed in such absurd nonsense that one must question his sanity. He believed that normal human brains contain millions of submicroscopic intelligences which he called "little people." The submicroscopic intelligences are supposed to be busy with chores given them by "master entities." Edison devoted considerable time trying to invent a machine that would make it possible to communicate with "the little people." Edison was easily hoodwinked by fake mind-readers, one of which used his own inventions of lights and a phonograph to send and receive phony psychic messages. He worked hard attempting to invent a machine which could communicate with the spirits of the dead.

The Edison laboratory produced the first motion-picture camera, but Edison opposed projecting motion pictures on a screen. He was blind to the commercial potential of the cinema. He was a doctrinaire fanatic in his insistence that cylinders make better recording devices than the more practical discs, and in his promotion of low voltage direct current, as opposed to high voltage alternating current, for the transmission of electrical power to homes and industry. He said that AC high voltage "is too dangerous," and he predicted it would never be used. He said, "It's just a waste of time," and to prove his point, he gave demonstrations by electrocuting dogs with AC. His low voltage DC transmission system was a total failure because high power losses made it impractical. Nowadays, AC is used universally. Edison's motivation was not love of knowledge. It was love of money and lust for personal glory. Said he, "Anything that won't sell, I don't want to invent."

Nikola Tesla invented the AC transformer (the Tesla coil) and alternating current motors. He was another eccentric genius who possessed a strange admixture of stupidity and intelligence. He was ridden with a complex of phobias. Because he feared contamination, he refused to shake hands with anyone. He was obsessed with the idea of inventing a machine capable of reading the thoughts in the minds of his enemies from photographs of the retinas of their eyes. At the time of his death he was working feverishly on an impractical death ray gun.

Albert Einstein was one of the most creative intellects, and the greatest theoretical physicist in human history. He heralded the Atomic Age with his famous equation: $E = mc^2$. The evidence of his genius was slow in making its appearance. He didn't begin to talk until the age of three. One of his early teachers scolded him: "You will never amount to anything!" He failed the entrance exam for the Swiss Federal Institute of Technology in Zurich, and would not have graduated, if a classmate, Marcel Grossmann, had not helped him cram for two major exams in 1900. The famed mathematician Hermann Minkowski called him a "lazy dog." Yet, as human intelligence goes, he was among the greatest. He demolished the Newtonian concept of absolute time and space, and showed their dependence on the relative motion of the observer. Separately, space and time are relative, but the space-time continuum is invariant. The only absolute, is the velocity of light. He disproved the concept that matter can neither be created nor destroyed, and proved not only the equivalence of matter and energy, but also their interchangeability.

Einstein's equation, $E = mc^2$, explains why the sun can burn for billions of years without shrinking appreciably. His equation laid the theoretical basis for atomic energy. It was Einstein's letter to President Franklin D. Roosevelt urging quick action on atomic bomb research which spurred the origin and success of the Manhattan Project. However, it must be said to Einstein's eternal credit that when he visited Japanese physicist Hideki Yukawa after World War II, he apologized in tears: "Had I known that the Germans would not succeed in developing an atomic bomb, I would have done nothing for the bomb."

Experiments have verified most of Einstein's deductions, but he did make serious mistakes which were due to the normal human propensity to project subjective belief into objective reality. He did not believe in the God of traditional religion, but he did "believe in Spinoza's God, who reveals Himself in the orderly harmony of all that exists, not in the God who concerns Himself with fates and actions of human beings," which is tantamount to atheism for the practitioners of traditional religion. His belief in a precisely engineered universe induced him to postulate the "cosmological constant," but American astronomer Edwin Rubble's proof that all distant galaxies are receding from one another in an expanding universe caused him to reverse himself and admit to the worst mistake of his scientific career.

Einstein rebelled against the conception of chance and probability in the universe, as postulated by Max Planck's quantum mechanics and Werner Heisenberg's uncertainty principle, saying, "God does not play dice with the universe." Physicist Niels Bohr chided him: "Stop telling God what to do!" Einstein's conception of a mathematically precise, orderly Cosmos is an artifact in the same sense that the Hebrew Yahweh is an artifact. Scientists are people, and whether people are politicians, physicists, priests, or physicians, rational modality has a common denominator.

Einstein was scurrilously denounced for his "Jewish physics" by his fellow German scientists. Even physicists are constrained by the same bigotry and prejudice as fanatical religious cults. Einstein's property was confiscated in 1934 by the Nazi government, and he was deprived of his German citizenship. He found sanctuary in the United States, having accepted a post at the Institute for Advanced Study at Princeton. America gained a true *Homo sapiens*, gained atomic power, and won World War II. Germany lost a bona fide *Homo sapiens*, and lost both the technological struggle for supremacy, and World War II. She paid dearly for her colossal stupidity.

When Einstein dallied in political theory, his naivete was egregious. He was an ardent pacifist and a devout socialist because he falsely assumed that all human beings shared his own rare intelligence, humanity, and compassion. Pacifism and socialism are perfectly workable ideals for the Einsteins who comprise less than 56/ 100 of 1 percent of the human race; but for the 99 and 44/ 100 percent of mankind which share the normal predatory instincts, war is an inevitable and practical necessity, and capitalism is the only eminently successful economic system.

We must always be cognizant of man's very limited intellectual potential. Human reason did not evolve as an instrument to penetrate the intricate secrets of the universe. The utilization of human intellect for the pursuit of exact science was an accident of evolution. Feathers seem to have been designed to make flight for birds possible, but such was not the case. Feathers most likely evolved originally for thermo-regulation; but once evolved, they were available, and facilitated the evolution of flight. Hence, an unplanned function (flight) arose from a totally different primary function. The same with human intelligence which evolved for a set of complex reasons having to do only with survival, but once evolved, it became fortuitously available for "solving the riddle of the universe," but only to a very small minority. This process of evolving for one purpose, and the adventitious use for a completely different purpose is known as EXAPTATION.

Human reason has blighted the world with far more absurdities, ignorance, and superstition than it has profited it with objective knowledge or intelligent behavior. Inexact science abounds with ignorance and stupidity. Louis Agassiz, the most influential naturalist of the nineteenth century, argued that the ice ages were a dispensation of divine benevolence, created to churn and enrich the soil. Said he, "We have our answer (to the ice age) in the fertile soil which spreads over the temperate regions of the globe. The glacier was God's great plough." He argued that "The animal world designed from the beginning has been the motive for the physical changes which our globe has undergone." Oxford's geologist William Buckland asserted in 1836 that the rich coal deposits in England were so expertly arranged in the bowels of the Earth that only God could have done it millions of years in the past, in loving preparation for its use by the English, probably so that they could conquer one quarter of the world during their imperial heyday.

Scientists are professedly dedicated to truth, but they are not above perpetrating hoaxes for reputation, position, or money. One of the most famous hoaxes was the "missing link" or Piltdown Man hoax. From 1908 to 1950, most anthropologists accepted the Piltdown Man as our early ancestor who lived from two hundred thousand to one million years ago. Charles Dawson was a highly respected lawyer, amateur geologist, and fossil hunter who "discovered" fragments of a human skull and the jaw of an ape among mammal remains in the sedimentary rock of the lower Pleistocene epoch at Piltdown, Sussex, England. Anthropologists, after several years of investigation, accepted the Piltdown Man as the authentic missing link.

Dawson was acclaimed one of the world's most brilliant scientists.

The Piltdown Man was known as *Eoanthropus dawsoni* (Dawson's Dawn man) in scientific circles. The "discovery" verified the preconceptions of the anthropologists of that day; namely, human intelligence evolved prior to the evolution of human anatomy. Erect posture and the "precision" grip were thought to have evolved because human intelligence directed the body to such posture and such a grip. In 1950, fluorine tests and X-ray analysis exposed the Piltdown Man as the most elaborate and carefully prepared hoax in the history of anthropology. Dawson perpetrated the hoax by artificially aging the bones with abrasives and by staining them with chromium and acid iron sulfate solutions. Millions of textbooks and encyclopedias had to be revised.

Anthropologists now know that the human brain evolved AFTER upright walk, precision grip, and tool making. Actually, it is now known that many animals other than man are proficient tool users. Apes make simple tools. Egyptian vultures use rocks to break eggs open. Satin bower birds use wads of bark as paint brushes. Galapagos woodpecker finches use cactus spines to probe for insects. Sea otters use rocks to crack open shellfish for food. Chimps shape twigs for termite probes. They make sponges from leaves to soak up water. The great apes learn and speak sign language with vocabularies of several hundred words. Man is not unique in either using tools, making tools, or using language. He is unique only in his proclivity for incredible stupidity and unspeakable savagery such as is unseen anywhere in the animal kingdom.

It is not at all uncommon for the great truth-seekers, the scientists, to tamper with truth for their own profit. The Austrian geneticist Paul Kammerer injected India ink into the feet of his laboratory toads in his attempt to prove the Lamarckian Theory, which holds that acquired traits are genetically passed onto the next generation. Sloane-Kettering Institute's Dr. William Summerlin confessed to painting mice to give the appearance of successful skin grafts. Dr. Leroy Wolins of Iowa State discovered that out of thirty-seven authors of scientific studies, twenty-one could not produce their raw data, and the seven who did had such flawed data that it could not pass as scientific fact. The Director of the National Bureau of Standards, Dr. Richard W. Roberts, asserted, "Half or more of the numerical data published by scientists in their journals are unusable because there is no evidence that the researcher accurately measured what he thought he was measuring or no evidence that possible sources of error were eliminated." Scientists belong to that same species of human predator to which we all belong. Therefore, they are subject to normal greed, cunning, dishonesty, egotism, and superstition.

John Darsee, a research fellow at Harvard, was accused of fakery by the National Institute of Health. He recorded test data from experiments which were never performed. Darsee was barred from receiving federal grant funded contracts for ten years. Harvard was asked to refund its grant of $122,371. According to Time magazine of February 28, 1983, fraud in the scientific laboratories is on the increase. "Yale, Cornell, and Boston University have each had to contend with embarrassing cases of scientific fraud." Whether a human being is a politician, evangelist, businessman, union labor leader, or scientist, he is first of all a predatory animal in which cunning, deceit, fraud, stealth, deception, and hypocrisy are the basic working tools of his trade.

Textbooks on subjects like chemistry, physics, anatomy, and mathematics are basically the same all over the world. They are the same because they contain impersonal facts which do not normally arouse human emotion, and they are easily proved or disproved by any person with a trace of sanity. Hence, there is uniformity in the exact sciences. However, the inexact sciences are as ridden with prejudices, superstitions, naive beliefs, and ignorance as witchcraft and religious cults. We are talking about psychology, psychiatry, sociology, anthropology, and the many other pretenders to legitimate science. Anthropology is ridden with racism, bigotry, and ignorance, as we shall see in the next chapter. The beliefs and conclusions of psychiatrists are as varied and absurd as religious cults. Regardless of the trappings of science, psychiatry is on a par with witchcraft.

A defense attorney can obtain any number of psychiatrists to testify in any criminal case that his client was insane at the time of the alleged crime. The prosecuting attorney can match him with a plethora of psychiatrists to testify that the defendant was perfectly sane. The evidence of any psychiatrist can be easily countered with nullifying "expert rebuttal." The judge or jury is swayed by the most impressive panjandrum. It would be better to determine the sanity or insanity of the defendant by the toss of a coin. Every day, psychiatrists discharge criminally insane patients as "cured", only to have them immediately resume their bloody forays on decent society. The suicide rate among psychiatrists is TWICE the national average, and THEY are entrusted with therapy that purports to save other people from self-destruction. The ancient Greeks had a word for it: "Physician, heal thyself!"

Psychiatrists are three times more likely to go insane or suffer emotional disorders than the average person. According to Dr. Ferris N. Pitts Jr., a professor of psychiatry at the University of Southern California School of Medicine, "Psychiatrists—the doctors who are highly trained to solve the problems of the mentally ill—are many times the individuals who need help the most . . . Many who select the field do so because they are searching for a solution to their own problems." These emotionally disturbed clowns receive fabulous fees to cure emotional problems in other people which they cannot cure in themselves. They dignify primitive witchcraft with scientific gobbledygook, confuse abstruseness with profoundness, and con the gullible like slickers conning pigeons.

Psychiatrists are trained to help married couples cope with their marital problems; but their own divorce rate is three out of five, as compared to two out of five in the general population, according to the Census Bureau. The blind lead the blind, but these blind predators have their hands in the pockets of their blind prey while leading them. Psychiatrists are like bald-headed barbers selling surefire hair restoratives to bald-headed patrons. This is no joke. It actually happens. Small wonder psychiatrists turn the criminally insane loose upon society to commit murder, rape, and robbery. Perhaps the root of the problem is the turning loose of psychiatrists upon society.

Psychiatric schools of treatment are as numerous as religious cults; and like religious cults, they each claim a monopoly on truth. The primitive method of treating psychiatric symptoms was to gouge out a hole in the skull (trephining) in order to allow the offending demons to escape through the hole. Modern therapists of the Transformation School use electricity and insulin to shock the demons out of the patient. Several schools of somatotherapy sprang up. They use chemotherapy and pharmacotherapy, including drugs such as chloral hydrate, various bromides, tranquilizers, MAO inhibitors, and antidepressants. Some schools employ electroconvulsive therapy, electronarcosis, and neurosurgery, including prefrontal lobotomy.

Other psychiatric cults take an entirely different approach in that the practitioner communicates with the patient mind to mind. These cults employ psychotherapy which spawned many related cults including Freudian Psychoanalysis, Jungian Analysis, Adlerian Analysis, Gestalt Therapy, Interpretive Therapy, Supportive Psychotherapy, Group Therapy, Behavioral Therapy, and so forth.

Psychotherapy is a term made up of two Greek words: psyche, meaning "mind", and therapia, meaning "treatment." Greek and Latin are as useful to physicians and psychiatrists as mirrors are to magicians. For example: The patient goes to his doctor complaining of loss of appetite. The doctor diagnoses his problem as, ANOREXIA. The patient is amazed at his doctor's proficiency and erudition in making such a quick diagnosis. He doesn't know that his doctor merely told him what he already knew, but he told him in Greek. Anorexia is the Greek word for "loss of appetite." Language is a fantastically effective way to dress ignorance in the raiment of knowledge.

Demonology is a strong force in the world even today, but it dominated seventeenth century psychiatry. Dr. Johann Weyer was ahead of his time. A little girl had a problem. She spewed needles, thread, and bits of cloth from her mouth. Dr. Weyer took the rare naturalistic approach and diagnosed hysteria. He believed that she had swallowed those objects, unbeknownst to her father, because she was crying out for paternal attention. The Church attacked Dr. Weyer as a stupid quack because he had failed to recognize a classic case of an entombed demon in the body of the girl which required the emergency therapy of immediate exorcism. Psychology was religious heresy those days. It has since blossomed into many independent cults which resemble religion more than science

John Broadus Watson founded Behaviorism, a school of psychology. He discarded consciousness and introspection as legitimate methods of observation and substituted the study of behavior. To him, thinking is merely sub-vocal speech. He taught that, "'Instincts' do not exist as such; they are all learned from parents and the environment." He derived his "proof" from the studies of behavior in human infants. From these studies, he concluded that only three unlearned instinctive reactions exist in human beings: 1) Fear of loud noises. 2) Rage induced by inhibiting the infant's movements. 3) Love as elicited by tickling, rocking, and stroking the infant. He used the proof of these three congenital instincts to prove that no instincts exist in human beings. Ashley Montagu in *The Human Revolution* makes Watson's illegitimate conclusions the bedrock of science. Says he, "The fact is, that with the exception of the instinctoid reactions in infants to sudden withdrawals of support and to sudden loud noises, the human being is entirely instinctless." His dogma reads like a Papal Bull.

Actually, Watson, Montagu, and other so-called scientists of their ilk are religious cultists, not scientists. Because instincts are not evident in infancy does not mean they do not exist. A freshly hatched chick doesn't build a bird nest or mate. The nesting and mating instincts are time-released. If Watson had placed a male and female nude human infant together, he would have detected no inclination for them to copulate. If he had repeated the experiment eighteen years later, he would have noted a vast difference. He would have made the amazing discovery that the human male didn't need parents or society to teach him how to get an erection or what to do with it once he got it. Perhaps it then would have dawned on him that INSTINCTS ARE TIME-RELEASED. Human beings grow into instincts, but not out of stupidity. Behaviorism has instinctive appeal, not unlike religious cults. It appeals to man's overweening ego because he wants to dominate instinct, not be dominated by instinct. Behaviorism flowered into Neobehaviorism, which was preached by Clark L. Hull and B. F. Skinner.

Burrhus Frederic Skinner made extensive experiments with rats. The experiments were designed to prove that learning is an exclusive function of reward and punishment. According to his reinforcement theory, and the theory that man is a rational animal, the North Vietnamese were supposed to learn from the brutal punishment of saturation bombings, the punishments of agonizing torture from napalm splattered on them, and the starvation induced from spraying Agent Orange on their sources of food that it would behoove them to forget about liberation *a la* Ho Chi Minh style, and start thinking about liberation *a la* USA style. The United States dropped many times more bombs on the North Vietnamese than she dropped on Germany and Japan during World War II, but Neobehavioristic cultism was as ineffectual as witchcraft, magic, or prayer.

Subscribing to Neobehavioristic psychology led the United States into a humiliating defeat. The North Vietnamese were not motivated to stop fighting because of punishment. On the contrary, it only gave them greater resolve. They were motivated by their territorial instincts. Some children will not respond to whippings even if they are beaten to death. Reward and punishment are aids to learning, but they are totally impotent when they conflict with basic instincts. Skinner failed to understand that rats will learn to solve a maze because of instinctive satisfaction. Human beings will defend territory, seek confreres, propagate, and domineer, regardless of reward and punishment, because they are mechanistically driven by instinct. Pleasure derived from satisfying instinct is its own reward. Sex teaches us this, if nothing else. The Vietnam experience should teach us that psychology cults are as dangerous as witchcraft cults.

The Sobell Experiment was a six-week behavioral modification program designed to convert alcoholics into social drinkers without the necessity of maintaining total abstinence. It would have been an unqualified success, provided B. F. Skinner's Behaviorist psychology of behavioral control by reward and punishment were valid. In 1982 and 1983, CBS's *60 Minutes* programs featured an expose of this experiment: twenty subjects were given drinks during the period of the experiment, but if they drank too fast or too much, they were administered mild electric shocks. The experiment was conducted on the theory that human behavior can be modified by reward and punishment. The Sobells published six-month, one-year, and two-year follow-ups on the experiment, all of which indicated that it was a whopping success. Nineteen of the twenty were reported to be "functioning well" after two years. The Sobells achieved international fame, and they became highly respected in the scientific community.

Reporters on *60 Minutes* interviewed the subjects in the Sobell Experiment and found that instead of nineteen out of twenty successes, it was nineteen out of twenty failures—if not twenty out of twenty. The first thing many of the subjects did after the experiment was concluded was head for the nearest bar or liquor store and get stinking drunk. Fourteen out of the twenty were back in a hospital within a year. When *60 Minutes* reviewed the experiment in 1983, four subjects had died (presumably from alcoholism), eight were still alcoholics, and the remainder of them sought traditional treatment consisting of total abstinence.

What passes as good science in the scientific community is frequently exactly the same as the most absurd nonsense of religious cults. Scientists form conclusions before they conduct experiments. Evidence which tends to disprove their preconceived conclusion is ignored, altered, swept under the rug, or distorted by rationalizations. One can find as much science in the *Bible* or in the *Koran* as in the textbooks of the inexact sciences.

Not only is much of what passes for science indistinguishable from fanatical religion, but some is unadulterated prostitution in disguise. Dr. Domeena Renshaw admits that psychologists employing sex surrogates are in a gray area at best. A licensed psychologist is considered unethical if he has sex with his patient, even under the pretense of sex therapy, but he can hire an unlicensed person or persons to have sex with his patients. Does he then become a pimp? Sometimes it is difficult to discern the difference between a sex surrogate and a prostitute; but one thing is certain, and that is that "sex surrogate" is an excellent euphemism for "prostitute," and "psychologist" can be an excellent euphemism for "pimp."

Psychology is similar to religion and mythology. That is why there are as many psychology cults as there are religious cults. There is only one school of mathematics. Two plus two equals four all over the world, but if there were any way two plus two could equal any assignable number, mathematics would also be broken up into endless cults. Actually, two plus two equals four because two plus two is DEFINED as the sum of two plus two. Arithmetic is tautology rather than knowledge, but psychology isn't even tautology. It is mythology. To mention but a few of the psychology cults we have: Structuralism, Functionalism, William James' Stream of Thought, Freudian, Gestalt, Biopsychology, Psychopharmacology, Cybernetic Psychology, *et cetera.*

The kinship of inexact sciences with superstition and religious cults was suggested in Robert Ardrey's *The Social Contract.* He says cultural anthropologists insist that man is solely a product of his culture, but the fact that culture is a product of man is ignored. The cart is put before the horse. If youth is solely a product of culture, how is it possible for youth to revolt against it? How can gravity, solely a product of mass, revolt against mass? Planets cannot leave orbit and go flying off into space!

Behaviorist psychology maintains that all human behavior flows from conditioned reflexes responding to associations of reward and punishment. Why, then, did pickpockets in Olde England thrive in crowds which consisted of spectators to the hangings of other pickpockets; and why hasn't the penal system been a success in the United States? Why are some children unresponsive to punishment, and why do children of rich parents who are extensively rewarded with every worldly luxury seek the thrills of crime? Why do men give their lives for their country with no other reward than pain, suffering, and death? Why do religious fanatics kill and die for their gods? Instinct overrules any and all reward/punishment-oriented behavior! Cheetahs and leopards are solitary creatures for the same reason lions and human beings are social creatures—INSTINCT! No amount of reward and punishment will make cheetahs and leopards social creatures or lions and human beings solitary creatures.

Environmentalist sociology denies that biology has any effect on social arrangements. How then, could man possibly learn language, music, art, ambulation, or reproductive behavior if the faculties for them did not preexist in man's biological patterns? The great apes can communicate in sign language, but they cannot communicate vocally because they lack the biological pattern of vocal cords. In the beautiful words of Ardrey, "cultural anthropology, Behaviorist psychology, and environmentalist sociology [are] like three drunken friends leaning against a lamppost in the enchantment of euphoria, all convinced that they are holding up the eternal light when, in truth, they hold up nothing but each other." Man is, indeed, unique. He is the only animal who even deceives himself.

Medical science, as an exact science, was a fantastic human achievement. It saved millions of lives. But we cannot credit the hoi polloi with this achievement. It was the abnormal bona fide *Homo sapiens*, the eccentric oddball who had flashes of genuine intelligence, that gave the world medical science, but it is not uncontaminated with superstition and nonsense. Much of so-called education is really indoctrination with ignorance. Millions of people who enter college or read books for the purpose of acquiring knowledge actually only acquire new names for old forms of ignorance. For example, if one goes to medical school to learn medicine according to the germ theory, he is probably increasing his knowledge; but if he goes to school to learn healing art from medical cultists or religious exorcists, he is increasing his ignorance and superstition. Some of our most prestigious universities teach national myths rather than historical facts; religious and superstitious ignorance rather than scientific fact; and pseudo-science rather than true science.

Even with medical science available to the modern world, much of the world is incapable of appreciating its value. More than half of the world's population rely on yoga, acupuncture, herbs, and witch-craft, rather than modern scientific medicine. The minds of most people in the world are in phase with primitive cults and one hundred eighty degrees out of phase with modern medical science. A leading Peruvian neurosurgeon, Dr. Fernando Cabieses, says, "Our studies show that 80 percent of rural Peruvians prefer to have folk healers treat them, rather than medical doctors." Many hospitals in Peru are almost empty. In several countries, Nigeria for example, witch doctor techniques and remedies are preferred over modern drugs. Why not! Witch doctors have proved their ability according to the usual criterion of human reason. An eclipse of the sun occurs. The populace is terrified. The witch doctor waves his magic wand, and the eclipse ends. The multitudes now have absolute confidence in the powers of the witch doctor. Even in the United States, religious groups such as Christian Scientists and Jehovah's Witnesses reject modern medical science. In addition, millions of Americans place their faith in worthless medical cults rather than authentic medical science.

There are no essential differences between medical cults, religious cults, and witchcraft cults. One of the first "modern" medical cults was founded in the late-eighteenth century by an Edinburg, Scotland, physician named Dr. John Graham, O.W.L. (stands for "Oh Wonderful Love"). He opened the sumptuous Temple of Health in London where he treated the sick with special baths, then placed them on "magnetic thrones" where compound magnets "poured forth curative magnetic waves." The magnetic waves were augmented with mild electric shocks, which his patients associated with cosmic healing powers.

Dr. Graham's assistant boasted the impressive title, "The Rosy Goddess of Health." She was none other than Emma Hart, the future Lady Hamilton and Lord Nelson's mistress. Dr. Graham offered a special treatment which was supposed to render barren couples fecund. It consisted of allowing the childless couples to spend a sexual night on his Celestial Bed for fees up to two thousand five hundred dollars. The bed featured electric coils, and the room featured soft music, incense, and colored lights caressing the lovers. The Celestial Bed didn't beget children so much as it begot wealth for Dr. Graham and Emma Hart.

Wilhelm Reich was a one-time professor at the New School for Social Research at Manhattan. He considered himself a biophysicist. He modestly admitted, "I have discovered the laws of living. [My discovery is addressed] to the culture of one thousand or five thousand years hence as was the first wheel of thousands of years ago to the Diesel locomotive of today." He "discovered" orgone energy which "is the basis of sexual energy in the human body." He theorized that the Russian Revolution failed and general disorder resulted from "the lack of full and repeated sexual satisfaction." His "science" maintained that sexual frustration from inadequate orgasms spills over into the thwarting of political consciousness. He said that the answer to the world's neurotic problems is the achievement of a true "Reichian orgasm," which is a full and complete orgasm attainable only by means of Reichian therapy.

Reich taught that "blue is the specific color of orgone energy within and without the organism." That is why the sky, the oceans, static electricity, *et cetera*, are blue—they contain orgone energy. In 1940, Reich invented the "Orgone Energy Accumulator," a phony therapeutic box which Dr. Theodore P. Wolfe described as "The most important single discovery in the history of medicine, bar none." A patient was supposed to accumulate orgone energy in the therapeutic box and be cured of anemia, cancer, arthritis, ulcers, sinusitis, *et cetera*.

Reich believed that the world could "learn to counteract the murderous radiation of atomic energy with the life-furthering function of orgone energy and thus render it harmless." Regarding cancer, he said, "Many cancer cells have a tail and move in the manner of a fish." Only the early death of a cancer patient prevents him from changing "completely into protozoa." His Orgone Energy Accumulator was declared a fraud by the Food and Drug Administration. He died in 1957 while he was serving a two-year prison term in a federal penitentiary for violation of the Food and Drug Act. If he had said God was the source of orgone energy, or even claimed to be God, and made a religion of his "science," he would have been protected under the constitutional guarantees of religious freedom.

"Doctor" John R. Brinkley became a millionaire during the 1920s by opening a clinic in Milford, Kansas, for rejuvenating sexually impotent old men, grafting goat glands onto them for a fee of up to one thousand five hundred dollars. His radio station license was revoked, but he bought a station in Mexico across the Rio Grande from Del Rio. He claimed he could cure prostate problems with blue dye and hydrochloric acid. People are frequently unable to distinguish between ignorance and knowledge. Consequently, this quack became so popular that he almost defeated Alf Landon, one-time Republican Presidential candidate, for the governorship of Kansas. Brinkley even polled thousands of write-in votes in Oklahoma where he was not a candidate.

John Humphrey Noyes pioneered the "medical science" of "COITUS RESERVATUS" which prescribed desisting from orgasm by the male and a gradual subsidence of desire after the female had achieved climax. Noyes maintained that coitus interruptus conserves male energy and leads to increased health and virility. He opposed marital fidelity because he called it a sin of selfishness. Coitus reservatus as a method of prolonging life had many advocates, chief of which was Dr. Alice Bunker Stockham who renamed it "KAREZZA," but she prescribed the withholding of sexual climax for both the male and female. She praised KAREZZA as an "exquisite exaltation [which results when] the physical tension subsides, the spiritual exaltation increases, and, not uncommonly, visions of a transcendent life are seen and consciousness of new powers experienced." She recommended interludes between infrequent sexual encounters of as long as three to four months to enhance "the reciprocal delight (and anticipation) of the ultimate union."

Dr. Stockham made a fortune from her books. This encouraged other predators to share in the rewards of phony medical science. Marie Stopes of Britain credited the female's absorption of the male's fluid from the prostate gland with vitalizing and health-giving effects. Joseph Yahuda wrote in his *New Biology and Medicine*, in 1951, that both the male and the female mutually benefit from absorbing secretions from sexual intercourse. Rejuvenation is an age-old dream. The search for the legendary Fountain of Youth on Bimini Island in the Bahamas led Ponce de Leon to the discovery of Florida in 1513. Many quacks and humbug artists arose to milk the dream. Dr. Johann Heinrich Cohausen promoted a physical-medical cult in the name of science which claimed it could prolong life to the age of 115. How? By its members inhaling the breath of young maidens. He said that young ladies exhale invigorating elements which are produced by their blood and organs. His therapy was known as "HERMIPPUS REDIVIVUS." Some eighteenth century London doctors not only prescribed it for their elderly patients, but they also took rooms in the buildings of girl schools so that they, themselves, could prime their slow and sluggish blood and quicken their pulses by inhaling the breath of young maidens.

Twelfth century alchemist Artephius claimed he was over a thousand years old when he revealed his secrets for longevity in his *De Vita Propaganda*. Fourteenth century Parisian Nicolas Flanel was believed to have discovered the secret of the Elixir of Life and remained ageless. His followers claimed that Flanel never really died, but had a wooden dummy buried in his place, and he departed with his wife for the Orient. Three hundred years later, a believer visited the Orient where he met a dervish who said he knew both Flanel and his wife, and they were still in excellent health.

Count Saint-Germain was also supposed to have discovered the Elixir of Life and become impervious to death. The ladies of the Paris salons whispered that the count had met Jesus Christ and Pontius Pilate personally. A Monsieur Gauve posed as Count Saint-Germain and gave lectures on his experiences with the Holy Family and Pilate nearly two thousand years in his past. He found no shortage of believers. *Homo nonsapiens* always lives up to his expectations. Seventeenth century "scientists" like Richard Lowers "rejuvenated" old men by giving them transfusions of blood from young men, but many died because of mismatching blood types.

Samuel Christian Hahnemann, of Leipzig, Germany, launched the famous medical cult known as Homeopathy with the publication of his magnum opus, *The Organon*, in 1810. In it, he "enlightened" the world to the "Law of Similia" which decrees that "like cures like." In other words, to discover a drug which will cure a disease, one must but find a drug which will produce the symptoms of the disease in a healthy person. The idea was borrowed from sixteenth century Paracelsus, the father of pharmaceutics, who said, "What makes a man ill also cures him."

Paracelsus was credited with curing plague victims in A.D. 1534 by administering orally a pill consisting of bread and a small amount of the patient's excreta. The first lesson he taught his students at the University in Basel was to burn all the standard textbooks on medicine. He preferred to learn from old wives, gypsies, sorcerers, astrologers, and occult personalities. As an alchemist, he tried to transmute lead into gold. It was said that he castrated himself so that carnal desires would not interfere with his medical interests.

Drugs used by the nineteenth and twentieth century Homeo-pathic physicians include Lachryma Filia (tears from a weeping girl), Asterias Rubens (powdered starfish), Mephitis (skunk secretion), Cimex Lectularius (crushed live bedbugs), and Acidum Uricum (human urine or snake excrement). The *materia medica* of Home-opathy contained three thousand of these zany drugs. Fortunately, Hahnemann believed that the more minute the dose, the more its potency. It was like saying, "The less brains one has, the more intel-ligence he has," which just happens to be true in the case of human beings. He called for the dilution of his compounds to one decillionth which was the same as placing a drop of his compound in the Pacific ocean, mixing it thoroughly, and giving a spoonful to his patients. Such dilution would even render the most deadly poison perfectly harmless, and the most effective medicine absolutely useless.

As with religious cults, political cults, economic cults, or any other human cult, Homeopathy split into factions. It splintered over dis-putes concerning the proper Homeopathic dosage. The Hahnemann purists reduced the dilution to the point of nonexistence, claiming that with the loss of material essence, the medicine gained spiritual essence; hence, greater curative powers. The "low potency" faction insisted that at least a few molecules of the compound must be left in the medicine. The "high potency" faction called for an even less dilu-tion of the drug. Pharmacologists have proved that the weird drugs were so diluted, they could produce neither symptoms nor cures, but since when have human beings allowed themselves to be prejudiced by facts?

Twenty-two Homeopathic colleges were founded in the United States by 1900. Many books and dozens of periodicals were published which were monumental contributions to human ignorance. A large memorial to Samuel Hahnemann was erected on Washington, D.C.'s Scott Circle. Homeopathy flourished in Europe, India, and South America. There are thousands of doctors in the United States who follow the Homeopathic tradition, but occasionally resort to Allo-pathic remedies (standard medical practice).

Homeopathic splinter-group doctors include Dr. Loyal D. Rogers of Chicago who published *Auto-Hemic Therapy* in 1916. He advertised that he cured patients "without use of drugs or bugs (by merely) attenuating, hemolizing, incubating, and potentizing" a few drops of blood from the patient. Dr. Charles H. Duncan of New York City published his *Autotherapy* in 1918 which explained how he cured dysentery by injecting the patient with filtered excretions from the patient's own waste matter; tuberculosis by injecting the patient with the patient's own sputum; boils from the pus taken from the patient's boils, *et cetera*. Much of the nonsense which posed as twentieth century medical science was as absurd as 50,000 B.C. witchcraft. Religious, medical, and science prophets write zany "Bibles" this very day, and they never lack for resolute believers.

Naturopathy is a worldwide medical cult with complete reliance on nature for healing. It rejects medicine and surgery out of hand. There are hundreds of splinter groups. Some advocate hydrotherapy (water cures). Louis Kuhne's *The New Science of Healing* opposed all drugs and promoted steam baths, sun baths, meatless diets and whole wheat bread. John H. Kellog founded the Nature Therapy Sanitarium at Battle Creek, Michigan. Bernarr Macfadden published health magazines and wrote books proposing home treatments for diseases as serious as polio and cancer. The treatments included exercise, diet, and water therapy. At one point, he became convinced that cancer could be cured by a diet of grapes alone, and he offered ten thousand dollars to anyone who could disprove his theory. Hundreds of medical cults sprang up advocating ridiculous diets, special massages, and various hydrotherapies, such as enemas, "to rid the body of poisons." Will Durant was addicted to hydrotherapeutic enemas.

George Bernard Shaw wrote that drugs merely suppress symptoms. He claimed that germs are the products of disease, not the cause; but once developed in the unhealthy body, they become infectious. He said that nature cures disease in spite of drugs, not because of them. Many naturopaths joined this cult. Eugene Debs, the famous labor leader, joined the cult as espoused by Bernarr Macfadden and Upton Sinclair. When he became ill, he fasted to the point of malnutrition and dehydration. Naturopaths administered a worthless cactus juice remedy for his faltering heart, and he died a victim of naturopathic medicine.

Jerome Irving Rodale, former publisher of *Prevention* magazine, editor of *Encyclopedia of Organic Gardening*, and several health books, insisted that milk is only for babies, and he denounced the cooking of food because it devitalizes food. He plugged organic farming, various secrets for longevity, and vitamins. On June 9, 1971, Dick Cavett was taping a TV interview with Rodale, who was in the process of assuring both Cavett and the world that his health secrets, which included the popping of over seventy vitamin pills a day, would guarantee him life to well beyond a hundred years. He was energetically expounding on the thesis that Vitamin E protects the heart from an attack when he suddenly pitched forward in his chair and became motionless. Dick Cavett thought he fell asleep. Actually, he died of a heart attack, age seventy-two, some thirty years short of his prediction. His disciples apparently concocted the canard that he always had a serious heart defect, and that it was a miracle he hadn't died thirty years sooner. This reassured the true believers, and helped to secure the future of *Prevention* magazine.

A Budapest doctor by the name of Ignatz Peczely "discovered" Iridiagnosis, a method of diagnosing illness by examining the iris of the eye. He made his "discovery" at the precocious age of ten when he associated variations in his pet owl's eyes from the time of an accidental breaking of the bird's foot to the time of its final healing. Naturopath Henry Lindlahr developed this basic concept into a discipline with his 1917 work, *Iridiagnosis and Other Diagnostic Methods*. He divided the iris into forty zones running clockwise in one eye and counterclockwise in the other. The zones are supposed to connect to all major parts of the body by nerve fibers. Any spot on the iris is a "lesion" which indicates malfunctioning in the corresponding part of the body. Imagine the embarrassing moment for the doctor when, after an expensive and exhaustive iridiagnosis, the patient jolts the doctor with the bombshell that he had examined his glass eye. J. Haskell Kritzer recognized the seriousness of the problem, and in his 1921 textbook of Iridiagnosis carefully explained how to identify artificial eyes and avoid the embarrassment.

Another medical cult was founded and exploited by the senior nose and throat surgeon, Dr. William H. Fitzgerald, of St. Francis

Hospital at Hartford, Connecticut. He and his associate Dr. Edwin F. Bowers collaborated in 1917 on the book called Zone Therapy. They revealed the esoterica that the human body is divided into five zones vertically on each side, and each zone terminates in a particular finger or toe. With this revelation came the "cure" for all pain and illness. It was simply a matter of applying pressure to the appropriate finger or toe. Pressure was usually applied by either wearing rubber bands or snapping spring clothes pins on the correct finger or toe. They claimed to cure whooping cough in a few minutes by applying pressure on a particular spot on the back of the throat. The "trailblazing doctors" testified that, "In experiments with several hundred cases of whooping cough, we have not yet seen a failure from the proper application of Zone Therapy." They neglected to mention where to apply pressure to cure human stupidity; but, if they had, and it were a true cure, they, and others like them, would have died in poverty.

Benedict Lust also wrote a book entitled *Zone Therapy*. It described how to treat goiters with pressure on the first and second fingers, but "if the goiter is extensive it becomes necessary to include the ring finger . . . One of the most effective means of treating partial deafness is to clamp a spring clothes pin on the third finger, on the side involved in the ear trouble." He revealed that Zone Therapy is a boon to dentists. By merely snapping rubber bands on the finger related to the zone associated with the particular tooth, the tooth becomes insensitive to pain and no anesthetic is required. It's even simpler than acupuncture. The treatment for falling hair "is simplicity itself. (It is performed by) rubbing the fingernails of both hands briskly one against the other in a lateral motion, for three or four minutes at a time, at intervals throughout the day. This stimulates nutrition in all the zones, and brings about a better circulation in the body, which naturally is reflected in the circulation of the scalp itself."

Didn't we meet the twentieth century medical cultist at some other time and in some other place? Wasn't he the same blathering idiot at the summit of the Hill of the Stars who saved the world from darkness by ripping out living human hearts and offering them to the gods?

Many breakfast food manufacturers advertise their "all natural" products and "organically grown" products as if they are *ipso facto* good for one's health. People don't realize that most poisons are "all natural." The poison hemlock is a natural plant, and so is rosary pea, purple locoweed, corn cockle, daphne, larkspur, foxglove, and hundreds of other "all natural" poisonous plants. Some springs are naturally poisoned with arsenic. Drinking this natural water causes sudden death. On the other hand, many drugs which naturopaths denounce as "unnatural" are merely purified compounds found in nature.

Some people believe that "health food" purchased in Health Food Stores necessarily promotes health, but it is not so. Health food addicts are notoriously absent from the roster of centenarians. The label "health food" on a natural poison does not effect any miraculous transubstantiation *a la* a Catholic priest changing wine into the blood of Christ in the ceremony of the Mass. However, it does effect the non-miraculous transposition of money from the health food addict's pocket to the pocket of the health food store owner. Even health food promoters find their natural predatory weapons of cunning and deception very useful.

Henry Lindlahr "discovered" that disease is nature's way of healing, and not as Louis Pasteur taught, the result of harmful microbes invading the body. Naturopaths who accept this dogma oppose vaccination and drinking pasteurized milk. Dr. Wood, in his August 1950 letter to the American Mercury, asked the rhetorical question, "If atmospheric bacteria bring about disease as claimed by the medical profession, then why is it millions of Indians . . . bathe daily in the filthy Ganges river, a river teeming with billions of germs, (and) to my knowledge, there has never been a serious epidemic outbreak of any disease?" The fact is that the death rate from infectious diseases in India is about the highest in the world.

If naturopaths had their way, and everyone drank raw milk, and refused to be vaccinated, millions of people would succumb to diseases that are now rare only because of pasteurization and vaccination. They would die today just as millions of people died of Black Death and Bubonic Plague before the advent of true medical science when human intelligence, such as it is, encouraged the faithful to cling to their ancient faith in prayers and their God. Man's total incapacity to learn when belief is resolute is the wonder and disgrace of the species. Given the tyranny of instinct over the intelligence of man, it is, indeed, a miracle that any members of the human species were ever capable of creating modern science and technology.

Many medical cults are founded on principles of posture, exercise, and diet. Dr. William Horatio Bates wrote *Sight Without Glasses* in 1944. He claimed he could cure every eye defect from presbyopia to amblyopia with eye exercise. Gayelord Hauser wrote *Better Eyes Without Glasses* which "revealed" the secrets of curing diseases of the eyes and gaining better sight from a combination of exercise and diet. Frederick Matthias Alexander established a school in London and gained an illustrious following from his system of treating voice problems with exercise. Anyone with a message people WANT to hear is assured a copious supply of patsies.

Several cults claimed to cure disease through relaxation therapy. Edmund Jacobson wrote *Progressive Relaxation* and *You Must Relax*. Dr. David H. Fink wrote *Release From Nervous Tension*. Chicago doctor, E. H. Pratt invented "Orificial Therapy," a relaxation system designed to cure all the common ailments. Relaxation Therapy worked best for its promoters because it made them rich, and wealth is a wondrous aid to relaxation. In like manner, many modern diet cults have proved successful in making their promoters rich even though many were dangerous, some even fatal.

Andrew Taylor Still was the father of Osteopathy. He was a self-declared genius. His autobiographies were laden with false data. One of his books contains a picture captioned, "Professor Peacock" which illustrates how "we learn God's plan of governing the body from peacock feathers." Like religious mystics, he claimed divine inspiration; but he was, in fact, inspired by the Swedish massage movement which was the rage in his day of the late nineteenth century. He coined the word " osteopathy" (Greek meaning " diseased bones") for his theory that diseases are the result of malfunctioning of nerves or the blood supply, which is caused by dislocations of small bones in the spine which he called "subluxations of the vertebra." Pressure on nerves and blood vessels caused by subluxations are supposed to prevent the body from manufacturing its own curative agents. The function of the osteopath is to locate subluxations and "adjust" them, somewhat like locating demons and exorcising them.

Andrew Still wrote a textbook on osteopathy in 1910 which taught methods of spinal manipulation to cure yellow fever, malaria, diphtheria, rickets, piles, diabetes, dandruff, constipation, and obesity. He had no interest in laboratory medical tests or tracking down bacterial causes of diseases because, as he said, "We have but little time to spare in analyzing urine, blood lymph, or any other fluid substance of the body because we think life is too precious to dilly-dally in laboratory work." He "recorded many astonishing cures," one of which was the growing of three-inch-long hair on a head bald as a billiard ball. Not bad! But even if spinal rubbing can't grow hair, it is excellent for a patient with repressed sexual desires.

Osteopathy, like many cults, has a flock of fanatical believers. Medical cults, if and when they effect cures, cure by the same process as religious cults and faith healing; namely, hypnosis and suggestion. Up to a point, they provide good results for the true believer, but total failure for the skeptic. Actually, they did little for the millions who died in germ-related epidemics. Meanwhile, medical cults, as well as religious cults, provide perfect hunting grounds for human predators.

Considerable evolution has taken place among the thousands of modern osteopathic doctors. They have succeeded in entering orthodox medicine through the back door. They no longer confine themselves to massaging spines. They prescribe drugs, perform simple surgery, give anesthetics, and administer water and electrical therapy. Some have extended their practice to psychiatric problems. They have "discovered" that schizophrenia is caused by subluxations in the upper bones of the neck. Incredibly, at least to some of us, osteopathic physicians are licensed to practice medicine in all states of the United States, and have the same privileges as legitimate M.D.'s under federal law and statutes of forty-eight states. There are over thirteen thousand osteopathic doctors in the United States, three hundred hospitals and many "accredited" schools of osteopathy. You have come a long way, baby!

In 1895, a grocer and fish peddler in Davenport, Iowa, by the name of Daniel D. Palmer, "discovered" that he could cure people by "animal magnetism." He then closed shop and entered the magnetic healing business full time. Shortly after this, he claimed that he made a revolutionary discovery. A patient who had been deaf for seventeen years came to him for treatment. The patient explained that he had become deaf a few minutes after hearing a popping sound coming from his spine. This clue led Palmer to palpate a great subluxation (displacement) in his spine whereupon he adjusted the bump (subluxation), and "the patient's hearing was restored to normal. " It is suspected that Palmer's "discovery" was a repetition of the common theme among founders of religious and medical cults; that is, the deaf patient story was a fabrication, and he purloined his techniques from another cult—osteopathy.

Daniel's son, Bartlett Joshua Palmer, expanded chiropractic into the thriving business it is today. He made several "outstanding discoveries", typical of which was that diphtheria is caused by the subluxation of the sixth dorsal vertebra. However, a textbook used by a Chicago chiropractic college contradicts this and insists that diphtheria is caused by subluxations in the third, fifth, and seventh cervical vertebrae. Treatment and cure calls for adjustments to these subluxations. The fact the diphtheria is actually caused by *Corynebacterium diphtheriae* which should be treated with antibiotics is irrelevant to staunch believers in chiropractic.

Bartlett Palmer believed that scarlet fever should be treated with adjustments to the sixth through the twelfth dorsals. The Chicago textbook instructs that the treatment should consist of adjustments to the second through the fifth cervicals and tenth to twelfth dorsals. There is obvious heresy here somewhere, but at least the heretics weren't burned at the stake. Actually, scarlet fever is a streptococcal infection, and antibiotics have practically eliminated the disease, but since when have human beings allowed facts to disturb their dogmatic slumbers? Chiropractic nonsense enjoys equal billing and prestige with legitimate medical science, just as "creation science" nonsense enjoys equal prestige with legitimate evolutionary science. Chiropractic treatments for germ-caused diseases are on the same primitive level as prayers and sacrifices to the gods. Except for specific problems, the curative powers of ALL cults are subjective and hallucinatory, generated only by suggestion and hypnosis.

Bartlett Joshua Palmer invented the neurocalometer, an electrical contraption which supposedly makes spinal diagnoses. It didn't improve the nation's health, but it certainly did improve Bartlett's wealth. Chiropractors often displayed spinal charts in their offices which indicated the correlation of the spine to specific areas of the body and diseases of these areas. They were as scientific as phrenological charts which relate head bumps to mental faculties. Another famous chiropractic diddenbobble was the ELECTROENCEPHALONEURO-MENTIMOGRAPH, which occupied as much room as its name. It was to chiropractic what ceremony is to religion—OSTENTATION!

Modern chiropractic did not evolve into orthodox medical practice as did osteopathy. The National Chiropractic Association does not include the Palmer schools in their list of "accredited" colleges. It places less emphasis on psychic energy, but still maintains that all diseases result from a disruption of the function of the nerves caused by subluxations of the vertebrae of the spine, joints, and muscle tissue. The therapy includes hand manipulation, massage, exercise and applications of heat, cold, and light. Like faith healing, the greatest value of chiropractic is to true believers. To the skeptic, it has very little value except in specific and appropriate cases. However, sometimes even skeptics are converted when cure follows treatment, even though the cure would have taken place anyway through natural healing processes. Few people escape the *post hoc ergo propter hoc* fallacy trap. The tedious process of the scientific method of inductive logic is an aberration of normal human thought processes, and thoroughly unpalatable for 99 and 44/100 percent of the human race.

There are almost endless medical cults, just as there are countless religious cults; and, objectively, they are all mostly nonsense, but they are excellent means of predation. Subjectively, they are as useful as one's faith in them. The curative powers of faith healing, witchcraft, religious, or medical cults are derived from the same source: namely, autosuggestion and hypnosis. Acupuncture also belongs to this category. It has become something of a fad in the United States.

Acupuncture was developed in China about 2,800 B.C. It was exported to Europe by Jesuit missionaries and became fashionable in France during the nineteenth century and again in the 1930s. It currently enjoys popularity in the United States where the populace has become blasé to the miracles of science and fatally fascinated by the fatuities of primitive cultures. Chiang Kai-shek banned it in China during the 1930s and 1940s in an effort to modernize his nation. Chairman Mao Tse-tung revived it during the Cultural Revolution, hoping to provide at least some form of quick and easy medical care for the masses.

Briefly, acupuncture is the insertion of thin metal needles into the skin at some of the two hundred to one thousand acupuncture points (the number varies with the acupuncture school) to precise depths. They are then twirled or vibrated in specific ways. Acupuncture therapy is supposed to correct blockages, excesses, or imbalances in the flow of vital life-force, i.e., the ying (negative) and the yang (positive) energy. Sometimes batteries are connected to the needles to provide mild shock. Herbs are often taken in conjunction with acupuncture. The principal use of acupuncture in the United States is for pain relief. It is an INEFFECTIVE anesthesia in children and many adults. As in most religious and medical cults, its physiological therapeutic value is largely psychological and depends upon faith, belief, hypnosis, and suggestion; in other words, gullibility.

We can but skim the surface of medical cults, folk medicine, "you are what you eat" cults, quackery, hoax, and humbug. The product "Hadacol" was typical of medical humbugs. Its impresario, the flamboyant LeBlanc, promoted it with colorful medicine shows. When people complained that it tasted like dirt, he pulled a Barnum and told them it was supposed to taste like dirt because it contained vitamins, and vitamins come from dirt. Its sickening taste actually enhanced its placebo effect because if medicine doesn't taste bitter, people don't think it has curative powers. One time on the *You Bet Your Life* TV show, Groucho Marx asked LeBlanc what Hadacol was good for. Without batting an eye, LeBlanc replied, "It was good for five and a half million for me last year."

It certainly must occur to some people that the reason so many human beings are so easily hoodwinked by messiahs, religious leaders, medical cults, fakers, frauds, and quacks, is not due to their uniquely superior intelligence. It is due to their unique stupidity. Dr. Elisha Perkins of the American Revolutionary era made a fortune with his "Perkins Patented Metallic Tractor", which he fanned over the infected part of the ailing patient. The metallic rods in it were supposed to draw the disease out of the infected part, much as a priest would exorcise a demon and draw it out of the body of the possessed patient. George Washington and his family used and recommended the Perkins Metallic Tractor. Elisha's son, Benjamin, became extremely wealthy selling the ridiculous device.

By the time Dr. Albert Abrams of San Francisco died in 1923, he had amassed a fortune from his absurd medical contraptions. They included the "Dynamizer" (a box of useless wires); the "Oscilloclast", which was supposed to vibrate at the same frequency as the disease and destroy it; and the "Reflexophone", which was supposed to permit Abrams to diagnose medical problems over the telephone. These devices were so ridiculously childish that it seems incredible anyone with an IQ above a moron could be taken in by them; but tens of thousands of people swore by Dr. Abrams and his contrivances including the famous Upton Sinclair, who wrote books praising the genius of Abrams and crediting him with discovering "the great secret of the diagnosis and cure of all major diseases."

Not many years ago, Dr. Ruth B. Drown of Los Angeles "invented" and wrote books about the science, philosophy, theory, and technique of "Drown Radio Therapy." She preserved droplet blood samples of her patients on blotting paper, and when they telephoned her for medical consultation she simply took out the patient's file containing the blotch of blood, and "diagnosed" the disease from "vibrations" coming from the blot of dried blood; and then she broadcasted "healing rays" to the patient at his or her home over the radio waves. She treated Tyrone Power and his wife, who were in Italy, by sending them shortwave radio therapy from her office in Los Angeles. She was acclaimed by thousands of delighted patients. The sale of her moronic instruments to chiropractors, osteopaths, and naturopaths became the source of additional wealth for her.

Abbott E. Kay claimed that his mysterious "Vrilium" cured disease by means of radiation. Robert T. Nelson sold "Magic Spikes" containing Vrilium for three hundred dollars each. They were worn around the neck like a flea collar, and were supposed to kill bacteria and germs inside and outside the body to a distance of twenty feet. Many important political bigwigs swore by the device until 1950, when government investigators discovered that the "Magic Spikes" contained nothing but cheap rat poison. The human predator is always seeking prey, and to facilitate his predations, he will don many garbs, including those of priests, physicians, businessmen, labor union leaders, patriots, politicians, et cetera. There is always good hunting for a wily predator.

Dr. Fred Urbuteit treated patients at his Sinuothermic Institute in Tampa, Florida, with his Sinuothermic Machine, a device to inject electricity into the body and "miraculously cure" incurable diseases. Arthritis was one of the many diseases the machine was supposed to cure, but Dr. Urbuteit, himself, was confined to a wheelchair because of arthritis. This fact in no way discouraged his many arthritic patients from taking and paying for his Miracle Cure. *Homo sapiens*? You must be kidding!

Colonel Dinshah Pestanji Framji Ghadiali discovered "Spectro-Chrome Therapy" in 1920 at Malaga, New Jersey. He "discovered" that each disease responded to a specific color, and by radiating the affected part of the body with this color, the disease disappears. Gonorrhea succumbs to green or blue-green rays. Diabetes responds to yellow and magenta, et cetera. In 1924, Ghadiali's Spectro-Chrome Institute boasted over ten thousand members. Wealth poured into the Colonel's coffers from leases on his Spectro-Chrome and his Favoroscope. The Favoroscope determined the most favorable time to use the Spectro-Chrome. When Ghadiali was put on trial for fraud, he easily rounded up one hundred twelve witnesses to testify that they had been miraculously cured by the ludicrous therapy. People simply cannot deal with causality rationally. Even the great Sir Isaac Newton who formulated the laws of motion displayed normal human stupidity when he departed from his narrow range of rationality. Total rationality is beyond the capacity of the human species. Modern science and technology evolved against impossible odds.

Dr. Seth Pancoast of Philadelphia simplified colored light therapy to the two colors of red and blue. It was a natural evolution in economy: something like the merging of the many gods into either one God, or three Gods in one divine person. There are many variations on the theme of color therapy such as Dr. George Starr White's "Rhithmo-Duo-Color Therapy," "Biodynamochromatic Diagnosis," et cetera. In 1932, Bruce Copen predicted that "color healing is a science of the future." That may be questionable, but the prediction that "human stupidity is a certainty of the future" is unquestionable.

Dr. William F. Koch taught histology and embryology at the University of Michigan. He was professor of physiology at Detroit Medical College. In 1919, he gave "Glyoxylide" to the world, even though the world would have been better off without it. He claimed that Gloxylide was a cure for every disease from cancer to leprosy. He said that it was a catalyst which stimulated the body to such a frenzy of health that all diseases were overwhelmed by the body's awakened ability to destroy them. Koch became filthy rich. When government chemists determined that Gloxylide was nothing but distilled water, he was put on trial for fraud—not once, but twice. He could not be convicted because, as with most quacks and phonies, he had no trouble rounding up a slew of witnesses to testify to the miraculous healing powers of his distilled water. Osteopaths and chiropractors found Glyoxylide injections a lucrative supplement to their battery of useless treatments.

The list of phonies and quacks goes on and on, and naturally so, because a sucker is born every minute. Kenneth Walker, in his 1951 Venture with Ideas, blends yogi with occult systems. Andrew Jackson Davis, the "Poughkeepsie Seer," practiced psychic therapy. Edgar Cayce was a famous psychic diagnostician who first went into a trance then rendered rambling diagnoses and prescribed spinal manipulations. He sold nostrums such as "Bedbug Juice" and "Fumes of Apple Brandy." He demanded absolute faith of his patients because he assured them that any doubt in their minds would invalidate the diagnosis and prevent the cure. He was smart enough to know that it is faith and faith alone which gives the phony religious prophet, the mystic, and the medical quack power over the gullible.

Current cancer cure quackery includes Carey Reams' distilled water, lemon juice, vegetable, and vitamin cures. He was indicted for fraud. Dr. William Kelley's Malignancy Index and Ecology Therapy (infamous Steve McQueen therapy). He was suspended from practice in Texas whereupon he moved his operations to Mexico. Kenneth Sheldon MacLean M.D.'s magnetic waves as used in his Institute of Cancer Cytology. Vlastimil Brych's "ultra secret" therapy, *et cetera, et cetera.*

One of the most notorious and dangerous humbugs foisted upon the gullible public was Laetrile and Amygdalina, which were promoted as cancer cures with the slogan: "Surgery slashes, radiation burns, chemotherapy poisons, but Laetrile is a risk-free treatment of cancer." Actually, some doses contained lethal sources of cyanide. Some laboratory tests even hinted that Amygdalina can cause cancer. Many people doomed themselves to a cancerous death by abandoning legitimate treatment and switching to Laetrile exclusively. The promoters even induced the faithful to believe that there was an AMA conspiracy to block the use and sale of Laetrile because "it is an effective cure, and it eliminates huge profits for medical doctors." Laetrile has a plethora of testimonials and die-hard believers like most religious, science, or medical cults.

Dr. Victor Herbert, professor of medicine at State University of New York Downtown Medical Center, says, "Quacks operate on the fact that four out of five patients are going to get well anyway. So the quacks are going to have four out of five patients swear by them . . . 80 percent of the problems presented to doctors will go away in a week or two weeks by themselves." Remissions are normal for untreated chronic diseases, but when the diseases are treated, the gullible patients credit the quacks with their improved health during the periods of remissions. The naive patient complaining of an arthritic shoulder visits the quack who promises that his daily treatment of shoulder manipulations at thirty-five dollars a visit will relieve the pain in two weeks; but he doesn't tell the dupe that the pain will disappear in two weeks even without treatment because of normal remission. Dr.

Alexander M. Schmidt, who once headed the FDA, says that, "This is a boon time, a 'golden age' for certain kinds of quacks." Actually, all times are golden ages for all quacks.

Orthodox medical science is of unquestioned value, but because it is practiced by the normal run-of-the-mill *Homo nonsapiens*, scientific medicine is transformed into witchcraft. One brighter than average M.D., Doctor Robert S. Mendelsohn, admits in his 1979 *Confessions of a Medical Heretic*, "I believe that despite all the super technology and elite bedside manner . . . the greatest danger to your health is the doctor who practices Modern Medicine." Every family has been stricken with a fatality, near-fatality, or some sort of a disaster as the result of medical treatment by a licensed M.D. Most people are not even aware of the danger because doctors do, indeed, bury their mistakes, sew up their mistakes, or wait for nature to heal their mistakes.

I can point to several deaths in my own family and near-family which are attributable to physicians' stupidity or ignorance. My seven-year-old brother had measles. The physician opened all the windows in the bedroom during the dead of winter and removed his bedclothes saying, "He needs plenty of fresh air." He quickly contracted pneumonia and died. My sister-in-law repeatedly complained to her doctor about stabbing pain and a lump on her breast. Her doctor repeatedly assured her it was nothing to worry about, and promised her that it would soon go away. When she finally lost faith in her doctor and went to a cancer clinic for tests on her own, it was too late. The cancer had metastasized throughout her body, and it killed her. She was a victim of a witch doctor who impersonated a bona fide medical doctor. My father suffered from rheumatic pain. His doctor prescribed hydrocortisone whereupon he developed peptic ulcers and hemorrhaged to death. One of the serious side effects James W. Longs *Essential Guide to Prescription Drugs* lists for hydrocortisone is "development of peptic ulcer."

Physicians are notoriously ignorant in pharmacology. If one wishes to learn about drugs and side effects, he should ask his pharmacologist, not his doctor. Better yet, he should buy Longs Essential Guide to Prescription Drugs and get it right out of the horse's mouth.

No one should have blind faith in his physician, priest, economist, parent, offspring, political leader, or any two-legged animal that is top-loaded with a hominoid cerebrum.

My young friend smashed his arm in an accident. His doctor insisted he had to amputate the arm to save his life. The boy's father said, "Over my dead body you'll hack off his arm!" Today, his arm is perfectly normal except for some scars. When my ex-wife was pregnant, her doctor briefly but seriously considered treating her for a tumor. My brother-in-law suffered from stomach cramps and pains. His doctor diagnosed intestinal flu. As the days passed, and the pain intensified, my brother-in-law suggested that appendicitis be considered as a diagnostic possibility, but he was pooh-poohed by the high priest of medicine. At painful long last, my brother-in-law nearly demanded an appendicitis operation. When his doctor finally yielded and operated, he discovered that the inflamed appendix was about to rupture.

Four doctors examined me, and they all agreed that I suffer from hypertension. One of them confided that my readings were in the neighborhood of 185/90, which is a high neighborhood. I was put on pills. Fortunately, before long I heard KGO's radio doctor, Dean Edell, explain that some people have high blood pressure ONLY when they are in the doctor's office because they get terrified when the doctor places the cuff over their arm. Blood pressure is supposed to be high when one is frightened or angry. It is nature's way of preparing one's muscles for the fight-or-flight response. It is nature's mechanism to promote survival. Blood pressure readings are standardized for perfectly relaxed and calm states of mind. I bought my own sphygmomanometer, calmed myself down and recorded perfectly normal readings of 120/70 where they have remained to this day.

Doctors told my son he had high blood pressure. I took his reading, but I also noted the terror in his eyes as I placed the cuff around his arm. His reading was 180/90. I explained my experience to my son, expounded on the idiocy of doctors, and within fifteen minutes his reading was down to 140/80. The next day, I continued my diatribe on the stupidity of physicians, calmed him down completely, and found his pressure a perfectly normal 122/75, which is about where it remained these many years. Pharmaceutical companies make big money from anti-hypertensive drugs, and when you hear over radio and TV the advice "Take your medication and live!" you can be assured someone out there is more interested in your money than your life. The pharmaceutical companies camouflage their sponsorship of "public service messages" under titles like "Citizens' Committee Dedicated to the Nation's Health."

Thousands of people die each year because physicians misdiagnose *angina pectoris* for either acute gastritis or indigestion. Thousands die because physicians confuse Reye's syndrome with drug addiction. A CBS *60 Minutes* program exposed the brutal treatment and death of a youth because both the police and the doctor thought the boy was jagging from drugs. Had he been treated for his actual ailment, Reye's syndrome, he probably would have lived. The parents of another youth saved their son's life only because they vociferously demanded that their doctor treat him for Reye's syndrome rather than drug addiction.

I honestly believe that even legitimate medical doctors may kill as many patients as they save. My mother visited many doctors in her lifetime. They prescribed pills and medicine for her all her life, but she seldom took them. They scolded her, "Mrs. Lorentz, you simply must take your medication, if you want to live!" One by one, her doctors passed away—and she outlived them all. At the time of her death, past age one hundred and two, her house looked like a drug store with unopened pill boxes and unopened medicine bottles scattered all over the place. All drugs have side effects. Sometimes the cure is more dangerous than the disease. Nature frequently cures in spite of the physician's treatment, and not because of it. Sometimes medication is needed; but many times, prayer is better than medicine not because it has intrinsic value, but because it can be a harmless substitute for dangerous drugs.

Elvis Presley's death certificate states that he died of a heart condition on August 16, 1977; but the Tennessee Board of Medical Examiners found that Elvis' physician had illegally dispensed six hundred doses per month of uppers, downers, and pain-relievers, which turned him into a prescription junkie. Sylvia Grant, age forty-four, of Kansas City, Kansas, had a promising future. Her doctor, James B. Mercer, prescribed six thousand doses of twenty-three different medications during twenty-one months of treatment to correct menstrual irregularities. Most of the drugs were prescribed to correct symptoms that were caused by previous drugs which he prescribed. Sylvia became a psychotic vegetable in a nursing home. Dr. Mercer was sued for malpractice. He settled out of court and surrendered his license.

There are probably tens of thousands of doctor-made prescription junkies (often Valium) suffering paranoia, painful muscle contractions, blackouts, convulsions, memory and concentration difficulties, suicidal tendencies, and shortened life-span because of idiotic physicians. Dr. William Thomas of Long Beach, California, became a Valium junkie because of his internist. The dosage of many drugs must be continually increased because the patient develops a tolerance for the drugs. After nine years of addiction, which caused intense mental and physical agony, Dr. Thomas quit cold turkey, but it required a month in the hospital to detoxify him, and he suffered a year and a half of withdrawal torment.

Dr. Edgar Berman's *The Solid Gold Stethoscope* estimates that twelve thousand people die annually from unnecessary operations. Ralph Nader places the figure at sixteen thousand. Of the unnecessary operations in one year alone, one hundred seventy thousand perfectly sound ovaries are removed. One hundred seventy three thousand uteruses are needlessly excised. Sixty-six thousand healthy gall bladders are removed per year, along with sixty five thousand good prostate glands. When doctors went on strike in England and the United States, the mortality rate dropped significantly. According to neurosurgeon Dr. C. Norman Shealy: "Between two hundred thousand and four hundred thousand laminectomies are performed each year in the country . . . nine out of ten back operations to relieve chronic pain are unnecessary!" Surgeons diagnose patients by feeling their purse instead of their pulse.

Surgeons and M.D.'s are members of the same race of predators and carnivores as the rest of us. They look for the same fast-and-easy buck as capitalists, union labor leaders, medical quacks, religious cultists, and all others. In England, profit has been removed from surgical operations because of socialized medicine. Therefore, there are very few operations performed. The frustrated medical predators flee to the United States, the Predators' Paradise, where they are unshackled and can blithely prey on the sick, the dying, and the poor. And so, there is a world-wide brain-drain which empties into the United States, where predation is the *summum bonum*, and predators savor the raptures of the Predators' Dream. People of wealth throughout the world converge on the United States for medical treatment and surgical operations where they are sometimes relieved of their maladies, but always relieved of a good hunk of their money.

Surgeons often hack away at human flesh with complete impassivity, like butchers hacking away in a meat market. And why not? The primary object of surgery in a predatory society is profit for the surgeon, not health for the patient. As a case in point, in 1963, a young Florida woman suffered from severe backaches. Her doctor advised an operation to ADJUST her MISPLACED uterus. When the operation was over, the young woman was minus her uterus, one ovary, and she sustained injury to her bladder which required a second operation to repair the damage from the first operation. But this is not the end to the story. Her backaches persisted. An orthopedist discovered that one of her legs was slightly shorter than the other. A simple lift in her shoe corrected the disparity and relieved her backaches which were supposed to have been caused by a MISPLACED uterus. The unfortunate woman suffered the needless loss of her uterus, ovary, and considerable money which truly became misplaced when it was replaced in the pocket of the surgeon.

It is relatively commonplace for surgeons to sew up patients with sponges and surgical instruments left in the victim's body. In one case, a thirty-inch towel was sewn into a patient. Elaine Mezich of Seattle lived five years with a six-inch pair of forceps sewn up in her abdominal cavity until sharp pain brought her to Cabrini Hospital where X-rays exposed the cause of her pain.

Dr. Michael Baden, deputy medical examiner for New York City, concluded from the autopsies which he oversaw, "maybe hundreds of times" the fatalities resulted from medical incompetence. Perhaps indifference also played a part. Attorney Matthew Lifflander, chief of the New York State Assembly Task Force, declared, "What we found is that the level of incompetence among surgeons is a lot greater than anyone imagined." A typical case: Franklin Mirando checked into Smithtown General Hospital in New York for the implantation of an artificial hip joint. When he left the hospital, his right leg was two inches shorter than his left leg, and he was unable to walk without crutches. Besides that, he was in constant pain.

Dr. Thomas Preston, head of the Department of Cardiology at USPHS at Seattle, demonstrated that mock surgery is more successful than actual surgery. A 1959 University of Washington study of seventeen heart patients in which eight were given actual surgery, 32 percent showed improvement; but of the nine who were given sham operations, 43 percent showed improvement. Said Dr. Preston, "I reviewed one hundred unsuccessful coronary bypass operations in which the bypass became blocked, yet 75 percent of those patients feel better anyway and 50 percent are free from any symptoms." The power of the placebo effect is tremendous. In neurotic and non-germ related afflictions, medical cults, prayer, and orthodox medical procedures seem to have equal success rates.

Fifty-seven-year-old Pearl Arnold of Roanoke, Virginia, was told by her doctors that she had less than a year to live because of incurable liver cancer. She was given gut-wrenching chemotherapy which left her bald; and, in her own words, "My brain felt like it was burning. My knees would buckle under me. I'd retch at the very thought of what was going on inside my body." She even picked out her burial site in the cemetery. Her own physician, Dr. Stephen Rosenoff, suspected misdiagnosis. He performed another biopsy and diagnosed her problem to be an allergic reaction to aspirin. Mrs. Arnold filed a 5 million-dollar malpractice suit in November of 1980. Another woman complained of pain in her breast. Her doctor said there was nothing wrong with her. The pain persisted. She went to a second doctor, who confirmed the diagnosis of the first doctor. Eventually, and after the pain became unbearable, she went to a third doctor who found that cancer had spread throughout her body and she was terminal. Even many M.D.'s with twenty years education, two years of internship, and several years of medical practice are basically the same absurd *Homo nonsapiens* as primitive witch doctors.

In June of 1977, at Nassan Hospital in Mineola, New York, doctors operated on forty-nine-year-old New York real estate appraiser Nick Lombardo. He was told that he had inoperable, terminal cancer of the colon, and had three months to live. For sixteen months, Lombardo underwent agonizing chemotherapy. He lost his hair, and nearly his sanity. When he didn't die as predicted, he got a check-up at the Memorial Sloan-Kettering Cancer Center in New York where the doctors found he had nothing but an inflammation of his large intestine: absolutely not cancerous and certainly not fatal.

Horror stories abound. Some years ago, a little girl in one of our Southern states was diagnosed as having retinal cancer, and removal of both eyes was recommended because the "sympathizing effect" would involve the good eye. This diagnosis was confirmed by nearly a dozen local ophthalmologists. Fortunately, the girl was sent to the Mayo Clinic in Rochester, Minnesota, where her problem was diagnosed to be simple retinitis. Prognosis: Do nothing, and the eye will fully recover within three months. That is precisely what happened. That rare, singular, admirable creature, a bona fide *Homo sapiens*, saved her eyes.

What are the indicia of a good physician and surgeon? One must wonder when people like Barry Vinocur—who flunked out of medical school in his first year and dropped out of the army premed school—impersonated a physician by using a genuine doctor's credentials and won the plaudits of men like Dr. J. Sheldon Artz at Mount Sinai. Said Dr. Artz: "[He is] one of the brightest guys I have ever worked with." Vinocur was even invited to join the faculty as an assistant professor of pediatrics and anesthesiology at the University of California Medical Center at San Francisco.

The Great Impostor Ferdinand Waldo Demara, using the credentials of a doctor friend, was commissioned surgeon-lieutenant in the Royal Canadian Navy during the Korean War and successfully performed daily surgical operations and amputations. His first task was to pull a tooth from a captain's mouth. He sat up all night reading a book on dentistry, expertly gave the captain a shot of Novocaine, and pulled his tooth in the morning. The Great Impostor was hailed and publicized as one of the greatest of surgeons. His phenomenal success was his undoing. The publicity of his superior performance exposed him to the world and disclosed his true identity. He also successfully posed as a doctor of philosophy, teacher, psychologist, theologian, and prison officer.

The cost of medical care constantly increases up to nearly twice the CPI rate. The same doctors who dominate three-fourths of the regional boards which set the rates of payment to the doctors for Blue Shield are also the beneficiaries of the high fees. The government complains about the high cost of Medicare. It increases the deductibles so that the poor and the elderly have to pay more and become even poorer. It even considers eliminating some benefits entirely, but the root cause of the problem of impending Medicare bankruptcy—INSATIABLE GREED OF THE MEDICAL PROFESSION AND HOSPITALS—is NOT addressed. There are no plans to curb the greed of doctors, nurses, and hospital owners and administrators because this would encroach upon American freedoms: namely, the freedom of medical predators to prey on the ailing, the infirm, the dying, the poor, and the elderly. THE EAGLE IS OUR NATIONAL EMBLEM—NOT THE DOVE. Naturally, the rights of the predator take precedence over the rights of the quarry.

The profits of hospitals have increased at confiscatory rates while care has deteriorated to utter indifference. According to David Louis' book *More Fascinating Facts*, 1.5 million people a year develop diseases which come simply from being in the hospital. Over fifteen thousand people die of such diseases each year.

It would seem that there is something intrinsically reprehensible and odious about a profession that makes enormous profits from the pain, suffering, and ills of fellow creatures, and whose escalating greed knows no limits. However, this statement must be qualified. Natural predators are not supposed to feel revulsion or remorse for their victims because it is their natural right to prey on quarry. In other words, charge what the traffic will bear. Only prey (victims), or one with the instincts of prey, can experience empathy for victims of predation. Do we Americans lie awake nights with guilt pangs for our quarry, the American Indians? HELL NO! WE REVEL IN THE PLUNDER, AND CALL IT OUR AMERICAN DREAM!

In many instances, there is more evidence of intelligence in animals than in human beings. Dr. Charlotte Tatro points out that many animals share parental responsibility better than human beings. When animals face food shortages, they reduce their birth rate. When human beings face food shortages, they increase their birth rate, as we see in China, India, Africa, Indonesia, and even in the United States among the poor whites and poor blacks. Animals retreat from a losing battle. They know that discretion is the better part of valor, but they are called dumb animals. Human beings fight to the death, and their stupidity is euphemized and glorified as heroism and valor. Human beings fret, worry, and stew over problems they, themselves, create. Animals do not worry over self-created problems. Animals kill other species to eat. Human beings kill all species, including their own, for God, country, sport, money, power, envy, thrills, and amusement. *Homo* is the last animal in the world that should be called sapient.

Ridiculous cults permeate general science as well as medicine and religion, especially the inexact sciences like anthropology, sociology, economics, psychology, and so forth. The most absurd of these cults are the pseudo-sciences such as astrology, oineromancy, physiognomy, numerology, alchemy, and the metaphysical sciences. The vast majority of people are more attracted to these daffy cults than to authentic science. Millions of people are acquainted with their astrological signs and horoscopes, but pitifully few are conversant with the legitimate science of astronomy. Considering the average person's instincts, interests, and intelligence, the existence of modern science and technology is a complete anomaly. Two million years of Homo's presence on Earth has maintained a consistent pattern of predation, stupidity, and cruelty.

The astrological cults date back to the times of the ancient Chaldeans and Assyrians. They saw the heavenly bodies as exerting influence upon the lives of individuals and the destinies of empires. The popes condemned astrology in the sixteenth and seventeenth centuries because it conflicted with the dogma of divine intervention. Incredibly, early astronomers and scientists such as Copernicus, Tycho Brahe, Kepler, Galileo, Descartes, and Newton were practicing astrologers. Devotees insist that astrology is a very real science based upon the law of astral heredity. From the true fact that the sun is responsible for life on Earth, and that the moon influences tides, astrologers jump to the absurd conclusion that planetary positions govern the destinies of man. The planets shed only minuscule, reflected light from the sun, and they are so remote that they could not possibly exert enough influence on newborn infants to determine their futures. As Will Durant said, "(The) sane uses of the heavens were exceptional; astrology antedated—and perhaps will survive—astronomy; simple souls are more interested in telling futures than in telling time."

In 1931, Charles Silvester de Ford of Fairfield, Washington, wrote the following inspiring words: "To me truth is precious . . . I should rather be right and stand alone than to run with the multitude and be wrong . . . The holding of the views herein set forth has already won for me the scorn and contempt and ridicule of some of my fellow men. I am looked upon as being odd, strange, peculiar . . . but truth is truth, and though all the world reject it and turn against me, I will cling to truth still." What sublimity and grandeur of human contemplation! What truth was de Ford defending? His belief that the EARTH IS FLAT—not an oblate spheroid. *Homo sapiens*? If human beings are wise, how is it possible to define stupidity? The insane look upon the sane as insane, and the sane look upon the insane as sane. "All the world's mad, but me and thee, and sometimes I even suspect thee."

Many thousands of volumes have been written on science cults (pseudo-sciences). It is possible to mention but a few in passing. Numerous attempts have been made to put them on a sound scientific basis. For example, Francis Joseph Gall attempted to put phrenology on a scientific basis. Gall and his fellow science cultists maintained that human personality traits and mental faculties are localized in specific areas of the brain. The larger the size of each region of the head (head bump) where the trait is localized, the stronger this faculty or trait. Hence, an examination of the size and contours of a person's head is supposed to reveal individual personality traits and character. Phrenology as a true science simply falls far short of the rigid requirements of the scientific method.

Physiognomy looks to the shape of the face, nose, ears, lips, and color of the hair and eyes for clues to the psychological traits of the individual. Cesare Lombroso claimed that criminals have "stigmata" which distinguish them from other people. Professor Earnest A. Hooton of Harvard correlated criminal types to structural parts of the face. For example, robbers have diffused pigment in the iris, attached ear lobes, and so forth. Students of psychology tend to lose faith in physiognomy when they identify saints as criminals and criminals as saints from photographs handed them in laboratory experiments.

The ancient cult of palmistry is divided into three branches: 1) Chiromancy, which foretells the future and determines character from lines in the palm of the hand. 2) Chirosophy, which reads character and the future from the shapes of the fingers and features of the hand. 3) Pedomancy, which foretells the future and analyzes character from features of the feet. Millions of people, even in this modern age, are firm believers in these ridiculous cults. There is no essential difference between modern man's belief in these cults and the ancient belief in the augurs who predicted the future by observing the flight of birds; the ancient Greek belief in the power of oracles to predict the future; or ancient Roman belief in soothsayers who predicted the future by examining the entrails of sacrificed animals.

Superstitious nonsense has a fatal fascination for most people. Even the science and technology of Western Culture which the modern world now enjoys was in nip and tuck competition with absurd cults throughout its development. True science is so foreign to human mentality that it could only have evolved in Western Culture because of a long series of lucky accidents. What chance does true science have when people have absolute faith in fortune-tellers, but don't have the simple intelligence to wonder why the seers of the future are not wealthy from betting on the outcome of horse races, political elections, or sports events. Surely they should be able to predict the outcome of these events if they are bona fide fortune-tellers. One need not be a fortune-teller to predict that there will never be a shortage of dupes on which predators can prey.

The modern flying saucer craze began June 24, 1947, when Kenneth Arnold observed nine distant circular objects moving at high speed while he was flying his private plane near Mt. Rainer. Arnold told a reporter that the objects "flew like a saucer would if you skipped it across the water." The word "saucer" caught on with the wire services, and the flying saucer mania was underway. Within weeks, flying saucers were reported in every state; in Canada; England; the Near East; and Australia. David Lawrence of the U.S. News said they were secret United States aircraft. Walter Winchell identified them as new technological breakthroughs by the USSR. Flying saucer hoaxes were perpetrated by pranksters, psychotics, publicity seekers, and those who wanted to sell phony yarns to adventure magazines. Wild stories circulated that the flying saucers were manned by a race of Titans returning to Earth after two hundred centuries; that intelligent beings from another planet were putting the planet Earth under close surveillance; that atomic explosions on Earth alerted intelligences from outer space to put Earth under surveillance; that flying saucers were piloted by a race of Martian super-bees two inches long but with intelligence superior to that of human beings; *et cetera*.

The flying saucer mania grew to such vast proportions that the U.S. Air Force set up "Project Saucer" to investigate the phenomenon, but the fifteen-month study found no evidence fur flying saucers which could not be explained as illusion, hoaxes, or misinterpretations of balloons or other familiar objects. Actually, Arnold's first sightings coincided with the Navy's 1947 launching of huge Skyhook balloons, designed for cosmic ray research. In fact, many of the lost Skyhook balloons were traced and recovered simply by following press reports of flying saucer sightings. But the flying saucer/UFO mania would not go away. The Air Force was accused of a cover-up.

Continuing pressure led the U.S. Air Force in 1968 to sponsor a UFO study at the University of Colorado called, "A Scientific Study of UFO's" under the direction of E. U. Condon, a renowned physicist. The study was reviewed by the National Academy of Sciences and released in 1969. London flatly rejected the extraterrestrial hypothesis and declared that no further investigation was warranted. According to Ronald Schiller, "The one inescapable fact that emerges is that, despite the millions of UFO landings that have supposedly taken place on earth, not a single piece of tangible evidence—neither a nut, bolt, artifact, instrument, or defector from a flying saucer, nor even a convincing picture of one—has ever been produced."

Richard Locke wrote a series of satires for the New York Sun which fabricated the story that the British astronomer Sir John Herschel had seen ape-like creatures on the moon through the then new Cape Town, South Africa, telescope. The articles went into great detail describing life on the moon. Half of New York believed the story, and many continued to believe it even when reporter Locke admitted it was a hoax. When Orson Wells presented a radio version of H. G. Well's *War of the Worlds* on Halloween night in 1938, hysteria and panic raged from coast to coast. Thousands of people wept, prayed, and slammed their doors and windows shut to keep poison gas from killing them. Many fled their homes in anticipation of the end of the world. Would a wise God pervert his wisdom by giving these ridiculous creatures an immortal soul?

But human beings are unique! They cannot be dissuaded from their superstitious predilections easily. They were never impressed by drab facts. Facts never impressed the Second Coming believers, the flat earth believers, the UFO freaks, or those who believe that the Apollo space flights and lunar landings were elaborate hoaxes. When facts conflict with belief, they are denounced as delusions created by the Devil, simply ignored, ridiculed, or swept under the carpet. People are intrigued by conspiratorial theories, such as blaming the cause of the troubles of the world on the Tri-Lateral Commission conspiracy, the Jewish conspiracy, or the Communist conspiracy. Capitalists see Communist devils lurking under every bed, and Communists see capitalist devils lurking under every bed. How much can be expected of a species that wallowed in ignorance for five hundred thousand years and is still, in the latter twentieth century, more attracted to the glamour of ignorance than the dreary exactitudes of science?

Mediums, psychics, clairvoyants, spiritualists and their ilk can always boast a large following for reasons that should now be clear. Attempts have been made to legitimize their nonsense by putting their cults under an umbrella of scientific respectability by giving them the equivocal designation of psychic phenomena, or parapsychology. Dr. Joseph Banks Rhine of Duke University is one of the most reputable psychologists whose work with ESP and PSI phenomena was supposed to lend them scientific credibility; but his own irrational and preconditioned belief in psychic phenomena made objectivity an impossible dream. Besides, psychology itself is something of a cult when it departs from the exact sciences of physiology, neurology, and biology.

Could a mother be impartial if she were to judge the guilt or innocence of her own son? Wouldn't it be natural for her to be more interested in the acquittal of her son than the truth of his guilt? The only passion and emotion involved in true science is the passion to arrive at truth, regardless of the consequences, not the passion to arrive at preconceived conclusions.

Fake mediums, phony clairvoyants, and fraudulent spiritualists were exposed by Harry Price, Baron Schrenck-Notzing, the famous Houdini, and many others. The tricks employed by mind-readers and mentalists like Dunninger and Dr. Bert Reese are well known to magicians. Thomas Edison was convinced that Reese was a genuine psychic, in spite of Reese's denial. Luther Burbank was a firm believer in psychic nonsense. Sir Arthur Conan Doyle, who wrote Sherlock Holmes, was absolutely convinced that Harry Houdini could only perform some of his amazing tricks by dematerializing his body and again rematerializing it, even though Houdini assured him that it was all a trick. If the will to believe utter poppycock countermands reason in the most intelligent of human beings, what hope is there for the human race at large?

Houdini was known for his personal "challenge to any medium in the world to present psychical manifestations that I cannot reproduce or explain as being accomplished by natural means." He did, in fact, accomplish by natural means psychical manifestations which the mediums and psychics were unable to accomplish by supernatural means. He exposed mediums by tricking them into receiving messages from dead husbands, wives, parents, and children who had never lived in the first place.

Houdini exposed many phony seances by concealing a photo-flash camera and photographing the medium as she held hands with believers on either side of her, but deftly removed her shoes, rang bells and shook tambourines with her feet. One time he smeared a megaphone resting on the seance table with lampblack when the medium wasn't looking. After the seance was over, and the believers had listened to the muffled voices of "their dead relatives," and the lights were turned back on, they were treated to the ludicrous sight of the medium's mouth and hands smeared with lampblack. Needless to say, the faith of the true believers was unshaken. Nothing can shake intelligence into a burn again fideist. Absolutely nothing will cause a true believer to lose faith in his gods, mediums, UFO's, psychics, astrologers, country, or beloved leader.

Philosophers have written many tomes on the subject of art and beauty, the theories of which come under the study of aesthetics. There are endless theories of beauty and art, just as there are endless cults in religion, science, *et cetera*. For purposes of this discussion, we will embrace the theory of Descartes and Durer that the criterion of beauty is variable and is decided practically by the generality of pleasure. In other words, just as sound does not exist on the moon because there is neither an atmosphere to conduct sound waves nor an ear to convey them to a brain which transforms vibrations into sound, there is no beauty or art where there is no brain to create them or sensorial entity to enjoy them. In a word, beauty is in the eye of the beholder.

The purpose of art is to give pleasure. Hence, if a man looks at a girl, and it gives him pleasure, she is beautiful. If the sight of her pains him, she is ugly. Exact science is the rational response to the demand for information. Art is the response to the demand for entertainment and pleasure. Different kinds of entertainments, or art, give pleasure to different people. A complex mathematical equation expressed by tensor analysis is a thing of beauty to an intellect of Albert Einstein's caliber. To others, the equation is a meaningless scribble on a piece of paper, perhaps even ugly. To a small child, its own creation of a mud pie is a work of art, but to most adults it is just a gob of filth that must be cleaned up. Beauty and art are entirely relative to the individual.

Every sane person must admit that a dog is higher on the scale of evolution than a worm, and a bona fide *Homo sapiens* is higher on the scale of evolution than a dog. The reason for this conclusion is that a dog has more intelligence than a worm, and a bona fide *Homo sapiens* has more intelligence than a dog. Most classical music, such as symphonies, and classical dances, like the ballet, appeal to intellect.

The audience and spectators to the fine arts sit in their seats without any irrational, emotional compulsion to put their bodies into wild, barbaric gyrations or rhythmic jungle contortions characteristic of primitive people. They are intellectually stimulated by complex tonal forms and euphonious structures, and their minds go into ecstatic frenzies, not their torsos and limbs. On the other hand, rock 'n' roll, and "modern" music in general, appeals to the raw, primitive emotions, and sends the body into frenetic undulations of jungle rhythms. Uncivilized music is euphemized as "soul" music. So-called modern music, or dance, is indistinguishable, in essence, from the music, or dance, of savages, barbarians, or cannibals dancing around a jungle bonfire preparatory to tribal warfare. It is the avatar of bestial man.

The 1969 Woodstock Music and Art Fair in Bethel, New York, attracted several hundred thousand young people. They called themselves the "Woodstock Generation", and, indeed, they were. This was a generation that had liberated itself from music which had evolved faster than their minds. As creatures of instinct rather than intellect, they atavistically reveled in Stone Age rhythm. They were the "Atavist Generation," that could find beauty only at the level of their own competence. Classical music is like rational science in that they are both antithetical to the nature of 99 and 44/ 100 percent of the human race. Rock 'n' roll is like cults and superstition in that they are in tune with the basic nonsapient nature of man. If the youth at Bethel had been subjected to classical music, it would have been like subjecting a Neanderthaler to a prolonged lecture on thermodynamics: that is, it would have been sheer torture.

Civilization is a very thin veneer. Contrary to Jean-Jacques Rousseau's drivel that civilization is a corruption of man's natural goodness and the source of human inequalities, civilization tamed man to the extent that he can be tamed. Roman civilization tamed the German barbarian. European civilization tamed cannibalism in black Africa. It interdicted the ritual murders of the Thugs in India, and the sacrificial human murders by the Aztecs in Mexico. Civilization made modern science and technology possible; but it is easy for civilized man to slip back to his natural state of barbarism, as we have seen in Nazi Germany, and in Japan under the warlords. (Actually, for any nation to go to war is for it to revert to barbarism.) It was far easier for the civilized world of art, dance, and music to backslide to the primitive art, dance, and music of savage man. The music of 50,000 B.C. was rediscovered, and it was hailed as a twentieth century innovation. The artistic devolution of the twentieth century was the triumph of primitive man over civilized man. The barbarians have conquered.

The interminably repetitious sound of the jungle beat affords immeasurable pleasure for the vast majority of people because it concurs with their level of appreciation. A condemnation of this fact will not change it. America has been liberated from the intellectual imposition of music for the mind, and it is not about to relinquish its newfound freedom to enjoy the natural pleasures derived from primitive instinct and emotion. Violence is a fact of human existence, and so is the music and dance of violence. The sexual revolution and the music and art retrograde evolution complement each other, and they are affirmations of the autonomy of instinct over reason.

Experiments were performed at New York University and Louisiana State University to determine whether there is any correlation between intellectual performance and the kind of music listened to while performing intellectual tasks. It was found that students scored HIGHER on intelligence tests when they listened to classical music than when they listened to no music at all. However, their test scores were LOWER when they listened to rock 'n' roll than when they listened to no music at all. The classical music stimulated intellectual performance, but rock 'n' roll inhibited intellectual performance. The evidence for the intellectual character of classical music and the barbaric character of rock ` n' roll is overwhelming.

Meanwhile, the Attila the Huns of barbaric music not only conquered the civilized musical world of Beethoven, Mendelssohn, and Mozart, but they also looted fortunes from the economy of the civilized world in salaries and fees. They are totally incapable of creating a world of science and technology, but they are very capable of plundering it. This is the hallmark of a true barbarian. The Stone Age atavists rock 'n' roll the world back to the twilight of civilization, amid the rabid approbation of the shrieking masses. But outrages to bona fide *Homo sapiens* are the motifs of all human history.

There are as many art cults as there are religious cults and inexact science cults, and many of them are equally absurd. They include Expressionism, Dadaism, Surrealism, Cubism, Orphism, neo-plasticism, purism, neo-impressionism, and Futurism. And we also have Suprematism, Constructivism, synthesism, Realism, neorealism, *et cetera ad nauseum*. Abstract expressionism, like others, consists of several subcults. Pollock, the dean of Abstract Expressionism, practiced Action Painting by dripping commercial paints on raw canvas. One prizewinning painting in an Abstract Expressionism contest was "painted" by a fascicle of worms which were dipped into paint and allowed to freely squiggle on a canvas. When the judges were apprised of this embarrassing fact, they rationalized that the worms were reacting to cosmic forces in their squigglings.

One artist got the bright idea of submitting his old canvas, which he had used to clean his paint brushes, to an Abstract Expressionism art contest. This hodgepodge of variegated colors swiped across his cleaning canvas won a prize. Confronting the judges with the embarrassing facts did not faze them one bit. They easily rationalized that a subconscious design guided the artist when he cleaned his brushes. Yet another time, a chimpanzee was given a painter's brush, paint, and a canvas to amuse himself. The chimpanzee's "work of art" also won a prize in a contest. The judges did not lack for rationalizations. Mankind and stupidity are inseparable companions.

Henrik Willem Van Loon wrote of stupidity in the art forms in his book, *The Arts*: "Having lost all touch with reality [the artists] went from one strange ism to another, finally leading up to that strangest of all emotional expressions, the nonobjective art, which went so far in its reaction against everything that had gone before that it composed its masterpieces out of old matchboxes, chicken feathers, and the offal of the barbershop floor."

It is as impossible for human beings to evaluate themselves objectively as it is for a mother to evaluate her own child objectively. Were it possible, they would see that they are not evolving into more intelligent creatures—bona fide *Homo sapiens*, that is. If anything, they are devolving into creatures who even surpass themselves in infinite stupidity, and they are inching their way to the abyss of nuclear suicide. The one hope for mankind is the one thing of which he is least capable: DISCIPLINED REASON. Even those who fastidiously employ impeccable logic in the pursuit of the exact sciences immediately lapse into the ludicrous absurdities of superstition upon their departure from the narrow field of their discipline. The supernatural and the occult are instinctive modes of human thought. Like Dante's Inferno, we must speak of the Human Comedy in the jeremiad words, "All hope abandon, ye who enter here!"

Chapter 7
NONSAPIENS AND RACE

As mentioned in Chapter 5, the first great American taboo is the rational, scientific analysis of religion. We now come to the second of the great taboos, and that is the rational, scientific study of RACE. Again, the reason for the taboo is the same. Science demolishes cherished prejudices: a state of affairs society will not tolerate. Again, we will be foolhardy and rush in where angels fear to tread. If the results of the scientific analysis of human races reinforced the national myth of equality, it would not only not be taboo, it would be a legal requirement ordered, like bussing, by the federal courts.

Our very existence and survival on Earth are intimately involved in the struggle for existence and natural selection of the fittest. Indian culture and Indian populations became almost instantly extinct with the arrival of Europeans in the Americas for the same reason marsupials became extinct in South America when the Isthmus of Panama formed a land bridge to North America and more advanced mammals invaded South America, eliminating primitive mammals in the struggle for existence. Marsupials survived in Australia because they were protected from invasion by the island continent. Primitive apes, the lemurs, are found only on Madagascar because they were protected from competition with advanced apes through insular isolation. Florida is now experiencing a revolution in its fauna and flora because of the introduction of superior animal and plant forms. The struggle of human cultures for survival is largely racial. The law of nature decrees that inferior people CANNOT create superior, survivable cultures.

The first six chapters of this book should give pause to those who are overawed by human intelligence. Anthropology, sociology, and ethnology are inexact sciences. Therefore, when they deal with the subject of race, they splinter into fanatical cults which are on a par with religion and witchcraft. The same bigotry, prejudice and intolerance pervade racial dogmas as religious dogmas, and abysmal ignorance masquerades as profound scientific truth. Some anthropological cults deny the existence of human races. This cult is typified by Paul R. Ehrlich and S. Shirley Feldman's statements in their book *The Race Bomb*: "The discordance of human variation means there are no natural units within *Homo sapiens* that permit the species to be divided into four or forty evolutionary entities that can be described as races . . . Biologically there are no races of *Homo sapiens*." On the other hand, Dr. Theodosius Dobzhansky, who resembles a scientist more than a cultist, says in his book *Heredity and the Nature of Man* "Race is however, also a biological phenomenon; there are races of man, and of animals and plants, and the races exist regardless of whether there is someone who wishes to classify them."

Childish nonsense is frequently dignified as science. To deny the existence of human races for the usual reason that they overlap, merge, and are in many cases indiscernible, is to deny the existence of day and night because they overlap, merge, and become indiscernible twice a day: dusk and dawn. Fatuity can be carried even further by denying that colors exist because they overlap, merge, and become indiscernible as in a rainbow or in the mixing of primary color pigments.

Racism is a frequently bandied epithet. The neologism, racism, is defined as "A belief that race is the primary determinant of human traits and capacities." Ethnic egalitarians have made it a hate word because of the implication that "racial differences produce an inherent superiority of a particular race." Social reasons, not scientific reasons, have made the recognition of racial differences taboo. Racism is a tool of bigots. For over two thousand years, Jews have been the saddest victims of bigotry, but the bigots were not always clear as to whether they were discriminating against a religion or a race.

Jacobs and Stern wrote in their *General Anthropology*, "Although, as will be shown, the Jews are not a race, they have recently been singled out for special attack in most racist propaganda . . ." On the other hand, Will Durant affirms Jewish racial identity in his *Our Oriental Heritage*: "but the Jews were the purest of all, for they intermarried only very reluctantly with other peoples. Hence, they have maintained their type with astonishing tenacity; the Hebrew prisoners on the Egyptian and Assyrian reliefs, despite the prejudices of the artist, are recognizable like the Jews of our own times: There, too, are the long and curved Hittite nose, the projecting cheekbones, the curly hair . . . "

The Hebrews, or Jews, were originally desert Arabs who migrated to the land of the Canaanites and Hittites around 1400 B.C. It is not certain whether they entered Egypt as freemen or slaves. They did go forth and were fruitful. They multiplied rapidly in Egypt. Led by Moses, they escaped enslavement during the period Egypt was ruled by racial relatives of the Hebrews, the Hyksos. The Hebrews adopted Yahweh (Jehovah) as their national God. It was the God worshipped by the Kenite nomads at Mount Sinai. Belief in this bloodthirsty God charged the Hebrews up with the killer ferocity needed to conquer the Promised Land in the ancient tradition of another hungry nomad horde raiding a civilized community. They slew the vanquished inhabitants in the name of Yahweh and married the remainder. The great judge of Israel, Gideon, slaughtered one hundred twenty thousand men in the capture of two cities. Joshua was cognizant of the supreme fact of human history: only the superior killer survives. The Jews inherited the Promised Land as we inherited the American Dream: *i.e.*, legacies of superior human slaughter.

About 1,100 B.C., the Hebrews conquered the Philistines and Saul became their first king. His successor, David, made Jerusalem the capital and expanded the kingdom using tactics as ruthless as any Assyrian monarch. His son, Solomon, ascended the throne by slaughtering all rival claimants. He then embarked on a life of epicurean enjoyment. He collected a harem of several hundred concubines. His attempt to unify the twelve tribes of Israel failed. To finance his luxuries, sumptuous palace, and magnificent temple, he taxed the people heavily. When he died, Israel was exhausted, and the suffering people began to transform their warlike cult of Yahweh into the religion of the prophets. After many defeats, poverty, and exploitation, the Jews lost hope for earthly triumphs and glory, and began to accept the Egyptian and Persian beliefs in a life to come.

Only the inhabitants of the southern two kingdoms of Judah

preserved their religious and racial identity to the present day. The ten tribes of the northern kingdom were dispersed after the Assyrian conquest of 721 B.C. and became assimilated by other peoples. They vanished from history, victims of miscegenation. When we speak of racial purity, we should know what we are talking about. All races mixed. The hybrids formed new races which may be termed "pure" as we shall explain later.

The religious prohibition against marrying Gentiles was introduced by Ezra and Nehemiah after the return of the Jews from captivity in Babylonia. Thus, a distinguished hybrid race preserved its relative purity. Obviously, if a black joins Judaism, he doesn't alter his race. There are qualifications to the term "Jewish purity." Jews would have been assimilated by Greeks after the conquests of Alexander the Great and the Hellenizing pressures exerted by Antiochus IV, were it not for the Maccabees, who resisted it. One indisputable fact emerges: ASHKENAZIC JEWS HAVE MAINTAINED AN EXTRAORDINARILY LARGE MEASURE OF ETHNIC PURITY.

With the distinctive religious and racial identities of the Jews came bigotry, prejudice, and discrimination by other groups who also possessed religious and racial identities. All early Christians called themselves Jews, but a Greek-Jewish tentmaker, Saul, who was later known as Saint Paul, or Paul of Tarsus, created a new religious identity by breaking from the Jewish tradition and founding the new religion of Christianity. He almost immediately embarked Christians on a course of hatred and destruction for Jews. He defined Jews as "vessels of wrath, fit for destruction", upon his failure to convert them to his doctrines. The same failure of Mohammed to convert the Jews to Mohammedanism induced him to turn his wrath on the Jews. When Saint Paul created his New Judaism (Christianity), he turned on his own people, and became apostle to the Gentiles.

The separation of Jew and Christian was completed when Christianity became the official state religion of the Roman Empire. Discrimination against the Jew because of his religion then went into high gear. In A.D. 329, Emperor Flavius Valerius Aurelius Constantinus inaugurated an official program of discrimination against Jews. In A.D. 330, any person in the Roman Empire who either converted or encouraged any Gentile to convert to Judaism was subject to the death penalty. Any Jew who married a Gentile was also subject to the death penalty. Imperial edicts referred to Judaism as the *SECTA FERALIS* (Bestial Religion). With the establishment of Christianity in the Western world came a built-in hatred of Judaism, and the basis for the future slaughter of millions of Jews not because of their race, but because of their religion.

Jews were persecuted more than any people in the history of the world. Hitler-like holocausts took place many times, but on a smaller scale. In A.D. 480 at Constantinople, when the Party of the Green burned a synagogue and hundreds of Jews in it, Emperor Zeno complained because ALL the Jews were not exterminated so as to end the Jewish problem once and for all. The Crusaders destroyed Jewish trade centers in southern Europe. Jewish-owned ships were pirated and sunk, and many of Europe's docks were closed to Jews. Christians burned Jews at the stake on the false charge of having poisoned the wells and causing the fourteenth century Black Death.

When the Jews were persecuted in Western Europe, they fled to Eastern Europe, but it wasn't long before the Christians whipped up hysterical hatred against them with accusations of performing ritual murders. The first pogroms were begun in Poland about A.D. 1500, but the Roman Catholic Poles, themselves, soon learned a lesson on inhumanity, as taught by the Greek Orthodox Cossacks who mutilated infants and sliced open the bellies of nuns, noblewomen, and Jewesses, into whom they sewed live cats. Ten years of carnage left the countryside strewn with the severed bodies of perhaps a million people, including one hundred thousand Jews.

After A.D. 1500, many Russians converted to Judaism, which so alarmed the Russian Orthodox Church that it began to stamp out the Jewish heresy with the same savagery the Roman Catholic Church used to stamp out the Albigensian heresy in France, which accounted for the murder of over a million Frenchmen. Ivan the Terrible ordered all Jews who would not convert to Greek Orthodoxy drowned in the river Duna. The Jews fled to Lithuania, but Peter the Great conquered the Baltic States, and Jews were banished by his daughter Empress Elizabeth. Pogrom is a Russian term meaning "riot"; but, specifically, it came to mean the violent attacks against Jews in the nineteenth and twentieth centuries. Pogroms increased in severity after the assassination of Alexander II in 1881. They were encouraged by the silent connivance of Russian soldiers and police. The anti-Semitic policies of the czarist government encouraged the emigration of Russian Jews to the United States. Pogroms increased in frequency and violence after the abortive Russian Revolution of 1905.

In the early Middle Ages, Jewish confinement to ghettos was voluntary. Spain and Portugal made it compulsory in the late fourteenth century. The ghettos were walled-in communities with gates which were locked at night from the outside. Any Jew not confined in the ghetto at night faced harsh penalties. The ostensible reason for the confinement was the preservation of Christian faith from Jewish contamination. When the Jews left the ghettos, they were forced to wear demeaning star-shaped yellow badges of identification and humiliating garb. They were required to step aside when a Christian passed. The restrictions placed on Jews by Christians were severe and much like the restrictions placed on Christians by Moslems when they controlled Spain. In A.D. 1460, all Jews in Frankfurt, Germany, were required by law to live in the ghetto, where women and children were sometimes murdered by mobs led by villainous men like Vincent Fettmilch. "Fatmilk" and his henchmen received retribution when the emperor chopped off their heads in the Frankfurt marketplace. Ghettos existed in Western Europe until the late nineteenth century and in Russia until 1917.

Jews were victims of religious and racial prejudice and bigotry throughout most of their history. Before the nineteenth century, the emphasis was on religion. Jews were accused of killing (crucifying) God, ritual murders, desecrating the Host by piercing it with sharp instruments to make it bleed (about as ridiculous a charge as human lunacy can invent), and Talmud-burning. They were hated because they refused to believe that Christ is the true Messiah, when, in fact, the Jews were in a better position to assay their own Messiah than strangers in distant lands who accepted flimsy hearsay evidence. But distance lends enchantment to a myth, and wishful thinking robes it in sparkling hues of truth.

The word "anti-Semitism" did not exist until 1879 when it appeared in a pamphlet. After the "Enlightenment" of the eighteenth century, religious bigotry against Jews abated somewhat, but it was quickly replaced by racial bigotry and prejudice. Before the "Enlightenment," Jews could become non-Jews by converting to Christianity. When the prejudice became a racial thing, Jews were stuck with their stigma for life. Hitler's Jews could not convert to Christianity and save themselves as they could before the nineteenth century. Anyone suspected of having as little as one-tenth Jewish blood was guilty of the crime of being a Jew, *a la* American Negroes.

Jews became scapegoats for every ill and every disaster. They were denigrated for either being exploiting capitalists or subversive Communists. They were accused of being all-purpose arch conspirators. They were denounced for either plotting to dominate the world by wielding international financial power (House of Rothschild), or for organizing a Bolshevik Revolution (Karl Marx and Leon Trotsky). Capt. Alfred Dreyfus was accused and convicted by the French for selling military secrets to the German embassy, even after the General Staff knew that Major Esterhazy was the culprit. The streets of Paris rang with the cry "Death to the Jews!" In 1898, Emile Zola came to the defense of Dreyfus and accused the army and the government of being the real traitors—traitors not only to France but to humanity. Through his efforts, and with great danger to himself, the French Supreme Court finally set the innocent Dreyfus free in 1906.

Racial bigotry had greater success in Germany than in France. A Frenchman, Count Gobineau, published *The Inequality of Human Races* in 1853. In it, he advocated white racial supremacy. He believed that civilizations fell because the superior blood of the aristocracy became diluted with the blood of common people, and he feared the contamination of the Aryan elite blood with the blood of non-Aryan hordes which is promoted by democratic governments. His theory was embraced by the German philosopher Friedrich Nietzsche, who became the father of Nazism. Said he, "Not mankind, but Superman is the goal! What is good? All that increases the feeling of power, the will to power! What is bad? All that comes from weakness." He called democracy a "mania for counting noses," and he plumped for its eradication. He did not share Hitler's consummate stupidity, as indicated by his advice: "We require an intergrowth of the German and Slav races; and we require, too, the cleverest financiers, the Jews, that we may become the masters of the world. We require an unconditional union with Russia."

Nietzsche understood the role of force and power in human society. We Americans are fond of repeating, "The only thing Russians understand is force." Actually, force is the universal language of predators, and it is the only thing any human being understands clearly. That is why strikes and violence were prerequisites to labor union power; and demonstrations, riots, and the burning of cities were prerequisites to civil rights for blacks. Everyone listens to reason when it is explained with a Colt .45 jammed to his temple. Logic can never command the respect of menacing physical power.

Nietzsche proved that he understood the predatory nature of man when he wrote, "(Men) live in ambush for one another; they obtain things from each other by lying in wait . . . They seek the smallest profits out of every sort of rubbish . . . When the instincts of a society ultimately make it give up war and conquest, it is decadent . . . Those races that cannot bear this philosophy are doomed." The United States can definitely bear this philosophy, as illustrated by the worldwide deployment of her troops and her nuclear arsenal which can obliterate all life from this planet. The United States became great because of war, and it can sustain greatness only by unchallengeable military power. The denial of this obvious historical fact is sheer hypocrisy.

An Englishman living in Germany during the early twentieth century by the name of Houston Stewart Chamberlain, took Gobineau's shibboleth, "Supremacy of the Aristocracy," and substituted "Nordic Racial Supremacy," which was essentially the same as Hitler's Aryan Supremacy. Drumont's *La France Juive*, published in 1886, transformed the prevailing attitude toward the Jew from an uncouth, flea-bitten lout to an evil creature possessing both superior cunning and the designs of a dangerous conspirator. Czar Nicholas II commissioned Sergei Nilus, a monk, to invent a rationale to discredit Jews. Nilus forged documents to "prove" that conspiratorial Jews known as the Elders of Zion planned to conquer the world, just as contemporary Communists try to prove that conspiratorial capitalists plan to conquer the world, and capitalists try to prove that conspiratorial Communists plan to conquer the world.

In 1930, Nazi Alfred Rosenberg wrote *The Myth of the Twentieth Century* which argued that Germany should rebuild herself by embracing the Nietzschean philosophy of power which glorified the Superman. Rosenberg equated the Superman with the German people. He decried Christian ethics which exalt weakness and gentleness. (America professed Christian ethics, but practiced power ethics. If she had not, the Manhattan skyline would now be dotted with tepees instead of skyscrapers.) Rosenberg maintained that Christianity should be extirpated as a Jewish disease; and that Germans, as representatives of the superior Nordic race, were entitled to dominate Europe by the natural law of predators; that is, the right of MASTERS to dominate SLAVES. It may have been wiser if he had employed predator cunning along with power by emulating America and conquering Europe in the name of Manifest Destiny and the Prince of Peace. *The Bible* in one hand and a gun in the other is superior strategy to *Mein Kampf* in one hand and a gun in the other.

Rosenberg identified "Russian Tartars" and "Semites" as Germany's enemies. To him, Semites were not only Jews, but all Latin peoples and all Christians. He looked upon Christianity as basically a Jewish religion, which it was originally. Having lost World War II, he was adjudged a war criminal by the Nuremberg trials and then hanged by the votaries of Christian ethics who exalt love, mercy, turning the other cheek, and forgiveness.

Adolf Hitler, the son of Alois Hitler, who was the illegitimate son of Maria Schicklgruber, believed he could make Germany great again after her humiliating defeat in World War I by outlawing Communism, by exterminating the Jews, whom he blamed for Germany's defeat in World War I, and by repudiating the Versailles Treaty. His magnetic personality and stirring oratory of hate and power, plus his mastery of deceitful strategy, swept him to political control of Germany. In 1935, Hitler pushed the infamous "Nuremburg Laws" through the Reichstag which disenfranchised all Jews, including anyone with one Jewish grandfather. Until 1939, Jews could leave Germany upon the payment of a ransom. After 1939, Jews had to forfeit their entire wealth for the privilege of emigrating from Germany. Germany soon demanded a 1.5 billion reichsmarks ransom from world Jewry for the release of the Jews. After 1941, Hitler embarked on genocidal extermination as the "final solution to the Jewish problem."

Adolf Eichmann was assigned the task of implementing the Final Solution. The Jews, as well as Czechs, Poles, and Russians, were forced to dig trenches, undress, and line up in front of the trenches where they were machine-gunned. Those who didn't fall into the trenches were bulldozed into them. The dead and the living—adults, children, and infants—all were buried in the dirt. Some Jews were used as guinea pigs for medical experiments. German ingenuity produced Zyklon B, a hydrogen cyanide which was cheap and easy to manufacture and was capable of killing thousands of people in a few minutes. Zyklon B gas chambers were built to resemble large rooms. The victims were told to undress and enter the rooms for a shower. The steel doors were then closed, sealed, and the hydrogen cyanide released. Thousands of gasping, retching human beings quickly turned into pink, green-spotted, contorted, grimacing corpses. Peepholes were provided for the sadists who could enjoy several performances per day. Technicians removed the gold fillings from the teeth of the dead.

The efficient and enterprising Germans used the hair from their murdered victims for the manufacture of cloth and mattresses. The ashes from the crematoriums were used to fertilize German victory gardens. Human fat was used to make soap. One recommended soap formula called for twelve pounds of human fat, ten quarts of water, and from a half to a pound of caustic soda boiled for two hours then cooled. The Auschwitz concentration camp was a major source of human raw material supplied by the victims of mass murder. Seventeen tons of gold were recovered from the mouths and bodies of the victims.

If a Jew resisted extermination, Nazi diabolical cunning knew how to deal with it. He was thwarted by attacks on his loved ones. The Nazis would pull an infant apart by its legs or bash a child's head against a tree, then hand the bloody remains to its mother, or they would rape a young daughter, sister, or mother in view of the family and impale her on a bayonet. Even when the German armies were in full retreat on both the Eastern and Western fronts, Nazi death trains kept rolling to Germany's gas chambers. Poland fed over 3 million of her Jews to the Nazi slaughterhouses, and the Germans showed their gratitude by murdering over a million and a half Poles. Clearly, the savage tribesman in the jungle and the urbane citizen of the civilized city are identical creatures. They are born killers, but the killer instincts of the latter are held in temporary abeyance.

At the end of World War II, the Nazi killers pleaded innocent to all charges of war atrocities. They tried to evade moral culpability by saying they blindly followed Hitler like sheep. The war's killing spree had cost the lives of seventeen million people in battle; 30 million people were maimed; 18 million civilians died as a consequence of the war; and the Nazis murdered 12 million people, including 6 million Jews—all in only six years of the civilized world's greatest mass murder binge. If the slaughtered corpses were placed end to end, they would encircle the Earth nearly two times. It has been predicted that if the Nazis had won the war, they would have killed 10 million non-Aryans a year pursuant to their "eugenic" racial policies. The Nazi outrage against reason and humanity in the name of eugenics was identical to the Christian outrage against reason and humanity when infidels and heretics were killed in the name of the God of Love.

The supreme irony to the Nazi atrocities is that were it not for Hitler's stupid anti-Semitism, he may well have won the war. The "inferior" Jews whom he expelled were, in fact, superior. Bigotry and prejudice make the mind opaque to truth. Germany could have become the world's first nuclear power. The German-Jew Albert Einstein laid the theoretical basis for atomic energy with his famous equation: $E=MC^2$. Lise Meitner, the Jewess professor at the University of Berlin (1926-1933), bombarded uranium nuclei with slow-speed neutrons and calculated the vast amounts of energy released as a result of nuclear fission. Niels Bohr was forced to flee Nazi-occupied Denmark. As a result, he gave valuable assistance to atomic research at Los Alamos.

Einstein, Meitner, Fermi, Szilard, and Bohr were all eminent research atomic scientists who were driven out of Europe by Hitler and came to the United States to develop the atomic bomb. Edward Teller, a Hungarian-Jew, was the father of the hydrogen bomb. Robert J. Oppenheimer, an American-Jew, was the father of the atomic bomb. Hyman Rickover was the father of the American atom-powered submarine. Isidor Isaac Rabi, an American-Jew, was chairman of the General Advisory Committee to the Atomic Energy Commission. Max Born was another Jew who contributed to nuclear knowledge, but was forced to flee Nazi Germany. Hitler's bigotry blinded him to truth as it does to all religious fanatics, racist bigots, and science cultists.

Germany was not the first country to suffer cultural and scientific deprivation after her Jews were expelled. In A.D. 711, the Arab-Moslems conquered southern and central Spain. They gave the Jews considerable freedom for three hundred years, during which time, a golden age of Spanish-Judaism flourished. The Jews advanced medical science to a level never before seen in the civilized world. The Jews created a great merchant marine and a merchant trade to all parts of the world, and specifically made Spain a center for the China silk trade. They gave literature, culture, and progress to Spain. In A.D. 1136, the Moslem Almohades conquests and cruelties ended the golden age for the Jews, but Christian northern Spain and Christian Portugal wanted to benefit from Jewish mercantile skill and technology. Consequently, they welcomed the persecuted Jews with open arms.

Unfortunately, terror and horror were cresting on the wave of the Spanish Inquisition. Dominicans persuaded the Christian Spaniards to make the Jews an offer they couldn't refuse: either accept mass conversion to Christianity, or face mass extermination. Probably three hundred thousand chose conversion circa A.D. 1400. The "converts" were called Marranos, a Spanish word meaning "swine." As a result of the "conversion" of the mercantile and nobility class of Jews into the Spanish mainstream, nearly every aristocratic family in Spain became at least partly Jewish. The aristocratic merchant-prince-Jew infused Christian Spain with tremendous vitality. He was the architect, engineer, geographer, and physician. Almost immediately, Spain became the leader of Europe. This vitality was soon destroyed, and the leadership role was lost because religious fanaticism and bigotry led Spain in the same suicidal path racist bigotry led Nazi Germany.

The Marranos were hated by the Church because they were actually Jews who only took on the facade of Christianity to save their own lives. Commencing in 1478, Marranos were burned at the stake for heresy, and their property was split between the Church and the Crown. Marranos fled the holocaust by ship, on foot, and every way possible. Art, science, and culture perished overnight. In 1492, Queen Isabella and King Ferdinand submitted to the pressure exerted by the Church, and expelled the Jewish population from Spain. The year 1492 was eventful. It was the year Columbus discovered America, the year Christians, with the help of the Jews, captured the city of Granada and destroyed the last remnant of Moslem power on the Spanish peninsula, and the year the Jews were expelled from Spain. They were expelled from Portugal in 1497. Most of the Marranos left Spain during the next two hundred years, and Spain's intellectual lights went out. Spain declined, never to regain her greatness.

The great nations and peoples of the ancient Western World have disappeared from the modern world. They lie buried under the sands of time, victims of genocide and miscegenation. Only the Jews, who are a hybrid related to the ancient Assyrians, Hittites, and modern Armenians, maintained racial continuity from ancient times, and it was because of Judaism. In the words of John R. Baker, "The contributions (to civilization) of the Assyrians, Hittites, and Armenid Jews are too well known to require emphasis here." The Canaanites and Hebrews intermarried after 1400 B.C. The ancient Greeks called the Canaanites "Phoenicians." Carthage was a colony founded by the Phoenicians in the ninth century B.C. It was a leading business center in the western Mediterranean. Carthage created an empire of colonies in Spain, Sardinia, Corsica, and Sicily. Under the military leadership of Hannibal. Carthage almost defeated the invincible Romans on their own home ground in Italy. The point being made here is that the Jews are a hybrid of superior people, and it is this HYBRID which we refer to as a pure race. But more of this later.

Jews have been a credit to the world and to host nations from the beginning of history. They were taken into captivity by Nebuchadnezzar of the Chaldaean (New Babylonian) Empire in 586 B.C. Even as captives, they rose to the top echelons of Babylonian society, of the business world, and were leaders in scholastic achievement. This same Jewish phenomenon exists in the world today. Any place in the world, even where there are but small Jewish minorities, they are leaders in science, art, finance, business, medicine, and scholarship. After the seventh century A.D., and Islam rose to challenge Western Civilization, the Jews rose with Islam to become philosophers, physicians, businessmen, and scientists. When the Jews were liberated from the ghettos of the Middle Ages, they almost immediately became prime ministers, military leaders, business leaders, and intellectuals. The list of the illustrious Jews is almost endless: Great Britain's Benjamin Disraeli, Sir Moses Montefiore, and Sir Rufus Isaacs; France's Adolphe Cremieux, Isaac and Emile Pereire, and Achille Fould; and so forth.

Karl Jacobi was the founder of modern mathematical physics. Other Jewish contributors to modern mathematics were Georg Cantor; Willgenstein; and Hermann Minkowski, who originated the concept of the relativity of time and space. Leopold Kronecker contributed to the theory of numbers and equations. Luigi Cremona developed birational transformation theory. Tullio Levi-Civita and Gregorio Ricci developed absolute differential calculus, which made it possible for Einstein, another Jew, to express his theory of relativity in appropriate mathematical equations. And there were great Jewish astronomers such as Sir William Herschel and Karl Schwarzschild.

Jews shaped world history not only in their contribution to three of the world's great religions—Judaism, Mohammedanism, and Christianity—but also as founders of the two great economic systems. David Ricardo, a Jew, is regarded as the father of capitalism. Karl Marx, a Jew, is the father of communism. Jewish scientists are legion. They include Fritz Haber, Richard Willstatter, Henrich Hertz, Wassermann, Ehrlich, Schick, *et cetera, et cetera*. In Soviet Russia, Jews constitute but one and one-half percent of the population; but 12 percent of Russia's top scientists, 15 percent of all doctors, and 10 percent of all lawyers are Jews. Jews comprise only one half of one percent of the world's population, but they won over 20 percent of all Nobel prizes in physics and medicine between 1901 and 1939. But they excelled in all fields of culture. Great painters like Pissarro, Soutine, Modigliani and Chagall were Jews. Great musical composers like Mendelssohn, Mahler, Saint-Saens, Schonberg, Bloch, and Offenbach were Jews. The Jewish literary greats are Proust, Kafka, and Zweig. Baruch Spinoza was one of the greatest philosophers of all time. Henri Bergson was another notable Jewish philosopher.

There is nothing particularly distinctive about Judaism *per se* that is conducive to the production of great intellects. It is merely another insult to intelligence which appeals to the blind faith of its adherents and is founded on ridiculous myths and legends. THE RELEVANT FACTOR IN JUDAISM IS ITS BONDING OF AN ETHNIC (RACIAL) GROUP THROUGHOUT THE MANY CENTURIES SINCE EZRA'S AND NEHEMIAH'S PROSCRIPTION AGAINST INTERMARRIAGE WITH GENTILES. The myth of being God's chosen people contributed to the reality of Jewish superiority.

Judaism expressed the nationalistic aspirations of an ethnic group as well as its "spiritual" needs. Other religions, Christianity, for example, actively proselytized American Indians, Chinese, Japanese, Negroes, Arabs—any race of people whatsoever. Even Mohammedans actively proselytized Asiatic Indians, Turks, Europeans, Indonesians, Filipinos, or any racial group. Races other than the original ethnic group have converted to Judaism, including blacks, but ethnic integrity has been central to the Jewish faith. The basis of Zionism is more ethnic than religious. Religion is merely the glue. The only other comparable ethnic religion in which religion and national aspirations are inseparable is that of the Black Muslims, who copied the format of the Jewish religion. They believe that "the Honorable Elijah Muhammed, Holy Prophet and Messenger of Allah" was divinely chosen to unite black Americans under Islam for "liberation" from white rule. Here again, religion is the adhesive for the ambitions of an ethnic group.

It is important to examine the ethnological relationship to religion in regard to Judaism. A group of anthropologists and geneticists under the auspices of UNESCO assembled in Paris in 1951. Like the pope in Rome speaking *ex cathedra* (infallibly), which is the way of religious and science cults, they pronounced that "Moslems and Jews are no more races than are Roman Catholics and Protestants." They were correct about Moslems, but dead wrong about Jews. Anthropologists, geneticists, psychologists, and sociologists have more in common with fanatical religion than with true, objective, exact science. To repeat the observation of Will Durant: "But the Jews were the purest of all, for they intermarried only very reluctantly with other peoples. Hence they have maintained their type with astonishing tenacity; the Hebrew prisoners on the Egyptian and Assyrian reliefs ... are recognizable like the Jews of our own time."

Because of political and social pressures, which translate into votes and riots, the scientific study of human races (ethnology) is taboo in America. There is but one and only one overriding reason why ethnology is taboo, and that is because a truly scientific, unbiased, unprejudiced study always yields the same repugnant conclusion which contradicts the nation's current dogmatic credo. In other words, it yields heresy, and human beings have always dealt with heresy in predictable ways. The public burning of heretical books is too crude for our sophisticated hypocrisies, but there are equally effective measures like creating taboos, not publishing heretical books and removing them from the libraries, or condemning them in the name of God, reason, science, and humanity.

If it is known by all previous studies that a new study will likely produce the same undesired results, what is better than to make the investigation, itself, taboo? Today, IQ tests are practically outlawed in the United States. There is no doubt that if the scientific study of human races yielded the conclusions desired by the bigots, they would welcome and DEMAND it. The curricula of all schools would include compulsory courses containing the data obtained as a result of studies on racial differences in intelligence.

There are other equally effective tactics which left-wing racist bigots employ. If the scientific study of human races yields heresy, why not deny that human races even exist in the first place? What a fertile field for left-wing racist bigots! If undesired racial differences are detected, why not blame them on the environment? A very effective weapon of left-wing bigots is to accuse their opponents of bigotry. If a study produces undesired results, simply accuse the study itself of having built-in prejudices. There is no fanatical religious cult that can match left-wing racist bigots or egalitarian zealots when it comes to deception, prejudice, falsification, and outright lies, as we shall show later in this chapter.

Dr. John R. Baker wrote a book called *Race*. It is scientific in the true sense. It is unbiased and apparently free of preconceived conclusions. It is also conspicuous for its absence from book store shelves, libraries, and schools. Dr. Baker points out that there are several Jewish communities throughout the world which comprise religious groups that are NOT ethnically related to the ancient twelve tribes of Israel. The "black Jews" of Ethiopia, otherwise known as the Falasha, are an admixture of Europid and some Negrids. They claim kinship with the ten Lost Tribes of Israel who were transported to Assyria by Tiglath-Pileser; but so, too, do the holy Shindai class of Japan, the Nestorians of Mesopotamia, some North American Indians, and many others. According to Falasha legend, the Queen of Sheba visited Jerusalem where she bore Solomon's son, Menelik, who returned to found a colony of Jews in Ethiopia. The actual facts are obscure.

The "Cochin Jews" in south-west India are indistinguishable from the Indian populations. The "Bene-Israel Jews" are conspicuously Indian. The "Tsung Jews" of China are almost purely Mongolid. The "Khazar (Cozar) Jews" were converted Tartars. The "Judeus (Judeos) Jews" of West Africa near the Congo river were Negroes. However, all of the above mentioned "Jews" comprise but a very small proportion of the Jews, and they are NOT genetically related. The vast majority of Jews are of the Ashkenazic stock which IS genetically related to the Armenian and Armenid subraces (Hittites and Assyrians), with Orientalid elements in its ancient ancestry.

We can legitimately use the expression "pure race" ONLY in proper context, and with the full knowledge that "pure races" are often "pure hybrids." The fundamental point is that the hybridization which produced Ashkenazic Jews was eugenic, a fact the history of the Assyrians, Hittites, and Armenid Jews clearly bears out. The second important point is that a large measure of ethnic purity was maintained for the Hybrid "Jew" by the Judaic ban on intermarriage with Gentiles. It was as effective as AKC rules for pedigree breeding. There are two groups of European Jews: the Ashkenazim of Russia, Poland, and England, which comprise 90 percent of all Jews; and the Sephardim (Hebrew word for Spaniards), who were expelled from Spain in 1492, and drifted into Asia Minor, North Africa, the Balkan States, Italy, and Holland. These two groups of Jews remained separate peoples until relatively recent times. They even had their own separate synagogues. The distinctive physical character of the Ashkenazic stock, which contains large Armenid elements, makes it recognizable from other European stock. These are the physical characters which Will Durant describes as "the long and curved Hittite nose, the projecting cheekbones, the curly hair and beard . . . The scrawny toughness of body, the subtlety and obstinacy of spirit that have characterized the Semites from the 'stiff-necked' followers of Moses to the inscrutable Bedouins and tradesmen of today." The Sephardim display far fewer Armenid elements because they have been bred out of the race by intermarriage with Mediterranids.

The modern tendency to intermarry not only between the Sephardic and the Ashkenazic Jews but also between Jews and Gentiles in general is breaking down the racial integrity of the Ashkenazic Jews. Modern bigots and self-professed intellectuals applaud this tragedy in the name of enlightenment, and they urge it Godspeed. We know the consequences. The ten tribes which had lost their racial integrity descended into less than mediocrity. The destruction of thorough-bred horses by interbreeding is unthinkable, but the destruction of the amazing Jews by miscegenation is accounted the highest good by the high priests of the anthropological and sociological cults. These benighted cultists will accomplish what all the Hitlers, Roman Emperors, pogroms, Inquisitions, massacres, and slaughters of history failed to accomplish: the extermination of the Jews as a race.

The ancient Greeks produced a fabulously advanced civilization over two thousand two hundred years ago. Francis Galton ranked the mental capacity of ancient Athenian Greeks two grades above the modern Englishman. Greeks have never been able to rise to a comparable level of greatness again. Jews maintained their superiority throughout the ages. The ancient Greeks lost their potential for greatness when they lost their racial identity. The Jews (Ashkenazim, of course) did not lose it. They demonstrate this fact throughout the world, wherever they live. The Greeks preserved the integrity of their language, but not their race. If we compare the average modern Greek to the statues of the ancient Greeks, we see little resemblance. Greece had been conquered by Romans, Huns, Avars, Slavs, Bulgars, and the Seljuk Turks with whom they interbred. The Ottoman Turks occupied Greece from A.D. 1456 to 1827. A visitor to modern Greece and Turkey cannot fail to see a striking resemblance between these people.

A breeder of thoroughbred horses would be aghast if a draft horse were to breed with his horses. The same applies to the owner of an American Kennel Club registered purebred dog, if he saw his dog breed with a mutt. Human beings recognize the value of quality breeding in other animals, but they are totally blind to quality breeding in their own species. What is even worse, they are proud of their blindness. They perform the miracle of transubstantiation by changing ignorance into broadmindedness, then denouncing knowledge as bigotry and prejudice. Wise men are made to look ridiculous in the company of fools. But, of course, if mankind displays incredible stupidity in his religious, political, and science cults, why should he suddenly become wise in matters of ethnology? He doesn't! Human beings, like all animals, reproduce to the call of blind instinct. Reason has absolutely nothing to do with human reproduction. A man was never known to have worried about, or inquired about, the genetic background of his sex partner prior to the insertion of his penis. To put it bluntly, a stiff dick has no conscience.

Nature's purpose for sex is reproduction, not pleasure. Pleasure is nature's lure which accompanies the compulsion of sexual drives. The primary consideration of mating couples is pleasure for themselves, as realized by obeying the commands of instinct; not the procreation of intelligent offspring. Intelligent offspring would be the major consideration of a purely rational creature, which man is not. When human beings marry, they seek mates who can make them happy, not mates who give them superior offspring. They want sexual satisfaction. In other words, human beings select their mates on the same instinctive bases as all animals. The male bird displays, and the female selects; or the alpha mammal establishes hegemony among other males, and the females are instinctively attracted to his alpha qualities. It works because every birth is an experiment of nature which is tested in the crucible of survival of the fittest. The unfit are disposable.

Nature is prolific, but very wasteful. Every man produces 400 BILLION spermatozoa in his lifetime—more than all the human beings who ever lived. Every time a man has an orgasm, he ejaculates enough sperm to populate the entire United States. The human female produces a quarter of a million ova in her lifetime, only a small fraction of which can be fertilized and evolve into human beings. Unfit ova perish, and unfit spermatozoa perish in the struggle for survival, just as unfit human beings have perished, and as all unfit creatures have perished for billions of years—until some misguided human beings adopted humanitarian philosophies.

A humanitarian society like the United States not only protects the unfit but also subsidizes their reproduction. However, humanitarian sentiments of natural predators never spill over to the out-group. There was no sobbing humanitarian sentiment for the Japanese victims of the nuclear Holocaust, or for the Vietnamese victims of 7 million tons of blockbusting demolition. The high priests of anthropology and sociology defend government subsidies to the unfit for their survival and reproduction because they abjectly support the mores and folkways of their society in the same spirit that Nazi physicists supported anti-Semitism and denounced Einstein.

Our science cultists deny that genetics plays a role in human destiny, and yet they know that the only reason they are human beings rather than mice, male rather than female, black rather than white, tall rather than short, normal rather than Mongoloid idiot, *et cetera* is because of their parents' genes and chromosomes. They know the difference between a thoroughbred horse and a draft horse is genetic, but they believe in the cult of magic: once an animal is defined as *Homo sapiens*, it instantly and automatically becomes impervious to natural law. This trick is as good as walking on water, rising from the dead on the third day, or bodily ascending into heaven, and why not?

There is no difference between religious cults and science cults!

Paul Harvey recognized our absurd, irrational attitude towards human reproduction when he pointed out that strict mental and physical qualifications are required of people who adopt children, but absolutely no qualifications whatsoever are required to produce children. Parents can be morons, physical wrecks, poverty parasites, or throwbacks to the missing link, but these are not legal barriers to their reproduction. Regardless of your mental or physical condition you can beget children who determine the future of the human race, the nation, and the world; but you can't even get a license to drive a motorcycle if you are mentally or physically unfit or a drug addict. You must be both mentally and physically qualified to adopt a child of mentally and physically unfit parents, but you can have all the children you want, if you, yourself, are both mentally and physically unfit. Man is a rational animal? Only an irrational animal would believe that.

Sammy Ho of Seattle, Washington, was reading the *Encyclopedia Britannica* at the age of three. Albert Einstein didn't begin to talk until the age of three. The genetic time-releases were different. One time the Ho family was working on a difficult jigsaw puzzle for hours when Sammy, who was less than two at the time, selected the correct pieces. When Sammy was nine years old, he passed his university entrance exams with higher grades than people twice his age. He went to Washington University at the age of nine years and three months. His mother is a biochemist and his father is a doctor. Any anthropologist or sociologist who thinks Sammy's genius is due to environment rather than genes is thinking like the Aztec priests who ripped out thousands of human hearts annually in sacrifices to the gods because their intellects told them that human sacrifices were necessary to guarantee the recurring miracle of sunrise.

The importance of genes and genetic factors can best be seen in the study of dogs. All domesticated dogs belong to the genus "*Canis*" and the same species, "*familiaris*", even though there are over two hundred breeds, one hundred sixteen of which are recognized by the American Kennel Club. Human beings are arbitrary in their methods of classifying themselves and other animals. Species classification differs in accordance with the method used. It may be typological, morphological, nondimensional, or biological. If we adhere strictly to the typological method, Negroes, Caucasians, and Mongolians could be classified as distinct species. The biological method is generally employed. Its criterion is whether or not the breed (race) can interbreed.

All races of man are included in the same species because they can all interbreed. We come to a contradiction when we see that all members of the genus *Canis* can interbreed, and yet they are classified into many different species. Dingos can interbreed with all breeds of dogs, but they come in heat only once a year while the latter come in heat twice a year. The gray wolf (*Canis lupus*) and the red wolf (*Canis rufus*) can interbreed with the domesticated dog (*Canis familiaris*), but they are all segregated into distinct species. Foxes (*Canis lagopus*, *Canis vulpes*, and so forth) can interbreed with dogs. The domesticated dog can interbreed with the coyote (*Canis latrans*), the hybrid of which is called the coydog; and it, like the coyote, is very intelligent, cunning, and swift. Regardless of the fact that it can interbreed with the dog, the coyote is differentiated from the dog by classifying it as a distinct species.

Jackals are classified into several species, chief of which are *Canis aureus*, *Canis mesomelas*, and *Canis adustus*, all of which interbreed with each other and with domesticated dogs. In spite of the fact they all can interbreed with each other, they are segregated into distinct species. In fact, some authorities even classify jackals as a separate genus. Thus we see that wolves, coyotes, jackals, foxes, and dogs are all segregated into distinct species, and some even into distinct genera, even though they can interbreed, but the varieties of *Homo* are all integrated arbitrarily and artifically by lumping them all into one distinct species. The typological method of classification was used for dogs, but the biological method was used for mankind. Carolus Linnaeus, the founder of the binomial system of nomenclature and the originator of modern scientific classification of plants and animals, found it necessary to differentiate four subspecies in the human race: *americanus, europaeus, asiaticus,* and *afer* (African).

Our anthropological cultists arbitrarily place all humanoids in the "unique" genus *Homo*, and all breeds in the identical species *sa-*

piens. Therefore, they are all bestowed with semantical equality and uniqueness. The cultists deal with abstractions: that is, language, not things. They infer racial equality from the word-magic of equating reality with abstractions. The absurdity of this kind of reasoning becomes apparent in the syllogism: American Indians are disappearing. He is an American Indian. Therefore, he is disappearing.

We stated that Ashkenazic Jews are a relatively pure ethnic group, even though they are ethnogenic hybrids. Purebred dogs and thoroughbred horses are all hybrids, but they are considered pure breeds. The thoroughbred horse is a hybrid of an English mare and Arabian stallion. The purebred German shepherd dog is a hybrid of herding and farm dog. Racial, or breed, purity refers only to preserving the favorable hybrid from contamination by other races, breeds or hybrids. The value of maintaining breed purity can be clearly seen in animals. The German shepherd, for example, is an intelligent, alert, and loyal dog which performs invaluable service to the blind, the police, and the military. To destroy this proven breed by mongrelizing it would be a major disaster. To destroy the superior Jewish subspecies by intermarriage would also be a major disaster.

The differences between breeds of dogs are obviously genetic. Only a madman could attribute the differences between dogs to environmental factors. The differences between dogs, coyotes, wolves, foxes, and jackals are far greater than the differences between breeds of dogs; but these differences do not prevent them from interbreeding, which should qualify them for membership in the same species. The only identity that can be inferred from membership in the same species is obviously semantical. The ability to interbreed is the only ability shared by all peoples, and word-magic will not increase them.

Over two hundred breeds of dogs were created by human intervention through selective breeding. Wolves, coyotes, foxes, jackals, and man were created by natural selection (nature's method of selective breeding) acting on genetic mutations, sports, drifting, *et cetera*, and by geographical isolation, which prevented the contamination of the gene pool by crossbreeding. If isolation had continued long enough, the differences between human races would have eventually become so great that they would no longer have been able to interbreed. If all variants of *Ramapithecus punjabicus* had immediately interbred, we would all be as primitive as the apes are today. If all variants of *Homo erectus* had immediately interbred, we would be going to caves seeking protection from predators more deadly than ourselves instead of going to the moon. Miscegenation is no virtue. It stops evolution dead in its tracks.

Genetic differences produce different behavior. Sporting dogs such as pointers, retrievers, setters, and spaniels hunt by air scent. Hound dogs such as beagles, fox hounds, and bloodhounds track their prey by ground scent. The greyhound types such as whippets, borzois, and salukis hunt chiefly by sight. Working dogs such as the collie, German shepherd and the Saint Bernard are bred for guards, guides, and herders. Toy dogs such as the Pekingese, pomeranian, and pugs have one function; the nonsporting dog such as the Boston terrier, bulldog, chow, Dalmatian, and poodle have another. Different genes yield different breeds (races) and different behavior. Researchers are now learning that alcoholism in man has a strong genetic component. Genetic studies of mice by Collins and Marks of the University of Colorado suggest that smokers are born, not made.

The bulldog was originally bred in the British Isles as a bullbaiter and pit fighter during the Middle Ages. As a result, it became endowed with ferocity, truculence, and tenacity. The cruel bullbaiting and pit fighting were outlawed after 1835, and the viciousness and intractability were progressively eliminated from the breed, but not entirely. Some ferocity and tenacity have been retained by the pit bull, much to the sorrow of several owners who have been sued because their dogs have attacked children whom they bit and held onto with such tenacity that they had to be nearly killed before they would release their jaws.

The point is that nearly any behavioral, physical, or mental characteristic can be bred. In physical size, dogs range from the huge mastiff group, including the Saint Bernard and Great Dane, to the miniature Chihuahua. Human beings display similar range, from the Pygmies of Africa and New Guinea, to the Tehuelches of Patagonia, and Hottentots of Africa. The reason dogs and human beings can be bred in so many varieties of physical and mental types is the unusually wide polymorphism of their genetic systems which provides the great range of heterozygous states. Adverse changes in environment determine the superiority of some ethnic groups over others in meeting the new challenges. Nature selects races for survival in the manner that man selects different breeds of domesticated animals.

The fact that different breeds (races) of the same species can have different genetic behavioral patterns was demonstrated by Van T. Harris in 1950. He created an artificial laboratory environment of grassland and woodland into which he released wild prairie deer mice and wild woodland deer mice. The wild prairie deer mice immediately selected the artificial grassland, and the wild woodland deer mice immediately selected the artificial woodland. The environmental "scientist" would say, "Naturally, they selected the environment to which they had become conditioned." BUT HARRIS'S LABORATORY DEER MICE, WHICH HAD NO CONTACT WITH EITHER PRAIRIE OR WOODLAND FOR SEVERAL GENERATIONS, ALSO MADE THE APPROPRIATE SELECTION. The way different breeds of dogs are produced is by selecting the dogs with the desired characteristics from among the normal variation within the dog species (or genus, *Canis*); hope for some lucky shuffling of genes and mutations; then mate offspring which contain the desired characteristics for about eight generations, after which time, the line usually breeds true. The selected hybrid becomes a "PURE BREED" in the same sense we refer to human races as "pure races." Human beings obey the same laws of nature as all animals, the ramblings and ravings of science and religious cultists notwithstanding.

Differences exist in human races as they exist in other animals, but when the same differences exist in other animals, they are classified as different species. The pygmy hippopotamus is considered a different species from the full-sized hippopotamus, and the pygmy chimpanzee is made a different species from the full-sized chimpanzee, but the human pygmy is considered the same species as the full-sized human being. Human races differ physiologically, psychologically, and anatomically from one another just as other animals differ from one another. Bigots attempt to obscure these facts by reducing deep-seated racial differences to superficial skin color. Human races can easily be identified by skulls alone. Alpinid and Nordid skulls differ greatly. The high and narrow Eskimid skull with its massive maxilla is vastly different from the short and wide Lappid skull with its small mandible. Dr. John R. Baker points out the fact "that anyone trained in physical anthropology could at once distinguish a typical Europid from a typical Negrid or Australid skull." Bigots thrive on ignorance, and they promote their bigotry by capitalizing on the ignorance of the masses.

The genetic differences between typical Europeans and typical blacks are far more profound than simple skin color differences. Before the *Encyclopedia Britannica* yielded to ethnic egalitarian bigotry it printed the following: "In certain of these (physical) characteristics, the Negro stands on a lower evolutionary plane than the white man, and is closely related to the highest anthropoids. The characteristics are length of arm, prognathism, a heavy massive cranium with large zygomatic arches, flat nose, depressed at base, and the tendency of the frontal bones to fuse together and form an eminence of peculiar shape. But in respect to the character of the hair, the white man stands in closer relation to the higher apes than does the Negro."

Different races are subject to different diseases. Black children are genetically susceptible to sickle-cell anemia (an evolutionary protection against malaria). Northwestern Europeans are genetically susceptible to cystic fibrosis. Thalassemia is a genetic disease of Mediterranean people. Tay-Sachs disease is an inherited genetic disorder most common in Ashkenazic Jews.

It is a curious fact that human beings take greater interest in breeding better dogs, cats, horses, and other animals than they take in reproducing their own species. Man breeds not as a rational animal concerned with intelligent offspring and the future of the human race, but as an irrational animal guided exclusively by blind sexual instinct. But this should be expected, provided we recognize the fact that man is NOT a rational animal. He is an animal programmed by nature with instincts in the same fashion as all other animals. Absolutely no rational provisions are made to prevent the racial deterioration of those who have risen on the scale of evolution to the heights of our modern Computer Space Age. Does anyone seriously believe that if the world consisted only of people like, for example, Australian Aborigines, an Australian Aborigine would have stepped from a lunar vehicle to the surface of the moon? Unfortunately, planned reproduction is as alien to man as a planned economy, and for the same reason. This is why neither Communism nor eugenics can ever succeed.

A personal note, please. I, as a young college student, dreamed of a Brave New World in which man would be guided by reason in every facet of his life. I dreamed of the time when the rationality of exact science would supplant the irrationality of religion, and the rationality of socialism would supersede the irrationality of the marketplace and boom and bust cycles of unplanned economy. I dreamed of the day cooperation would supplant exploitation, and eugenic breeding would elevate humanity to dizzying heights of rational excellence. Alas, it was an impossible dream born of pristine innocence. I had embraced the delusion of my science and philosophy professors—the delusion of all mankind—the delusion that man is a rational animal.

In respect to human breeding, the ancient Greeks were more rational than the modern Western World. They eliminated their imbeciles, idiots, deformed, and incurably ill by exposure so that they could not be a burden on society and live to breed a substandard race. People like the Kallikaks and the Jukes are now subsidized by the government and encouraged to reproduce. The "Kallikak" family was studied by H. Goddard. Martin Kallikak produced a feebleminded son by mating with a feebleminded girl. After that, he married a normal woman and produced several children all of whom were normal and contributed to society. The illegitimate, feebleminded son, however, sired a degenerate line of 480 descendants, 143 of whom were feebleminded, 46 normal, and the remainder unknown or doubtful.

The "Jukes" family was studied by Richard Dugdale and Arthur Estabrook. From the marriage of a shiftless farmer's son and a prostitute, a total of 2,094 descendants were identified. Of the total, 299 were paupers, 118 were criminals, 378 were prostitutes, and 86 were brothel keepers. There was a general record of intemperance and illegitimate births, and half of the total was feebleminded. The cost to the State of New York for jails—institutions for the insane, fee-bleminded, and delinquent—totaled up to several million in today's dollars: all of which was due to that one mating between the shiftless farmer's son and the prostitute.

Because of dysgenic breeding, there are several million people in the United States with an IQ of 70 or lower, all of whom are encouraged by public welfare, food stamps, and government subsidies to reproduce more feebleminded juvenile delinquents, problem children, and cases for public charity and relief. The bills to care for the unfit mount, as do the costs of the crimes they commit. As should be expected, the conclusions of the "Kallikak" and "Jukes" studies have been questioned by science cultists who question any scientific study with heretical conclusions that contradict their own cherished dogmas.

The survival of the unfit is a phenomenon peculiar to modern times. Modern "civilization" has suspended the normal process of natural selection and encouraged dysgenics. Modern medicine was created by the fit, but it prolongs the life of the unfit and swells the ranks of the unfit. The problem is compounded by the government which subsidizes their prolific reproduction. War drains the best blood on the battlefields, and permits defectives to reproduce at a faster rate than the fit. Modern humanitarian society insists upon keeping the worst types alive and functioning in the gene pool. It objects to the execution of criminally insane murderers on the basis of word-magic which labels them human beings; but it blesses the slaughter of millions of the fit with the simple expedient of more word-magic: that is, by labeling them "the enemy."

From Cattel's study of one thousand American scientists, it was found that the fertility of this superior stock was cut in half in one generation. The more educated and higher types of women are failing to beget children. Not the least of the problem is dysgenic racial crossbreeding. Using the thought processes of religious fanatics, many people religiously believe that by accepting the gospel of ethnic egalitarianism, they automatically join the ranks of the born-again intelligentsia, and they thank God that they have been blessed with broadmindedness and granted dispensation from the sin of racist bigotry. They refuse to be tempted by devils masquerading as facts and evidence.

In sharp contrast to the Kallikaks and the Jukes, we have the Edwards family. Jonathan Edwards made a study of this family of 1,394 descendants, 13 of whom were college presidents; 60 were physicians; 75 were army and naval officers; many were lawyers, judges, senators; a vice president of the United States; and the remainder held prestigious positions. It is known that gifted men rise rather easily through social and economic barriers, but individuals lacking such gifts cannot achieve eminence in spite of social advantage. Breeding in the Edwards family was eugenic, and it preserved greatness much as the breeding of the Jews in the past has been eugenic and accounts for the many great Jewish scientists, philosophers, statesmen, financiers, businessmen, physicians, and so forth.

It is often said that ability and intelligence are not related to the color of a person's skin. This is CERTAINLY true in the case of the Japanese, a people of the yellow race. Historically and geographically, Japan was to Asia what England was to Europe. As an island protected by water, Japan was twice saved from conquest by the great Kublai Khan. Like the Jews, the Japanese were an eugenically mixed race of people, a hybrid, who maintained a good measure of ethnic integrity by their isolation and cultural xenophobia. In fact, many people in the United States disparage Japan's monolithic ethnic structure with the same pejoratives they reserve for "racists." Our nationalistic bigots transform Japan's virtue into vice, and their own vice into virtue.

The ethnogeny of the Japanese involved hybridization with primitive white "Ainu" from the Amur River in neolithic times, a yellow Mongol strain from Korea that entered Japan about the seventh century B.C., and a brown-black Malayan and Indonesian strain coming from the south. Mahayana Buddhism was imported from China and began to make rapid headway in A.D. 522. The Buddhist missionaries introduced Chinese civilization to Japan. The Japanese adopted both it and Chinese writing. Even the name the Japanese gave to their islands, Nippon, originated in a letter a Chinese emperor wrote to the Japanese ruler.

As in Europe during Medieval times, a fighting class arose in

Japan. It was needed to protect the people against both the lawless and the Ainu who had remained segregated. The fighting class was called the "samurai." They correspond to the English knights. The samurai code of right conduct was called the "bushido", which was equivalent to the European knight's code called "chivalry." If a samurai failed in his duties, he was expected to perform "hara-kiri": that is, suicide by ripping open his own bowels with a long knife.

Life was difficult in Japan, and natural selection of the fit was relentless. Japan is mostly mountains. Eighty-five percent of the islands cannot be cultivated. Emperors had ruled Japan, but in A.D. 1192, a clan chieftain became the *de facto* ruler and assumed the title of "shogun." From A.D. 1192 until A.D. 1868, Japan was ruled by shoguns who were the overlords of the samurai. The emperors were puppets residing at Kyoto, but they were revered as descendants of the Sun Goddess. The shoguns were the actual rulers, and they resided in Tokyo. Japanese militarism flourished during the Age of the Knights (Samurai). Militarism intensified in modern times and culminated in World War II.

Saint Francis Xavier and two other Jesuit missionaries went to Japan in A.D. 1549 where they converted over one hundred thousand Japanese to Christianity by the year A.D. 1600. The shogun was fearful that the religious conversion was the first step to military conquest and ordered all missionaries to leave the country. It must be remembered that at the very time that the Spanish missionaries were converting the American Indians, the Spanish military were conquering them. After A.D. 1622, Christians were put to death in Japan because it was feared they would form a fifth column for European invaders. By 1641, all European foreigners were driven from the country, and all Japanese were forbidden to leave the island or build ships.

Japan was isolated from the outside world for two hundred years, except for some contact with the Dutch on the small island of Deshima in Nagasaki Harbor. An historical change took place in 1854 when Commodore Matthew Perry of the United States Navy steamed into Tokyo Bay with ten warships. The shogun was so impressed by the steamships which Japan had never seen before, and by the show of naval power which Commodore Perry commanded, that he signed a treaty which opened up Japan to American shipping. The United States gained extraterritorial rights in Japan, which were also soon granted to England, France, Russia, and Holland.

The granting of humiliating extraterritorial rights to foreigners so angered many Japanese that they attacked the foreigners. The British retaliated by destroying Kogoshima in 1863. In 1864, an allied fleet of British, French, Dutch, and American ships entered the Straits of Shimonoseki and demolished all forts along the coast. The wrath of the Japanese was then turned against the shogun, whom they deposed. They then made the emperor the ruler in fact as well as in name. This was in 1868, and the imperial palace was moved to Tokyo.

NOW THE GREAT MIRACLE OF MODERN HISTORY BEGAN TO TAKE PLACE. In 1871, Japan's ancient and primitive feudalism was abolished. Almost overnight, the Japanese transformed their medieval, agricultural nation into a modern industrial power. Railways were built and telephone and telegraph systems were installed. Much business was turned over to private capitalists, which promoted industrial growth on a huge scale. No other people in the history of the world ever duplicated the feat of the Japanese. Within fifty years, Japan changed from a feudal society into a modern, industrial state. She quickly absorbed Western science and technology. At first, French officers were hired to train the new Japanese army; but after Germany soundly trounced France in the War of 1871, German military experts were hired in their stead.

The amazing speed in which Japan transformed her primitive society into a modern industrial society is but a one part of the massive evidence attesting to the superior quality of the Japanese people. In 1894, Japan abolished the extraterritorial rights of all foreigners. In the same year she declared war on China and won an empire including Formosa, the Pescadores, and virtual control of Korea. In 1899, Japan helped the Western powers put down the Boxer Uprising. On February 5, 1904, Japan struck at Russian warships at Port Arthur in a sneak attack which was a preview of the Pearl Harbor sneak attack on December 7, 1941. What followed amazed and confounded the world.

Little Japan, only a few years out of the Feudal Age, massacred mighty Russia which had begun to industrialize in A.D. 1700 under the leadership of Peter the Great. Russia was defeated on land and on sea in engagement after engagement. Japanese forces quickly advanced in Manchuria and down the Liaotung Peninsula, inflicting defeat after defeat on the Russians. Port Arthur fell to the Japanese in February of 1905. The Russians were decisively beaten in the Battle of Mukden and lost one third of their forces. The Japanese annihilated the Russian fleet in May of 1905. Russia surrendered, and the peace treaty at Portsmouth, New Hampshire, on September 5, 1905, gave Japan Port Arthur, the Liaotung Peninsula, the south Manchurian railroad, and the southern half of Sakhalin Island. Japan soon took full control of Korea and renamed it Chosen. Only the rivalry of Imperial Russia and the Western nations prevented Japan from gobbling up most of China.

During the Middle Ages, when Europe was floundering in the mire of the Dark Ages, China was the most cultured nation on Earth, and the model for the rest of Asia, including Japan. However, China revered the past and held the newfangled ideas of the Western "barbarians" in contempt. Western troops and merchants gained more and more control of China. Foreign conquest was not so much of a shock to China as to Japan. She had been conquered and she absorbed her conquerors many times in history. The Ming Dynasty, who were the successors of Kublai Khan, ruled China from A.D. 1368 to A.D. 1644. Another foreign line, the Manchu Dynasty, who were related to Mongols and Tartars from southern Manchuria, ruled China from 1644 to 1912, at which time, a revolutionary movement overthrew the Manchus, and Dr. Sun Yat-sen became president of the New Republic of China. He died in 1926, and Generalissimo Chiang Kai-shek came to power. He united China and attempted to Westernize it

In Japan, the samurai were eager to imitate the West so that they could remain military masters. Industrial progress was amazingly rapid in Japan, but it was painfully slow in China. Even today, little Japan is an industrial and technological giant while huge China is industrially backward. However, in this case, the cause is probably due more to nurture (Communism, partly) than to nature.

Japan and China both joined the Allies during World War I, but industrialized Japan was of greater service to the Allies, and so she was allowed to invade China and practically make her a protectorate. The militarists were very powerful in Japan. They embarked the nation on a course of domination of the Far East. Essentially, Japan followed in the footsteps of England, Spain, and other Western imperialistic powers. She invaded Manchuria in 1931. By 1934, it became a virtual protectorate of Japan, who renamed it Manchukuo. In 1937, Japan increased her military pressure on China (Chiang Kai-shek) and also came in conflict with American interests in the Far East. She sank the United States gunboat Panay and some Standard Oil Company tankers, but was forced to apologize and pay damages to the American Government.

The United States began to obstruct Japan's efforts to dominate the Far East, issuing warnings and trade embargoes of needed war materials. Nevertheless, Japan took advantage of France's defeat at the hands of Hitler and took possession of French Indochina. Japan now became a threat to British possessions such as Burma, Singapore, Malay, and the East Indies, as well as to American possessions such as the Philippines. President Franklin Roosevelt demanded that the Japanese withdraw. They refused, whereupon the United States and Great Britain froze all Japanese funds. General Tojo became Premier of Japan. He ordered the sneak attack on Pearl Harbor of December 7, 1941. The United States was now in World War II. Britain declared war on Japan immediately.

The Japanese who were in a primitive Feudal Age until 1871, and lived on a few rather small islands which are 85 percent useless for agriculture, miraculously transformed themselves into such a formidable industrial and military power within a scant seventy years that they were able to challenge the world's greatest nation, the United States, and all its naval and military strength, as well as the mighty fleet of the British Navy which wasn't committed to the war in Europe, in addition to other countries such as China.

"By their fruits, ye shall know them," and by the accomplishments of the Japanese, we know them to be a superior people just as we know the Jews to be a superior people: not by revealed or intuitive truth, but by solid facts and hard evidence. Like the Jewish Empire of King David, the Japanese Empire was short-lived, but the superiority of both peoples continue to live in their genes, at least until bigoted ethnic egalitarians expunge it through miscegenation. The Jews survived their military defeats to become the great scientists, physicians, philosophers, financiers and businessmen of the world. The Japanese failed to dominate the Far East militarily, but they survived to dominate the entire world economically. The Japanese were able to build an economic empire as rapidly as they had built a military empire. They excel in electronics, optics, automobile manufacturing—almost everything intellectual, industrial, or technological. Technological consumer innovations originate in Japan more frequently than in the United States.

The United States faults Japan for her monolithic social and ethnic structure, but Japan is steadily progressing, and the United States is steadily declining. The United States graduates functional illiterates from her high schools and ranks a poor fifth in education among the nations of the world. Only one in one thousand American students scored as high as the top 10 percent of the Japanese on the same math test according to a recent study. Japan graduates scholars, but she is not handicapped by open enrollment or affirmative action programs, the purpose of which is to accommodate inferior elements in society. The quality of workmanship in Japan is superior to that of the United States. While American labor unions, motivated by greed and lust for profits (high wages and benefits) show indifference to workmanship and drive up prices beyond the reach of the poor and of world markets, Japanese workers cooperate with their employers and give quality work priority over lust for money. Melting-pot United States, which alloys the superior with the inferior to form the amalgam of mediocrity, is definitely NOT the paragon for the monolithically superior Japanese to emulate.

The Japanese are known for their courtesy, politeness, kindness, consideration, respect for their elders, and refinement, to which any visitor to Japan will attest; and yet, they can be brutal. In the 1937 undeclared war against China, Japan practiced the most uncivilized cruelties and terrorism imaginable. She bombed and maimed thousands of noncombatant civilians in populous cities. Japanese soldiers reportedly gouged out living fetuses from Chinese pregnant women with their bayonets. American prisoners of war and participants in the infamous Bataan Death March got a taste of Japanese barbarism as did the victims of Pearl Harbor. But Japanese, Jews, Germans, and Americans are all members of the same species of predator and born killer. They have all had histories of unspeakable barbarism.

Certain statistical attributes and qualities can be ascribed to races, groups, and classes, even though they do not necessarily apply to particular individual members. To illustrate the point, if one were to say that men are stronger than women, few would accuse him of being a male chauvinist pig or a bigot because it is a fact that, as a class, men are stronger than women. And yet, there are thousands of women stronger than millions of men. The real bigot is the person who denies physical differences between men and women as classes. Imagine the mayhem in the sporting ring if the ultra-liberals managed to open the heavyweight boxing and wrestling championships of the world to female contestants. Only a brainless bigot would refuse to admit that the best super females would get the bejesus knocked out of them. Where is the woman who could have lasted over a few seconds with Muhammad Ali?

It is also fair to say that men are taller than women, even though millions of women are taller than millions of men. By the same token, it is fair to say that some races are more intelligent than other races (as classes), even though millions of individuals in the less intelligent race are far more intelligent than millions of individuals in the more intelligent race. If random groups of people are graphed with coordinates of frequency and physical and mental abilities, the graphs form bell-shaped curves of standard deviation which normally overlap. There is overlapping and skewing in the graphs of intelligence of members of different races, just as there is overlapping in the strength and heights of the sexes, but the fact of overlapping does not alter the fact of statistical class differences.

The performance achievements of Japanese and Jews correlate to the results of intelligence tests. Miss Ruby Kerr gave the Pintner-Paterson Performance test to 276 Japanese elementary school children in Vancouver, British Columbia. Their median IQ was tested at 114.2. This prompted Professor P. Sandiford of Toronto University to conclude that the Japanese are the most intelligent of all racial groups living in British Columbia.

Apologists for low black scores on IQ tests protest that they are culturally biased and rigged by the white man and naturally favor the white man. But the same tests which indicate black inferiority to the white man also indicate yellow man superiority to the white man in spite of the fact of vast differences between Japanese culture and language *vis-a-vis* white man culture and language. The superior performance of the yellow man and the inferior performance of the black man are reported in nearly every textbook on psychology since intelligence testing has been performed.

Robert S. Woodworth's, *Psychology*, a textbook copyrighted in 1921, says on page 56, "It is, however, important to notice that Chinese and Japanese children, tested in California, British Columbia, and Hawaii, obtain an average IQ of just about 100, being thus on a par with white children; from which we learn that the white man's tests do not give a low standing to every alien group." Let us quote from one more of the many textbooks on psychology, all of which have the same message. In Glenn Devere Higginson's textbook of 1931 called *Fields of Psychology*, we read on page 329, "The yellow race is apparently the only race, aside from the white, which lifts its head high in defiance of any race prejudice, invades the American universities, and demonstrates both ability and interest in education. In these two qualities, they appear to be the white man's equal. "

Thus, the evidence clearly contradicts the fanatical dogmas of ethnic egalitarian bigots such as Paul R. Ehrlich and S. Shirley Feldman who wrote in *The Race Bomb*, "It has been shown, for example, that the conclusion of Black vs. White IQ studies can be predicted from the background of the investigator. Upper-class scientists tend to conclude that Blacks are innately inferior intellectually." Then, in defiance of the scientific method, and in the spirit of religious fanaticism, they write, "Scientifically, Shockley and Jensen notwithstanding, the claim that Blacks are genetically inferior to Whites in intelligence is just plain silly. " We shall present absolute proof of Ehrlich's and Feldman's prejudice and bigotry later in the chapter.

Japanese and Chinese, both of whom come from a totally different culture, and speak an entirely different (and more difficult) language from the white man, yet have the capacity to beat the white man at his own game of intelligence testing. But the superiority is more than academic. There was a wave of Japanese immigration to California in 1900. Even though they were severely discriminated against, they were such successful farmers that by 1920, they controlled 10 percent of the farmland but comprised scarcely 2 percent of the population. Cream rises to the top. The Japanese even beat the white man at his own game of science and technology. Little Japan, devoid of necessary raw materials and petroleum, outproduces in quantity and quality the huge and mighty United States with all her resources and petroleum.

Ethnic egalitarian bigots have a religious hatred of facts. They are committed to the national gospel of equality which, in essence, is identical to the Nazi dogma of the inferiority of Jews and superiority of Aryans because both are national gospels sustained by religious faith and not by scientific evidence. Intelligence testing, contradictory evidence, and facts must be made taboo and suppressed in a nation that places a higher priority on racial appeasement, social harmony, and political expediency than on scientific truth. It is better to sustain racial myths than racial riots. Like huge government budget deficits, it has short-term benefits, but it spells disaster for the future.

Like the Japanese, Jews also do well on intelligence tests. One test of five thousand school children from ages five to eighteen, all offspring of immigrant parents, described in Henry E. Garrett's *Great Experiments in Psychology*, show Polish Jews leading in intelligence with an average of 102.8, followed by Swedes with 102.1, English with 100.7, Russian Jews with 99.5, Germans with 98.5, and much further down the list were Russians with an average IQ of 90.0. Some of the greatest brains in both Germany and Russia were not Germans or Russians, but Jews. Soviet Russia would do well to take note of Santayana's admonition: "Those who cannot remember the past are condemned to repeat it."

All scientific data confirm the intellectual superiority of Jews and Japanese AS CLASSES. However, no Jew, Japanese, or European as an individual has the logical right to claim superiority over another individual of an inferior class, say an Australian aborigine, simply because he belongs to a superior class. Class comparisons are statistical, and they MUST NOT be confused with individual comparisons. For example, there are thousands of blacks who are superior to millions of Europeans, Jews, and Japanese. There are moronic Europeans, Jews, and Japanese, and there are extremely brilliant blacks. It is the STATISTICAL inferiority of blacks that has prevented them from producing superior societies.

From a study of California children, and the data given by F. L. Goodenough in the Journal of *Experimental Psychology*, 1926, 9:394, we find that Jewish children top the list with an average IQ of 106; followed by Scandinavians with 105; Chinese with 103; white Americans with 100; Japanese with 100; Germans with 99; and much further down are American Indians with 86; and lastly, blacks with 83. Again, we see that Orientals equal and even surpass the white man in spite of different cultural roots and tremendous differences in language. This data correlates to European supersession of Indian cultures in the Americas in the evolutionary tradition of the survival of the fittest, just as mammals superseded marsupials in South America when a land bridge formed at Panama to permit an invasion of more advanced mammals. We must never forget that unfit creatures do not and cannot create fit cultures for survival in the struggle for existence.

According to the environmentalist cult as preached by the apostle of behaviorism, John B. Watson: "Give me a dozen healthy infants . . . and I'll guarantee to take any one at random and train him to become any type of specialist I might select: doctor, lawyer, artist, merchant-chief and, yes, even beggar-man and thief, regardless of his talents, penchants, tendencies, abilities, vocations and *RACE* of his ancestors." (italics added) Those are brave words. They read like revealed truths out of the ethnic egalitarian's Bible.

Instead of accepting behaviorist dogma on blind religious faith, the disciples should test their faith with the scientific method by taking a dozen healthy Australian aborigine infants and setting about the task of training them to be mathematicians and theoretical physicists of the caliber of Albert Einstein. If these cultist disciples could produce scientific evidence as prolifically as they produce rhetoric, the entire world would be convinced that they are true scientists rather than fanatical religious cultists. But they cannot use the scientific method, and for the same reason religion cannot use it—it would destroy their faith. Nay, more—it would destroy all religion and all science cults, which human instinct will never tolerate.

Many evangelists of the anthropological, sociological, and psychological cults of environmentalism and behaviorism assure us that the ONLY reason many blacks are not in the top echelons of American society and leaders in science is because they were held back. They blame society, not genes; and nurture, not nature. They are the Flat Earthers of ethnology who look inside their heads for truth rather than to the external world of reality. The best evidence against their dogmas is the biography of great black intellects like the great black agricultural chemist George Washington Carver. He was born in the early 1860s of a slave woman who was owned by Moses Carver, a plantation owner in the southwest corner of Missouri. It was difficult to protect slaves in Missouri from slave-raiding night riders who struck from out of the South during the Civil War; so, Moses sent all his slaves to Arkansas.

After the war, all his slaves disappeared, including young George Washington's mother. Her small child was ill with whooping cough. He was brought back to the Carver plantation, and nursed back to health. He was a lovable little fellow who often went alone in the woods and fell asleep with a wildflower in his little black hand. He was so appealingly honest that the Carvers named him George Washington, and they gave him their own surname.

The fortunate shuffling of genes in George Washington Carver's zygote was such that conceived a most remarkable human being. There was only one book in the Carver home. It was a little blue-backed *Webster's Speller*. The boy's instinctive hunger for knowledge was so great that he quickly memorized the entire book. He had a delicate sense of color and form, and he taught himself to draw. He also loved music and became a singer and an organist. His unquench-able thirst for knowledge induced him to leave the Carver plantation at the age of about ten or twelve. He went to Neosho, eight miles away, and attended a one-room log schoolhouse. It was 1874. George Carver was penniless. He slept in barns, worked at odd jobs, and ea-gerly soaked into his thirsty mind all the book-learning his teacher could provide. There were more educational worlds to conquer, and so he went to the nearest high school, which was sixty miles away at Fort Scott, Kansas, where he "took in white folks' washing" to pay his way.

After George Washington Carver's ravenous mental hunger ab-sorbed all that the Fort Scott teachers could provide, he spent his entire savings on train fare to a college in Iowa where his letter of application had been accepted. It was the era of right-wing racist bigots. When Admissions Office saw that he was black, he was told that blacks were not accepted. The Land of the Free enslaved the black intellect as well as the black body. This intellectual giant, whom American society would make a dwarf, had no money with which to leave the college town. He took odd jobs, worked as hotel cook, and started a laundry from his savings.

Having saved sufficient funds, Carver enrolled in Simpson Col-lege in Indianola, Iowa, which cost him all his savings except for a single dime on which he had to live for over a week while he looked for odd jobs. He studied piano and art, and subsequently transferred to Iowa State Agricultural College at Ames where he received a degree in agricultural science in 1894, and a master of science degree in 1896. The college was so impressed with his wizardry in agricul-tural chemistry and his uncanny skill with plant life that it appointed him to a teaching position. He became famous for his work in the bacteriological laboratory. He won universal honor and respect, even from die-hard bigots.

George Washington Carver was instinctively and genetically driven to seek knowledge just as a predator is instinctively driven to seek prey. His environment dictated a life of crime or poverty, and especially ignorance; but his genes dictated a life of culture, learning, and respectability. His genetic superiority drove him to the top, in spite of vaulting racial prejudice and social pressures to keep him down. He could NOT be held down, even in the heyday of discrimination. Cream rises to the top.

Carver learned of Booker T. Washington's efforts at Tuskegee Institute in Alabama to advance blacks in America through self-improvement and education rather than political agitation; and so, in the fall of 1896, he joined Tuskegee's new department of agriculture as its director. However, by 1910, Booker T. Washington relieved him of his administrative duties because that was not wherein his talents lay. Carver was now able to devote most of his time to research. Using the laws of soil fertility as established by Justus von Liebig, he was able to harvest unprecedented plush crops in Alabama.

Because the boll weevil was destroying all cotton fields, Carver urged farmers to switch to peanuts and sweet potatoes. People began to refer to him as "the peanut man." Farmers heeded Carver's advice, but they soon overproduced peanuts and sweet potatoes which rotted in the fields for want of a market. Carver was a sensitive man, and it distressed him. According to his own story, he walked into the woods and repeatedly asked, "Mister Creator, why did You make the peanut?" He buried himself in his laboratory to learn the "why" of the peanut, and to correct the evil for which he felt responsible—overproduction of peanuts.

George Washington Carver's intellect and industry wrought many scientific miracles in his laboratory. From sweet potatoes, he made or synthesized starch; vinegar; shoe-blacking; ink; library paste; dyes; candy; tapioca; ginger; coconut and chocolate compounds; stock feeds; coffee substitute; molasses; rubber; flour; *et cetera* for a total of one hundred eighteen separate and widely used products. From peanuts, he created milk; butter; cheese; coffee; shaving lotion; breakfast food; flour; soap; ink; cosmetics; pickles; sherbets; salad oils; soft drinks; wood stains; axle grease; tan remover; insulating boards; dyes; *et cetera* for a total of three hundred different products. He synthesized many products from cotton waste, soy beans, and local clay. He saved the peanut and sweet potato farmers and created an industry which now runs in the billions of dollars. Carver was elected fellow of the London Royal Society for the Encouragement of Arts, Manufactures and Commerce in 1916. He received the Spingarn Medal in 1923. At one time, Thomas Edison offered him a position in his laboratory with a salary of over one hundred thousand dollars a year, but he refused it. Presidents Coolidge and Franklin Roosevelt visited him. Joseph Stalin invited him to Russia in 1931 to superintend cotton plantations.

George Washington Carver contributed his life savings to a foundation for research. Farmers and industrialists from all parts of the world sought his chemurgic counsel, and they got it free of charge. When he gave Florida peanut farmers his diagnosis and treatment for a disease which was blighting their crops, and the grateful farmers sent him checks, he returned them saying that God did not charge for growing peanuts, so he could not charge for curing sick peanuts. Because of his generosity, he had little money, but what he had went to his school to educate youngsters of all races. He wore tattered old clothes and shoes that were more patches than shoes. He could have been a wealthy man and lived in luxury, but he did not possess the avaricious instincts of a predator. His instincts gave him an insatiable thirst, not for money, but for knowledge, and they gave him a predisposition towards kindness, generosity, and sympathy.

According to all the dogmas, rules, and theories of the cultural anthropologists, behavioral psychologists, and environmental sociologists, Carver's dire poverty and deprived environment should have been the root cause for him to be a streetwise, tough mugger—certainly not a kindly, brilliant scientist. His stultifying environment should have been the root cause of ignorance, not wisdom. John B. Watson could no more have taken George Washington Carver as an infant, and trained him to be a beggar-man or a thief than he could have taken a dove chick and trained it to be a hawk.

Benjamin Banneker was another Negro whose genes impelled him to intellectual greatness in spite of the fact that he lived in the heyday of black slavery; that is, 1731 to 1806. He had an innate hunger for knowledge. He became a mathematician, astronomer, inventor, and writer through self-education from reading borrowed textbooks. His achievements were acclaimed by the scientists of his day. Cream rises to the top. If the statistical distribution of the

George Washington Carvers and Benjamin Bannekers were more widespread, Negro culture would have eclipsed Western European culture, and the corollary of superior predatory capability would mean that Europeans would have been hauled off to Africa as slaves, instead of vice versa.

In contrast to George Washington Carver—a brilliant, kindly, generous, sympathetic lover of all mankind, and a socially disadvantaged black whom society had "set up for a life of crime," according to most science cultists—we have two socially advantaged Jews: Leopold and Loeb. Richard A. Loeb was the son of Albert H. Loeb, who was the wealthy vice-president of Sears, Roebuck and Company. Richard Loeb was born in wealth and raised in the exclusive Kenwood district of Chicago, Illinois. He graduated from the University of Michigan in 1924 at the age of seventeen. His weekly allowance was two hundred fifty dollars which was far more than the monthly wage for most Americans at that time. He was 5' 11" tall and had an athletic build. According to environmental science cultists, both he and his friend. Nathan F. Leopold, son of a multimillionaire shipping magnate, should have become pillars of upper-class American society. Their environments provided them with the root cause of social preeminence; but, instead, both Leopold and Loeb spent a four-year apprenticeship committing petty thefts, vandalism, and fraud prior to conceiving the ultimate crime: the perfect murder.

Loeb was the born, genetic criminal who evidently seduced Leopold to a life of crime by the attractive force of their homosexual relationship. Fourteen-year-old Bobbie Franks was the selected victim for the perfect crime. Loeb stabbed him in the head four times, and blood gushed forth in rivers. Loeb, the genetic killer, reveled in the gore. Leopold, who was not a genetic killer but an environmentally conditioned killer, sickened at the sight of blood. The killers were apprehended. Had they been black, right-wing racism would have decreed their execution. The killers' parents hired the famous criminal lawyer Clarence Darrow to defend their sons, at the cost of a million dollars. The "fun" killers were spared execution. They were sent to Northern Illinois Penitentiary at Statesville where they lived in luxury. Genetic variability is a fact of biology. All Jews are not Albert Einsteins, and few blacks are George Washington Carvers.

There is no denying the importance of environment, but heredity must provide the raw material. If one is born without vocal cords, he cannot be taught to speak. If one is born with Down's syndrome, no environment is going to make him a straight "A" student in college. If one is genetically coded for Edwards' or Patau's syndrome, he is lucky to survive beyond his first year of life, and he will he mentally retarded. Racial differences in intelligence are genetically coded, statistical phenomena. They spell the difference between racial survival and extinction; for example, Indian and European struggle for survival in the Americas. All ethnic groups are simply not genetically coded to create a space-age technological society. It is miracle enough that sufficient people of ability ever appeared even among the most gifted of races to provide us with our fantastic world of modern science and technology.

There is no super-race, and if there were, every individual in it would not be a super-individual. We have spoken of the superior Jews, Orientals, and Europeans, and yet there is an extreme paucity of individuals even among superior races who could match the intelligence and ability of George Washington Carver. If one is tempted to think of the white race as a super-race of intellects, he had better review his history. White men slaughtered each other by the millions in the name of the God of Love, and they are still slaughtering each other. The white man made science a religious crime, a heresy, and burned scientists at the stake. The most nonsensical religious cults, healing cults, science cults, and ethnic egalitarian bigotry are products of the white man's intellect. Less than 56/ 100 of I percent of white men gave the world true science. More than 99 and 44/ 100 percent of them gave the world absurd nonsense.

At one time, right-wing racist bigots predominated in America. Blacks were denied dignity, jobs, education, advancement, and basic human and civil rights. In the 1920s, millions of the Ku Klux Klan— posing (originally) as ghosts of the Confederate dead returning from the battlefields in garbs of flowing white robes and masks, and riding horses draped with white sheets and skulls mounted on their saddle horns—terrorized blacks, and even whipped and lynched them under any pretense to maintain white supremacy; but many of the lynched blacks were actually intellectually superior to their lynchers. With the decline of these dastardly and reprehensible right-wing racists came the ascendancy of left-wing racists. Bigotry merely turned its ugly head and presented society with its obverse face.

To learn about left-wing racism, let us hear from another black man of superior intelligence. He is Walter Williams, an economist, author, and college professor. Even though he is black, he finds affirmative action and open enrollment despicable because any quota system by race is obviously racist. These programs assay people not by ability or qualifications but by race. He points out that President Johnson's Great Society, i.e., government give-away programs, are run by poverty pimps. In other words, by people who profit from poverty not only by getting elected on the poverty issue, but also by receiving high salaries working for government agencies set up under poverty programs. He opposes discrimination, and favors laws outlawing discrimination, but he says that because he has the right to sit at a white lunch counter doesn't give him the right to force whites to pay for his lunch. Walter Williams, like George Washington Carver, and Booker T. Washington (men of intellectual accomplishment, rather than firebrands of rhetoric like Martin Luther King. Jr.), wants economic advancement for blacks to come through their own efforts and participation in capitalism and not as parasitic recipients of government handouts. Superior blacks find affirmative action and open enrollment demeaning to their intelligence.

Professor Williams points out that when the poor Irish came to America in 1848, they had no food stamps. What they had and what they needed to rise above poverty was capitalism and free enterprise. Now that the laws protect blacks from unfair discrimination, participation in capitalism is all they need. To say that they need ancillary assistance is to admit they are inferior, loudly and clearly. When liberal Tom Braden confronted Williams with the fact of historical discrimination against blacks in America, Williams told him all people had their problems. Braden retorted, "But your people were enslaved! Would you want to be a slave?" Williams shot back, "Six million Jews were exterminated in Nazi Germany, and Jews were slaughtered all through history. I would rather be a slave than exterminated, and I believe you would, too."

Professor Williams is not against the government helping the down-and-out, but he is against government handouts and welfare programs which keep the down-and-out down-and-out by discouraging them from seeking gainful employment so long as they are provided with handouts. He says that the welfare state encourages illegitimate babies because the government subsidizes illegitimacy with welfare checks and food stamps. According to him, illegitimacy among blacks in 1940 was 8 percent, but in 1983 under welfare state conditions black illegitimacy, often among sixteen-year-olds, jumped to 55 percent of all births. As Williams says, you can't blame the high illegitimacy rate on racism in America. Births are the results of sexual intercourse, not racial attitudes.

Open enrollment and affirmative action are reverse forms of racism. New evils cannot rectify old evils. Walter Williams is opposed to the liberal whites and the NAACP stand against competency tests for students and teachers because, as he says, it promotes mediocrity in education. In his own words, "It graduates functional illiterates who can't read a parking ticket." Any special privilege to anyone "because of the color of his skin" whether black or white is racism, pure and simple.

Left-wing racism is usually rationalized by saying it makes up for past right-wing racism and discrimination; but Jews, Chinese, and Japanese are not in need of special privilege. How is it possible for white America to make up for the past theft of the Americas from the Indians? Should the Catholic church make up for her past atrocities of the Inquisition? If a qualified white is denied a job "because of the color of his skin," what will compensate for this discrimination? Everyone can rationalize anything. Hitler rationalized his extermination of the Jews.

One of the most racist acts of the left-wing bigots was the making of Martin Luther King Jr.'s birthday a national holiday. It was an affront to America's greatest men like Abraham Lincoln and Thomas Jefferson because they are NOT so honored. It was a racial sop, and a prostitution of integrity to garner votes and suppress riots. But nothing should be surprising in a nation whose "intellectuals" tout with a straight face a man like Jesse Jackson—who probably wouldn't qualify to manage a McDonald's hamburger joint—as presidential timber to manage the world's greatest superpower.

Former Governor of New Hampshire Meldrim Thomson said that Martin Luther King Jr. was a man of "immoral character whose frequent associations with leading agents of Communism is well established." Francis X. Cannon's *Biographical Dictionary of the Left* says that King's legal immunity was acquired by his friendship with the Kennedys and Lyndon Johnson, and by his having "taken shelter behind a clergyman's cloth." According to Representative John M. Ashbrook, King's disregard for the law was deplorable, but "his disregard for the laws of God (was) almost inconceivable." J. Edgar Hoover called him "the most notorious liar in the Country." Harry Truman labeled him a "troublemaker. "

Incriminating evidence against Dr. King, FBI tapes and documents, were hidden from the light of day by U.S. District Judge John Lewis Smith Jr.'s court order; and what little evidence filtered out through the Freedom of Information Act was heavily deleted by government censors for "national security" reasons, the same reasons given by Richard Nixon to obstruct justice. Truth must be suppressed at all cost. Nothing must tarnish the ICON.

Martin Luther King Jr. was a charismatic minister with impressive oratorical powers, but rhetoric did not take us out of the Stone Age. The entire nation owes a debt to George Washington Carver, not to King. But a nation that worships its rock 'n' roll performers but ignores its scientists would certainly make a hero of King rather than Carver. A nation that pays reporters who cover the White House higher salaries than the President of the world's greatest superpower has to be a little whacky.

Left-wing racism has made profound changes in the United States, few, if any, for the good. Glorification of mediocrity, even stupidity, is the national vogue. Excellence is looked upon with suspicion, and elitism is as repugnant as right-wing racism. The gifted child must hide its head in shame rather than lift it high with pride.

The United States has a national guilt over looking with favor upon a superior individual. The educational process has ignored the superior student and tailored its needs to the least fit students. There is now a pervasive feeling that a qualitative classification of students violates a basic principle of democracy by admitting the heresy that all men are not created equal. Intelligence tests have been excoriated and virtually banned because they consistently show Jews, Japanese, Chinese, and whites surpassing blacks in intelligence. Our national policy is the policy of all fanatical religious cults from Nazism to Inquisitorial Christianity: BAN EVERYTHING THAT CONTRADICTS OFFICIAL DOGMA!

Books have been banned in libraries and as school textbooks because they contain ethnic heresies. Minorities protest and demonstrate against "demeaning" books, and they are promptly removed from library shelves and school classrooms. This is *de facto* book burning, and it is as effective as the *de jure* papal *Index Librorum Prohibitorium* of the dreary Dark Ages. Truth is not determined by the scientific method. It is decreed by edicts of the federal government and by pontificating court orders. Human beings never change.

But the banning of books in the United States is covert. There are no public ceremonies in which offensive books are heaved into fires to the screams of "Down with the racists!" The books simply vanish from the library shelves and schools. Nazi and Fascist dictatorships openly and proudly displayed public book-burning of publications offensive to the national ideal. The "burning" of books in the United States is covert, sneaky, insidious, and in the name of social justice. Therein lies a double contradiction: to burn books publicly would contradict the national ideal of freedom of speech, but not to burn books would permit the racial heresy of inequality to survive. The solution to the dilemma is the surreptitious, *de facto* burning. Book burning follows a custom respected and hallowed by antiquity. Only the hypocrisy is new. Constitutional guarantees exist on paper in both the Soviet Union and the United States. The play's the thing, and the show must go on!

A good case in point to illustrate the fanatical banning of truth which contradicts the ethnic egalitarian dogma of the United States can be seen in the difficulties Robert Ardrey experienced when he was writing *The Social Contract*. To quote Ardrey, "In 1966 an enormous Federally financed study, *Equality of Educational Opportunity*, reported on the educational achievements of some six hundred thousand students in American schools. Referred to usually as the "Coleman Report," it became instantly unavailable at book shops and from normal distributors of scholarly literature. After some eight months of trying, I pried a copy out of the U.S. government printing office. Why it had become unavailable became evident only after long exploration of its seven hundred-plus pages of statistics. The Negro had failed in American schools—failed catastrophically, beyond statistical doubt or sentimental apology, beyond all explanation. It was not a document to be freely circulated in congressional areas wherein the Negro commanded the swing vote."

Ardrey went on to explain that this study revealed 15 percent of black students are superior in achievement to half of all white students, BUT 85 PERCENT ARE INFERIOR REGARDLESS WHETHER THE STUDENT HAD COME FROM A SEGREGATED OR INTEGRATED SCHOOL, AND EVEN THE SOCIO-ECONOMIC LEVEL OF THE FAMILY MATTERED LITTLE. Most devastating was the record of Oriental Americans who also suffered rigorous discrimination in America, but still either equaled or excelled the records of white students. To quote Ardrey, "A consequence of the Coleman Report was the hysterically received study by California's Arthur Jensen, published in early 1969 in the Harvard Educational Review, suggesting the genetical inferiority of Negro intelligence." He continues, "It is a persuasive document, so persuasive that there were those who could provide no better answer than to threaten Jensen's life."

Ardrey suggests there may be a deep-seated problem when millions of human beings who successfully survived the conditions on the African continent through the processes of Darwinian evolution are transported to a different continent and a totally different environment. Natural selection for white Americans who evolved through ten thousand years of highly developed civilizations, including those of the ancient Cretans, Greeks, Hebrews, and Romans, would certainly tend to evolve a different creature from one evolving under African jungle or semi-jungle conditions. Orientals evolved under conditions of ancient civilizations similar to white Americans.

Results of intelligence tests have correlated to cultural performance from their very inception at the beginning of the century. This fact cannot be denied, and so the left-wing racists attack the validity of qualitatively categorizing cultures. They say that if Indians, Eskimos, or Negroes devised intelligence tests, the tests would favor skills necessary for survival in their cultures, and the white man would test inferior. True, but if these ethnic egalitarians cannot distinguish between the quality of Einstein's intelligence coping with abstract and abstruse problems of the Cosmos, and the primitive hunter's intelligence coping with the problem of killing prey, rational discourse is hopeless.

Ethnic egalitarian bigots equate all human cultures; but, for themselves, they want the benefits of Western Culture: namely, automobiles, refrigerators, computers, and television sets. When they are in sub-zero weather, they press a button and on comes the heat in their luxurious rooms. They should try starting a fire by rubbing sticks together and huddle by its flickering flames in freezing cold for a few years before they glorify primitive cultures. Anthropologists and sociologists who study primitive societies and exalt them are never far from an airport where they can quickly fly back to the comfortable world of modern science, medicine, and technology. If they really want to be broadminded, they should admit that they would test lower than a hopeless idiot in an intelligence test on communication via the dance as administered by a common honey bee.

We have shown in previous chapters that freedom in our "free" society is freer on paper than in practice. Freedom of information is a vaunted American value, but it is hypocrisy because there is no freedom of information. Information is on a tether. It cannot exceed the limits imposed by dogmatists. Libraries, book stores, newspapers, magazines, radio programs, and TV programs abound with ethnic egalitarian propaganda. Readers are inundated with left-wing racist dogma in endless books like Jacobs and Stern's (college outline series) *General Anthropology*, Ashley Montagu's *The Human Revolution*,

Desmond Morris's *The Human Zoo*, Paul R. Ehrlich's *The Race Bomb*, *et cetera, et cetera*. The scientific fact of racial inequality is treated like religious heresy and suppressed.

Left-wing racists outrage intelligence by falsifying history, falsifying records, employing deception, outright lies, and every indoctrinational device invented by fanatical religious cults; but publications exposing them and their methods are "unavailable." Sometimes, the falsifications of history are positively ludicrous. Bantam Books published *Black Heroes in World History*, which not only included Hannibal in its stories of great Negroes, but it also included a picture of him which was the head of a 100 percent Negro. Bantam Books also published the book *Hannibal*, by Harold Lamb, and its cover displays a picture of the head of a 100 percent white man who is also supposed to be Hannibal. Almost every school child knows that Hannibal was a Carthaginian, which was an ethnic Phoenician with racial ties to Ashkenazic Jews. The real Hannibal was white, and wishing will not make him black.

Also typical of the tactics of left-wing racists is that of Desmond Morris in his *Human Zoo*. We could say that Morris employs deception, but it more nearly approximates outright lies. In his chapter on in-groups and out-groups, he writes, "The first travellers to penetrate black Africa were astonished by the grandeur and organization of the Negro empire. There were great cities, scholarship and learning, complex administration and considerable wealth." He continues, "Let us take one glimpse at an ancient Negro city in West Africa, as it was seen over three and a half centuries ago by an early Dutch traveller." Fortunately, we were able to track down his source which was apparently Roland Oliver and J.D. Fage's *A Short History of Africa*, where this city is identified as Benin. The center of the Benin Kingdom was also known as Edo. Needlessly to say, Morris's source was NOT included in his bibliography.

In the first place, it was not an ancient city. According to the 1982 *Encyclopaedia Britannica*, Benin was only founded some time before the fourteenth century A.D. by the Edo people. In the second place, to even begin to equate Benin with ancient cultures such as existed in Greek Civilization of TWO THOUSAND YEARS EARLIER is a sacrilege. It is indicative of either skulduggery or unfathomable ignorance. Ancient Greek and Hellenistic philosophy, science, medicine, and mathematics had to be relearned during the Renaissance if modern science and technology were ever to develop. Aristarchus of Samos (310-230 B.C.) taught the heliocentric theory of the solar system one thousand five hundred years before Copernicus. Euclid's geometry of 300 B.C. is still taught in mathematics courses. Aristotle's deductive logic was not improved upon until recent times. The ancient Greek plays are still performed. Ptolemy mapped out the heavens in detail and named the constellations which we still use. Ancient Greek temples were masterpieces of architectural and sculptural perfection. It is utterly ridiculous to compare the best of black culture, modern or ancient, with the ancient Greek Culture of over two thousand years ago. In the third place, Morris's Dutch traveller is never identified by name, and the entire story sounds more like the account of a UFO freak telling of his visit with people from outer space aboard a flying saucer.

Let us assume, however, that the account given by the "Dutch traveller" is perfectly true. Morris's skulduggery is positively proved by comparing his quotation with the actual passage in *A Short History of Africa*. In order to create a false image of the grandeur of black culture, and to promote his brand of bigotry, he quoted in his *Human Zoo*, and this is an exact quotation, "The town seemeth to be very great; when you enter into it, you go into a great broad street . . . seven or eight times broader than Warmoes street in Amsterdam." The three periods represent the deletion of six key words. The original quotation from the history book reads, "The town seemth to be very great; when you enter into it, you go into a great broad street, *NOT PAVED, WHICH SEEMS TO BE* seven or eight times broader than the Warmoes street in Amsterdam." (Italics added.)

Morris wanted the reader to visualize a Parisian boulevard or an ancient Roman road. Since when has a dirt road indicated an advanced culture of grandeur? Besides, there is a deal of difference between "seems to be" and "is." Morris continues, " . . . you see many streets on the sides thereof." He deliberately tried to create the illusion of a great modern city with a broad boulevard and interlacing streets. In addition to all this, there is question about the authenticity of the "Dutch traveller" in the first place, and the "traveller's" reliability in the second place.

Morris continues his quotation, "The houses in the town stand in good order, one close and even with the other as the houses in Holland stand . . . The King's Court is very great, within it having many great four-square plains, which round about them have galleries." Morris again practices deception. He again omitted key words which, if they were not omitted, would give the reader the impression of a primitive village rather than a highly civilized city. His ". . ." replaces the deleted words "at the gate where I entered on horseback, I saw a very high bulwark, very thick of earth, with a very deep broad ditch." How could the reader form the illusion of a great, modern city if the true facts of thick mud walls, big ditches and dirt roads were made known to him? Morris ends his quotation with, "Hardly a crude mud-hut village." If he had not deleted key words from the original source, it would certainly have read exactly like a crude mud-hut village.

Morris also omitted other pertinent information from the original source such as, "There are also many man slaves seen in the town, that carry water (*et cetera*)." Morris wanted to perpetuate the myth that the white man was the villain who must now compensate the black man for past crimes against human rights by paying reparations. The truth is that Negroes enslaved their fellow man to the limits of their primitive capability, and the human rights issue is merely a change in the weather of moral climate. If Negroes had been capable of creating a superior culture, Europeans would have been hauled to Africa in slave ships, and Europeans would now be petitioning for their own civil rights in black Africa. With this scenario, America would have been "discovered" by a Negro, not a Caucasian, and the United States would now be a black nation with a minority of former white slaves demanding affirmative action and open enrollment

To quote Morris again, "As early as the middle of the fourteenth century a sophisticated visitor remarked on the ease of travel and the reliable availability of food and good lodging for the night. He commented, 'There is complete security in their country.'" Morris neglected to mention that the "sophisticated visitor" was Ibn Battuta, that the country was Mali, that it was an empire, and that the Mali kings were either Moslems or had deep ties to Moslems. Moslem travelers and writers always exaggerated the importance of Islamized countries. Morris played down the slave-owning and slave-trading by black countries which was frequently discussed in his source material, *A Short History of Africa*. He wanted to promote the fiction that a highly moral and civilized race of Negroes were reduced to barbarism "by white brutality and greed."

The truth is that blacks were as barbarous, greedy, and lustful for conquest and empires as whites, yellows, or reds. They had the same instincts as all human beings, but not the same abilities. They were not great imperialistic powers for the very simple reason that they never advanced to the necessary level of competency to create mighty empires. When Japan attained this level of competency, she immediately embarked upon empire-building. India had its Asoka Empire of 250 B.C.; China had its Han Empire of 100 B.C.; Cambodia had its Khmer Empire of A.D. 1000; the Aztecs and Incas had their empires; and black Africa had what empires and slaves its competency permitted. Before one is tempted to dispense liberal portions of sympathy, he should contemplate that the master would have been the slave had their genetic endowments been reversed; and, parenthetically, the bleeding hearts for the Hiroshima and Nagasaki victims would, themselves, have been the victims if Japan had been able to acquire the atomic bomb before the Americans.

Left-wing bigots attempt to prove ethnic egalitarianism by categorizing an accomplished mixed-breed possessing as little as 3 percent Negro blood as a Negro. Some years ago *Time* magazine ran an article purporting to prove Negro ability by means of vignettes of "Negro" successes in the United States, but they were conspicuously European hybrids. One time, a group of "Indians" were on a TV talk show expounding on Indian rights. One observant spectator remarked, "You don't look like Indians to me. You look like white men dressed up as Indians."

There were advantages to crossbreeding, but they were unilaterally enjoyed by Indians and Negroes. Booker Taliaferro Washington had an European father according to his autobiography *Up From Slavery*. Jan Ernst Matzeliger (1852-1889), the black inventor who "revolutionized the shoe industry," was the son of a Dutch father and a black Surinamese mother.

Left-wing bigot Paul Ehrlich says in *The Race Bomb*, "Biologically there are no races of Homo sapiens. The race-IQ controversy is really just a skin color-IQ controversy." All bona fide biologists agree with *The New Columbia Encyclopedia*: "The differences among races are essentially biological and are marked by the hereditary transmission of physical characteristics." Raciation is incipient speciation and fundamental to the evolutionary process. Asiatic Indians are at least as black as Negroes, but they are Caucasians (whites). The color of one's skin does not define race. A black Asiatic Indian is blacker than most American Negroes. Many American "Negroes" are whiter than millions of Caucasians, but a white "Negro" is a black man, and a black Asiatic Indian is a white man. It may seem illogical, but that is how man, the "rational" animal, sees it. Negro-Caucasian hybrids predominate in Mauritania, parts of Mali, and Rio de Oro to the river Senegal. Much of progressive "black" Africa is mostly Europid stock, but credit for intellectual progress is given to "Negro nations."

Space limitations do not permit a full disclosure of Paul Ehrlich's bigotry except to point out that he says in *The Race Bomb*, "Nigerians developed a magnificent tradition of sculpture centuries ago that has never been approached in England or America . . ." According to the *Encyclopedia Britannica*, it was derived "partly from the varied racial elements in the population." When the glory of ancient Greece was flourishing, Nigeria "where superstition still waxes strong," was featuring "late Stone Age terra-cotta heads associated with the Nok culture." The Yoruba naturalistic sculptural style of the Middle Ages was flawed by "bulging eyes; flat, protruding, and usually parallel lips; and stylized ears."

Many people insist that the black's lack of intellectual and social progress in the United States is due SOLELY to white society holding him down, but men of intelligence like Carver and Banneker made it even in the days of slavery. Any world traveler who has visited the Caribbean islands, Central America, South America, and black

Africa knows that wherever there are large numbers of blacks, there is a notable lack of industrial progress and widespread poverty. In Brazil, which has long boasted of her freedom from discrimination, and even purposely sought interracial breeding, the lack of black advancement is conspicuous. There, as in the United States, blacks achieve notable superiority only in sports—Pele, for example—and in primeval music. Some of the worst slums in the world are Just outside Rio de Janeiro, the chief inhabitants of which are blacks, as they are in the slums of Panama, Venezuela, Haiti, and many other parts of the world.

In Durban, South Africa, the Asiatic Indians are discriminated against as religiously as the blacks, but they have a thriving Indian Village which attracts tourists from all over the world. The economic status of blacks is higher in Apartheid South Africa than any part of black Africa. *Time* magazine (Jan. 16, 1984) admits that South Africa is an outstanding exception to the interminable inventory of failures in black Africa. When I visited the black nation of Tanzania and its capital of Dar-es-Salaam, I was amazed to see that the Asiatic Indians were the aristocrats, and blacks were in poverty. The Indians had the beautiful homes, new automobiles, and big businesses. Blacks had the shacks, bicycles, and poverty. Did Asiatic Indians hold blacks down in their own country? Tanzania could have adopted the action taken by Nazi Germany and expelled a superior people, as Sudan and other African countries had when they expelled their Indian and European populations, only to suffer decline, but Tanzania was wise not to duplicate the blunder.

Left-wing bigots, like all bigots, refuse to face facts. They either deny them, sweep them under the rug, or intimidate fact-finders with names like "racist," or threats against their lives. It is one thing to rationalize away 10 percent of the facts, 50 percent of the facts, or even 90 percent of the facts; but when one must rationalize away 100 percent of the facts, it would seem that the most fanatical, dyed-in-the-wool left-wing bigot would begin to question his dogma. But, of course, science cults are religions, and the dogma of religion must never be questioned, no matter how stupid or asinine.

There is a long catalogue of evidence with which every rational person must come to grips. By simply watching TV without closing one's eyes to that which he doesn't want to see, one will detect that in TV quiz shows the more the quiz depends on intelligence or knowledge rather than luck, the less chance a black has of winning. Very few blacks won at the old "Jeopardy" quiz show. What children win spelling bees? They are Jews, Orientals, and Europeans. Watch the TV screen! Blacks predominate in sports and primitive music, but are conspicuous for their absence among scientists and astronauts. Perhaps liberals who count noses in the job market and scream discrimination ought to do the same in TV contests of knowledge and intelligence. Whenever pictures of intellectually gifted children are shown, blacks are usually among the missing. Why don't liberals count noses in Mensa International and scream discrimination? Apparently, there is a limit to stupidity.

Left-wing racism has spelled decline for the United States, The federal government's requirements of affirmative action and open enrollment as a condition for government contracts and federal money for education have sent the economic and educational superiority of the United States into a nose dive. In the one area the United States refused to compromise quality for racial appeasement, the space program, it has remained supreme in the world. The government desperately wanted to boost its liberal image in the eyes of the world, especially Third World countries, by putting unqualified blacks into space, but it resisted affirmative action and maintained superiority. A woman preceded a black into space. Why didn't the liberal politicians count racial noses when spacemen stepped on the moon? Evidently, even politicians draw the line on absurdity somewhere.

William Bennett, coordinator of humanities under the Reagan Administration, was on the *Larry King* talk show one morning. A listener asked him whether the integration of the races in schools, which started about 1960, had anything to do with the lowering of SAT scores and educational performance because they both occurred at the same time. Bennett replied to the effect, "Definitely not! Recent studies indicate that black scores have actually gone up. Only white scores have declined." What an amazing reply! He gave the best reason in the world to prove racial integration is the cause of lowering national educational performance, but he offered it as proof integration is not the cause.

Low SAT scores for blacks are blamed on environment. Why, then, does the identical environment lower white scores? If educational performance were due to causes other than integration, poor teachers, for example, both races would be equally affected adversely, and BOTH races would suffer diminished performance. To say an incompetent teacher would lower white scores but improve black scores is to speak absolute gibberish. If you mix white and black paint, the result is gray paint: each color becomes more like the other and less like itself.

Ashley Montagu tells us in *The Human Revolution*, "All of us are mongrels, and we are all the better for being so." If he told a thoroughbred horse breeder that his horses would be the better for being mongrelized with draft horses, the breeder would know that Montagu is insane. If we think in terms of mongrelizing the two hundred breeds of dogs and thus reduce them to ONE SINGLE BREED OF DOG, we realize that Montagu should be cutting out paper dolls instead of writing books. There are many contributing genetic factors to a superior stock: mutations, sports, genetic drift, and sometimes hybridization; but unrestrictive hybridization destroys the favorable strain that mutations, sports, and genetic drifting provide. Selection (natural) must act on the genetic factors to winnow the superior from the inferior.

If early forms of life had immediately hybridized whenever a favorable mutation appeared, evolution would have stopped dead in its tracks. Life would still be confined to the primordial seas. Geographical isolation (segregation) makes raciation possible; raciation is incipient speciation, and speciation is the name of the game of evolution. Nature produces endless varieties—some good, most bad—and then selects the favorable varieties for survival, as she had in the sixteenth through the nineteenth centuries of struggles for survival between Indian and European cultures and peoples. Montagu would never have lived to see a Computer Age society if modern man's finest were Australian aborigines and Yanomamo mongrels.

Montagu, along with anthropologists like Margaret Mead and

Ruth Benedict, consider Western culture with its man-walks on the moon, jet airplanes, TV's, and computers, just another human culture, separate but not superior. Smoke signals are as remarkable as radio and TV because they are identical in that they are but modes of communication at a distance. These mad cultists say that all cultures and all people are equal. Paul Ehrlich asks, "How would white children perform on an Eskimo (intelligence) test?" He goes on to explain that the Eskimo intelligence test would involve questions on hunting seals, selecting snow for an igloo, and so forth, and a white child would be scored a moron on such a test. Ehrlich should also have noted that all human children would flunk an intelligence test given by animals like migratory birds and fish on finding direction.

If a science cultist's intelligence is such that he cannot distinguish the qualitative difference in intelligence between a Computer Age society and a primitive hunting society, and he sees no difference between an Einstein solving the riddle of the Universe and an Australian aborigine solving the problem of cold-conking a kangaroo with a boomerang, we have entered the twilight zone of the mad, and rational discourse is at an impasse.

Repressive white society could not hold superior blacks down, and supportive white society cannot hold inferior blacks up. The black greats like George Washington Carver, Benjamin Banneker, Booker T. Washington, and Jan Matzeliger rose, like cream, head and shoulders above millions of inferior whites. On the other hand, no amount of busing or open enrollment can improve the IQ of less-gifted blacks. Phillis Wheatley was a slave born in Africa and brought to Boston at age ten where a merchant, John Wheatley, purchased her. Recognizing her superior intelligence and wit, he educated her and encouraged her talents. He named her Phillis Wheatley. She became America's first important black writer and anti-slavery advocates' most prized exhibit to prove Negro mental equality.

Emancipationists trampled each other in rushing to acclaim the first exemplar of Negro literary talent. Phillis Wheatley was given her freedom, and she traveled to England where poets were better appreciated. Her poems were first published in London in 1773 when she was seventeen. Right-wing bigots belittled her achievement calling it,

"A single example of a Negro girl writing a few silly poems, to prove that the blacks are not deficient to us in understanding." Eighteenth century right-wing bigots had as little regard for truth as twentieth century left-wing bigots.

Phillis Wheatley was intelligent, sensitive, and much admired, but she died in poverty in 1784. Times, fads, national myths, values, and mores have changed since then. Alex Haley is a modern black author of considerable repute but probably less talent than Phillis Wheatley. He is the author of *Roots*, which won him a Pulitzer Prize and 2.6 million dollars in hardcover revenues alone. In 1978, the courts forced Haley to pay Harold Courlander a reported five hundred thousand dollars for plagiarizing from his book *The African*. Said Haley rather lamely, "Somewhere, somebody gave me something that came from *The African*. That's the best honest explanation I can give."

It was asked by the nineteenth century proponents of slavery, "If the Negro was naturally the equal of the white man, why was he so notoriously barbarous in his natural state?" If Desmond Morris had been around in those days, he would have simply falsified history and insisted that the black natural state was "grandeur and organization . . . of great cities, scholarship and learning (*et cetera*)"; but bigots like Morris were not around then, and so the emancipationists replied, "Excessive heat had depraved them." The trouble with this excuse is that while Negroes inhabiting the tropical rainforests of central Africa did not make even a start in mathematics, the Maya of the Guatemalan tropical rain forest who were also cut off from civilization made astounding progress in mathematics.

Cream rises to the top. When blacks were guaranteed equal opportunity, they instantly rose to the top in sports. In mathematics, physics, computer science, *et cetera*, it was an entirely different story. Affirmative action was not needed for Negroes to gain equality in sports—the white man needed affirmative action. In spite of open enrollment, athletic scholarships, racial scholarships, and every possible racist advantage, black achievements in science and technology are not impressive. It was thought that school integration was the answer to the problem, but once integrated, black students began to demand special black facilities, black studies, Black English courses, and so forth. The whole idea behind integration was to produce black parity in Western culture, not to create nostalgia for a primitive culture. Europeans want to put as much distance as possible between themselves and their primitive, barbaric roots, and so do blacks like Booker T. Washington who understood modern realities. Said he, "No race that has anything to contribute to the markets of the world is long in any degree ostracized. "

Statistical achievements in intelligence testing correlate to national achievements. The Japanese quickly took on national greatness. They also took on the greatest military powers of the world. They lead today's world economically. The Jews founded the modern state of Israel in 1948. It immediately became the model of democracy in the Middle East, if not in the world, and "a power to be reckoned with." The Jews converted a barren desert into a garden spot. They made their country an industrial giant, and defeated Arab nations ten times more populous than themselves. Hong Kong, Singapore, and Taiwan became showcases of modern industry and technology in Asia. The Chinese, once free to function in an economic system natural to the human predator, capitalism, rose to the top immediately, just as Japan had risen to the top.

As we mentioned, if genetic endowments had been reversed, black Africa would have dominated Europe, Africa, and the Middle East—not vice versa. In recent years, when black nations were given their independence, they went nowhere. Of course, excuses abound. One is that more time is needed to overcome the effects of colonialism. Liberia was founded in 1822 (when Japan was still a backward, feudal state) by black freedmen from America who settled at Monrovia. It became a republic on July 26, 1847, with a constitution modeled on that of the United States. The government went bankrupt in 1909. Scandals broke out in 1930 which were investigated by the League of Nations. The League upheld the charges that the Liberian government was involved in slave trading. Native peoples and Americo-Liberians fought each other constantly. Military dictatorships took control of the government. A bloody coup took place April 12, 1980. President Tolbert was murdered and Sgt. Samuel Doe took over.

The black nation of Haiti fared no better than Liberia. Independent since 1804 when Toussaint L'Ouverture scored a brilliant victory over Napoleon's forces, it remained in dire poverty and under the control of the Duvalier family dictatorships. In 1984, CBS's *60 Minutes* exposed the country's poverty, corruption, filth and hopelessness. Nigeria has been hailed as black Africa's finest. In November of 1983, *60 Minutes* ran an expose of Lagos, the capital, largest city, and economic center of Nigeria. It showed that poverty, corruption, infestation of rats, uncollected garbage, and economic stagnation was incredible. The nation's oil wealth is funneled into Swiss banks to feed individual greed instead of promoting the national weal. Stagnation is ubiquitous.

In February of 1984, CBS's *60 Minutes* ran an expose of Zaire. It was the old familiar story. Instead of a showcase for black African progress, it became a cesspool of black African corruption, poverty, and deterioration since independence. The CIA installed Joseph Mobutu as president. He is supported by the United States. He bled Zaire of its copper, cobalt, and diamond wealth to amass a fortune of 5 BILLION DOLLARS for himself. The economy is in shambles, and the people wallow in garbage, poverty and infestation.

Time magazine (Jan 16, 1984) described the deterioration of Black Africa since independence in unequivocal terms: the decline in agriculture and the encroachment of jungle bush upon the cities, railways, and roads built by European technology and engineers. From an objective, scientific etiology, the genetic component is evident; but people are moved by emotion and religious fanaticism, not by scientific evidence; and so the evidence is as unacceptable as the evidence of man's mortality and God's nonexistence.

We are dealing with facts. To left-wing racist bigots, they are unpleasant facts, and man has a unique way of dealing with unpleasant facts. For example, the fact of his mortality is unpleasant. Therefore, he invents an immortal soul for himself. Human beings are idiotic enough with living brains, but thinking with dead brains, seeing with dead eyes, and hearing with dead ears are tricks the likes of which are made possible only by the magic of religious, racist, or science cultists. The fact of race, itself, is denied. An infinite variety of excuses are conjured up by left-wing racists, and they live smug and content in fantasyland.

Arthur Jensen is America's most hated heretic. He has the impudence to confront left-wing racists with facts. Jensen showed that blacks do better on verbal tests than nonverbal tests, which disproves the theory that blacks are disadvantaged by cultural and linguistic barriers. Blacks perform better on "culture-loaded" tests than on "culture-fair" tests. He proves that the notion that culture-fair tests devised by whites will favor whites is false because Japanese children outscore white children by six points in the Wechsler Intelligence Scale for Children. He showed that the tests used by schools, employers, and the armed forces accurately predict success or failure for native-born English-speaking Americans. He also found that when white and black children of equal socioeconomic status are tested, whites score an average of twelve IQ points higher than blacks. Says Jensen, "None of these attempts to create highly culture-reduced tests has succeeded in eliminating, or even appreciably reducing the mean differences between certain subpopulations—races and social classes—in the United States." Nevertheless, left wing bigots advance their bigotry, and they do it by countering facts not with facts but with blind rage, threats of physical violence, and smoke screens of false charges of bigotry.

The United States, the Land of the Free, does not tolerate heresy any more than the Church tolerated heresy during the days of the Inquisition. Arthur Jensen suffered personal abuse because he employed science in a field where religious faith is demanded. Science yields heresy, as in the days of the Inquisition, and it must be squelched! He was mobbed and shouted down at lectures and had to be rescued by the police. Bodyguards had to protect his life. Threats on his life forced cancellation of his lectures in Australian universities. When a colleague defended him in London, he was beaten up and taken to the hospital. Jensen lost many personal friends. He is America's twentieth century martyr to science.

Many American scientists, like Nazi scientists, prostitute their science because it is more profitable to peddle official state dogma than to defy it with heresy. The prostitutes of science sail to prosperity with the prevailing winds of racial bigotry rather than flounder on uncharted reefs in storms brewed by scientific inquiry. Human beings behave today as they have since the dawn of time. Now that left-wing racism is in vogue, it, like the Ku Klux Klan, compensates for intellectual impotence with physical violence to the cheers of public approbation.

The American philosopher and poet George Santayana (1863-1952) is one of America's most frequently quoted authors for his famous observation, "Those who cannot remember the past are condemned to repeat it." He made other perspicacious observations which America would do well to note. In his *Life of Reason*, specifically, 'Reason in Society,' he wrote, "Some races are obviously superior to others. A more thorough adjustment to the conditions of existence has given their spirit victory, scope, and a relative stability. It is therefore of the greatest importance not to obscure this superiority by intermarriage with inferior stock and thus nullify the progress made by painful evolution and a prolonged sifting of souls. Reason protests as much as instinct against any fusion, for instance, of white and black peoples."

Santayana thought that intermarriage is perilous, except between races of acknowledged equality and stability. Evidently, he would have approved of intermarriage between either Japanese or Chinese with Europeans. He believed that CONTACT with ALL PEOPLES by a superior stock is extremely beneficial, but CONTACT SHOULD NOT LEAD TO INTERMARRIAGE because "mixture with an inferior stock can only tend to obliterate" the superior stock, as has happened with the Ten Lost Tribes of Israel, ancient Greeks, and so forth. Santayana wrote, "The Jews, the Greeks, the Romans, the English were never so great as when they confronted other nations, reacting against them and at the same time, perhaps, adopting their culture; but this greatness fails inwardly whenever contact leads to amalgamation." The United States, blinded by the bliss of ignorance and euphoric in the delusion of racial enlightenment, is playing with fire. The fire may consume America's potential for future greatness as it had for the Lost Tribes of Israel, the ancient Greeks and the ancient Romans.

Santayana was no right-wing racist. He would certainly have acknowledged that there are many very intelligent blacks who are superior to millions of Europeans. But greatness in a society is dependent upon pervasive statistical greatness rather than limited, discrete, individual greatness, and it is derived from its gene pool. Santayana clarifies this point, "Individual gifts and good intentions have little efficacy in the body politic if they neither express a great tradition nor avail to found one." In the words of John Heywood, "One swallow maketh not summer." Thus, we see that the Jews, ancient Greeks, ancient Romans, Europeans, and Japanese have been able to create great cultures and societies, but Negroes have not. Santayana continues, "The common soul will destroy a noble genius in absorbing it; and, therefore, to maintain progress, a general genius has to be invoked; and a general genius means an exceptional and distinct race."

Our Earth passes through great geological cataclysms, upheavals, and diastrophisms which put every species, breed and race through the test of its qualifications for survival. Dinosaurs, for example, were tested and found wanting. Droughts alone in recent years of relative climatic stability have accounted for the lives of millions of human beings. Widespread progeny, volcanism, and climatic severity ushered in the Cenozoic Revolution and brought about mass extinction of the unfit. It was called "the Time of the Great Dying." The great Ice Ages also tested survival qualifications and spurred human evolution. When Europeans invaded, the Americas Indians were tested and found wanting. When the next great test comes, nature will be deaf to man's protestations of racial equality. She will define racial inferiority and racial superiority in her own relentless way, as she had for billions of years.

Eugenics is the most important factor in the survival and advancement of the human race; but, as a human goal, the most impossible of dreams. The importance of an eugenic race is best expressed by Santayana, "Environment, education, fashion, may be all powerful while they last and may make it seem a prejudice to insist on race, turning its assumed efficacy into a sheer dogma, with fanatical impulses behind it, yet in practice the question will soon recur: What shall sustain that omnipotent fashion, education, or environment?

Nothing is more treacherous then tradition, when insight and force are lacking to keep it warm. Institutions without men are as futile as men without institutions."

The horror of Hitler's Holocaust in the name of eugenics, but in the practice of dysgenics, was an outrage against reason and intelligence the world can never forget. But, in addition, the basic stupidity of even the most intelligent of human beings will immediately transform the theoretically rational science of eugenics into an irrational, inquisitorial, fanatically religious saturnalia of persecution. A superior race is vital to a superior society, but it cannot be planned, even as a successful economy cannot be planned, a la Communism. Man's nature will not have it so. Success must come from the adventitious interplay of human instincts adjudicated at the court of natural selection, just as the success of capitalism comes not from rational planning but from the interplay of irrational instincts of greed, egoism, and selfishness driving creatures on to effort and achievement. Capitalism weeds out unfit businesses, and nature weeds out unfit races. Superiority is attained not via planned economy or planned eugenics, but via economic selection and natural selection. What is the ultimate answer to quell the searching soul? The answer is: "THERE IS NO ANSWER!"

Humanitarianism and left-wing racism have guaranteed the successful breeding of the unfit. Government subsidized dysgenic human breeding has become a social *summum bonum* with global consequences. A people who have never advanced technologically to the point of shipbuilding, to permit them to transport themselves and disperse their genes to the far flung corners of the world, are parasitically transported by a people who HAVE created a superior culture. The armed forces of the United States have changed the complexion of the world.

The proliferating unfit, unable to integrate into a technological society in significant numbers, turns to crime and public doles. The fit become an endangered species, and excellence is derided. The ubiquitous sounds of the jungle tom-toms bruit the decay of an elite culture, and music of the intellect is threatened with extinction for lack of appreciative psyches. The intellectually gifted child becomes a pariah in the mainstream society of the unfit. The King's English is ridiculed, and Black English is glorified. Says Paul Ehrlich in *The Race Bomb*, "Black English is a coherent system with richness and complexity that is obscured if one simply considers it as a deviation from the norm or as erroneous speech." Some extreme left-wing racists even demand that Black English be taught in the schools. Some bigoted judges agree.

Is Black English rich and complex, or is it just plain Stupid English? If you consider the expression, "Man, yuh doesn't know noth'n," for example, it violates basic logic and the rules of enunciation and pronunciation. A double negative is a positive in grammar, just as it is in algebra and elementary logic. The idea the expression is intended to convey is, "Man, you don't know anything." The statement, "You know nothing," means you are ignorant, but if you DENY this statement by saying. "You DON'T know nothing," it means you are NOT ignorant and must know something. "I have no money," means I am broke. "I ain't got no money," denies that I am broke. It actually says the precise opposite of what I intend to say. Black English is illogical, and a stupid confusion of number and person of subjects and their verbs. It is indicative of either the inability to learn simple rules of English grammar or indifference to learning, and to glorify it is to glorify ignorance and stupidity. The decline and fall of civilization into a Dark Age is not new to history, and our left-wing racist bigots are doing their level best to repeat history and drive us back into the murky Dark Ages.

Intellectual elitism is deplored in the United States, but athletic elitism is exalted. As Joseph N. Bell noted, "The athlete who can throw a football 70 yards with uncanny accuracy is considered praiseworthy and justified in receiving special treatment and rewards. So is the actor who is capable of projecting a charismatic ego trip with someone else's words." Physical prowess receives the acclaim intellectual prowess would receive in a society of predominantly intelligent human beings.

Boxing and basketball, for example, sometimes approach a black monopoly. There are no racial nose-counters to demand affirmative action and to demand a racial reapportionment to reflect the racial composition of our society in the world of sports. Affirmative action would mean that 85 percent of all athletes must be white, but it would also reduce the quality of the athletes and make America inferior in world competition. The superior performer would be denied his rightful place in the sun because of his race. This would constitute right-wing racism. It would be deplorable and stupid, but its effects on national greatness would be negligible compared to left-wing racism which denies the superior intellectual performer his rightful place in the Sun, and it has the potential to eventually reduce superpower United States to just another banana republic.

The pressures to reduce the United States to the status of a banana republic are everywhere. As Dr. Emery Stoops, professor emeritus of education at the University of Southern California said, "When the courts demanded that children from all social and economic classes must be thoroughly mixed within a school system, educational and behavioral standards had to be further lowered to accommodate those not able to compete with their new peers."

It must never be forgotten that the United States has risen to the status of the world's greatest superpower by not compromising the principles of Darwinian evolution. Man, the predator, must be a superior predator if he is to survive in a species of predators. Left-wing racism and concomitant decline in excellence are post World War II phenomena.

But racism is here to stay, especially if we understand that racism has two faces. Left-wing racism is currently in vogue, and right-wing racism is anathematized. Popular propaganda has it that prejudice is not innate. A child is not racist by nature. It must be taught prejudice; but what is overlooked is that left-wing racism and prejudice must also be taught, and it is being taught with a vengeance. Left-wing racists preach their brand of prejudices in the name of enlightenment, just as churches teach their superstitions in the name of eternal truths. Educationally, a child's mind is a *tabula rasa*. It can learn language, science, technology, and all the good things only by being taught. Unfortunately, it also "learns ignorance," superstition, misinformation, and prejudice by being taught, and the teachers are incapable of distinguishing knowledge from ignorance.

The physical superiority of blacks, (as a class, of course, in the sense that men are physically superior to women, and Japanese are intellectually superior to Australian aborigines), is a consequence of evolutionary principles: *i.e.*, genetic variation acted upon by natural selection resulting in the survival of the fittest. This process occurred not only under natural environmental conditions on the continent of Africa, but also through human selection of the physically fittest slaves, and the elimination of the physically unfit because of the harsh conditions of transportation to America and subsequent brutal slave existence. Human selection determined human evolution, just as it determined canine and equine evolution.

Negro genetic superiority cannot be denied. In the words of Robert Ardrey, "Despite all hybridization, all cultural disparity, all environmental divergence, such common traits as superb teeth and the capacity to run forever or jump over the moon or knock a baseball from San Francisco to Los Angeles must find an explanation in some dominant genetic complex inherited from common West African ancestors." When the direction of human evolution made the fateful shift from brawn to brain, from jungle to city, and to science and technology, physical superiority became obsolete. That is why women have achieved social equality.

The United States is sucked into a maelstrom of genetic declension in the same manner that white girls are sucked into the trap of becoming white slaves for black pimps. The adolescent runaway is approached by a black pimp as she gets off a train or a bus in a strange city. The pimp tries to strike up a conversation with the white girl. If she is hesitant, he says, "What's the matter? Are you prejudiced against black people?" She doesn't want to be a social leper in today's society; *i.e.*, a social heretic who defies accepted articles of faith, and so she converses. She proves that she isn't prejudiced by dating him. She gives absolute proof of her "enlightenment" by having sex with him. Before she knows what happened, she is a prostitute working for a black pimp. He lives in luxury and drives Cadillacs or Lincoln Continentals while she has the bare necessities to sustain her existence.

Our nation is seduced by this same process. It wants to appear "enlightened," and free from racism (right-wing), but SAT tests, IQ tests, and college entrance examinations indicate black inferiority. Therefore, these tests are condemned as racist, and open enrollment is substituted. Job qualification tests flunk out black applicants therefore, they, too, are condemned as racist, and affirmative action is substituted. Natural unequals are proclaimed equal by judicial and legislative decree much as if the United States Supreme Court were to declare the law of gravity unconstitutional.

Meanwhile, the United States, oblivious to true reasons, begins its nose dive into decline and fall. To think the truth would be to think the unthinkable. Our nation is committed to suppress racial heresy with every means at its command, and with the effectiveness of Inquisitorial severity "for the good of the nation" in the spirit of Pope Pelagius I, who quieted the scruples of soldiers in the service of brutalizing heretics by assuring them that "to prevent or to punish evil was not persecution, but love."

Chapter 8

NONSAPIENS AND FREE WILL

That we possess free will is the most natural of assumptions; yet, were it not instinctively assumed, it would be the most impossible of conclusions. Human beings have always assumed that the Earth is flat until relatively recent times. Knowledge of geology, geography, and astronomy exposed the assumption as a product of ignorance. We experience a flat Earth, but it is actually an oblate spheroid. What we experience, and what is true apart from our experience, are two entirely different things. A dream is an experience, but it is a figment of the mind, and it exists only in the mind. Even our immediate sensations and perceptions are entirely different from external reality. We believe a baseball bat is something solid, for example, especially if we get hit on the head with it; but physicists tell us that it is mostly empty space. Solidity is an illusion of experience.

All matter with which we have experience on Earth, whether it be a baseball bat, a bar of steel, or we, ourselves, is actually almost entirely empty space. The electrons and protons of all objects with which we have experience are separated by vast space, comparable to the space between our Sun and its nine planets. If the matter in our bodies were compressed so that its electrons and protons were close together, we would become so small that we would be invisible to the naked eye.

Compressed matter (compact, solid matter) actually exists in the universe. It is the stuff of white dwarf stars, supernovae, neutron stars, and black holes. The matter of white dwarfs weighs more than a ton per teaspoonful on Earth. If the matter in Mount Everest were compressed to the density of a black hole, it would be reduced to the size of a proton. We cannot walk through each other, even though we are more than 99 and 44/100 percent empty space, because of the impenetrability of electronic fields. If we try to make two powerful magnets of the same polarity touch each other, we can readily understand how electric and magnetic fields can be "impenetrable" without "solid" matter intervening. Cosmic rays and X-rays pass through us almost as if they are passing through empty space. Neutrinos emitted by the sun pass completely through Earth, almost as if it were not even there. Our insubstantiality approaches the tenuity of a dream.

There is no necessary relationship between experience and reality. We assume from our experiences that size, mass, and time are absolute. A six-foot, two hundred pound person believes that his six feet, two hundred pounds, and lifespan as measured in years are absolute values in the universe, but they are entirely relative. Our "HUGE" Universe could be compressed to the size of an orange, but there is no way we could possibly detect the shrinkage because all our measuring rods would shrink in the same proportion. It would still be 93 million miles to the Sun, even though a mile would be infinitesimal as compared to its pre-shrinkage length. A hundred years would be the same hundred years to us, even though it would be an infinitesimal second relative to pre-shrinkage time. Universes could exist in an electron; and Suns, planets, and life types could form, flourish, and become extinct every moment of our Earth time.

The world we know from our experience is entirely different from the real world which exists outside our minds. What we see as color, such as red and green, has absolutely no existence apart from our perceiving minds. Electromagnetic waves strike our retinas, which transmit nerve impulses to our brains, which, in turn, create the sensations of color. If there were no animals in the universe with minds capable of generating the sensations of color, there would be no such thing as color in the iniverse—only electromagnetic radiation. The beautiful, scintillating colors of the twinkling stars do not exist in the physical universe. They are the creations of the brain of an animal when it looks up into the evening sky. The beauty of the stars exists only in our heads—not in the sky.

We say that sugar is sweet and vinegar is sour, but they are neither. Sweetness and sourness cannot exist in anything but a mind which creates them. Every student of elementary psychology learns that taste is a chemical sense caused by gustatory cells in taste buds reacting to kinds of ions which transmit neuronic impulses to the medulla oblongata; thence to the thalamus; and finally to taste-receiving areas in the anterior cerebral cortex where the sensation of taste is created. The sensation of taste can be created in a subject simply by stimulating his anterior cerebral cortex with an electrode probe. To say that our sensations exist in the external world apart from our perceiving them is the same as saying that pain exists in the external object which causes it. Pain is not in the pin that pricks our skin. It is in our mind. By the same token, to say that we have free will is merely to say that our cerebrums produce the experience of our being free. Freedom of choice is a real experience in the same sense that hallucinations are real experiences, but it lacks objective reality.

We all have the experience that our behavior is controlled by our own free will. We experience freedom of choice; but, as we have seen, experience and reality are not necessarily related. We experience the illusion of free will because we are fully conscious of our desires, wants, and ambitions; but totally unconscious of how our desires, wants, and ambitions were implanted in us like programming in a computer. It is rather simple to prove by a simple theatrical demonstration how a person can be programmed like a computer, and how this person behaves like an automaton while believing that his behavior results from his own free choice:

A hypnotist can program the behavior of another person by hypnotizing his subject, and giving him a post-hypnotic suggestion while he is under the hypnotic trance. For example, the hypnotist says to his hypnotized subject, "After you are awakened from your trance, and upon hearing me mention the word `freedom,' you are to jump on the table and sing "The Star-Spangled Banner!" The subject is awakened and returned to his normal state of consciousness. In a few minutes the hypnotist blurts out the word "freedom." The subject immediately jumps on the table and sings "The Star-Spangled Banner." What is astonishing about this experiment is that the fully awakened subject obeys the commands of the hypnotist, but he is conscious only of the belief that he acted by his own free will. He is unconscious of the fact that his behavior was programmed.

When the awakened and normally conscious subject is asked why he did such a ridiculous thing as jump on the table and sing the national anthem, he indignantly responds that there was nothing ridiculous about his actions. He, like all human beings, is compelled to rationalize his behavior regardless of how bizarre it is. He defends his predetermined, automated behavior as if it were his own freely determined behavior. He says, in effect, that more people should demonstrate their love of country and love of freedom for which the United States stands by not being ashamed of being demonstrative. He is likely to ask the rhetorical question, "What better way is there to demonstrate one's love of freedom and love of America than by singing the national anthem loudly and proudly for all the world to hear?"

All the world can see how a person experiences the delusion of freedom at the very moment his behavior is controlled by post-hypnotic suggestion, as in the above experiment; but few realize that they, too, experience the same delusion of freedom, as they actually behave in a manner predetermined by a complex of instincts. The person acting out the will of the hypnotist was conscious only of the DESIRE to act in a predetermined way. He was unconscious of the fact that this desire was implanted in his conscious mind by another person. By doing what he felt he wanted to do gave him the delusion that he acted by his own free will, but he was not aware that he was robotized by drives which were implanted in his subconscious mind.

Nature robotizes human behavior by creating unconscious drives and conscious desires to behave in specific ways. These desires are implanted in our subconscious mind by a complex of instincts. Our gregarious instincts give us the desire to live in societies and have companions. Our reproductive instincts give us the desire to make love, preferably to the opposite sex.

Our territorial and acquisitive instincts give us the desire to make war in order to acquire and defend territory, and to acquire wealth. Our inquisitive instincts give us the desire to learn, and they eventually led a few very able men to create the modern world of science and technology. Our religious instincts give us the desire to worship and to pray to gods. Maternal instincts give mothers the desire to love and care for their young. Instincts are never experienced as instincts. They are experienced as desires, urges, ambitions, and wants. This is why we are nature's obedient robots who live out our lives in the delusion that we are masters of our fate.

All human beings are robotized by nature through her device of implanting drives and instincts, in the same manner that a human being is robotized by another human being through the device of post-hypnotic suggestion. Each human being differs from every other human being in that his genetic distribution of instincts and intelligence is somewhat unique. A human sex cell contains no fewer than ten thousand different genes, the combinations of which provide for a staggering amount of variability in an individual's instincts and intelligence.

A mother plentifully endowed with maternal instincts will insist, "My boy is a good boy," even though he may be a vicious rapist, murderer, or Mafia hitman. If she lacks these instincts, she may throw her baby in the garbage dump. A person who is well endowed with tribal instincts will write, "Our country! In her intercourse with foreign nations may she always be in the right; but our country, right or wrong." If the tribal instincts are lacking, but the egoistic acquisitive instincts dominate, the person, if he lives in a Communist country, would probably want to defect to the United States where he is free to exercise his egoistic-acquisitive instincts and partake of the predator's exquisite delights of economic predation. If he has potent sexual instincts, he will be an outstanding womanizer, or at least he will try his damndest.

There is conclusive laboratory evidence that human beings are unconscious of the true forces which control their actions. Dr. Wilder Penfold of McGill University in Montreal, Canada, performed many operations on the brains of human beings. Strange as it may seem, even though the brain is the cause of feeling the sensation of pain, the brain itself has no pain receptors, and it may be cut or manipulated without any sensation of pain. Therefore, only a local anesthetic applied to the scalp and surface of the bone is necessary to remove the top of the skull for brain surgery. The patient is fully conscious while his brain is being probed, cut, or manipulated, and he experiences no discomfort.

Dr. Penfold discovered that he could robotize his patients by touching various parts of the surface of their brains with a small electrical probe. He could make his patients move any part of their bodies, draw up their legs, roll their eyes, turn their heads, swing their arms, even sing songs, by simply stimulating particular areas of their brains. THE IMPORTANT POINT TO THESE EXPERIMENTS IS THAT THE PATIENTS WERE TOTALLY UNAWARE OF THE FACT THAT THEY WERE FORCED TO PERFORM THEIR ACTIONS EXACTLY AS A PUPPET'S MOVEMENTS ARE CONTROLLED BY A PUPPETEER. When the patients were asked why they moved, sang, or did what they were robotized to do while under brain surgery, they replied that they "felt an overpowering urge to do so." They behaved mechanically, but they believed that their mechanical behavior was behavior they, themselves, freely chose because they fulfilled their "own" desires and urges. After all, we define freedom of choice as the freedom to do that which we desire to do. Desire is the key, but the causes of desires is the rub.

The Swiss neurophysiologist Dr. Walter R. Hess discovered that he could compel practically all the normal functions of man by electrode stimulation of the appropriate portion of the brain. These results were confirmed by Dr. Jose M. R. Delgado of the Yale University Department of Physiology. The automated, mechanized, robotized human puppets always felt that their fully mechanized behavior resulted from the exercise of their own free will, not the will of someone or something else. There is a built-in delusion of free will in all normal human behavior. When human behavior is mechanized by subconscious drives, cerebral stimulation, or by instincts, it is never experienced as robotized behavior. It is always experienced as freely chosen behavior. There is a comic aspect to human beings in that they strut about like peacocks as if they were masters of their own fate, if not the fate of the world, but they are really fantoccini that move by networks of mechanical compulsions.

The delusion of free will is inevitable because of the limited nature of human consciousness. We are conscious of our urges, desires, wants, needs, and impulses, which we experience as parts of our individual essence; but we are not conscious of how our urges, desires, wants, needs, and impulses were programmed into our consciousness. The robotized human being, whether he is robotized by post-hypnotic suggestion, electrical stimulation of his brain, instincts, drugs, or brainwashing, is aware of the urge to perform certain acts, but unaware that what he feels as an urge is really a command to act in a prescribed manner. He is actually a marionette, but he feels that he is a completely free being. For example, a ladies' man seeking to seduce young ladies is fully aware of his sex urges, but he is totally unconscious of the mechanisms whereby his genetic programming creates his sex urges.

Our happiness lies in being obedient slaves to our genetic programming. The highly-sexed person must have sex if he is to be happy. The highly acquisitive person must pursue wealth, fame, and power if he is to be happy. One with strong religious instincts finds happiness by preaching his faith and saving souls, and his happiness may be enhanced by getting rich at the same time. The highly inquisitive person must pursue science and philosophy if he is to find happiness. The red-blooded young man with an abundance of tribal instincts seeks honor and glory on his nation's battlefields. He is unaware that he is automated by his tribal instincts like a robotized tin soldier. He is only aware of his desire to fight for his country, for freedom, for God, or for some other quixotic phantasm. Martial music played to the beat of two sticks on an ass's skin sends tingles up and down his spine, arouses his patriotic fervor, and he bristles to see action for whatever flatulent balderdash defecated by some idiotic panjandrum.

Experiments have been performed on rhesus monkeys to fully robotize them. Radio-controlled boxes were glued to the tops of their heads. The radio-controlled boxes contained electrodes which were implanted in the brains of the rhesus monkeys. There was no discomfort because there are no pain spots in or on the brain itself. The monkeys were actuated by the radio control operator. The robotized monkeys, like human beings in similar experiments, felt they were behaving according to their own desires.

There is a particular spot in the brain of monkeys and human beings which produces intense pleasure when it is stimulated electrically. The monkeys were not only behaving in what they experienced as voluntary actions, but they were made exceptionally happy because they were rewarded with extreme pleasure by having their pleasure spots stimulated periodically. They were happier being robotized by man than they were by being their natural selves; that is, robotized by the multiplicity of their genetic determinants.

Like the rhesus monkeys, human beings can also be robotized by other human beings (in a kind of chain reaction) by placing similar radio-controlled brain probes affixed to the top of their heads. Technology is soon, if not now, able to produce societies of human robots completely controlled by other human beings. Such a society could be called an Electroligarchy, if we use the terminology proposed by David M. Rorvik. Rorvik pointed out that the human robots in the electro-society would be eager and even dedicated to fulfilling the will of their masters because they would be programmed with the DESIRE to implement the goals set for them. In fact, they would war against anyone who would interfere with their "freedom" to perform as robots, much as suttee widows fought against anyone who tried to restrain them from the honor of burning to death on their husbands' funeral piles.

Would there be a moral problem involved in creating a society of human robots? There was a moral problem to black slavery because they were required to behave against their own desires. This moral problem would evaporate if they were willing slaves acting in accordance with their desires, especially if they fought against anyone who attempted to interfere with their freedom to be slaves, such as happens when religious cultists fight against those who attempt to deprogram them. Human robots in the electro-society would not experience or be aware of any coercion of their behavior, even though it would be mechanically determined by cerebral stimulation, because the process of robotization would be identical to natural robotization by the multiplicity of genetically determined human instincts. If happiness is the goal of human life, it would be better to be electro-society robots because the robots would be happier than normal human beings since they would enjoy the pleasure of performing in accordance with their own desires; and, additionally, their pleasure spots would be stimulated frequently by their electroligarchal masters so as to make them supremely happy human beings.

Every human robot in the electro-society would be as certain that he acted by his own instigation as any of us who function without the robotizing boxes affixed to our heads. Each human robot would be programmed to enjoy being a robot, and he would argue, with all the cogency of human logic, that he is the master of his own fate, and NOT a robot, just as some psychologists, sociologists, and anthropologists argue that human behavior is completely instinctiveless while they are blissfully unaware that it is their own instincts that robotize them into believing they are completely instinctiveless. The human robot could be made to dig ditches all day and cherish every moment of it while believing and insisting that he is fulfilling the great ambition of his life. He would be no more ridiculous than the millions of humankind who create gods in their own minds and devote their lives in service to these figments of their imagination.

A little thought on this subject should make any person who is capable of thought question the limitations to his imagined freedom of choice. No human being chose his own birth, his own sex, his own race, his own species, his own genus, or his own battery of instincts. No one chose his own parents, the ovum, or spermatozoon which make him what he is. Each plant, animal, or human being existing on this Earth is a product of forces acting under natural law, over which it or he had absolutely no control. At what point can any creature defy the mechanism which brought it into existence, and say, "You, the forces which brought me into existence and made me what I am, no longer control my destiny because I am NOW, at this precise moment, the master of my own fate?" Actually, at no point! Nature never relinquishes command. We are not apart from nature. We are a part of nature. Maturity only enhances the delusion of free will. If the electronic impulses which program a computer were felt as conscious urges to perform its predetermined functions, the computer, too, would be convinced that it has freedom of choice because it would be performing only as it, itself, desires to perform.

Man boasts that he exercises control over his environment, but he controls his environment in the same sense bees control their environment by cross-fertilizing flowers and creating new and better species of flowers from which they can extract nectar; or as beavers control their environment by building dams and altering the fauna and flora of the region. The only difference between bees, beavers, and human beings is that bees and beavers do not have a cerebral cortex to give them the delusion of freedom of choice. Modern science and technology would never have appeared on Earth if a few exceptional humanoids had not been genetically programmed with the fortunate combination of inquisitive instincts and intelligence.

The human being is a territorial predator who is programmed to establish and defend territory like any territorial animal. He can no more change his predatory nature than a wolf can change its predatory nature and become a lamb. The dream of universal peace on Earth is just that—A DREAM—AN IMPOSSIBLE, RIDICULOUS DREAM. A lion can be domesticated, and a human being can be civilized; but don't turn your back on either of them because behind the facade lurk dangerous predators. Remember Nazi Germany? Remember that the only good Indian is a dead Indian?

The plots of most novels, soap operas, and movies revolve about the thesis of violence and sexual love because violence and sex are what the human predator is all about. War is the common theme of history because man is a helpless victim of his blind, predatory, territorial instincts. Human beings have reproduced to the saturation point. He is dying of starvation by the millions throughout Africa and Asia, but he continues to overpopulate because he is driven to it by blind instinct. The poor in America proliferate against all dictates of common sense because they are helpless victims of blind instinct. Nature performed her task well when she robotized man for sexual behavior.

Religion has evolved naturally, and it has become an instinctive drive in man because it has survival value as explained in the chapter on religion. The concept of God is the personification of man's instinctual needs. The dream of immortality and the invention of the immortal soul are the natural consequences of the instinct for survival carried to the nth degree. Man's gods always reflected man's instinctual needs such as victory in war, refuge from the tyranny of nature, and ideal survival: that is, immortality. The instinctive quest for territory by the Hebrews (Promised Land) led to the invention of the murderous God, Jehovah. The word "Jehova" means "WARRIOR." When repeated defeats, massacres, persecutions, and endless suffering frustrated the Jews and Christians, their instincts demanded a new God: a God of Love. People who suffer greatly have a need for love, especially a God of Love. The vanquished have a greater need for love than the victors.

The Christian God has been a very handy all-purpose God. When Christians suffered, they could look to their God of Love for consolation. When Christians wanted conquest, they could also look to the same God for inspiration and divine help. The Christian God was the inspiration for the Crusades and the slaughter of Moslems, the slaughter of heretics, as well as the genocide of the American Indians. Christianity also fosters the instinctive delusion of free will. It teaches that man can choose between good and evil, but it fails to inform that good and evil are entirely relative. One man's good is another man's evil; for example, slaughter on the battlefields. Good and evil are the spurs and curbs of human automation. Actually, the Christian God is a thousand different Gods. Each Christian sect moulds his Christian God to better suit the instinctual needs of its members.

Subliminally, at least, religions have glimpsed at the role of determinism in human life. According to ancient Greek religion (now called Greek mythology by infidels who also call Christian religion 'Christian mythology'), three Fates, all sisters, sat near Pluto's throne. Clotho, the youngest, spun the thread of life. Lachesis, the second, was chance, the element of luck that a man had the right to expect, twisted the thread of life.

> *Twist ye, twine ye! even so.*
> *Mingle shades of joy and woe,*
> *Hope, and fear, and peace, and strife,*
> *In the thread of human life.*
> (Scott)

Atropos, the third sister, was armed with a huge pair of shears. She remorselessly cut short the thread of life.

Ancient Romans also believed in the Fates. They were called Nona, Decuma, and Morta. The religion of the ancient Germanic tribesman taught that the three NORNS wove the web of life. The Norse Fates were Verthandi (the present), Urth (the past), and Skuld (the future). Not even the gods could escape their fates in these religions. Fate is even recognized in the Christian religion. The Lord's Prayer includes, "Thy will be done on Earth as it is in Heaven." Christian sects like Calvinists (Huguenots) and Presbyterians taught that all men were predestined by the forewill of God to Heaven or Hell, in contradiction to the popular notion of free will.

The concept of the inexorable dominion of fate over the destiny of man is expressed with consummate perfection and beauty by the words of Omar Khayyam in his *Rubaiyat*:

The Moving Finger writes; and, having writ,
Moves on: nor all your Piety nor Wit
Shall lure it back to cancel half a Line,
Nor all your Tears wash out a Word of it.

We must ponder the question of how it could be possible for man—an infinitesimal speck in the staggering expanse of the vast universe, and a momentary flash in the eternity of time, a mere ephemeral accident of evolution and of clashing, relentless natural forces—to escape the overwhelming powers of the external forces which created him? How can he escape the infinite concatenation of causes and effects which prevails throughout all nature? That our Sun will one day die is a certainty. That the human race will one day be just another extinct species is also a certainty. If man cannot determine his origin or his end, why should he be capable of determining the interval? Some people argue that unpredictability of human behavior is evidence of indeterminism (free will). Weather is caused by mechanistic, meteorological forces, not the whims of gods; but even the weather of the next few hours cannot be accurately predicted in spite of modern technology—too many variables are involved. Unpredictability is no argument for free will unless one agrees that weather has free will.

The amazing technology of modern times is an overt miracle of gifted human beings, but it is a covert creation of nature. The great scientists and technologists who made our modern Space Age possible could have made nothing possible if a single chromosome or gene in their forming zygotes had shifted while in their mothers' wombs. People are nature's robots. Man's will merely fulfills the entelechy given him by nature, just as any germinating seed fulfills the entelechy given it by its determinants.

It is absurd to think of man—who is totally dependent upon nature for his evolutionary development and existence; entirely contingent upon the replicating strands of DNA in the double helix for his individuality; and is sustained only by air for his lungs; water, and food for his nutriment; the sun for his life; and sexual intercourse for his propagation—as an autonomous being, separate and apart from the autonomy of nature. How can a fertilized egg repudiate its genes and its destiny? Can an ape will itself to be a bird? We, like other animals, are products of sexual intercourse. How can a fortuitous combination of gametes which terminates an orgasm evolve a magical creature that can defy the mechanisms of the universe?

We are all spectators to the unfolding drama of our own lives as we are spectators to the lives of others. In the words of Shakespeare, "All the world's a stage, And all the men and women merely players." The Alexander the Greats, the Napoleons, the Hitlers, the Einsteins, the Christs, and the Edisons were nature's puppets whose destinies would have been aborted had a single gene in the sperm or ovum of their origins been mechanically altered. They acted out their roles like monkeys with radio-controlled boxes of electrodes planted in their brains, confident that the mere consciousness of free will was an absolute guarantee of its authenticity. Men left their marks on history, but only mechanistically, as earthquakes and meteoric impacts leave their marks on geological history. All actors of their fates have always sung the refrain of all mankind, "I am master of my fate; I am the captain of my soul," but they were not even masters of their own delusions.

The mechanisms of all life are perfectly obvious at their lower levels. The invariable response of plants towards a stimulus like light (phototropism) is duplicated by animals. Postitive phototaxis compels moths to fly into flames. The pupillary reflex causes the pupils of our eyes to mechanistically narrow with the stimulus of a bright light. The invariable mechanisms proceed up scale to conditioned reflexes, conditioned responses, and instincts which are a series or a chain of reflexes that are coordinated by the whole organism; until in human beings, the complex of invariable, interacting reactions become so complicated that we loose sight of the mechanism. They become completely unrecognizable and the end result (behavior), like weather, appears somewhat unpredictable or indeterminate.

The difference between the instinctive behavior of animals and the "intelligent" behavior of man is one of degree and not of kind. A greater number of predetermining forces act on man to give the illusion of free will. Even simple theatrical tricks can reach the point of complexity that an intelligent man like Sir Arthur Conan Doyle lost sight of the trickery and became absolutely convinced that Houdini could perform certain of his tricks only by dematerializing his physical body and rematerializing it later.

Human behavior is a matter of physics. It is the resultant sum of an infinitely complex tangle of internal and external vector forces. Many of these forces, such as our killer instincts, are programmed in us for deferred execution. We kill only when the deferred execution command is given. We may live our entire lives without killing anyone or anything, but the programming is stored in our DNA, ready for the deferred execution command. Hitler, for example, gave the command to the German people. Charles Manson gave the command to his "family." Popes gave the command to the Crusaders. Because killing is programmed in us as a DEFERRED EXECUTION COMMAND, and not as an immediate execution command, anthropologists like Richard Leakey are misled into believing that human beings are not wired for the killer instinct. His limited studies of peaceful African tribes, and his natural optimism, caused him to misread human nature. If the deferred execution command had been given to his peaceful tribes, he would have seen his peaceful tribes suddenly transformed into warring tribes.

Misreading animal behavior data is an understandable failing because programming for deferred execution is sometimes very elusive. Jane Goodall made extensive studies of chimpanzees in the Gombe Stream area of Tanzania, Africa, starting in 1960. In 1971, she published her book *In the Shadow of Man*. She noted that "the circuitry of the chimpanzee brain resembles the circuitry of the human brain more closely than does that of any other species," but she never dreamed of just how close until some twelve years AFTER she began her extensive studies. After many years of observation, she finally learned that chimpanzees are NOT the gentle vegetarians they are often depicted; but, like human beings, they can be formidable predators who hunt down and kill young antelopes, bush pigs, monkeys, and baboons. They can be cannibals who hunt down and kill the young of their own species and eat them.

Jane Goodall saw her chimps divide into two distinct societies with distinct territories in 1972. This division into the in-group and the out-group activated the deferred execution command in the circuitry of their brains. Three to six adult males in the larger group in the north made concerted gang attacks on single members of the group in the south and brutally attacked them. After four years of cruel warfare, the southern group was decimated. Seven males and a female disappeared. Had Goodall not continued her studies beyond her expected ten years, she would never have known the dark, human side to chimpanzee behavior. Chimpanzee behavior is programmed amazingly like that of human behavior. Human beings can live in relative peace and harmony only when they live in isolated communities. When they form discrete out-groups—that is, tribes, nations, and superpowers—strife, violence and war inevitably erupt because deferred execution commands in their programming are then given.

Jane Goodall discovered that violence can be triggered in chimpanzees even in the in-group (criminal behavior). One time when the chimps had access to a larder of bananas, their peaceful behavior immediately transformed into excitement and violent aggression. The sudden abundance of bananas activated deferred execution commands in the circuitry of their brains, just as money and wealth activate greed and avarice in human beings. The Mafia, gangsters, and drug ring leaders are prone to violence and murder because this behavior is triggered by the injection of wealth or the dream of wealth into their behavioral environment just as the chimpanzees were triggered for violence by the wealth of bananas. Nothing can trigger violence or the killer instinct in sheep because it is not programmed into their behavior either as an immediate execution command or as a deferred execution command.

The process by which human beings are mechanized is complicated. We can merely scratch the surface in this book. We previously mentioned that the ladies' man is mechanized by his sex instincts. Actually, the ladies' man and sex offenders are mechanized by hypergonadism, which is the enhancement of the secretion of testosterone, a product of the Leydig cells of the testicles. Testicular function is under the direct control of luteinizing hormones and follicle-stimulating hormones that are regulated by the hypothalamic-pituitary mechanism. This mechanism, in turn, functions by virtue of the DNA code which specifies genetic autonomy.

Testosterone determines specific behavioral patterns. It promotes aggression, boisterous behavior, and sexual activity. Excessive levels of testosterone induce uncontrollable biological urges leading, in some men, to rape, child-molestation, exhibitionism, and voyeurism. The compulsive behavior of these men is felt as an irrepressible urge or desire to act as they do. It is the same kind of urge that people of great ambition feel when they climb high mountains, seek acting career success or political power. In the former, the behavior is antisocial, and so it is condemned. In the latter, it is social, and so it is praised.

Dr. Fred Berlin of Johns Hopkins Hospital in Baltimore, Maryland, is doing research work on chemotherapy for rehabilitating sex offenders. He has found that Depo Provera can control the compulsive behavior of sex offenders by lowering their testosterone levels. Drugs, chemicals, and hormones are used to alter mental processes and behavior, and they will be used more extensively in the future. Their uses in chemical and biological warfare, and their potential for political robotization have frightening possibilities. They can be used as truth serums and brainwashing techniques to reduce populations to tranquil slavery in the manner of human beings reduced to robots by radio control boxes affixed to their heads, a subject we already addressed. We can have electro-societies and we can have chemo-societies of human robots.

The instinctive need for religion can he satisfied by religion's chemical surrogates. The Mescalero Apaches attained the mystical-religious experience by means of peyote. The Aztecs did it with their "sacred mushrooms." According to the *Encyclopedia Britannica*, "The American Indian with his peyote and the modern jazz musician with his marijuana have discovered . . . Dionysian ecstasy without formal knowledge of aesthetics." Consciousness-expanding drugs (psychedelics) produce a wide range of subjective and objective effects by stimulating the central nervous system. The sensation of light is intensified and becomes confused with sound. Colors become more vivid, and the perception of space is enhanced. Space seems boundless; one's body seems to float; and the subject fuses with the object. The LSD user becomes robotized like a religious fanatic in that he feels the need to convert others to the use of drugs.

Psychosis, paranoia for example, can be induced with the use of amphetamines. Marijuana (cannabis) produces various psychological manifestations with mood variations from euphoria and hilarity, to fear, anxiety, and panic. Sometimes, the user becomes depersonalized: that is, detached from reality. Sometimes, he experiences an enhancement of personal worth. Since normal human behavior and mental processes are mechanizations produced by natural hormones and chemicals, it should not be surprising that normal behavior and normal mental states can be altered by abnormal combinations of these hormones and chemicals, or by foreign drugs and chemicals.

The conviction that we enjoy free will persists in spite of all evidence to the contrary because it is a primary instinctive need of the human ego; and, besides, free will is a normal datum of human experience. Hans Vaihinger states in his *Philosophy of 'As If'*, "The idea of human free will and its corollary of moral responsibility not only contradicts observation which shows that everything obeys unalterable laws, but it is also self-contradictory, for an absolutely free, chance act, resulting from nothing, is ethically just as valueless as an absolutely necessary one."

Not only do we experience free will as an accompaniment of our "voluntary" actions, but our instincts demand that we accept it on philosophical grounds. It is the foundation of our moral and criminal law. We punish a criminal only if we think he has the capacity to choose between "right and wrong." If we think he does not, we treat him medically. Vaihinger considers the notion of free will a practical, ethical fiction, and a necessary complement to our repertoire of self-serving myths. We must act "AS IF" we are free, but, as Adolf Steudel says, "Even though we live, think and act as if we possessed absolutely free control over our volitions and actions, natural law fulfills itself with certainty just the same."

Human beings are so constituted that they cannot accept reality as is like other animals. We all, from Albert Einstein to Jim Jones, shatter the harsh and relentless world of the real into bits, and remold it into a fictional dream nearer to our heart's desire. We live "AS IF" our myths and dreams are real. We hypostatize our gods and reify our scientific abstractions. We are but transient conglomerates of atoms and molecules; but we live as if we are immortal entities of indestructible spiritual essence. We are but another species in the animal kingdom; but we live as if we are disjointed from nature by a discontinuity that transmutes us into unique, rational beings. We are purposeless, infinitesimal specks of ephemeral nothingness flashing on an inconspicuous particle of dust in the infinitude of time and space; but we live as if the vast universe were nothing but adornments to titillate our aesthetic sense, and we give it credence with our religious fictions of divine teleology to our lives.

Our national legacy is in the finest tradition of Adolf Hitler's *Machtpolitik*—Our ancestors exterminated the native American Indians. They robbed them of their beloved land bequeathed to them by the Great Spirit and which they possessed for thirty thousand years. They enslaved Africans and used them as beasts of burden. But we live as if America is God's loving gift to us, His chosen people, and as if our country had been founded upon pure justice and the noblest of principles. We reproduce sexually and by instinct, like other animals; but we romanticize our sexual loves as if they were ideal essences made in heaven. We are nature's robots, but we live as if we are masters not only of our own fates but also of nature's fate. We live, and indeed we must live, by the philosophy of "AS IF." When reality is not to our liking, we scorn it and proclaim our self-serving myths as the "enlightened" New Reality. But Omar Khayyam said it best:

> *Ah Love! could you and I with Him conspire*
> *To grasp this Sorry Scheme of Things entire,*
> *Would not we shatter it to bits—and then*
> *Re-mould it nearer to the Heart's Desire!*

Human behavior having been mechanized by nature, it can be remechanized by us. The most aggressive human predator can be permanently made into a person gentle as a lamb by the operation known as prefrontal lobotomy. In this operation, the fibers connecting the prefrontal lobes of the brain to the large nerve center within the brain (thalamus) are cut. The roaring lion of a man can be redesigned into a vegetable. An army of fighting human robots could be produced by fixing radio controlled electrode probes to their heads which would stimulate the lateral and anterior regions of their hypothalamus. Human beings are programmed by nature; but, like computers, they can be reprogrammed.

The protestation "I am master of my fate" is the voice reacting to cerebral compulsion like a phonograph record mechanically reacting to bumps in grooves. As adults we are programmed differently than as children. We felt we had free will when we were children just as we feel we have free will as adults because we responded to our desires and urges as children as we do as adults. In all instances, we are conscious of our desires, but ignorant of the causes whereby our desires have arisen in us. We behave differently as adults not because of newly introduced intelligence to control our behavior, but because of new time-released behavioral programming. People do not necessarily grow wiser with age. They often become more stupid. The behavior of adult dope addicts and cult fanatics is more stupid than the most stupid behavior of children. What is more stupid than religious fanatics slaughtering each other in the name of their gods, especially when it is the God of Love?

We do things when we are drunk that we would never dream of doing when we are sober; but at the time we do them, we feel that we are making free-choice decisions. The same applies to the modification of our behavior by drugs. We are not aware of the fact that our behavior is being modified mechanistically by chemicals and drugs. Alcoholics and drug addicts go for years thinking that their behavior and performance are unimpaired. We can see how behavior is mechanized and modified in other people, but we cannot see it in ourselves. We are never conscious of our own robotization.

Philosopher Baruch Spinoza uses the analogy that if a stone were given consciousness, it would feel it has free will as it travels through space, and it would think it determines its own trajectory and selects the place and time of its fall because all changes in acceleration and momentum would be experienced as urges or impulses to WANT to move precisely as the law of gravitation determines that it must move. The falling stone would not be aware of the external forces acting on it, *per se*, just as human beings are not conscious of the forces of nature working on them. The flight of the stone is to the behaving person what the law of gravity is to the law of instincts. The mechanistic forces with which human beings are robotized by nature are experienced as desires, wants, impulses, aspirations, ambitions, and urges which are complex and often conflicting. Whey they conflict, we experience it as deliberation, the predetermined resolution of which is experienced as an act of free will.

Abstract, logical science presupposes a deterministic world, and it is verified by objective observation and experimentation. Human behavior is, accordingly, completely explicable in terms of mechanics, bio-physics, and bio-chemistry. Both Newtonian and Einsteinian physics are deterministic. Even Heisenberg's Uncertainty Principle is conditioned by the Law of Probability.

Einstein's General Theory of Relativity is an avowedly deterministic doctrine. According to it, we do not and cannot make things happen. We merely observe things happening to us. We are marionettes in a four-dimensional space-time continuum which we observe as being played like a cinema. All events are unequivocally predetermined. We, ourselves, are tenseless, invariant, four-dimensional objects. We are tracks prescribed through space-time that are called our world lines in the absolute of the space-time continuum.

Our world lines are unalterable. Time is a dimension in the absolute space-time continuum, and like space, it can be read either way by different observers; that is, from the past to the future or the future to the past. However, our individual, normal consciousness permits us to read time in only one direction: from the past to the future, with the present standing as a barrier to the future. Our brain imposes the unidirectional consciousness of time in our minds. Because we are events—that is, points in space-time, or, in other words, world lines in absolute space-time—we can only EXPERIENCE the here-now; we cannot CREATE the here-now. That is to say, we have no real capacity to alter our destinies (world lines). We possess no free will.

The partition of the space-time continuum into space AND time is a subjective, relative experience. Some of the stars we see at night are thousands, even millions of light years away. They are no longer in the same positions which we now see them. In fact, some of them no longer exist at all, even though we see them as existing. They have exploded into supernovae eons ago. Observers having different coordinates in the space-time continuum all see the same absolute space-time event in different time frames. Individually, space and time are relative, but cosmically the space-time continuum is absolute and does not permit variance—free will, that is. The reading of free will into the space-time continuum is a subjective, relative experience. It is an illusion.

The prestigious American philosopher Alfred North Whitehead observed that the roots of scientific imagination are found in the great tragedians of ancient Athens: Aeschylus, Sophocles, and Euripides. Wrote he, "Their vision of fate, remorseless and indifferent, urging a tragic incident to its inevitable issue, is the vision possessed by science. Fate in Greek Tragedy becomes the order of nature in modern thought ... Let me here remind you that the essence of dramatic tragedy is not unhappiness. It resides in the solemnity of the remorseless working of things ... this remorseless inevitableness is what pervades scientific thought. The laws of physics are the decrees of fate."

Nobody can escape from nature and free himself from the decrees of fate any more than the moon can escape the gravitational attraction of the Earth and fly off into space in an act of defiance (free will). A person has the same chance of willing a fate other than what nature programmed for him as his automobile has of defying his driving maneuvers and taking off on its own chosen course.

The basis of the laws of physics, chemistry, and science in general, is the eternal and universal uniformity of nature, and the inexorable, ineluctable necessity of her laws. These same principles, fundamental to modern science, were anticipated by the ancient Greek scientists and philosophers of the fourth and fifth centuries B.C.: namely, Leucippus and Democritus. Leucippus laid down the basal scientific idea of atomism and the principle of necessary, unchanging, and uniform causation. According to Diogenes Laertius, he said. "As the world is born, so, too, it grows, decays and perishes, in virtue of some necessity. Nothing happens without a cause, but every thing with a cause and by necessity."

His pupil, Democritus, was born at Abdera in Thrace in 460 B.C. He taught that all things are composed of underived, indivisible, and indestructible atoms, and no purpose exists other than mechanical necessity, according to which all change and alteration arises. He urged equanimity and fortitude, and taught that intellectual activity which is free from greed, superstition, desire, and ignorance is the highest goal of living. That was almost two thousand five hundred years ago, and not many people in our modern world are capable of such intellectual insight or sublime sensibility. It is great men such as he that produce Great Societies. It would seem that the belief in determinism should predispose one to serenity and understanding of the errors and failings of one's fellow man. Why should one fret over that which he has no control? However, because man is a strange melange of conflicting instincts and little intelligence, it does not necessarily follow as it had in the case of Democritus, the "laughing philosopher."

Nineteenth century John Stuart Mill recognized that the postulates of causality and uniformity of nature must be primary assumptions of science; and, to be valid, the truth of these assumptions must be verified by the discovery of invariable laws in nature throughout the Cosmos—which they have. Science and religion are natural antagonists. Science deciphers the universe in terms of verifiable, inexorable laws. Religion deciphers the same universe in terms of the whims or decrees of fictitious gods who are amenable to flattery and human petitions. The universe is the sum total of all matter and energy. If one wishes to learn about the universe, he would do better to consult with his physicist and astronomer than with his priest or minister. As with Santayana, we may not know what matter is, but, in his words, "I wait for the men of science to tell me. But whatever matter may be, I call it matter boldly, as I call my acquaintances Smith and Jones without knowing their secrets."

We are truly such things of which stars are made. Our sun is a star. It contains the matter from which our Earth evolved. All life, including human life, arose from the matter and energy contained in our star, the Sun. The protoplasm in our bodies is the same as protoplasm in all life on Earth. The molecules in protoplasm are made up of the identical electrons and protons as in all matter throughout the Universe. In the words of Omar Khayyam:

With Earth's first Clay They did the Last Man knead.
And there of the Last Harvest sow'd the seed:
And the first Morning of creation wrote
What the Last Dawn of Reckoning shall read.

There is a fundamental unity and continuity of all life and all matter in the universe. All qualitative difference in all life and all matter is merely the quantitative difference in the number of orbiting electrons, the number of protons in the nuclei of atoms, and the lattice of the atoms and molecules. All matter and all life in the universe consists of approximately 102 elements which contain varying numbers of the same electrons and protons. For example, an atom of the element hydrogen contains one proton in its nucleus and one orbiting electron. An atom of the element oxygen contains eight protons in its nucleus and eight orbiting electrons. If we bind two atoms of the gas hydrogen with one atom of the gas oxygen, presto chango: we have something entirely different: not a molecule of gas, but a molecule of water, H_2O. With a different arrangement of electrons and protons, presto chango: we have an amoeba (LIFE)! Yet another combination of electrons and protons and presto chango: we have a human being who proclaims his mastery over the electrons and protons which automate him!

Herein lies the Cosmic Comedy: Nature created man after over 3 billion years of groping with varying combinations of electrons and protons in the evolutionary development of life; and man created the hydrogen bomb with which he can (and will) not only self-destruct, but also return all life on Earth to its pristine state of random electrons and protons, and thus undo in a fraction of a second an achievement which required over 3 billion years of trial and error experimentation. But man has always excelled in his ability to kill and to destroy. As nature comes full circle, the fictitious Goddess of Nature may well philosophize, "Remember man! Electrons thou art, and unto electrons thou shall return."

Death is a universal, necessary experience. The mere fact of birth presupposes its opposite, death. The fifth century ancient Greek philosopher Heraclitus was among the first to recognize the identity of opposites. We live in a world in which opposites define existence. How can there be an "up," if there is no "down?" Love can exist only because there is hate. Man is the only laughing animal because he is the only crying animal. There could be no light, if there were no darkness. Good cannot exist without evil. A god of goodness necessitates a devil of evilness. Those who are proud of their goodness owe a debt of gratitude to the existence of evil. Even the building blocks of the universe require opposites. The existence of the electron, which is a negatively charged particle, necessitates the existence of the positron, which is a positively charged particle having the same mass and magnitude of opposite charge as the electron. Every elementary particle of matter has its opposite which is a corresponding antiparticle. The particle opposite to that of the proton is the antiproton. When particles and antiparticles collide, both are annihilated. Antimatter is a fact of the universe as well as matter, and when they collide, they annihilate each other.

Death is the inexorable fate of all that is born. We share the same fate as the stars and galaxies. We, like stars and galaxies, are born, mature, age, and die. Our fate is inextricably woven with the fate of the stars and the relentless necessity of causation. Human life exists on Earth only because the physical environment favored its unfolding. It exists on no other planet in our solar system because the environments on the other planets do not permit it. A variation in our Sun's radiation by less than 1.5 percent would create an ice age which would spread ice cover over both land and sea, down to the middle latitudes. A variation of a few degrees in the Sun's radiation would extirpate all human life from Earth, either by roasting it or freezing it. The accumulation of a little more carbon dioxide in the Earth's atmosphere would create the greenhouse effect. This would make the Earth's surface like the surface of Venus which is so hot, it melts lead. It would cause the extinction of man; and along with the extinction of man would go the extinction of all gods, devils, good, evil, beauty, and ugliness in the solar system because they cannot exist without minds to beget them.

Man's instinct for survival induces him to vastly overrate the value of life. To paraphrase Santayana, what is life, if it "must wait for sun and rain to set it in motion? What is this life that in any individual can be suddenly extinguished by a bullet . . . or . . . that a little fall in temperature would banish altogether from the universe?" It is overweening arrogance and patent absurdity for a fractionally conscious, transient gathering of electrons and protons to proclaim itself immortal, and master of its own fate. Strutting gobs of human vanity are exterminated annually by the millions through earthquakes, typhoons, floods, tornados, tidal waves, and diseases; but man's delusions of mastery over his fate persist. Man, the natural predator, exterminates millions of his own kind by interminable acts of war and crime. A rational creature would not have killed countless millions of his own kind in stupid wars through the ages, nor would he have engaged in the unspeakable brutality characteristic of man. Only a creature driven by blind instinct is capable of such cruelty and senseless slaughter. Man is programmed: a stupid, cruel, vicious killer by necessity, not by choice.

If we accept the role of fate and determinism as compelling forces in human life, it would seem difficult to hate anyone. How can we hate anyone for doing what he cannot help doing? We can hate a puppeteer, but how can we hate the puppet? A murderer cannot help being a murderer. Why should we hate him? We definitely should not! When we hang, gas, or electrocute him, we should do so with the utmost love and understanding, especially with love for those innocent people who would have been his next victims had we not executed him. The executed criminal should also accept his fate with good grace and not hate his executioner for doing what HE must because of HIS role in the Chain of Necessity.

As we mentioned, it would seem that the logical implication of fatalism is submission, passivity, and tranquility. If we can't alter fate, why try, or why worry about it? Logic and reason are not applicable to human beings. Mohammed taught that man's every action was predestined by Allah's will (Kismet), but this doctrine of Kismet prompted aggression, not passivity. Believing it was fated for him to conquer the world in the name of Allah, he and his followers fought for Islam with uncommon ferocity. Omar Khayyam also accepted the doctrine of Kismet, but he took the rational approach. He was more in tune with science than religion, and logic than fanaticism. The belief in Kismet (FATE) prompted him not to conquer, convert or kill in the name of Allah, but to accept the inevitable in serenity and tranquility:

> *Yesterday This Day's Madness did prepare;*
> *To-Morrow's Silence, Triumph, or Despair:*
> *Drink! for you know not whence you came, nor why:*
> *Drink! for you know not why you go, nor where.*

Omar Khayyam was no fool. He was not duped by Mohammed's promise of eternal Paradise for those who died for Allah. Nor was he frightened by a threatened Hell of horrors for the unbeliever, who would be condemned to wear a cloak of fire and drink scalding water like a thirsty camel for all eternity. Nor was he dissuaded by Christian threats of Hell or promises of Heaven:

> *Oh threats of Hell and Hopes of paradise!*
> *One thing at least is certain—This life flies;*
> *One thing is certain and the rest is lies;*
> *The Flower that once has blown for ever dies.*

The brevity of life haunted Omar Khayyam as it must haunt every sensitive, thinking person. The contemplation of mortality awakens our survival instincts, which activate our imaginative brains to dream of immortality. And so, our brains invent the concept of the immortal human soul. If it were not for the irresistible power of our survival instincts to compel abject belief in us, our simple intelligence would expose the notion of human immortality for the ridiculous nonsense that it is; but instinct always has autonomy over reason. That is why people of great intelligence, even amazing geniuses, believe in the most absurd nonsense of religion and various cults. That is why people obediently follow their national leaders, believe the drivel that flows from their prevaricating mouths like excrement, and willingly die in nonsensical wars "for their country." They use their intelligence not to expose nonsense, but to sophisticate and rationalize it. Truth is beyond the reach of intelligent people when their inquisitive instincts do not have hegemony over their narcissistic instincts. When Shakespeare contemplated life's brevity and desultoriness, he had Macbeth soliloquize:

> *Tomorrow and tomorrow and tomorrow*
> *Creeps in this petty pace from day to day*
> *To the last syllable of recorded time,*
> *And all our yesterdays have lighted fools*
> *The way to dusty death. Out, out, brief candle.*
> *Life's but a walking shadow, a poor player*
> *Who struts and frets his hour upon the stage,*
> *And then is heard no more. It is a tale Told*
> *by an idiot, full of sound and fury,*
> *Signifying nothing.*

Omar Khayyam, as translated by Edward Fitzgerald, expressed the futile quest of human intellect (for answers which do not exist) in poetry unsurpassable in beauty:

> *There was the Door to which I found no Key;*
> *There was the Veil through which I might not see;*
> *Some little talk Awhile of Me and Thee*
> *There was—and then no more of Thee and Me.*

But futility is unacceptable to the human spirit—instincts, that is. Science and reason clearly tell us that human existence is an accident of evolution which serves absolutely no purpose in the scheme of things, if there is a scheme to things. Man is of no more importance in the universe than the bug he squashes when he steps on it, and nature doesn't distinguish between him and bugs when she destroys man by the millions in natural disasters. Man's blind ego-trip-producing instincts demand purpose to his life. If there is no purpose, and there isn't because purpose, itself, is an invention of man's mind, he must invent it. Enter religion! Religion invents the purpose which his instincts demand. To believe that an Almighty Egotist, God, created man to flatter His insatiable EGO throughout eternity borders on madness, but it assuages the instinctual need in man for purpose, and so blind instinct conquers noble reason and reduces it to a whimpering wimp.

We who live in this Atomic Age should be keenly aware of the brevity and futility of life. We live under the sword of Damocles, with each moment tenuously and precariously hanging by the thread of uncertainty. What does it profit a man to sweat and groan for a future that may terminate in the atomic rubble of the next moment? Why build a brave new world atop an active volcano? Power of nuclear destruction in the hands of politicians is like matches in the hands of children in a gunpowder factory. When the fantastically destructive power of modern science and technology, which was created by men of some intelligence, is transposed to the hands of men with little or no intelligence, the hour of doom cannot be far away. That the nuclear Armageddon will arrive is a certainty. Only the precise time is uncertain. It requires but the whimsical touch of a restive finger, dangling from the arm of a misguided religious fanatic hastening to do God's will to defeat the EVIL EMPIRE; or of a Communist doctrinaire hastening to assure the inevitable dialectical victory of socialism over capitalism; or of a fascist dictator who believes it is his destiny to rule the world. Faith in Fate can precipitate the end to all human fate.

The future does not present a pretty picture. But we do have our optimists, and when we speak of optimists we should consider Ambrose Bierce's definition of optimism in his Devil's Dictionary:

"Optimism: The doctrine, or belief, that everything is beautiful, including what is ugly, everything good, especially the bad, and everything right that is wrong. It is held with greatest tenacity by those most accustomed to the mischance of falling into adversity, and is most acceptably expounded with the grin that apes a smile. Being a blind faith, it is inaccessible to the light of disproof—an intellectual disorder, yielding to no treatment but death. It is hereditary, but fortunately not contagious."

There is little room for optimism in a world in which no magnitude of overkill can appease the appetite of its leaders for ever greater weapons of annihilation. The superpowers spend billions of dollars to facilitate the slaughter of people in Third World countries. They spend little to feed these people. Money that is spent on economic aid often feeds corruption instead of people. Perhaps it would be poetic justice for nature's *magnum opus*—the world's consummate predator—to make his finale in one supreme act of predation: a cosmic explosive flash of nuclear particles, blowing willy-nilly in the wasteland's winds. If there could be a collective tombstone over the debris, which will have been once the human race, erected for the edification of some future intelligences from some extragalactic worlds, it should be inscribed with the words of Omar Khayyam:

Into this Universe, and Why not knowing
Nor Whence, like water willy-nilly flowing;
And out of it, as Wind along the Waste,
I know not whither, willy-nilly blowing.

THE END

PROLOGUE

When we are born into this world, our brains are a *tabula rasa*.

We are fed information by our parents and our teachers. All animals are dependent upon their mothers to learn survival skills. It's more complicated for human beings. Their young are often fed with as much misinformation as true information, which accounts for the thousands of years delay in the inventions of computers, automobiles, airplanes, walks on the moon, and all advanced technology and science. Perhaps the real culprit is DNA. The genetic component of human nature, *i.e.*, human genes, bears a good deal of responsibility. These genes program us like computers. We are driven by powerful instincts. We are enticed to sex and reproduction not by reason but by nature, exactly as with ALL animals. We like to believe that we are rational creatures, but we are primarily animals of instinct. Reason is just another survival instrument like the opposable thumb, claws, or wings. Serendipity provides reason with the bonus of cognitive powers beyond the needs of survival. We can decipher the riddle of the universe with reason if we employ the scientific method, but first we must have the desire to WANT to understand the universe. That's where instinct enters the picture. Without that instinctive desire, we couldn't care less.

Carolus Linnaeus catalogued human beings in the binomial taxonomy of *HOMO SAPIENS* in 1758. That's the juxtaposition of the two words WISE and MAN. That nomenclature (*sapiens*) resulted from narcissism rather than evidence. It's very flattering so who's objecting? Well, I am. Why? Because truth should be given preference over myths and fables. What is wise about believing nonsense for tens of thousands of years? It was nearly 2,000 years before the world could accept simple truths first proposed by a few wise Ancient Greeks who theorized that the SUN and NOT Earth is the center of our solar system. People have been slaughtering each other in religious and territorial wars since their origination. Only man, of all the animals, is stupid enough to kill his fellow man in the name of gods of his own making. People fought for territory by instinct, exactly as all lower animals. A sapient creature would have used diplomacy instead of violence. World War I was fought on the false premise that it was the War to end all wars, just as the Iraq War is fought on the false premise of WMDs. The Vietnam War was fought because of the ludicrous Domino Theory. The insanity of man senselessly killing his fellow man continues, and there is no end in sight.

Human stupidity is pervasive. Some people are genetically programmed to murder other people by compulsion and obsession (instinct). We had serial killers like the Green River Killer, Gary Ridgway, who murdered 50 people. Do-gooders object to executing people like him because it's "inhumane" and the state should not be as brutal as the criminal. That's insane nonsense. If Ridgway had been executed after his first murder, 49 innocent victims would still be alive. The fact is that serial killers are a cancer on society and should be excised for the sake of society, exactly like any cancer. If you have brain cancer, do you refuse to have the cancer destroyed because they are living cells and all life is sacred? President Harry Truman ordered the dropping of two atomic bombs on Japan on the theory that it saved lives. At least that made sense because it undoubtedly saved many American lives and probably many Japanese lives as well because of Japanese fanaticism as shown by the Kamikaze.

The nonsapient flaw in human nature is as deep-seated as DNA. When, in 1969, Neil Armstrong became the first human being to walk on the moon, it was the most amazing feat in the history of the world. It was fantastic beyond belief, but how well is he appreciated by his fellow human beings? Many people forgot his name shortly after the achievement. Is he a wealthy man as a result? NO! Compare him to Tiger Woods. Everyone knows Tiger Woods because HE is a SUPERSTAR. What is HIS achievement? He has dexterity in knocking a silly little ball into a silly little hole in the ground; and so, he wins world fame and fantastic wealth while Armstrong is sidelined into oblivion. So I ask YOU. Are we dealing with *Homo sapiens* or *Homo stupido*?

Jonas Salk saved millions of human beings from horrible deaths resulting from Poliomyelitis. He saved millions of people from spending their lives in iron lungs or wheel chairs. The disease crippled Franklin D. Roosevelt. Salk developed a vaccine for polio, which was a fantastic boon to humanity, yet he was far from being wealthy or even well-known. Actually, most people never heard of Jonas Salk. Actors like John Wayne are much better known and much wealthier. An actor playing the part of the President of the United States is paid many times more than the REAL President. *Homo sapiens*? I don't think so.

If you study the lives of great people, you will see that they showed signs of their greatness when they were very young. The possibility for greatness itself arises at conception. Nature predominates over the power of nurture. It's impossible to make an Einstein out of a chimpanzee. It has been said that Einstein was a backward child, but that's far from the truth. At the age of four or five, he was profoundly impressed by the invisible force that guided the needle of a magnetic compass. He learned to play the violin before 5, surpassed other children in math, and was fascinated by geometry at the age of 12, all of which was indicative of his genius. As a child he hated playing soldier and was a lifelong pacifist. He had good genes. Environment is important, but in the order of importance, genetics is first and foremost.

Even Einstein was not immune to nonsapience. Granted, his idea of God was much different from religion's conception, yet he could not liberate himself from the ancient idea itself. He wanted to understand the mind of God, but God had nothing to do with the Big Bang. God didn't arrive until some 13.5 billion years after the Big Bang, when *Homo sapiens* evolved and invented the God concept. Einstein believed in a static universe, but Edwin Hubble proved to him that it is dynamic and expanding. Einstein admitted that his "Cosmological Constant" was one of his worst mistakes. He thought that God would not play dice with the universe; but Heisenberg's uncertainty principle, quantum mechanics, and chaos science all indicate "chance" exists in the universe. The great modern Sir Isaac Newton, Stephen Hawking, thinks that both the universe and human beings were chance events, as do I. Einstein did not observe the most important rule of separation of science and religion. That mistake was responsible for many of his embarrassing errors.

The scientific method is the key to knowledge. It involves the principles and empirical processes of discovery and demonstration: *i.e.*, investigation and observation, formulation of hypothesis to explain the phenomena, and experimentation and verification to demonstrate the truth or falseness of the hypothesis. For a religious person, it is blessed to believe and a sin to doubt. A doubting Thomas is in disfavor. In parts of the Islamic world, it's DEATH to the doubting Thomas (infidel). Jesus said, "Blessed is he who has not seen, yet has believed." That would be a death knell for science. For a person of science, the precise oppose is true. It's a sin to believe without evidence, and a virtue to doubt and search for truth. Which is better? Look at what science gave the world and look at what religion gave the world. It's NO contest.

Evidence is the source of knowledge, not intuition, revelation, or supposition. While absolute truth may require nearly infinite evidence, there's a point where virtual truth approaches absolute truth, and the gap is infinitesimal. Many people do not react to evidence well. A doting mother will not believe her serial killer son is guilty, despite the evidence. A religious fanatic will not believe in evolution, despite all evidence. Criminal trial juries are often totally incapable of handling evidence. The O.J. jury found O.J. not guilty of murdering two people despite the overwhelming evidence. When one juror was asked why she found O.J. not guilty, she replied, "There ain't no poof." When asked about the DNA evidence she replied, "DNA, what's DNA? It's only blood. Everybody got blood." Judge Lance Ito remarked on several occasions that he had an "intelligent" jury. So much for HIS sapience or lack thereof.

Geraldo sapiently remarked that Mark Furhman was the only person connected with the O.J. trial that was ever convicted of perjury, but he was probably the most honest of them all. Even O.J., after getting away with a double murder, was not charged with perjury, in spite of him denying under oath that he ever wore those "ugly dumbass Bruno Magli shoes"; yet there was a photo of him doing exactly that, and denying that he ever hit his wife, Nicole, even though there were photos, tape recordings, and massive evidence that he did. Barry Scheck, a DNA expert and attorney who helped O.J. get away with double murder, became dedicated to exposing wrongful convictions as director and co-founder with Peter Newfeld of the Innocence Project. His best credentials are helping acquit O.J. Simpson of a double murder, the guilt for which one would have to be nearly brain-dead not to recognize. If THAT isn't the epitome of irony, hyperbole, oxymoron, and perfect evidence to show that *Homo sapiens* is really *Homo absurdo*, I don't know what is.

Yes, "sapiens" of *Homo sapiens* is 99 and 44/100% more honored in the breach than the observance. Only *nonsapiens* is congruent with the foibles, wholesale slaughters, contradictions, and absurdities in human history. Ignorance and poverty abound in the world today. The wealth and technological progress in the world was brought about by an extremely minute minority. One may wonder why the wonders of science and technology were the exclusive creations of Euro-gene bearing individuals. The history of chemistry, physics, biology, geology, *etc.*; and the history of radio, TV, automobiles, airplanes, *etc.* are the confirmation of this ethnically tainted statement. The preceding three paragraphs (including this) are perfect examples of political incorrectness, but this book makes no pretense at being politically correct. It doesn't give a hoot about political correctness, but it is shamelessly committed to pervasive and universal TRUTH.

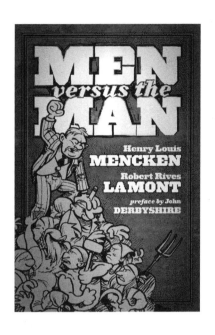

Made in the USA
Middletown, DE
05 May 2015